Technological Change in Health Care

Technological Change in Health Care

A Global Analysis of Heart Attack

Mark B. McClellan and Daniel P. Kessler, Editors

ANN ARBOR
THE UNIVERSITY OF MICHIGAN PRESS

Published in the United States of America by
The University of Michigan Press
Manufactured in the United States of America
⊗ Printed on acid-free paper

2005 2004 2003 2002 4 3 2 1

A CIP catalog record for this book is available from the British Library.

Library of Congress Cataloging-in-Publication Data

McClellan, Mark B.
Technological change in health care : a global analysis of heart attack / Mark B. McClellan and Daniel P. Kessler, editors.
p. ; cm.
Includes bibliographical references and index.
ISBN 0-472-11128-0 (cloth : alk. paper)
1. Myocardial infarction—Treatment—Developed countries. 2. Medical technology—Developed countries. 3. Medical technology—Developed countries—Costs. 4. Medical innovations—Developed countries. [DNLM: 1. Biomedical Technology. 2. Myocardial Infarction—therapy. 3. Technology Assessment, Biomedical—trends. 4. Cross-Cultural Comparison. 5. Health Expenditures—trends. 6. Myocardial Infarction—economics. WG 300 M4775t 2002] I. Kessler, Daniel P. II. Title.
RA645.H4 M38 2002
616.1'237—dc21 2002005411

Contents

Acknowledgments ix

Chapter 1. Introduction: A Global Analysis of Technological Change in Health Care, with a Focus on Heart Attacks 1
Mark B. McClellan and Daniel P. Kessler

Chapter 2. Technological Change in Heart Attack Care in the United States 21
Mark B. McClellan, Nathan Every, Alan M. Garber, Paul Heidenreich, Mark Hlatky, Daniel P. Kessler, Joseph Newhouse, and Olga Saynina

Introduction to the Canadian Chapters 55

Chapter 3. Technological Change in Heart Attack Care in Ontario, Canada, 1981–1995 58
Jack V. Tu, Peter C. Austin, and C. David Naylor

Chapter 4. Technological Change in Heart Attack Care in Quebec, Canada 72
Louise Pilote, Frédéric Lavoie, Vivian Ho, and Mark J. Eisenberg

Chapter 5. Determinants and Consequences of Technological Change in Health Care: Acute Myocardial Infarction in Alberta, Canada 88
Konrad Fassbender, David Hailey, L. Duncan Saunders, and Koon K. Teo

Chapter 6. Health Reform and Technological Change in Manitoba: Treatment of Acute Myocardial Infarction 106
Leslie L. Roos, Randy Walld, Ruth-Ann Soodeen, and Noralou P. Roos

Chapter 7. The Impact of New Technology on the Treatment and Outcomes of Acute Myocardial Infarction in Australia: Incentives for Technological Change and Their Consequences for Treatment Decision-Making 121
Jeff Richardson, Iain K. Robertson, Michael Hobbs, and Diana Edwards
Changes in Medical Treatments and Their Consequences for Patient Health Outcomes
Michael Hobbs, Brenden Bertuola, Elizabeth Geelhoed, and Richard Hockey

Chapter 8. The Causes and Consequences of Technological Change in the Treatment of Acute Myocardial Infarction in Japan 156
Aki Yoshikawa, Haruko Noguchi, Saburo Ide, Akihiro Koike, Toru Maruyama, Naoto Uemura, and Akinori Urae, with Tsuruhiko Nambu

Chapter 9. Technological Change in the Treatment of Acute Myocardial Infarction in Korea 184
Bong-min Yang

Chapter 10. Technological Change in Heart Attack Care in Taiwan 193
Joan C. Lo and Mei-shu Lai

Chapter 11. Technological Change in the Treatment of Acute Myocardial Infarction in Sweden 208
Alexander Dozet, Sören Höjgård, Anna Lindgren, Hans Öhlin, and Carl Hampus Lyttkens

Chapter 12. Determinants and Consequences of Technological Change in the Care of Acute Myocardial Infarction Patients in Finland 233
Unto Häkkinen, Ilmo Keskimäki, and Kimmo Asikainen

Chapter 13. Determinants and Consequences of Technological Change in Health Care: Acute Myocardial Infarction in Denmark 252
Ivar Sønbø Kristiansen, Jørgen Clausen, Terkel Christiansen, and Jes Søgaard

Chapter 14. Technological Change in Heart Attack Care in England 268
Michael B. Robinson, Rob Manning, Mark Pettigrew, Nigel Rice, Mark Sculpher, and Trevor Sheldon

Chapter 15. Technological Change in Heart Attack Care in France: Causes and Consequences 289
S. Jacobzone, Brigitte Dormont, and Isabelle Durand Zaleski

Chapter 16. Technological Change in Heart Attack Care in Belgium: Causes and Consequences 306
N. Maes, P. M. De Coster, M. C. Closon, and J. Perelman

Chapter 17. The Determinants and Consequences of Technological Change in the Care of Acute Myocardial Infarction in Italy 323
Vincenzo Atella, Simona Giampaoli, Lorenza Pilotto, and Diego Vanuzzo

Chapter 18. Technological Change in Treatment of Acute Myocardial Infarction in Switzerland, 1986–1993 343
Fred Paccaud and Alberto Holly

Chapter 19. Determinants and Consequences of Technological Change in Heart Attack Care in Israel 356
Jeremy D. Kark, Amir Shmueli, Sylvie Goldman, and Ziona Haklai

Chapter 20. Conclusion 384
Mark B. McClellan and Daniel P. Kessler

Glossary 399

Contributors 405

Index 411

Acknowledgments

A great many people and institutions contributed to the research reported in this volume. We have built on a large body of existing international health research, such as the World Health Organization's MONICA (Multinational Monitoring of Trends and Determinants in Cardiovascular Disease) project. Indeed, several of the MONICA investigators are collaborators in our research network, and the analyses we report have benefited greatly from their expertise.

The book initially arose out of a conference held at Stanford University in February of 1998, with substantial additional effort by contributors thereafter. We gratefully appreciate the generous support of the U.S. National Institutes of Health (through grant R01-AG 17154 from the National Institute on Aging), the Stanford Graduate School of Business, and the Stanford Institute for Economic Policy Research for the conference and the effort underlying this research. In addition, support from the Hoover Institution at Stanford and the Commonwealth Fund enabled us to integrate the conference papers into this collection.

The contributors were aided immeasurably by the generous assistance of a number of individuals. Victor Fuchs and Alan Garber provided intellectual encouragement, especially in the early stages. Kathryn McDonald from Stanford's Center for Primary Care and Outcomes Research and Abigail Moreland expertly managed every aspect of the project, ranging from research design and implementation to conference planning. It would not have been possible without their intelligence, grace, and good humor. Pam Renna's flawless administration was an invaluable contribution. Jean Agras and Julie Lee worked tirelessly to edit and format text, tables, and figures. Three anonymous reviewers provided numerous helpful comments. Our editors, Rebecca McDermott and Ellen McCarthy, guided us through the publication process and helped us refine the chapters into a more coherent whole.

Finally, we would like to thank our families, and especially our spouses, Stephanie and Karen, for their patience with us as we worked on this project.

CHAPTER 1

Introduction: A Global Analysis of Technological Change in Health Care, with a Focus on Heart Attacks

Mark B. McClellan and Daniel P. Kessler

In virtually all developed countries, health care costs are rising and population health is improving. Technological change in health care, one of the most salient features of the industry, may be a major contributor in both of these worldwide facts. Yet many previous studies have shown that medical treatment differs substantially around the world. If *changes* in medical treatment also differ across countries, then policies that affect technological change may have important implications for both the nature and the magnitude of growth in medical expenditures and improvements in health. Because technological change in health care is rapid, these dynamic differences could have much greater long-term consequences for the health benefits and resource costs of different kinds of health care systems than differences between health care systems at a point in time. Despite its central importance, little is known about whether the incentives for changing medical practice provided by different health care systems influence technological change, or about the consequences of these differences.

This book presents the first report of a global research network that is implementing a new approach to analyzing the causes and consequences of technological change in health care. This approach involves the analysis of medical care for consistently defined, common health problems in a broad range of countries. By analyzing technological change at the micro level, we are able to integrate economic, clinical, and epidemiologic perspectives for understanding technological change. We are also able to minimize problems of noncomparability across countries and to isolate the contribution of medical care to health changes that, at a broader level, are influenced by many other factors.

We focus on care for heart attacks in this book. A heart attack is a common and serious illness in all developed countries, including Asian countries. It is a clinical condition that is defined similarly throughout the world and has been studied in a number of previous international epidemiologic studies. Because most of the key treatments for heart attack are delivered in inpatient settings, the problems of data reliability characteristic of other treatment settings are minimized. Moreover, many innovations have occurred in heart attack treatment in recent years, providing considerable opportunities for differences in technological change and their consequences to emerge.

In this chapter, we place our comparative study in the context of previous international research and introduce our methods. We begin by reviewing what is known about differences in technological change in health care across countries. We then describe the approach implemented in each chapter in the book. First, we describe how the regulatory and financial incentives for technological change differ across countries, by demonstrating how they can influence medical decisions for treating a common health problem. Second, we define our approach to measuring technological change and the consequences of technological change for patient health.

Technological Change in Health Care: Context and Previous Studies

Technological Change and Medical Expenditure Growth

Large differences in measured spending on health care across developed countries are well known. For example, per capita spending in Japan in 1995 was approximately $1,400, compared to over $3,000 in the United States. Perhaps less well recognized is the fact that medical spending, whether measured by share of GDP or real expenditures per capita, has increased enormously in recent decades. Real per capita spending in Japan has more than tripled in the past 25 years, and per capita spending in the United States has increased by more than 2.5 times. Newhouse (1993) noted that similar—and substantial—real expenditure growth rates occurred in virtually all the OECD (Organisation for Economic Cooperation and Development) countries, at least through the 1980s. In the 1990s, trends appear to have diverged (Anderson and Poullier 1999), but the reasons for this divergence are not well understood. Increasing health care expenditures are consequently a global concern.

Considerable evidence suggests that technological change in health care is responsible for much of this expenditure growth worldwide. Most of this evidence is indirect: all the other factors that might contribute to such expenditure growth seem able to explain only a small fraction of it.[1] Population aging has been and remains an important policy concern, yet even in the most rapidly aging countries it can account for real growth rates of perhaps 1 percent per year, often much lower than medical expenditure growth rates. Per capita income has increased as a result of economic growth, but the medical spending increases are far greater than can be explained by higher income alone. There is little evidence that regulation or competition in the health care industry has changed in a way that, in a static context, could lead to substantial price increases. Many countries have implemented important policy changes, such as large expansions of the availability of insurance, that might also contribute to one-time increases in expenditures if technology and these other factors are held constant. Once again, however, reasonable estimates of the impact of these policy changes, at least in the short term, explain only a small part of the growth in most countries.

Recently, more direct evidence on the importance of technological change has emerged, though most of it is confined to the United States. These studies focus on particular illnesses, because the treatments used in different illnesses differ, and their use must be quantified explicitly if technology is not to be treated as a residual. For example, Cutler and McClellan (1998) and Cutler, McClellan, Newhouse, and Remler (1998) show that virtually all of the expenditure growth in heart attack care is associated with the use of new treatments, or with increases in the quantities of existing treatments; in general, prices for particular treatments increase only slightly or actually fall over time. Unfortunately, little comparable evidence exists for most other countries, though there is no obvious reason to think that technological change is much less important in other parts of the world.

Another fact suggesting the universal importance of technological change in explaining medical expenditure growth is that, in a fundamental sense, production in health care is global. Although patients receive the vast majority of their medical care locally, the knowledge base, drugs, devices, and procedures that comprise this care are far from local. Clinicians throughout the developed world read many of the same medical journals and attend many of the same conferences. Drug and device manufacturers either are global or sell national or regional versions of products that are largely globally available, often as part of international collaborative ventures. Differences in national systems of drug regulation and, to a lesser extent, device regulation may imply that specific products may not become available in all countries at exactly the same time. But a quick look at medical reports from particular countries and the many international collaborative clinical studies suggests that approximately equivalent versions of all commonly used products are available in all developed countries, at least within several years of each other. And because international exchanges of medical information are generally not regulated, medical procedures—which consist mainly of labor inputs of expert time, effort, and skill, and comprise the bulk of medical expenditures—generally become known quickly throughout the world. In our study, virtually all of the major treatments that were quantitatively important contributors to medical expenditures were available in all of our participating countries, generally within several years or less.

Yet despite the global nature of basic knowledge about health care production, and the global availability of important health care products, many comparative studies have shown that medical practices differ substantially across countries. Thus, although technological change in health care may be driven ultimately by discovery and invention of new techniques and devices, cross-national studies of the causes and consequences of technological change focus on differences in rates of actual use of technologies.

This research demonstrates that nonmedical factors, in particular the financial and regulatory features embodied in a country's health care system, may explain much of these variations in practices around the world at a point in time. The research highlights another notable feature of the health care industry: how differently it is regulated and financed in developed countries around the world. We do not attempt to review this vast literature here; instead, we summarize one recent study to illustrate these prior comparisons. The McKinsey Global Research Institute (1996) conducted a detailed review of differences in medical practices and their consequences in three countries with quite different health care systems: the United States, the United Kingdom, and Germany.[2] The study assessed the treatment of lung and breast cancer, diabetes, and gallbladder disease, based on medical practices around 1990. The investigators documented substantial differences in practices, with generally higher intensity of care in the United States and Germany. For example, cancer patients in these countries received more (and more intensive) chemotherapy or radiation treatments, and gallbladder patients were much more likely to be treated with surgical procedures. They also documented higher prices for nurse and especially physician services in the United States, and to a lesser extent Germany. These findings were consistent with the overall differences in health care expenditures across countries.

Though these international comparison studies provide some evidence to support the view that differences in technology use across countries are important explanations for differences in expenditures, they do not provide much direct evidence on the core questions in this book. First, and most important, very few of these studies have a dynamic perspective: they do not examine changes over time. Thus, they provide little direct evidence on the key question of the sources of expenditure growth. If expenditure growth rates are similar across countries with very different expenditure levels, is it because technological change is identical but prices are proportionally lower in the less-expensive country? Or is it because the nature or magnitude of change in real medical practice actually differs across countries? Does the less costly country use new technologies less extensively? Or does it tend to adopt different kinds of technologies? Or does it follow medical practices in the more costly country with a lag? The potential importance of technological change in explaining the rapid expenditure growth in health care suggests that these are all crucial policy questions, and direct evidence on them is lacking. Second, with the notable exception of the McKinsey study, most of these international comparisons have only evaluated clinical practices, and have not sought to compare medical resource use or expenditures across countries. Third, many of these studies have relied in large part on reviews of the medical literature (which in turn largely reflects practices at academic centers), interviews with clinical experts, or local datasets. Because variability in practice across local geographic areas is also a global phenomenon, none of these sources may provide a very representative picture of national differences in medical practices, changes in practices, and their expenditure consequences.

Technological Change and Health Improvement

Previous studies of international differences in health have also led to some notable, and perhaps puzzling, results. Differences in gross measures of population health, such as life expectancy at age 60,[3] show little relation to the differences in health care spending just described. Substantial behavioral, cultural, and genetic differences, as well as differences in public health, educational, and income redistribution policies, have been cited as the likely reasons that little gross correlation between spending and health exists. To avoid these problems, many studies have focused on the treatment of particular well-defined health problems, for which relatively similar patient populations in different countries can be identified. For example, the McKinsey study of health care productivity examined the extent to which the differences in medical practices described above could plausibly be expected to lead to differences in health outcomes. Through a combination of literature reviews of treatment effectiveness and actual data on patient outcomes in the study countries, as well as estimation of reasonable valuations of the outcomes, the investigators concluded that U.S. productivity was better for cancer and gallbladder disease care. However, care for diabetes in the United Kingdom was better, because the multidisciplinary teams used to treat diabetics did a better job of triaging patients with different types and severity of diabetes to the most appropriate level of care. Other studies (e.g., Tu et al. 1997) have found less evidence of differences in health outcomes despite substantially different practices across countries. Once again, however, virtually all of these studies have examined practices at a point in time, raising the possibility that the differences across countries may be due to other country-specific factors.

In contrast to these studies, we examine differences in *changes* in health across countries. Focusing on changes may allow many of the potentially confounding country-specific factors to be differenced out. Moreover, if technological change really does improve health, then the dynamic health costs to a country of having worse policies for technological change may quickly dwarf any cross-sectional differences. In fact, almost all developed countries have experienced notable improvements in life expectancy in recent decades. For example, life expectancy at 60 has generally increased at a rate of around one year per decade since 1975. Quality of life, as assessed through a variety of different measures, also appears to have improved substantially in most countries. Because these countries have also experienced substantial expenditure growth, it seems plausible that the two trends are closely related.

The World Health Organization's MONICA project (Multinational Monitoring of Trends and Determinants in Cardiovascular Disease) represents a major international epidemiologic effort to document and understand possible national differences in the most important contributor to the improved life expectancy: reductions in death rates from ischemic heart disease, of which heart attacks are an important component.[4] MONICA covers population areas from a large number of developed and less developed countries. The study implemented careful and consistent methods for capturing all fatal out-of-hospital coronary disease events, as well as all hospital admissions for coronary events (including both heart attacks and acute chest pains or other symptoms short of a heart attack that also result from heart disease). This careful attention to detail in describing changes in the burden of heart disease has led to a number of important findings. First, the study confirmed the importance of a substantial decline in heart disease event rates over time in explaining the falling mortality rates from heart disease. Second, the study also documented substantial reductions in mortality among patients who reached the hospital alive. Both of these findings suggest an important role for technological change in explaining improved population health. Primary and secondary prevention of heart disease includes medications to reduce blood pressure, cholesterol levels, and the workload of the heart, and these medications have become much more widely used over the past 20 years. Public health measures such as advertising campaigns, behavioral changes such as reduced smoking, and other nonmedical factors may also be important contributors to the declines in event rates.

However, these findings also illustrate why it may be difficult to discern the impact of medical treatment and especially changes in medical treatment even in disease-specific mortality trends. The importance of medical treatment in prevention, relative to public health and other nonmedical factors, is questionable. The medications involved in prevention comprise only a small share of medical care and changes in resource use in the treatment of heart disease. In contrast, the hospital treatments for patients who reach the hospital alive are more representative of the bulk of health care resource use. But the third major finding of the MONICA project illustrates the limited importance of these treatments in contributing to the total mortality trends: the bulk of heart disease deaths are out-of-hospital deaths. Because the role of the health care system in preventing these deaths is limited,[5] and because innovations in prehospital medical care have also been limited,[6] it is not surprising that the level or trends in aggregate health care spending appear to have little relationship to the levels or declines in heart disease death rates documented in the MONICA study. Similarly, prevention, behavior, and public health measures may be important in explaining variations and trends in other causes of death and disability, such as cancer and stroke.

For these reasons, MONICA has primarily had an epidemiologic focus on total and out-of-hospital heart disease events, and on public health and other interventions for disease prevention, rather than on the performance of the health care system in treating hospitalized heart attack patients. Thus, our research complements many of the MONICA studies reported to date by directing attention to the subset of heart disease patients for whom innovations in medical care may have important health consequences. The research also complements the MONICA focus on public health with attention to the role of economic and regulatory incentives in contributing to health improvements. Many MONICA investigators are collaborators in our research network, and the analyses we report have benefited greatly from their incorporation of MONICA data on heart attack patients.

Technological Change in Heart Attack Care: A Global Analysis

These studies illustrate why our analysis focuses on technological change in health care, and on heart attacks. Despite its potential importance for understanding differences in medical expenditures and possibly health across countries, few detailed comparative studies of technological change exist. Though many studies have documented substantial differences in medical practices across countries, they provide little direct evidence on how treatment differences arise or evolve over time, and how economic and regulatory incentives might influence these changes.

Our research seeks to fill this critical gap. Aggregate studies of medical expenditure growth do not provide specific insights into how technological change contributes to medical expenditure growth in different countries, and discerning the effects of technological change on aggregate measures of population health—or even disease-specific aggregate measures such as heart disease mortality rates—is even more difficult. For these reasons, we follow much of the recent literature on international differences in medical technology and on technological change within countries and adopt a micro focus in our analysis. We study patients hospitalized with heart attacks for several reasons. First, heart attacks are a common, serious illness for which many medical treatments may affect outcomes. Second, it is relatively easy to collect reliable data on the characteristics, treatments, important outcomes, and resource use of large populations of heart attack patients in each of our participating countries, because so much of heart attack treatment is inpatient-based. Third, we can build on a substantial international epidemiologic literature that has provided basic insights into heart attack treatment and outcome trends; these results can also help validate the data used in our analyses. In the concluding chapter, we discuss how our methods can be extended to other important diseases.

The Technological Change in Health Care Global Research Network: Overview of Methods and Results

This book reports on a global analysis of technological change in heart attack care. It represents the collaborative effort of 18 research teams in 15 countries, comprising the Technological Change in Health Care (TECH) Global Research Network. The members of the investigating teams are listed at the back of this book; they include health economists, physicians who conduct clinical investigations, and epidemiologists. Integrating these perspectives effectively was essential to achieve the project's research goals. Countries represented, which span four continents, include the United States, Canada, Japan, South Korea, Taiwan, Switzerland, Australia, Israel, Finland, Sweden, Denmark, United Kingdom, Belgium, France, and Italy.

The TECH research summarized in this book had five components, all of which required substantial international collaboration. First, the research teams conducted structured evaluations of the key economic and regulatory incentives that might affect technological change for heart attack care in their country, and any major changes in these incentives. These descriptions provide concrete illustrations of how *exactly* treatment choices and changes in treatment choices may be affected by incentives. By developing a common method of describing diverse incentives in different health care systems, this phase of the project represents an important step toward sifting through the many complexities and idiosyncrasies of all health care systems to identify the most important features for understanding technological change. Second, the research teams identified the best available data in their country for conducting a large-scale empirical analysis of how the treatment of heart attacks had changed. This component of the project also required substantial coordination, to assure that all major treatment changes were described as accurately and consistently as possible across countries. Together, these phases of the research project permitted a comparative analysis of the effects of differences in economic and regulatory incentives on technological change in heart attack care.

The other major aim of the research strategy was to provide a foundation for evaluating the consequences of differences in technological change for health outcomes and medical resource use. To accomplish this aim, the research teams developed the best available large-scale data from their country on changes in mortality and in subsequent heart disease complications for heart attack patients. They also compiled data on medical expenditures for heart attack patients—in countries where payments for care occurred at the patient level—and on many other measures of resources used by heart attack patients, such as lengths of stay in intensive-care units, in the hospital, and in rehabilitation programs. Especially for long-term health and expenditure outcomes, complete longitudinal data were not available in some countries. Even in these cases, however, the research teams were able to develop some comparable outcome measures, and to identify feasible approaches to reduce these data limitations in the future.

In the remaining sections, we outline our research methods. We begin with a description of the framework used to describe economic and regulatory incentives affecting technological change, with illustrations of the enormous differences in these incentives across countries. We then describe our framework for summarizing the dimensions of technological change that have occurred in heart attack care. We conclude by reviewing our methods for describing the changes in health outcomes and medical expenditures for heart attack patients.

Incentives for Technological Change

Based on our review of the international and country-specific literature on economic influences on medical treatment, and extensive discussions with the economists and other participants in the research network, we identified a set of economic and regulatory incentives of health care systems that we hypothesized might influence technological change in each country. This analysis includes a consideration of the effects of health care payment systems, regulations, and a range of other economic and policy factors. Many of these factors have been the subject of cross-sectional studies, for example of the effects of copayments or differences in physician payment on treatment choices. Following Weisbrod (1991) and others, we emphasize the *dynamic* consequences of these policies. For example, lower patient payments or more generous physician payments for a particular treatment may provide incentives to develop expanded uses of a medical treatment that would be less encouraged under different reimbursement systems. As a result, differences in health care incentives and regulations may have substantial dynamic implications.

Patient Payment Incentives

The out-of-pocket payments by patients when they use medical services are quite different in different nations. Patient payments range from trivial or nonexistent in countries like the United Kingdom and Sweden, to very high rates in some Asian countries. For example, many insurance plans in Korea reimburse only a fraction of the cost of hospital admissions, procedures, and drugs. And Singapore relies heavily on Medisave, a mandated savings account for expenditures on health care by an individual or their family member, with only limited reliance on catastrophic insurance and low-payment public medical services. Many of the countries with low patient payments in their "basic" public insurance systems have more or less extensive systems of private insurance, where patients are responsible not only for their premium payments but also for substantial copayments when they use services. Australia provides a good example of this system, in which more than one-fifth of the population (largely those with higher demands for medical care) have private policies that provide coverage for a substantial amount of medical care.

Provider Payment Incentives

Countries also differ enormously in their provider payment systems. We considered two principal dimensions in which payment methods and changes in payment methods for hospitals, physicians, and other health care providers may differ: the *level* of payment ("average" payment generosity), and the *responsiveness* of payment to the use of more costly treatments for a patient ("marginal" or incremental payment generosity). Countries in our study vary enormously in these incentives. For hospital reimbursement, systems range from global budgets with relatively high (Canada) and low (United Kingdom, Denmark) average payments per bed or admission, to fee-for-service systems with relatively high (United States, for its "traditionally" insured and preferred-provider populations) and low (Japan, Korea) payment levels.[7] Other countries use intermediate systems, ones that respond to some extent (or for some kinds of treatment only) to the use of more costly treatments. For example, Australia and Taiwan now rely on diagnosis-related group systems for hospitals, which are "prospective" payments that differ in amount based on the diagnoses and technologies used to treat a patient (McClellan 1997). These countries also differ substantially in their average payment rate.

Payment systems for physicians also differ widely, in ways that differ from hospital reimbursement systems. For example, Canada pays physicians on a fee-for-service basis, so that more intensive treatments lead to more reimbursement (up to a cap), while "traditional" Medicare in the United States features a relatively more generous fee-for-service system. Physicians in Japan, Korea, and Singapore are also reimbursed largely on a fee-for-service basis. At the opposite extreme, physicians in Denmark and Sweden are salaried. In between, the United Kingdom and many managed-care plans in the United States use a "fee-for-patient" (capitation) reimbursement system, again with quite different average payment levels. The level and responsiveness of payments for drugs, devices, and other medical services also differ across countries.

Technology Regulation

Countries differ equally widely in their regulation of medical technology and the use of various medical treatments. Our reviews of technology regulation suggested that countries differed primarily in two broad types of regulation: macroregulation of the adoption or aggregate level of use of medical technologies, and microregulation of the use of medical technologies in particular cases. At the *macro* level, countries including Canada, the United Kingdom, Denmark, Sweden, and Finland all strictly review and limit the capabilities of providers to perform costly, intensive medical procedures. These government regulations generally affect "high-tech" medical technologies such as MRI scanners, cardiac cath labs, and open-heart surgery facilities. At the opposite extreme, countries including Japan, Korea, and the United States have little or no macroregulation of technological capabilities. In between, countries including France and Australia regulate intensive technological capabilities on a limited basis, for example in public hospitals but not the large number of privately owned hospitals.

Microregulation of technology use in individual patients, particularly the use of costly technologies, occurs on a more limited worldwide basis. The preapproval requirements, second-opinion requirements, and other features of utilization review that are a major part of managed care in the United States are well known. However, other countries have also begun to regulate technology use at the micro level. For example, the province of Ontario uses a relatively detailed clinical evaluation system to prioritize its waiting lists for bypass operations and other procedures that are subject to macroregulation. The United Kingdom also has "gatekeeper" requirements, involving preapproval by a patient's primary physician, for visits to specialists and other intensive services to be covered.

Hospital Ownership

Our participating countries also differ in the ownership of their health care facilities. In the United Kingdom, Denmark, and Sweden, hospitals and other facilities are publicly owned. However, these countries differ in the level of government with institutional control, ranging from the national government to local municipalities. Many countries, including Australia, France, and the United States, have mixed systems of hospital ownership, and also differ in the extent to which private ownership is for-profit or nonprofit. Countries such as Japan and Korea rely relatively heavily on for-profit ownership, even of teaching hospitals.

Competition

Countries differ in the extent to which their populations have effective choices among medical providers and health insurance plans. For its nonelderly population, the United States has a high degree of choice and thus competition at the health plan level. Other countries, including Japan and Switzerland, also have some freedom of choice of health plans. At the opposite extreme, universal government-funded health insurance programs such as those in Canada, Denmark, the United Kingdom, and Sweden have no choice in primary insurance plans, and (in some of these countries) only limited choices in supplemental private insurance policies. Many countries with limited choice of insurance plans, such as France, do have considerable freedom of choice among health care providers.

Physician Supply

Many countries, including some that do not regulate technology use strictly or rely on public payment systems, strictly regulate their supply of health professionals. Regulations may affect both the total supply and their distribution across specialties. Countries with relatively strict limits include Belgium, Denmark, and Sweden; countries with relatively little regulation include the Japan and the United States.

Other Factors

Virtually all research teams suggested that the factors listed previously were likely important determinants of technological change in their countries. Research teams in some particular countries also noted some additional factors; these are described in the chapters that follow. For example, investigators from the United States but virtually no other country noted the potential importance of malpractice liability concerns or "malpractice pressure" as an important incentive for technological change. Investigators from several countries also mentioned the importance of public and private policies on the provision of information about providers and the effectiveness of medical technologies. For example, information provided to patients was noted by investigators in some Canadian provinces (press coverage of waiting lists) and the United States (direct advertising to patients). Information provided to physicians and hospitals on such topics as the effectiveness of treatments (e.g., policy initiatives to educate doctors on treatment effectiveness in the United Kingdom) and on how their practices differed from those of their peers (e.g., utilization review activities in the United States) was noted as an important determinant of treatment changes in some countries. However, many more research teams reported that such information provision was likely to become a more important determinant of medical practice in the future, with further improvements in data collection systems on medical practices and outcomes.

International Differences in Technological Change

In this section, we review our framework for describing technological change in health care and comparing it across countries. We divide technological change into three main categories: changes in *high-tech* care, *low-tech* care, and the *appropriateness* of medical care. As we discuss in the concluding chapter, the framework was designed to be applicable to the analysis of technological change for any health problem, not just heart attacks.

High-Tech Changes

We define high-tech treatments as those with high fixed costs for provision, or marginal costs with each use. We focus on three specific treatments in this book: cardiac catheterization, angioplasty, and bypass surgery. Cardiac catheterization, also known as angiography, is used for diagnostic purposes to provide an image of the extent of blood flow to the heart and the extent of damage to the heart muscle after an AMI. Catheterization is a necessary prerequisite to performing either of the two high-tech therapeutic procedures that we study. The provision of cardiac catheterization is a high fixed-cost technology, requiring hospitals to hire specialized personnel (not only interventional cardiologists, but also specialized nurses and cath technicians) and purchase substantial specialized equipment (e.g., cath tables and fluoroscopic imagers).

Angioplasty and bypass surgery, also known collectively as revascularization procedures, are therapeutic procedures that are designed to increase blood flow to and from the heart in response to damage from an AMI and to cardiac vessel blockage. Both of these procedures also require substantial fixed investments and are expensive to perform on a per-case basis. Each case requires substantial specialized surgeon, cardiologist, and nurse input, as well as costly supplies like blood products and heart-lung bypass filters and tubing (in the case of bypass surgery).

In keeping with the TECH research strategy, all of the chapters in this volume report on trends in the use of these three intensive procedures. This enables us to evaluate how changes in the use of an identically defined technology vary across countries, abstracting from fixed differences in treatment patterns across countries and from other issues of comparability. Several of the chapters in this volume report on trends in procedure growth rates for the average AMI patient, or for an AMI patient with particular demographic characteristics. If data on procedures per AMI patient were not available, papers report on the total growth in these high-tech procedures per million residents.

Low-Tech Changes

We define low-tech treatments as those with low fixed and marginal costs of use. Essentially, these are treatments that individual doctors or other health personnel could provide without the use of substantial input of labor, capital equipment, or materials. For example, clinical trials in the 1980s documented important survival benefits from the use of drugs such as aspirin and beta-blockers soon after a heart attack. These drugs have been available for some time in generic versions. Unfortunately, data on trends in the use of important low-tech treatments are more difficult to obtain in many countries, especially over long time periods. Since use of low-tech treatments by definition does not have important consequences for resource use or resource allocation decisions, it is often not tracked by large-scale administrative databases. This is an important area for further research, as we discuss in the concluding chapter below.

Some drug treatments do not fit well under either a high-tech or a low-tech label. Of course, most drugs have very low social marginal costs of production. But some new, patent-protected compounds may be sold at a relatively high price, even to very large public purchasers. Whether the high price of new drugs represents the true social cost of the research and development that was required for their invention, or merely a transfer to patent owners, is a debate we will not enter here. Records on the use of drugs that have high costs per use, or are used in conjunction with other high-tech treatments, are more complete. For example, use of ACE inhibitors, drugs that have recently been shown to increase survival of patients with heart failure after their heart attack, increased at substantially greater rates in the United States than in other countries such as the United Kingdom. Use of costly nongeneric ACE inhibitors is common, and patients must be diagnosed as having heart failure before they are considered candidates for ACE inhibitors. To the extent that high-tech treatments like cardiac imaging procedures are required to diagnose heart failure, this complementarity between high- and low-tech treatments may have implications for low-tech treatment changes. Similarly, some thrombolytic drugs—which break down the blood clot responsible for the heart attack, restoring blood flow to the affected heart muscle before it dies—have high costs per use and/or require other high-tech procedures for appropriate use.

Changes in Expertise or Appropriateness

We characterize technological change not only in terms of changes in the use of various types of technology, but also in terms of changes in the *appropriateness* or experience with which such technologies are used. For example, two countries may have similar rates of use of catheterization and aspirin, but if medical professionals in the first country do a progressively better job of targeting the technology to the patients who would most benefit from it, then the first country is likely to have better outcomes after heart attack. Judgments about changes in appropriateness or the skill of physicians using the technology require detailed medical data over time to assess these issues, and such data are not currently available in most countries. However, many of the research teams were able to review research studies relevant to this question, and to identify better data for future studies. We suspect that differences in the appropriateness of technological change are important determinants of differences in outcome trends given observed trends in technology use rates, and that higher average reimbursement levels may lead to more rapid changes in appropriateness. However, in the current study we are only able to develop speculative evidence on this topic.

Outcome Changes

We explore the outcome consequences of the substantial differences in technological change across countries that are associated with differences in economic and regulatory incentives.We consider both health outcomes, especially mortality, and expenditure and resource use outcomes. Together, these trends provide a foundation for exploring the consequences of different incentive systems for changes in the productivity of health care systems.

Health Outcomes

Our research teams attempted to assemble the best longitudinal data on important health outcomes for their heart attack populations. In some countries, investigators were able to obtain long-term mortality follow-up data for all patients, regardless of location or cause of death. In other countries, linkage to death records for large populations is not feasible. Some of these countries were able to obtain long-term data on in-hospital mortality, and on the occurrence of readmissions with complications from heart attacks, including heart failure and recurrent heart attacks, that reflect a patient's functional status and thus quality of life. Some countries were unable to obtain longitudinal outcome data; these analyses have focused on mortality outcomes during the initial hospital episode of heart attack treatment. Many of these groups were able to use data sources on more limited populations within their countries, such as longitudinal heart attack registry data collected through the MONICA program, to obtain detailed information on trends in health outcomes for a smaller part of their country's population. In all of these cases, the investigators discuss the representativeness of their outcome data, as well as the potential for improvements in outcome data in the near future.

Expenditure Growth

Our research teams also attempted to assemble and analyze the best available data from their country on trends in expenditures, costs, or real resource use in heart attack care. In countries with longitudinal data and per-case payment systems, for example Australia, Belgium, Japan, Singapore, and the United States, conducting an analysis of expenditures was relatively straightforward. However, no equivalent per-case expenditure or cost measures exist in countries like Canada, the United Kingdom, Sweden, and Finland that rely on global budget systems. Investigators from these countries discuss some alternative approaches for evaluating resource use; among other things, they present data not only on trends in high-tech and low-tech treatment but also on overall hospital utilization by heart attack patients. Investigators in a number of countries were able to obtain estimated charges or costs for representative hospitals, physicians, and other providers of heart attack care, as a complementary source of information on costs. As with health outcomes, all investigators sought to highlighted potential opportunities for the development of better expenditure and cost measures in the near future.

The following chapters present the initial results of the TECH research teams, all based on the methods outlined here. The chapter organizations are similar, facilitating the cross-country comparisons of technological change, its causes, and its consequences. Because regional health care systems have some important similarities—in the characteristics of their populations if not in their economic and regulatory features—we group the chapters by region. We begin with North America, move on to Australia and Asia, and conclude with Europe and Israel. After presenting our analysis of each country's health care system, we summarize our findings in our concluding chapter, and also discuss the implications of these results for future research. While we present many new results on technological change in health care, its causes, and its consequences, we do not resolve all of the difficult issues we have raised in this overview. But one conclusion is very clear. Our research is the consequence of recent progress in the development of more comparable data on medical treatments, outcomes, and health care costs, in the use of more standardized methods to promote more valid cross-country comparisons, and in the formation of interdisciplinary collaborative research teams. These achievements are likely to make possible a new kind of careful, detailed, micro comparative research on changes in health outcomes and medical care across countries that could yield many further insights about the benefits and disadvantages of the vastly different economic and regulatory features of health care systems around the world. As issues of health reform and the economics of health care become increasingly important national policy concerns, these studies are likely to become an increasingly valuable approach for guiding health policies.

Notes

1. Newhouse (1992) illustrates this evidence in the case of the United States; the qualitative issues in other developed countries are similar.
2. For a concise summary, see Baily and Garber 1997.
3. We emphasize differences in health at older ages, because the health problems contributing to death and disability at these ages include heart disease, cancer, cerebrovascular disease, and other illnesses for which many medical treatments exist.
4. For an overview of MONICA, see Tunstall-Pedoe 1988; for a summary of MONICA results on the decline in cardiovascular mortality and their principal causes in participating countries, see Tunstall-Pedoe et al. 1999, and Tunstall-Pedoe et al. 2000. Summary estimates of the decline in ischemic heart disease mortality are available from other sources, e.g., Uemera and Pisa 1988, and OECD 1999.
5. See the detailed discussion of the relatively limited innovations in prehospital care in the United States in Heidenreich and McClellan 1998. For example, the average time to hospital arrival has not declined substantially in 20 years, and ambulance technologies and advanced cardiac life support procedures are largely unchanged. Informal investigations of changes in prehospital care in other countries suggest that the U.S. experience is representative, with only a few exceptions.
6. We discuss some country-specific exceptions in the analyses for particular countries below. For example, the French SAMU system permits the rapid use of thrombolytic agents and other treatments for heart attack patients in the field, whereas these treatments remain hospital-based in most countries.
7. Many analysts have noted that Medicare payments and payments in the fee-for-service insurance systems remaining today in the United States are low relative to historic levels. However, as we describe later, these payment levels are relatively high from an international standpoint.

References

Anderson, Gerard, and Jean Pierre Poullier. 1999. "Health Spending, Access, and Outcomes: Trends in Industrialized Countries. *Health Affairs* 18, no. 3: 178–87.

Baily, Martin, and Alan Garber. 1997. "Health Care Productivity." In *Brook-*

ings Papers on Economic Activity: Microeconomics, ed. Martin Baily, Peter Reiss, and Clifford Winston. Washington, D.C.: Brookings Institution.

Cutler, David M., and Mark B. McClellan. 1998. "Technological Change in Medicare." In *Topics in the Economics of Aging,* ed. D. Wise. Chicago: University of Chicago Press.

Cutler, David M., Mark B. McClellan, Joseph P. Newhouse, and Dahlia Remler. 1998. "Are Medical Prices Declining? Evidence for Heart Attack Treatments." *Quarterly Journal of Economics* 113, no. 4: 991–1024.

McClellan, Mark B. 1997. "Hospital Reimbursement Incentives: An Empirical Analysis." *Journal of Economics and Management Strategy* 6, no. 1: 91–128.

McKinsey Global Institute and the McKinsey Health Care Practice. 1996. *Health Care Productivity.* Los Angeles: McKinsey and Co.

Newhouse, Joseph P. 1992. "Medical Care Costs: How Much Welfare Loss?" *Journal of Economic Perspectives* 6, no. 3: 3–21.

———. 1993. "An Iconoclastic View of Health Cost Containment." *Health Affairs* 12 (suppl.): 152–71.

Organization of Economic Cooperation and Development (OECD). 1999. *OECD Health Statistics.* Paris: OECD.

Tu, J. V., C. D. Naylor, D. Kumar, B. A. DeBuono, B. J. McNeil, and E. L. Hannan. 1997. "Coronary Artery Bypass Graft Surgery in Ontario and New York State: Which Rate Is Right?" *Annals of Internal Medicine* 126:13–19.

Tunstall-Pedoe, Hugh, for the WHO MONICA Project. 1988. "The World Health Organization MONICA Project: A Major International Collaboration." *Journal of Clinical Epidemiology* 41:105–14.

Tunstall-Pedoe, Hugh, K. Kuulasmaa, M. Mahonen, H. Tolonen, E. Ruokokoski, and P. Amouyel. 1999. "Contribution of Trends in Survival and Coronary-Event Rates to Changes in Coronary Heart Disease Mortality: 10-Year Results from 37 WHO MONICA Project Populations." *Lancet* 353, no. 9164: 1547–57.

Tunstall-Pedoe, Hugh, Diego Vanuzzo, Michael Hobbs, M. Mahonen, Z. Cepaitis, K. Kuulasmaa, and U. Keil. 2000. "Estimation of Contribution of Changes in Coronary Care to Improving Survival, Event Rates, and Coronary Heart Disease Mortality across the WHO MONICA Project Populations." *Lancet* 355, no. 9205: 688–700.

Uemura, K., and Z. Pisa. 1988. "Trends in Cardiovascular Disease Mortality in Industrialized Countries since 1950." *World Health Statistics Quarterly* 41:155–78.

Weisbrod, Burton. 1991. "The Health Care Quadrilemma." *Journal of Economic Literature* 29, no. 2: 523–52.

CHAPTER 2

Technological Change in Heart Attack Care in the United States

Mark B. McClellan, Nathan Every, Alan M. Garber, Paul Heidenreich, Mark Hlatky, Daniel P. Kessler, Joseph Newhouse, and Olga Saynina

Over the last few decades, the United States has experienced both substantial growth in medical expenditures and improvements in health outcomes, especially at older ages. To provide further evidence on the role of technological change in the United States in contributing to these trends in outcomes and expenditures, we analyze recent changes in medical care, health outcomes, and medical expenditures for acute myocardial infarction (AMI, or heart attack) in the United States. Mortality from heart disease, most of which is directly or indirectly related to AMI, has declined rapidly in the United States in the last three decades. Figure 2.1 shows the overall age-adjusted mortality rates from AMI and ischemic heart disease for the U.S. population, and figures 2.2a and 2.2b show mortality rates for elderly and nonelderly Americans, respectively (National Center for Health Statistics 1999). The absolute rate of decline is much larger for the elderly, who have much higher death rates from heart disease. Reductions in ischemic heart disease mortality account for almost all of the recent improvements in heart disease mortality, and in turn the decline in heart disease mortality accounts for most of the improvement in overall mortality rates during this period. In turn, many observers (e.g., Braunwald 1997) have attributed the survival improvements to the substantial changes occurring in the technology of treating AMI and other acute forms of coronary disease, suggesting that these changes were having valuable consequences for the health of the population.

We first describe the context of economic and regulatory incentives in which technological change occurs in the United States. Next, we use detailed microdata to describe the changes in AMI treatment

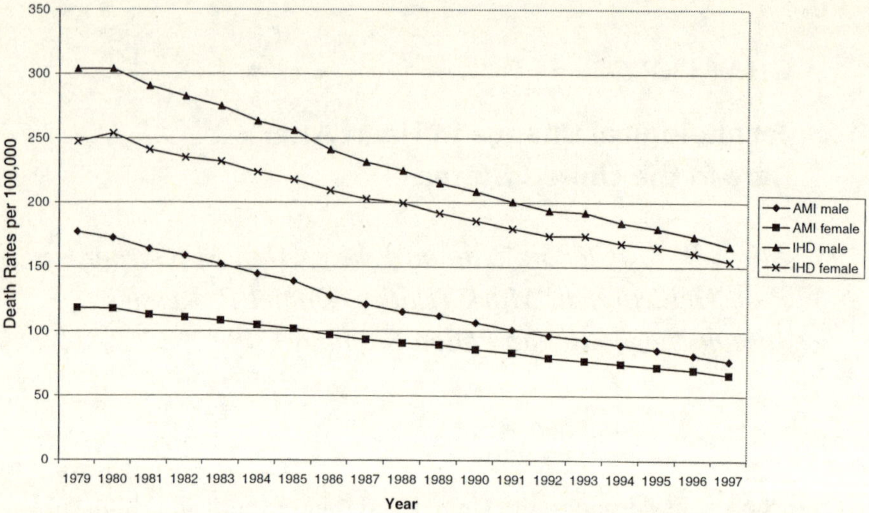

Fig. 2.1. Adjusted mortality rates from AMI and ischemic heart disease, U.S. population, 1990 population weights

that have occurred in recent years. We then discuss the implications of the incentives for understanding the technological change in AMI care that has occurred, and thus the effects of these incentives on changes in the health and medical spending of Americans. Many AMI treatments have changed, and summarizing the causes as well as the consequences of these changes is necessarily speculative. Nonetheless, the results presented here suggest that technological change in the United States has differed in some important respects from changes in other developed countries.

1. Incentives for Technological Change in the United States

Financing of Heart Disease Care

Americans receive health insurance from three major sources. Almost all elderly citizens are covered by Medicare, a federal (public) insurance program financed by premium payments by beneficiaries (which cover approximately one-fourth of program costs), payroll taxes, and general tax revenues. The principal source of insurance for nonelderly

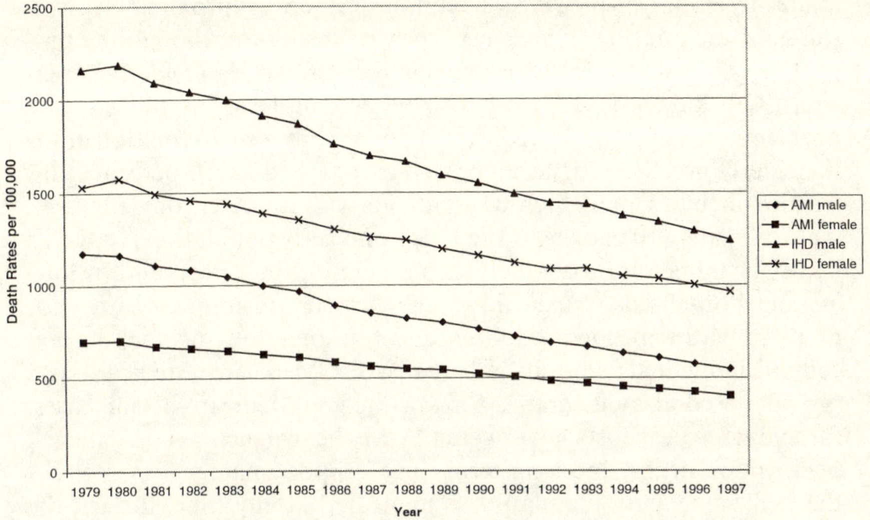

Fig. 2.2a. Adjusted mortality rates from AMI and ischemic heart disease, U.S. population ages 65-plus, 1990 population weights

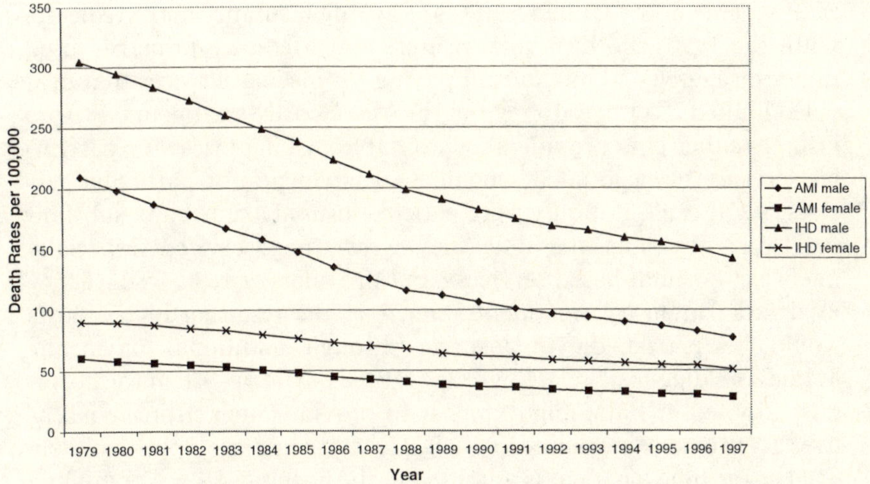

Fig. 2.2b. Adjusted mortality rates from AMI and ischemic heart disease, U.S. population ages 40–64, 1990 population weights

adults is employer-provided health insurance. Approximately two-thirds of the nonelderly have such private insurance, though the proportion covered has slowly declined in recent years. Nonelderly Americans with kidney failure and with other long-term disabling health problems are covered by Medicare. Though only a small fraction of the nonelderly are covered through Medicare (less than 10 percent), this fraction includes many high-cost patients with severe chronic illnesses. Approximately 10 percent of the U.S. nonelderly population is covered by Medicaid, a joint federal-state (public) insurance program for low-income households. Medicaid is the primary insurance source for mothers with dependent children and for some low-income, chronically ill individuals who do not qualify for Medicare. Medicaid also provides secondary insurance for low-income Medicare beneficiaries, for many medical costs not covered by Medicare (such as copayments, prescription drugs, and long-term care). Approximately 17 percent of the U.S. nonelderly population is uninsured at any time, though the fraction uninsured with serious medical problems is smaller. For example, only around 5 percent of individuals in their fifties with heart attacks have no health insurance by one to three years after their heart attack (Falba and McClellan 2000).

Thus, the principal sources of health care financing for heart disease patients in the United States are private insurance and Medicare. Until the 1990s, both private insurers and Medicare primarily used rather disaggregated methods of paying for medical services that provided limited incentives to restrict the use of costly treatments. Private insurers either paid providers' "reasonable" asking prices for particular services, or negotiated schedules of payments for particular services. As a result, not only were patients insured against any substantial expenditures at the time they were using services—especially intensive, hospital-based services—but providers were as well. If they used more intensive treatments, much of the resulting higher costs would be passed on to insurers through additional payments. Medicare's diagnosis-related group (DRG) payment system for hospitals, adopted in 1984, might appear to provide much stronger incentives to providers to limit costs. DRG payments are approximately fixed at the time a patient is admitted to the hospital. However, almost half of the DRGs (and most DRG expenditures) are "treatment based." In the case of heart attack care, for example, a hospital receives substantially greater Medicare reimbursement if it performs angioplasty or bypass on a heart attack patient, rather than treating the patient with drugs and monitoring alone. As a result, even the DRG system allows hospitals to pass on much of the additional cost of using intensive cardiac procedures (McClellan 1997b).

In recent years, managed-care plans have grown rapidly among privately insured Americans, from less than one-fourth of covered individuals in the early 1990s to more than four-fifths of individuals today (Kuttner 1999). Managed-care patients typically face even smaller out-of-pocket costs than those in traditional insurance plans. But managed-care plans typically use payment systems for providers that do not allow as much of the cost of intensive services to be passed through. For example, primary physicians and even specialists may receive fixed, capitated payments per patient enrolled in the plan, or be reimbursed for intensive services at substantial discounts. Hospitals are often paid according to per diem payments that do not vary much with the disease severity of the patient or the intensity of the service provided. Though the payment systems used by managed-care plans vary enormously, they generally make providers bear much more of the cost of intensive services. Managed-care plans have also started to grow in Medicare. But in the years after 1997, enrollment in such plans stabilized at around one-sixth of Medicare beneficiaries (*HCFA Statistical Supplement* 1999). Moreover, considerable evidence suggests that Medicare beneficiaries with serious health problems like ischemic heart disease were less likely to choose to enroll in such plans (Laschober 1997).

This discussion suggests that provider payments have become less responsive to the use of more costly treatments in the United States. Both private and Medicare payment systems are moving away from reimbursing specific minor treatments (e.g., particular drugs or blood tests) and toward more aggregated payments for services. Even so, payments for Medicare beneficiaries remain largely fee-for-service, at least at the level of a physician or hospital visit. And only a minority of managed-care plans use budgets for providers that are completely fixed. As a result, the financial incentives for adopting costly, intensive medical technologies may still be more favorable in the United States than in many other countries.

Technology Regulation

The initial adoption of new drugs in the United States is regulated by the U.S. Food and Drug Administration (FDA). The FDA's approval process for most new drugs has been criticized as excessively burdensome, with prolonged clinical trial and review requirements. However, this process has been streamlined in recent years (although the costs to bring a drug to market remain substantial). Moreover, after a drug is approved, there is little explicit regulation of its use and pricing. Though the FDA also is responsible for regulating new devices, in practice most new devices do not face substantial obstacles to adoption (they are often classified as "substantially similar" to existing devices). The use and pricing of devices also involves little direct regulation. Medicare and managed-care plans do regulate payments for drugs and devices used in the course of inpatient stays indirectly, because payment for these services is generally included in the aggregated payment that the providers receive. Medicare pays for drugs used in the outpatient hospital setting based on a system of regulated prices, but generally does not cover outpatient prescription drugs. Medicare beneficiaries pay for such prescriptions either out of their own pocket or through supplemental private insurance policies or Medicaid. Managed-care plans typically cover most of the cost of prescription drugs, but may negotiate discounted purchase prices in association with formulary restrictions (e.g., by only covering one or two particular compounds from a therapeutic class of drugs like beta-blockers with identical mechanisms of action).

Government "macroregulation" of technology acquisition by health care providers is minimal, whether for minor devices or major capital investments like cardiac catheterization laboratories.[1] Though few government regulatory barriers to technology use exist following their initial approval, so-called microregulation of technology use in the United States has risen. Both managed-care plans and "peer review" organizations sponsored by Medicare and Medicaid now undertake utilization-review and other activities to evaluate whether costly treatments are "appropriate" in particular cases, and to judge the quality of care in these cases. These case review programs are increasingly used to determine whether services are allowable for payment, to guide managed-care plan decisions about contracting with providers, and to provide information on provider quality for health care purchasers and consumers.

Competition

The United States relies rather heavily on competition among insurers and health care providers. Historically, insurers placed minimal restrictions on patient choices of either physicians or hospitals. Because provider payments depended entirely on attracting patients, and because patient out-of-pocket payments were limited, physicians had to attract patients primarily through intensity, amenities, or other aspects of quality. In turn, hospitals attracted patients and physicians by similar mechanisms, for example by providing pleasant work environments for physicians and intensive treatments for patients. More recently, managed-care plans have restricted physician and hospital choices of their enrollees. However, these restrictions have emerged in association with increased competition among managed-care plans to enroll patients. Thus, competition among plans and hence among providers now appears to be relatively more important (Feldstein and Buchmueller 1997; Kessler and McClellan 2000).

Other Incentives for Technology Adoption and Use

Several other influences on changes in treatment decisions have received particular attention in the United States. Though the direct costs of malpractice are relatively large in the United States, malpractice premiums only amount to a small fraction of total medical expenditures. Nonetheless, malpractice liability concerns are widely cited by doctors as a justification for additional diagnostic tests and therapeutic interventions (e.g., U.S. Congress 1994), and some evidence suggests that limitations on malpractice liability lead to reductions in expenditure growth through reductions in the growth of medical treatment intensity (Kessler and McClellan 1996). Whether limitations on malpractice liability have long-term effects on technological change, and whether the potentially higher degree of malpractice concern in the United States is an important long-term determinant of technological change, is less clear.

The United States also imposes relatively few regulatory restrictions on entry and earnings for medical specialists. Board certification in a specialty generally requires completion of a certified training program in the United States, and training program certification and testing are largely self-regulated by the specialty boards. Though some critics have suggested that the resulting entry restrictions give specialists monopoly power, the lack of any central regulation of specialization and financing of specialty education is probably responsible for the much larger share of specialists in the United States relative to Canada and European countries. To the extent that more specialization supports more extensive technological change, or at least more rapid or extensive adoption of specialized treatments, this difference in physician specialty mix may be an important contributor to differences in technological change in the United States.

2. Technological Change in AMI Care in the United States

We present evidence on technological change in AMI care in two parts. First, we use large administrative databases to describe changes in some key "high-tech" AMI treatments. By high-tech treatment, we mean the use of procedures and devices that require substantial fixed investments in equipment and specialized personnel, or that have high equipment and personnel costs with each use, or both. We use administrative records from the Medicare program to describe trends in high-tech procedure use for the entire U.S. elderly population with AMI for 1984–94, and we use hospital records from the state of California to describe trends in high-tech procedure use for the nonelderly population of the state for 1991–95. Reliable longitudinal data on large populations of nonelderly AMI patients is not available prior to 1991; for the 1980s, we review some relevant clinical studies to supplement our results for the elderly. The reasons for our emphasis on California include the large size of the state, and the high penetration of managed-care plans in the state by the early 1990s, allowing us to explore whether managed-care growth has substantially affected trends in technology use.

Second, we summarize previous clinical studies of treatment use as well as analyses of the U.S. National Registry of Myocardial Infarction to describe trends in the use of some key "low-tech" AMI treatments. By low-tech treatment, we mean procedures, devices, and drugs that do not require large fixed investments and that have relatively modest costs of use. These treatments are not recorded reliably (i.e., in a way that can be linked to the occurrence of heart attacks in a large, representative sample of patients) in most U.S. administrative databases for public and private insurance programs. We focus primarily on changes in drug treatment, which have been particularly notable over the past decade in AMI care, but we consider some other changes in technology as well.

We concentrate on treatment changes during the acute episode of AMI care. This clinical episode might reasonably be defined to include the 30- or 90-day period following AMI. As the following results show, however, the most dramatic changes in AMI treatment in the United States have occurred in the initial hours and days after the heart attack occurs. In addition to these acute treatments, we also briefly consider changes in treatments designed to prevent first AMIs, postacute treatments designed to prevent further complications of ischemic heart disease, and the postacute treatment of AMI complications.

Changes in High-Tech Care: Intensive Cardiac Procedures and Hospital Use

In the United States, treatment for AMI and ischemic heart disease has relied heavily on the "open artery" principle, the straightforward idea that reducing or eliminating blockages in coronary blood vessels supplying the heart will prevent heart damage and complications (e.g., Braunwald 1996). The gold-standard invasive diagnostic procedure used to assess artery status is cardiac catheterization, which may be followed by either coronary artery bypass graft surgery (CABG) or percutaneous transluminal coronary angioplasty (PTCA) to remove areas of blockage detected on catheterization.

Figures 2.3 through 2.6 show changes from the mid-1980s to the mid-1990s in the use of these intensive cardiac procedures within 90 days after AMI in the U.S. elderly. Use of all of these procedures has grown enormously in both the elderly and nonelderly. Less than 10 percent of elderly AMI patients underwent catheterization in 1984, compared to around half of all elderly patients by 1996 (fig. 2.3a). Figure 2.3b shows the trends in catheterization use by age and gender, including trends for nonelderly residents of California for 1991–95.[2] Though catheterization rates were increasing for the nonelderly as well, they grew somewhat less rapidly in the 1990s because they started from a higher level. By the late 1990s the catheterization rates for patients aged 65–74 had almost caught up with the rates for patients under 65, and more rapid growth was occurring in older AMI patients. (Rates for the California elderly are also slightly higher than for the overall U.S. elderly, but growth rates are similar.) Indeed, figure 2.3b suggests two different phases of procedure growth by age. Prior to 1989, although rates were increasing for all demographic groups, they increased relatively more rapidly for the younger elderly (65–69) than for the older elderly (80–89). Since 1989, the relative rate of growth for the older elderly increased, as procedure growth in the young elderly approached the "plateau" of younger patients. Greater use of intensive treatments in the older elderly has thus become an increasingly important component of technological change in AMI care in the United States. Moreover, essentially all of the growth in procedure use in the past decade has consisted of more use of procedures soon after AMI, that is, within 7 days.

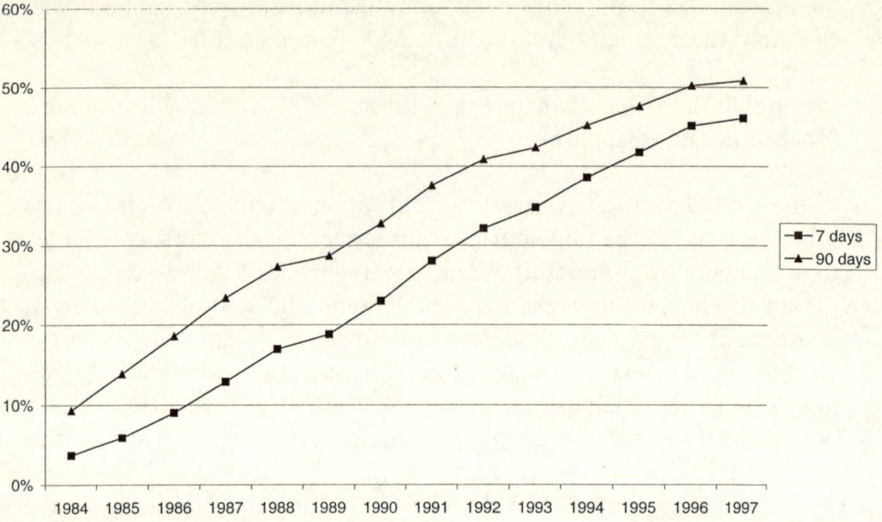

Fig. 2.3a. Cardiac cath rates for elderly U.S. AMI patients

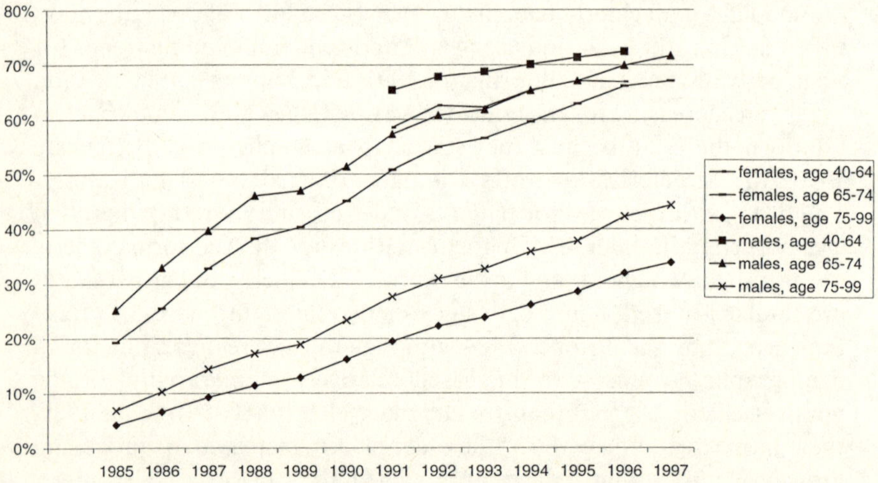

Fig. 2.3b. Ninety-day cardiac cath rates, by demographic group

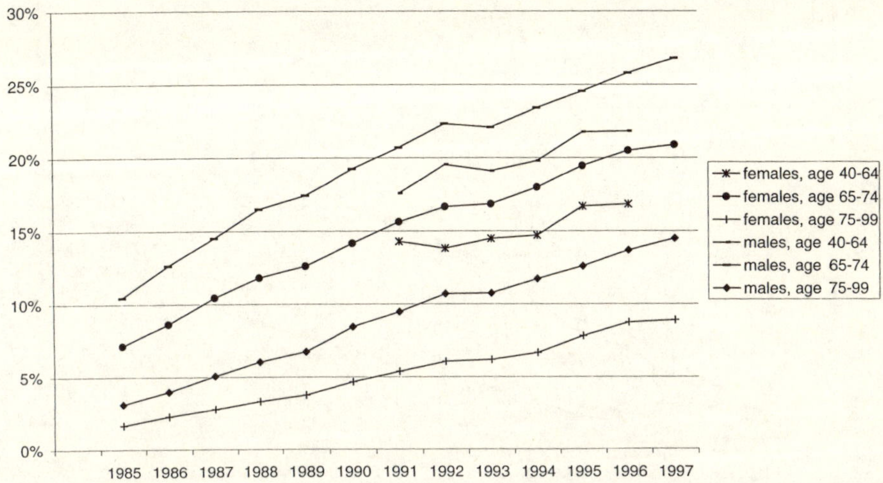

Fig. 2.4. Ninety-day CABG rates for U.S. AMI patients, by demographic group

Figure 2.4 shows trends in the use of bypass surgery. Over our study period, bypass surgery rates increased from less than 5 percent to around 15 percent. Growth rates for bypass surgery have also been somewhat more rapid in recent years for older AMI patients; indeed, the rates of bypass surgery are higher among patients aged 65–74 than they are among younger AMI patients.

Figure 2.5 shows trends in the use of PTCA, or angioplasty. PTCA growth has been even more substantial than CABG, from virtually no use in 1984 to over 20 percent of patients by 1995. Trends by age and gender are summarized in figure 2.5a. In contrast to bypass surgery, angioplasty has become relatively more common among younger AMI patients: younger patients by the mid-1990s were almost twice as likely to undergo PTCA as CABG, whereas the procedures were more equally used among elderly patients. Figure 2.5b illustrates trends in the timing of angioplasty as well as the use of stents for the elderly. As the figure shows, all of the procedure growth has occurred soon after AMI, and a substantial amount of growth has occurred in the use of primary angioplasty—that is, angioplasty within one day of AMI. Though most angioplasty and bypass surgery procedures are performed with the goal of secondary prevention after the patient has been stabilized, primary angioplasty is a method for restoring blood

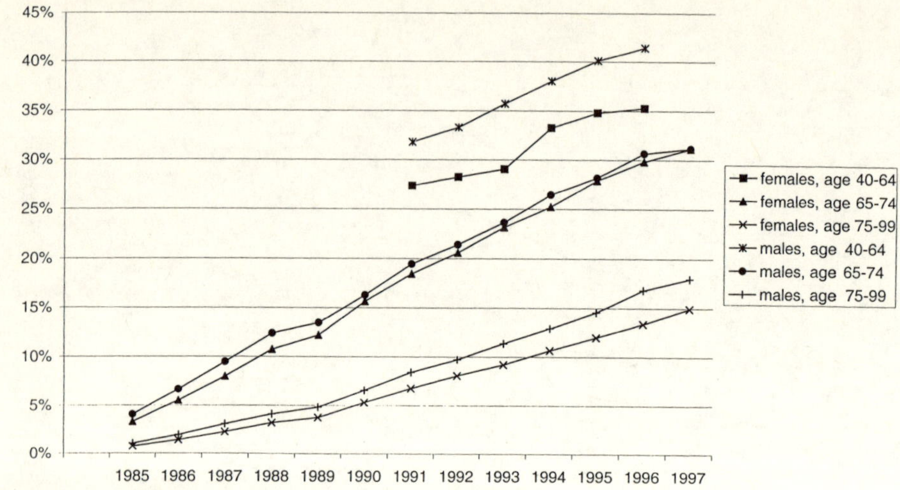

Fig. 2.5a. Ninety-day PTCA rates for U.S. AMI patients, by demographic group

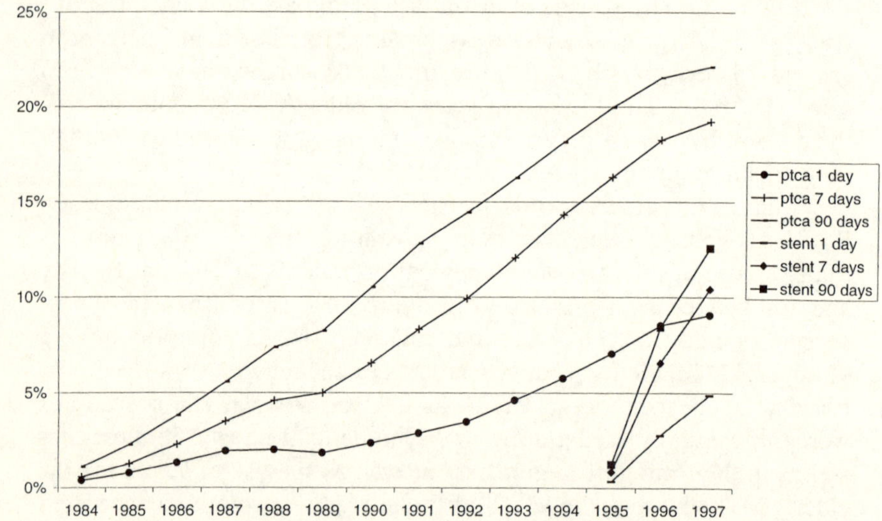

Fig. 2.5b. PTCA timing and stent use in U.S. elderly AMI patients

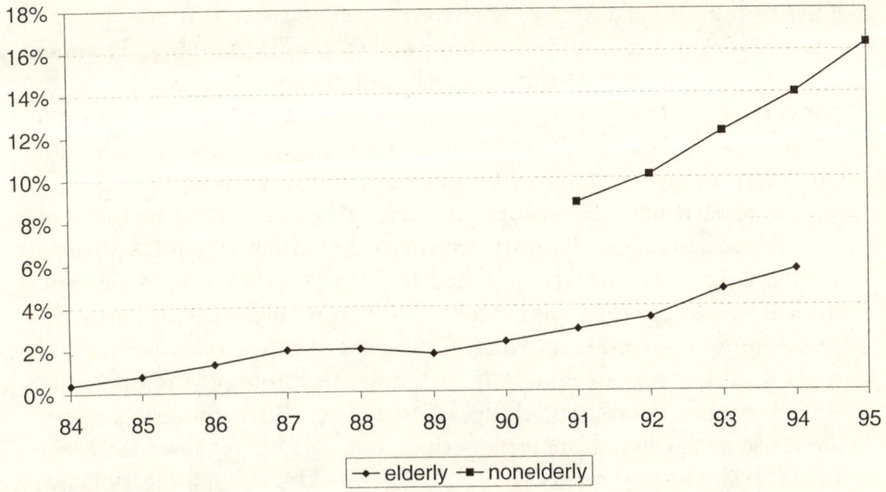

Fig. 2.5c. One-day angioplasty rates in elderly and nonelderly AMI patients

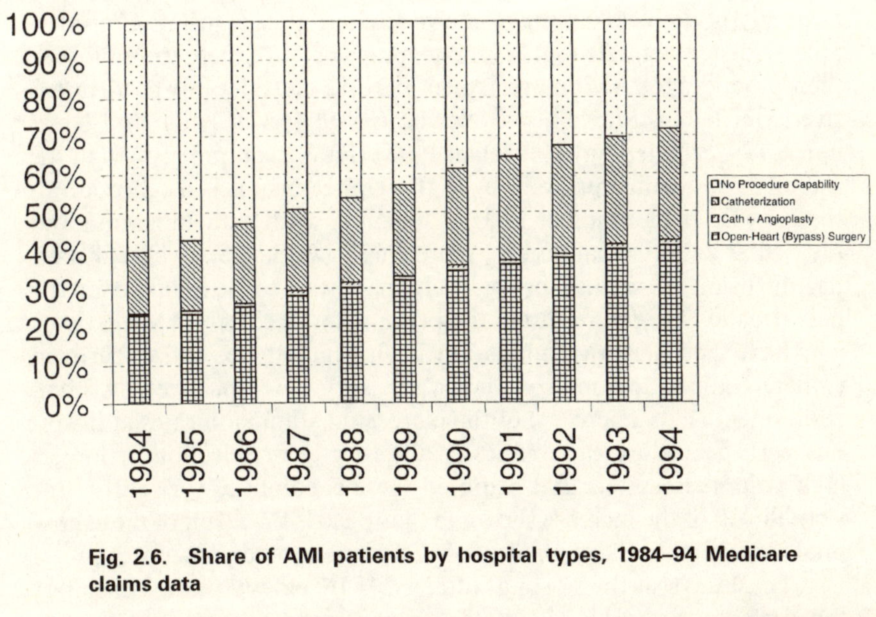

Fig. 2.6. Share of AMI patients by hospital types, 1984–94 Medicare claims data

flow to the affected area of the heart *during* an AMI. If successful, it can prevent much of the damage associated with the AMI. Trends in angioplasty use for nonelderly AMI patients have been similar to use for elderly patients—use of procedures soon after AMI accounts for all of the growth—except that primary angioplasty has become even more common. Figure 2.5c illustrates this more rapid trend.

A related new technology that may be contributing to the rapid recent growth of angioplasty use in AMI patients is intracoronary stents, wire rims that are designed to help keep a blood vessel open after it has undergone angioplasty. Unfortunately, as with many new technologies, hospital reporting of stent use appears to become reliable in U.S. data only around 1995, after the technology was first introduced. A large number of clinical studies (e.g., Bittl 1996) suggest that stent use has grown more rapidly than angioplasty use since 1993. Figure 2.5b shows that stents have diffused quickly; though the 1995 estimate may be understated, it is clear that a majority of angioplasties were done with stents by 1997.

Performing angioplasty requires the capability to perform catheterization and revascularization on site. Patients initially admitted to hospitals that do not perform catheterization or revascularization may nonetheless undergo the procedure after transfer. Considerable evidence suggests that, when hospitals acquire these technologies, their practices for AMI management become considerably more intensive (McClellan, McNeil, and Newhouse 1994; McClellan and Newhouse 1997; Cutler and McClellan 1998). Thus the rapid growth in the use of these cardiac procedures in the United States is a reflection of the growth in the number of U.S. hospitals with catheterization and revascularization capabilities. Figure 2.6 shows this relatively substantial diffusion of cardiac procedure capabilities to hospitals over the past decade. The figure shows the proportion of elderly AMI patients who have their first AMI admission at a hospital that is able to perform catheterization, angioplasty, and bypass surgery, respectively. A small component (1 to 2 percent) of the increasing admission rates at hospitals with procedure capabilities is due to greater selection of larger, high-volume hospitals that acquired these capabilities very early. But virtually all of the increase shown in figure 2.6 is the result of more hospitals investing in the capability of performing these procedures.

Total days in the hospital after AMI by elderly patients has not fallen much in the United States, in contrast to other countries, as figure 2.7a shows. The average number of hospital days in the year after AMI declined slightly in the early years following implementation

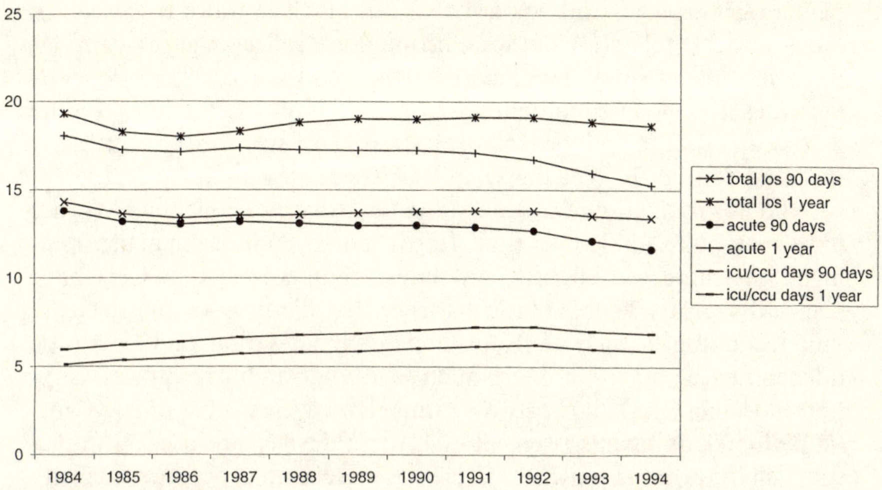

Fig. 2.7a. Average length of stay for elderly AMI patients

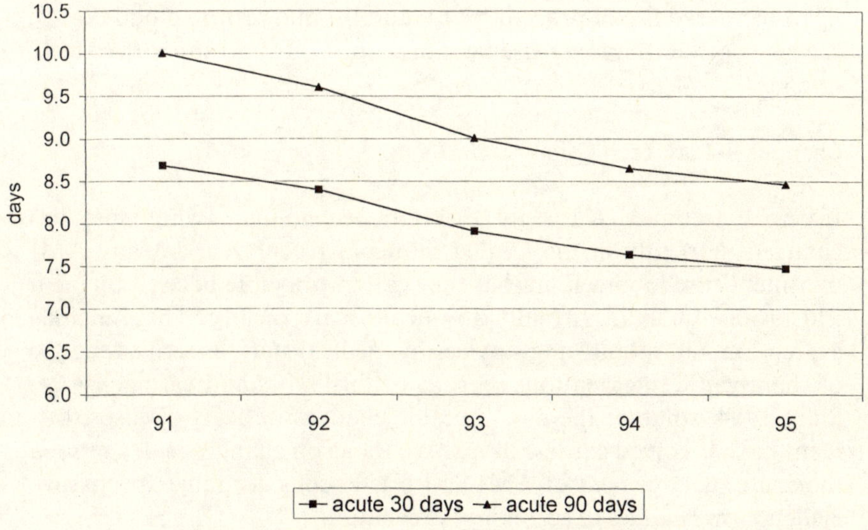

Fig. 2.7b. Length of stay in acute hospitals, nonelderly AMI patients

of the DRG system and has not changed much in more recent years. However, this relatively flat total hospital use reflects a more complex pattern: acute hospital days have declined, but they have been offset by increases in nonacute rehabilitation or skilled-nursing facilities. Figure 2.7b shows that the pattern in hospital length of stay for the nonelderly is similar to that for the elderly, at least for acute-care hospital use.

Trends in the use of coronary and intensive care units in AMI care have been quite stable over time. In particular, their use in acute treatment has increased slightly, but later readmissions to CCUs have declined slightly. There is little evidence that diagnostic intensive care unit technologies such as Swan-Ganz catheterization or therapeutic intensive care unit technologies such as intubation for respiratory support have increased markedly over time. However, the use of intra-aortic balloon pumps has risen, though these devices are used in only a small share of AMI patients. Thus, the increasing procedure intensity in AMI illustrates substantial growth in high-tech care for AMI in the United States, even for the oldest heart attack patients. But this intensity growth has not translated into much change in the total amount of time patients are spending in the hospital, and it has consisted primarily of increased use of procedures to monitor and restore blood flow to the heart rather than increased use of monitoring and supportive technologies.

Changes in Low-Tech Care

Intensive treatments are not the only technologies whose use has changed markedly in the United States in recent years. Many AMI treatments are low-tech, in that they can in principle be used by medical professionals in virtually any health care facility. These include evaluation and monitoring services by medical staff, as well as the use of therapeutic interventions such as defibrillators and cardiac drugs. Since 1984, some of the most notable changes in heart disease treatment have involved cardiac drugs. We focus on changes in drug use in the acute management of AMI and briefly consider more speculative evidence on changes in secondary prevention.

Clinical trials over the past two decades have shown clear benefits for acute survival of AMI from the use of aspirin, thrombolytics, beta-blockers, heparin, and nitrates. All of these treatments have become much more widely used in the United States for acute treatment. The treatment whose use in acute care appears to have increased most dramatically in the United States is aspirin, from around 15 percent of patients in 1980 to over 80 percent of patients by 1995 (Rogers et al. 1996; Goldberg et al. 1987; Burns et al. 1997). Beta-blocker use also increased, and this drug was used in over half of AMI patients in 1995, though most of the increase occurred before 1985 (Goldberg et al. 1987; Gurwitz et al. 1994; McLaughlin et al. 1996). Heparin use increased from around half of patients in the early 1980s to around three-fourths of patients in 1995, though other anticoagulants may have been widely used instead of heparin in earlier periods (Rogers et al. 1994; McGovern et al. 1996; Goldberg et al. 1991). Intravenous nitrates appear to have been widely used (more than 80 percent of AMI patients) by 1980, and some modest further growth in nitrate use may have occurred since that time (e.g., Goldberg et al. 1987).

Thrombolytic or "clot-busting" drugs, introduced in the mid-1980s, have gradually diffused into moderately widespread use. Around 9 percent of patients (virtually all nonelderly) received thrombolytics by 1987, and this proportion increased to 24 percent by 1992 and 31 percent by 1995 (Rogers et al. 1996; Chandra et al. 1997), with substantial use in the elderly under age 80. Tissue plasminogen activator (tPA, or alteplase), and not streptokinase or other generic thrombolytic drugs, has accounted for the vast majority of thrombolytic drug use in the United States. Although many studies have shown that time to thrombolytic drug use is strongly related to the drugs' effectiveness, the average time to thrombolytic use in the United States may be relatively high. Results from multiple sources show an average time to treatment of two hours or more, which has not improved significantly in recent years (Yarzebski et al. 1994; Rogers et al. 1994; GISSI Investigators 1997). One reason may be that, with the exception of a few rural areas, thrombolytics are administered only in hospitals under direct physician supervision.

At the same time as these dramatic increases in treatment use were occurring, other treatments were becoming less widespread. Calcium channel blockers, developed in 1982, became very widely used in AMI treatment by the mid-1980s, perhaps in as many as 64 percent of nonelderly AMI patients (McGovern et al. 1992; Gurwitz et al. 1994). However, with the publication of several observational studies and other clinical reports suggesting worse outcomes of AMI with short-acting calcium channel blockers, their use declined substantially, to 31 percent of patients by 1993 (Rogers et al. 1996). With studies showing adverse consequences from the prophylactic use of lidocaine (a drug intended to prevent irregular heart rhythms), its use declined from almost half of patients in the mid-1980s to around 15 percent of patients by 1995 (Goldberg et al. 1987; Chandra et al. 1996).

Figures 2.8a and 2.8b, based on data from the National Registry of Myocardial Infarctions,[3] show recent (1993–97) trends in drug use during AMI admissions and at discharge (a measure of the initial postacute treatment of AMI), respectively. Figure 2.8a shows that, for the most part, the trends discussed in the preceding literature review have continued. In particular, use of aspirin, beta-blockers, and ACE inhibitors has continued to rise, while use of calcium channel blockers and lidocaine acutely after AMI has continued to decline. Of note, the use of thrombolytic drugs in the United States has been declining; this distinctive trend appears to be a reflection of the rising use of primary angioplasty. Figure 2.8b shows that the greater use of aspirin, beta-blockers, and ACE inhibitors persists into the posthospital treatment phase.

Because few quantitative studies exist, evidence on changes in the use of prehospital and postacute AMI care other than drug therapy in the United States is more speculative. Advanced cardiac life support (ACLS) in the field and during transport to the hospital has become available in more geographic areas, though as noted above, this trend has not substantially reduced time to treatment. Postacute cardiac rehabilitation programs have expanded, particularly for the elderly, but it is difficult to obtain reliable data on how much their use has increased. The proportion of elderly AMI patients with admissions to nonacute hospitals after AMI has increased from around 5 percent to 15 percent of patients over the past 10 years, and around one-third of patients enrolled in the GUSTO (Global Utilization of Streptokinase and Tissue Plasminogen Activator for Occluded Coronary Arteries) trial were reported to be enrolled in some kind of cardiac rehabilitation program (Mark et al. 1994). Clinical trials in the past decade involving U.S. patients have shown significant reductions in long-term mortality for nonelderly AMI patients treated chronically with aspirin, beta-blockers, and cholesterol-lowering drugs (Lau et al. 1992), and informal clinical observations suggest that use of these three types of drugs has increased.

Changes in Expertise or Appropriateness of Care

The summary of changes in AMI treatment in the preceding sections has focused on changes in treatment rates. New clinical trials,

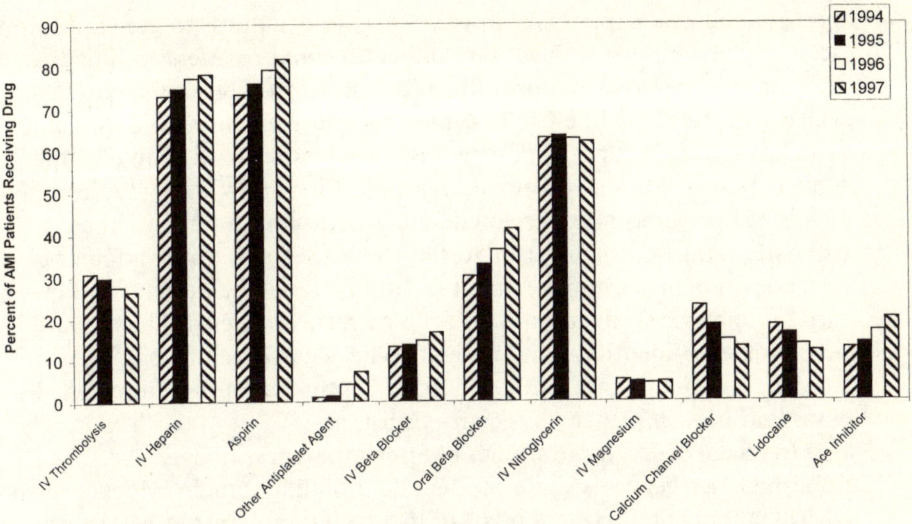

Fig. 2.8a. Trends in in-hospital medication use within 24 hours of AMI, U.S. National Registry of Myocardial Infarctions, 1994–97

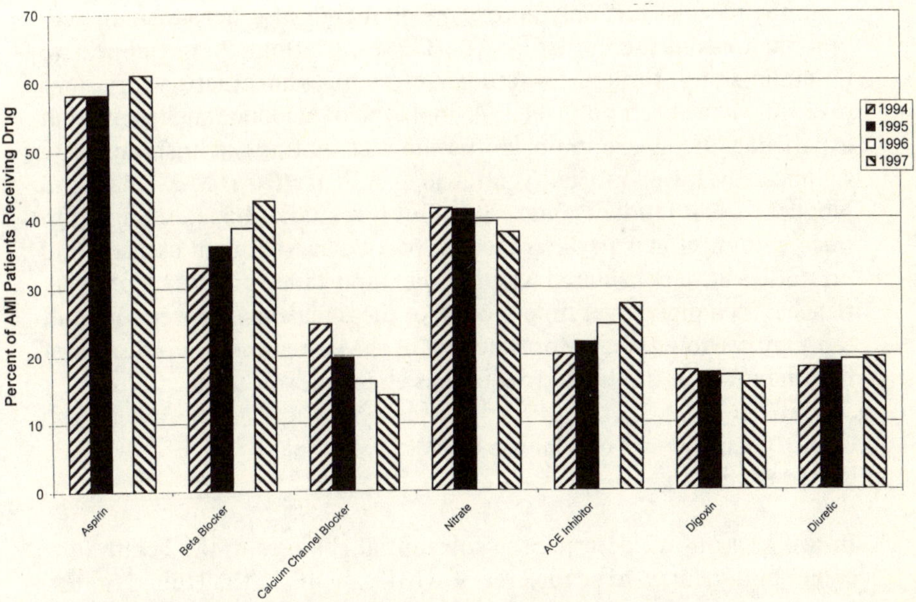

Fig. 2.8b. Trends in medication use after discharge, AMI patients, U.S. National Registry of Myocardial Infarctions, 1994–97

increased clinical experience, or other new information to guide practices may also improve the ability of health care providers to time the allocation of treatments more effectively, or target their use to patients who are particularly likely to benefit. Unfortunately, little longitudinal evidence on such "appropriateness of care" issues is available in the United States, for several major reasons. First, few large studies of U.S. AMI populations collected detailed information on patient characteristics and treatment prior to the 1990s. Second, appropriateness depends on many complex patient factors that may be difficult to capture for analytic study, even with detailed record reviews. Thus it may be possible to identify some patients who clearly would not benefit from certain treatments, but it is hard to capture all of the subtleties of cases that may influence physicians' decisions.

In recent years, more studies of appropriateness of care have been published. In general, these studies do not find much evidence of clearly inappropriate use of high- or low-tech treatments in AMI care. However, most of these studies classify large shares of patients in "equivocal" or "possibly appropriate" categories, where the benefits of the treatment are unknown or likely to be modest. Substantial variations in treatment rates, especially for intensive cardiac procedures, continue to exist not only across hospitals but also across small geographic areas in the United States. These variations do not appear to be diminishing, though few studies of changes in practice variations over time have been published. A final type of evidence suggesting that experience effects are important is the fact that larger hospitals have significantly lower mortality rates in AMI care (e.g., McClellan and Noguchi 1998; Dudley et al. 2000). But few studies have attempted to trace volume effects to differences in particular treatment choices, and no studies have considered whether the importance of volume or experience has changed over time. For all of these reasons, it is very difficult to quantify how the appropriateness of AMI treatment *given* rates of treatment use in the United States has changed over time.

3. The Consequences of Changes in AMI Care in the United States

In this section, we describe the substantial changes in the health outcomes and medical expenditures of AMI patients in the United States. The changes in the technology of AMI care just described may explain these trends, but so may other factors. First, the characteristics of AMI patients may have changed over time. The demographic characteristics of AMI patients have shifted gradually, toward a slightly older and more female population. Heidenreich and McClellan (2001) conclude that, over the past decade, AMI patients in the United States appear to have slightly higher rates of serious comorbid diseases on admission, and also slightly higher rates of shock. However, a larger share of patients have non-Q-wave infarctions and infarctions in territories other than the left anterior descending artery. Both of these case characteristics are associated with a better prognosis. These trends toward less severe cases might be expected to lead to some improvements in health outcomes and perhaps reductions in costs for AMI care. But it is also possible that the improvements in case characteristics are the result of treatment innovations (e.g., better revascularization treatment leads to lower rates of Q-wave infarcts). Thus, it does not appear that changes in AMI patient characteristics unrelated to heart attack treatment can account for much of the change in health outcomes and expenditures.

A second source of changes in outcomes and expenditures involves changes in treatment for other health problems. For example, new innovations in cancer care may lead to higher costs and better outcomes for AMI patients who also have cancer, and thus will contribute to the overall trends for AMI patients. However, almost no other common condition in the middle-aged and elderly population has undergone such dramatic changes in treatment as has cardiac disease. Thus, it seems unlikely that changes in treatment for these other conditions would be responsible for a large component of the AMI health outcome and expenditure trends.

We first summarize trends in health outcomes for elderly AMI patients in the United States, and then summarize trends in their medical expenditures, focusing on hospital expenditures. Even if changes in AMI treatment are primarily responsible for the observed trends, it is still difficult to disentangle the consequences of all of the different treatment changes we described above. Some treatment changes may have large consequences for expenditures or for outcomes, or for both or neither. For example, reasonable estimates of the effects of aspirin use, based on multiple clinical trials, suggest that this treatment change alone can explain roughly one-fourth of the observed improvement in 30-day AMI mortality over the last 15 years (Heidenreich and McClellan 2001), but this treatment change obviously had minimal direct implications for medical expenditures. In contrast, growth in primary and late angioplasty clearly has major consequences for medical expenditures soon after AMI, but might reduce later expenditures through reducing the incidence of later cardiac complications. We do not attempt to quantify these individual technology effects here.

Changes in Health Outcomes for AMI Patients

Figure 2.9 shows trends in the adjusted incidence of hospitalization with new AMIs in the United States, for the elderly and nonelderly. The figure shows that the age-adjusted incidence of AMIs declined slightly in the 1980s, especially for elderly males. But since then, hospitalization rates with new AMIs have been stable. Thus, changes in AMI incidence appear to explain only a small part of the decline in AMI-related deaths shown in figure 2.1. A more likely contributor to the decline is shown in figures 2.10 and 2.11: improvement in survival after AMI. Figure 2.10 shows that age-adjusted one-year case fatality for elderly AMI patients declined by eight percentage points, or one-fifth (from almost 40 to 32 percent) between 1984 and 1994. Shorter-term fatality rates shown in the same graph demonstrate that much of the mortality reduction occurred acutely, within 30 days after AMI. Almost all of the mortality improvement occurred between 1987 and 1996; notably, this improvement is not closely related to the growth in intensive cardiac procedure use, which continued before and after the period of greater mortality improvement.

Figures 2.11a and 2.11b show one-year and 30-day mortality trends for AMI patients by age and gender. As in the previous figures, the mortality data for the nonelderly come from residents of California. Case fatality declined for the nonelderly as well, primarily due to improved survival in the 30 days after AMI that persisted; however, because absolute mortality rates were much lower for the nonelderly, the absolute magnitude of the mortality gains was much smaller. In general, the magnitude of the gains in short- and long-term mortality was proportional to the case fatality rates in the base year, with gains of almost 10 percentage points for male patients aged 75 and above. Fatality reductions for women were smaller, particularly for the older elderly.

Figures 2.12 and 2.13 show that these mortality improvements were not obviously associated with worse health among the additional AMI survivors. Figure 2.12 shows the rates of readmission of elderly AMI patients with three common complications after a heart attack: symptoms of ischemic heart disease (*ihd* in the figure), a recurrent AMI *(ami),* or congestive heart failure *(chf).* Readmissions within 30 days of the initial AMI are excluded, because they are likely to represent fur-

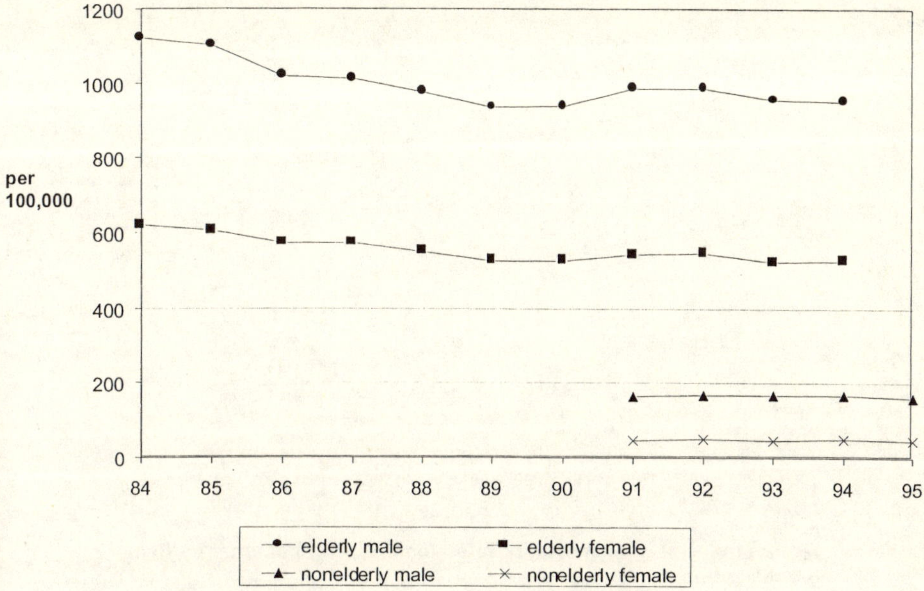

Fig. 2.9. Trends in AMI incidence, U.S. elderly and California nonelderly

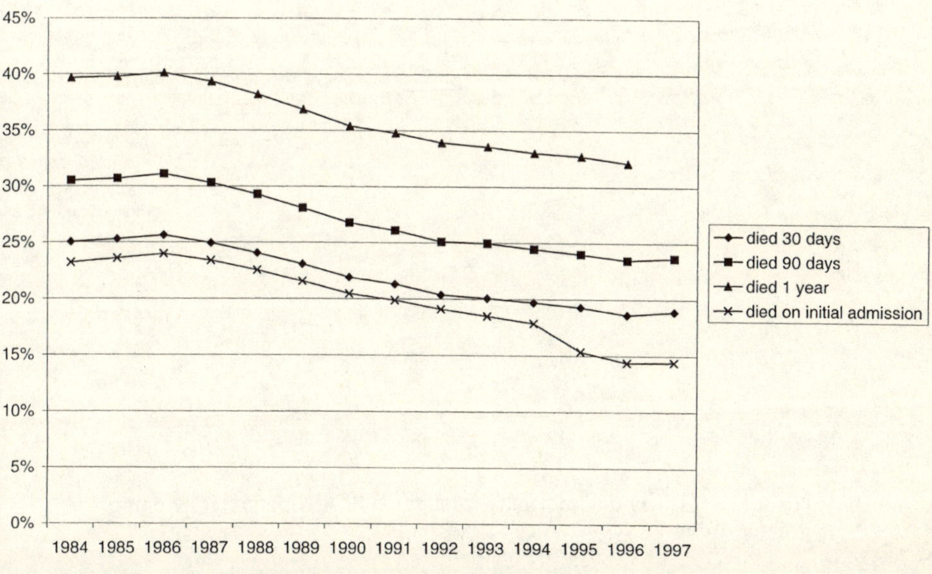

Fig. 2.10. Mortality rates for U.S. elderly AMI patients

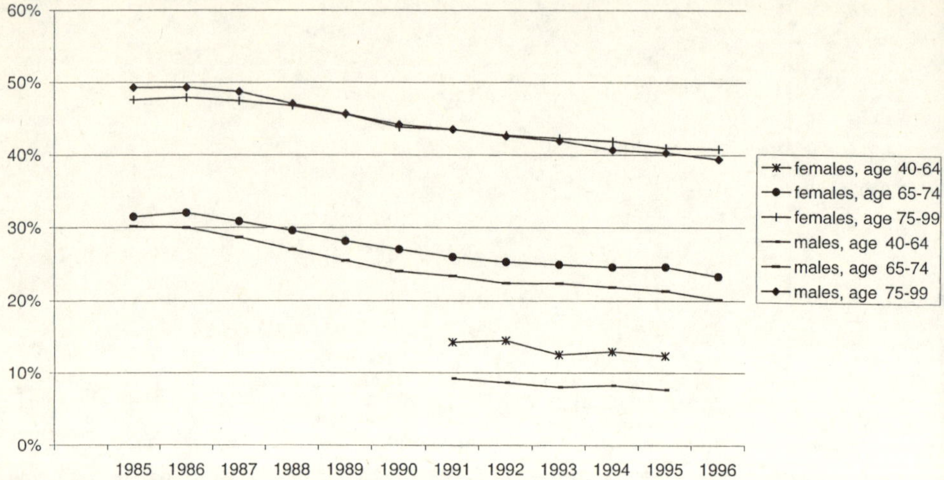

Fig. 2.11a. One-year mortality rates for U.S. AMI patients, by demographic group

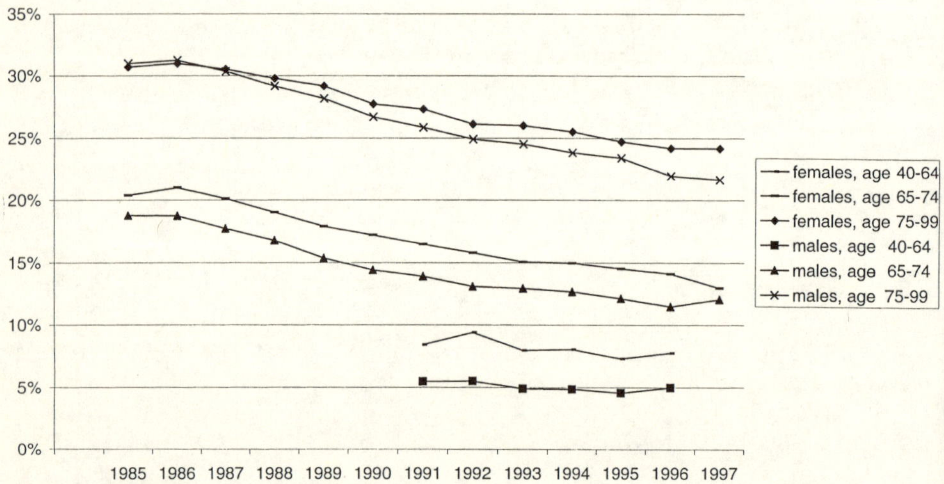

Fig. 2.11b. Thirty-day mortality rates for U.S. AMI patients, by demographic group

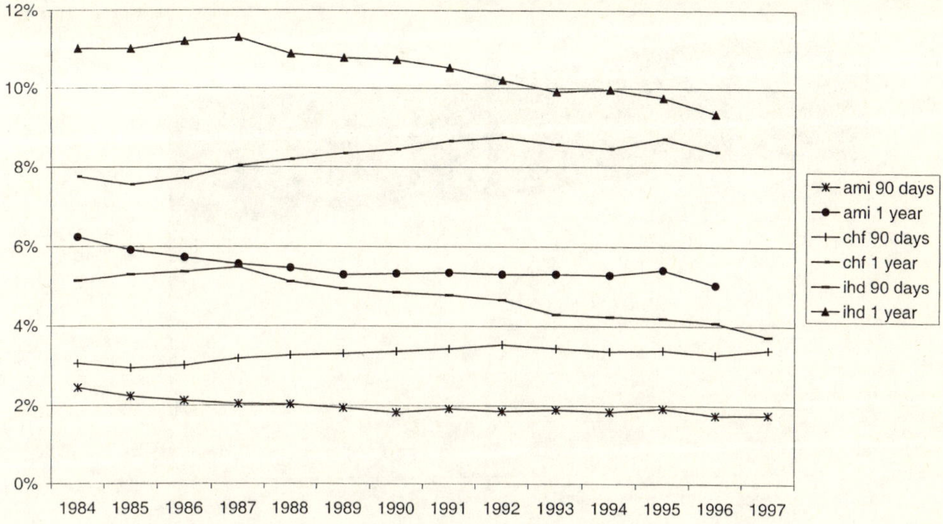

Fig. 2.12. Readmissions with cardiac complications for U.S. elderly AMI patients

ther care for the AMI itself. The proportion of patients readmitted within a year for heart failure symptoms increased slightly between 1985 and 1992 (from about 8 percent to about 9 percent of patients), while the proportion of patients readmitted with further ischemic heart disease symptoms or recurrent AMI declined. Thus, as figure 2.13a shows, the overall rate of major cardiac complications in the elderly declined. Figure 2.13b shows that nonelderly patients had considerably higher readmission rates with complications compared to elderly patients (including a much higher rate of readmission with ischemic heart disease), but their readmission rates also declined along with the mortality improvements. For all age groups, then, the cardiac health of AMI survivors appeared to improve over time in the United States.

Changes in Medical Expenditures

Inpatient hospital expenditures for elderly AMI patients in the United States have increased substantially, as figure 2.14 shows. The figure presents 90-day and one-year total hospital expenditures for elderly patients. Both are in constant 1995 dollars, using the U.S. overall CPI deflator. Both show real growth rates of over 4 percent per year. One-year hospital expenditures increased from around $12,000 per patient

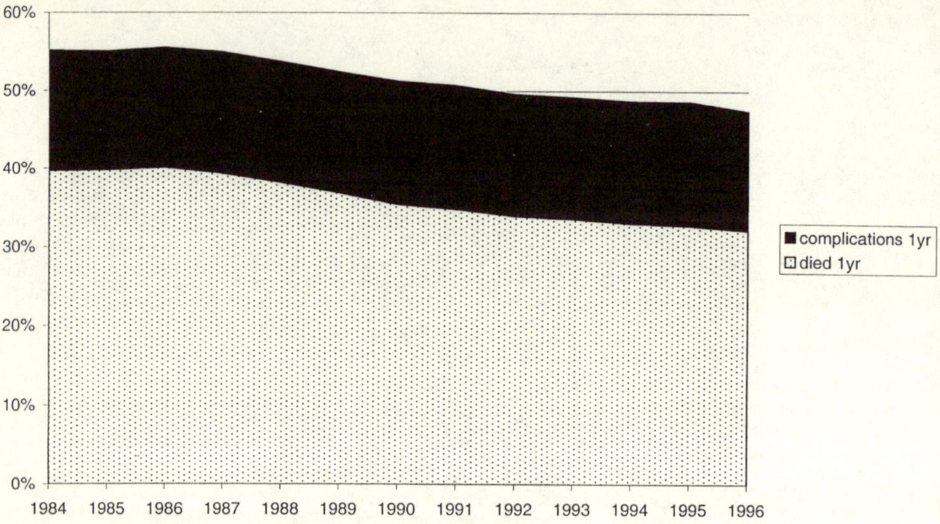

Fig. 2.13a. Adverse outcome rates for U.S. elderly AMI patients

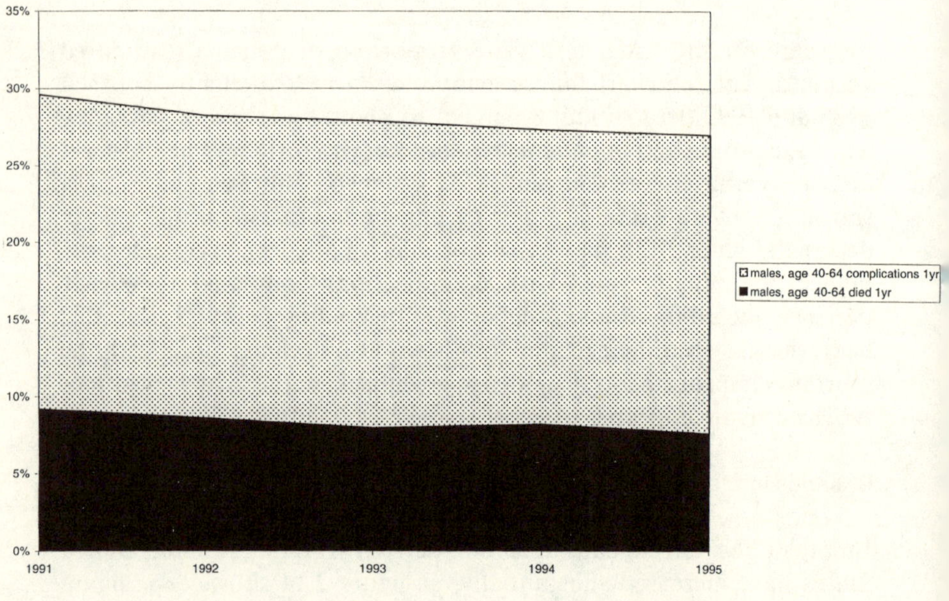

Fig. 2.13b. Adverse outcome rates for U.S. nonelderly male AMI patients

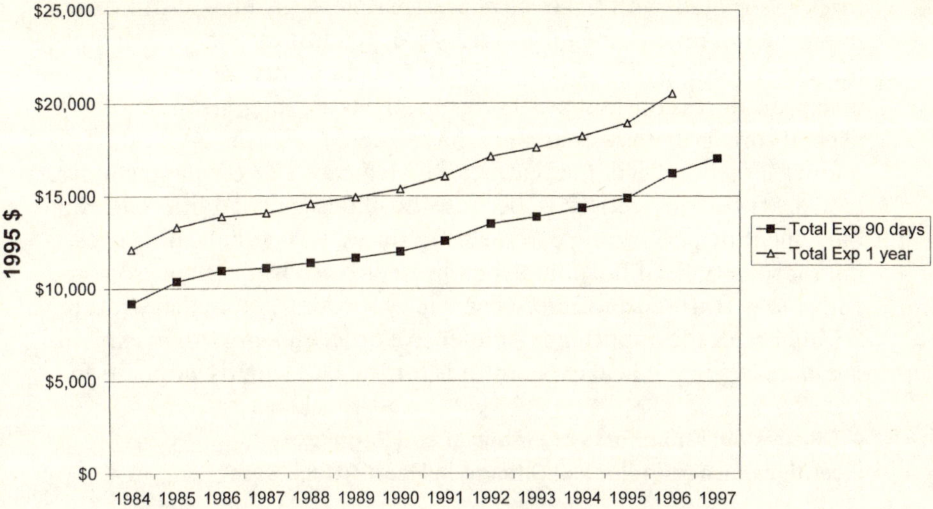

Fig. 2.14. Inpatient hospital expenditures for U.S. elderly AMI patients

in 1984 to over $20,000 per patient in 1996. Most (over three-fourths) of this expenditure growth is attributable to the first month after AMI. Though much of the change in technological intensity in AMI care has involved hospital care, other types of Medicare expenditures for elderly heart attack patients have increased even more rapidly than payments for hospital care. However, these other sources of growth are less important quantitatively, because they comprise a relatively small share (less than 30 percent) of total Medicare expenditures for AMI patients. Moreover, a major component of growth in these other types of expenditures was physician services in association with more intensive hospital-based treatments. Analyses using total expenditures had qualitatively similar results to those reported here, with proportionally larger expenditure amounts.

Table 2.1 illustrates the close association between Medicare expenditure growth and growth in the use of intensive cardiac procedures in the elderly. The first half of the table summarizes the proportions of elderly AMI patients receiving "medical management" only or intensive cardiac procedures (catheterization, angioplasty, or bypass surgery) after their AMI. As figure 2.3 shows, the proportion of patients undergoing all of these procedures increased dramatically. The bottom half of the table summarizes the average hospital expenditures associated with each of these treatment groups. Within each intensive-treatment category, average expenditures per patient have increased modestly if at all. Indeed, if we held the use of intensive cardiac procedures constant at 1984 levels, the table suggests that hospital expenditure growth would only have been one-fifth as great. This finding largely reflects the features of Medicare's DRG payment system described in section 1: because hospitals gain additional reimbursement by performing cardiac procedures, it is perhaps not surprising that the bulk of hospital expenditure growth is directly associated with the performance of more cardiac procedures. Nonetheless, table 2.1 illustrates the importance of intensive procedure growth in explaining increases in medical expenditures for the U.S. elderly population.

4. Discussion: The Effects of Financial and Regulatory Incentives on Technological Change in Heart Attack Care

Effects on Technological Change

The results of section 2 show that one of the most notable features of technological change in AMI care in the United States over the past decade has been rapid growth in the use of intensive cardiac procedures. This growth is apparent for both relatively young and old AMI patients; in recent years, growth in the use of intensive cardiac procedures in AMI patients over 80 has been particularly rapid. Primary angioplasty is also becoming widespread in the initial management of AMI, to the point that it is displacing the use of thrombolytics. The

TABLE 2.1. Shares of Patients and Expenditures for Intensive Cardiac Procedures

Treatment Regimen	1984	1991	Change[a]
Share of patients receiving treatment regimen			
Medical management	89%	59%	–4.2
Catheterization only	6	16	1.4
Angioplasty	1	12	1.6
Bypass surgery	5	13	1.2
Average cost of treatment regimen			
Medical management	$9,829	$10,783	1.3%
Catheterization only	15,380	13,716	–1.6
Angioplasty	25,841	17,040	–5.9
Bypass surgery	28,135	32,117	1.9

Source: Adapted from Cutler et al. 1998.

Note: Costs are in 1991 dollars, adjusted using the GDP deflator.

[a]Change is annual percentage points for treatment shares and annual percent for costs.

prominence of changes in high-tech procedure use in the United States is quite different from the changes in AMI care in many other developed countries. However, many other less intensive treatments for AMI have also changed in ways consistent with evidence on treatment effectiveness, including more use of aspirin, beta-blockers, and ACE inhibitors, and less use of lidocaine and calcium channel blockers soon after AMI.

The regulatory barriers to all of these technological changes have been limited in the United States, and the financial barriers have been considerably weaker than in many countries. For example, though delays in drug approval led to calcium channel blockers becoming available slightly later in the United States compared to some other countries, once they were approved by the FDA they became very widely used in just a few years. A far greater proportion of hospitals have adopted the capability of performing catheterization, angiography, and bypass surgery than in most other countries. This rapid and widespread diffusion of high-tech procedures is consistent with technology regulation having a limited role in the United States, and financing mechanisms being relatively responsive to the provision of more costly treatments. For example, procedures like angioplasty are reimbursed more highly in Medicare, not only in physician billing but also in hospital DRG payments, compared to less intensive medical management. Because physicians and hospitals have historically not borne much of the additional cost associated with these additional procedures, they have had little incentive to restrict their use. Indeed, hospitals and physicians face considerable competition for patients in the United States, and providing more intensive or "high quality" services may be a principal way to attract patients. With the growth of managed care and somewhat more powerful payment incentives in the 1990s, both price and quality competition appear to be important influences on technological change in the United States. It is too soon to tell whether these changes in incentives associated with managed care will have a lasting effect on the pace or nature of technological change, especially high-tech change, or whether it will simply lead to one-time price reductions. Our empirical results from California suggest that managed care may have had a modest impact on the rate of growth of high-tech procedure use.

Implications for Changes in Expenditures and Outcomes

The growth of high-tech procedures in the United States appears to be the principal source of expenditure growth in AMI treatment, especially for the elderly. Expenditures given the use of catheterization, angioplasty, and bypass surgery have risen only slightly; the bulk of expenditure growth has been associated with increasing shares of patients treated with intensive procedures. Lower-tech procedures may also contribute to some of the expenditure growth; for example, the use of the most costly thrombolytic drug and of rather costly cholesterol-lowering agents has increased rapidly.

Along with this rapid expenditure growth in association with changes in the high- and low-tech treatment of AMI, the United States has also experienced large improvements in heart disease mortality. For example, both death rates from heart disease and one-year death rates after AMI in the U.S. elderly population declined by one-fourth between 1984 and 1994. Much of the survival improvement appears to be survival in good health, as little increase in readmissions with long-term complications from AMI have been observed. Several studies (e.g., Hunink et al. 1997; Heidenreich and McClellan 2001) attribute about half of the observed improvements to changes in acute treatment, and much of the remainder to other changes in technology. Changes in patient behavior and health unrelated to medical technology, such as lifestyle changes to reduce cardiac risk factors, only account for a small part of the improvements in outcomes. With reasonable valuations of the improvement in quality of life, it is likely that technological change in AMI treatment has been worthwhile on average (Cutler et al. 1998). In other words, Americans are better off with recent medical technology for heart attack care, and its consequences for medical costs and health outcomes, than they were with medical technology from a decade earlier.

Nonetheless, it is unlikely that all of the changes in technology just described have been equally valuable. Considerable evidence suggests that the marginal (as opposed to the average) effect of the additional intensive cardiac procedures resulting from the diffusion of catheterization and revascularization is low (e.g., McClellan and Newhouse 1997; Tu et al. 1997; McClellan and Noguchi 1998). Moreover, Heidenreich and McClellan (1998) found that low-tech treatments such as aspirin and thrombolytic use appeared to be far more important in explaining improvements in acute survival after AMI than growth in the use of primary angioplasty and other acute revascularization procedures. On the other hand, the performance of additional cardiac procedures does appear to reduce the frequency of readmissions with heart failure and recurrent ischemic symptoms (McClellan and Noguchi 1998), and previous cross-sectional studies of American and Canadian practices suggest that more use of revascularization may be associated with significant improvements in heart disease symptoms (e.g., Rouleau et al. 1993). Further, several investigators have speculated that, because the performance of high-tech procedures are a principal mechanism of increasing hospital and physician reimbursement in Medicare and (historically) private insurance plans, the adoption of cardiac procedure capabilities may provide additional hospital resources for supporting experienced cardiologists and nurses, as well as many other valuable new AMI treatments.

Our conclusions about the causes and consequences of the United States' distinctive trends in technology use for AMI care are necessarily speculative. Further evaluations of the impact of managed care and related changes in regulatory and financial incentives in the United States, as well as comparisons to the experiences of technological change in other developed countries, should provide a foundation for firmer conclusions. If trends in medical expenditures and outcomes can be affected by differences in economic and regulatory incentives, such comparative research could have major policy implications.

Notes

1. Many U.S. states have "certification of need" regulations to require justifications for the adoption of expensive, high-tech capital investments such as cardiac catheterization labs. However, only New York State's program appears to limit capital investments substantially.

2. Because reliable longitudinal data for California residents is only available beginning in 1991, we are unable to exclude all cases of recurrent AMI in 1991. Approximately 6 percent of patients in subsequent years had prior AMI admissions within one year, and including these patients in our trend analysis did not substantially alter our results. The estimates for 1995 reflect AMI cases in the first three quarters of the year.

3. NRMI includes data from over 1,800 U.S. hospitals and a majority of hospital admissions. The trends reported here are unadjusted and include both elderly and nonelderly patients with confirmed new AMIs.

References

Bittl, J. 1996. "Advances in Coronary Angioplasty." *New England Journal of Medicine* 335, no. 17: 1290–1302.

Braunwald, E. 1996. *Heart Disease: A Textbook of Cardiovascular Medicine.* Philadelphia: W. B. Saunders.

———. 1997. "Cardiovascular Medicine at the Turn of the Millennium." *New England Journal of Medicine* 337, no. 19: 1360–69.

Buchmueller, T., and P. J. Feldstein. 1997. "The Effect of Price on Switching among Health Plans." *Journal of Health Economics* 16, no. 2: 231–47.

Burns M., R. Becker, J. Gore, C. Lambrew, W. French, and W. Rogers. 1997. "Early and Predischarge Aspirin Administration among patients with Acute Myocardial Infarction: The Second National Registry of Myocardial Infarction (NRMI 2)." *Journal of the American College of Cardiology* 29, no. 2: Abstract-738–1.

Chandra, H., J. Yarzebski, R. J. Goldberg, J. Savageau, C. Singleton, J. H. Gurwitz, and J. M. Gore. 1997. "Age-Related Trends (1986–1993) in the Use of Thrombolytic Agents in Patients with Acute Myocardial Infarction: The Worcester Heart Attack Study." *Archives of Internal Medicine* 157, no. 7: 741–46.

Chandra, N., R. Ziegelstein, J. Hilbe, W. French, L. Sanathanan, and NRMI Investigators. 1996. "Lidocaine Use in Acute MI: A Marker for Increased Mortality: Observations from the National Registry of Myocardial Infarction-2 (NRMI-2)." *Circulation* 94, no. 8: Abstract-2083.

Cutler, D., and M. B. McClellan. 1998. "Technological Change in Medicare." In *Topics in the Economics of Aging,* ed. D. Wise. Chicago: University of Chicago Press.

Cutler, D., M. B. McClellan, J. P. Newhouse, and D. Remler. 1998. "Are Medical Prices Declining? Analysis of Heart Attacks." *Quarterly Journal of Economics* 113, no. 4: 991–1024.

Dudley, R. A., K. L. Johansen, R. Brand, D. J. Rennie, and A. Milstein. 2000. "Selective Referral to High-Volume Hospitals: Estimating Potentially Avoidable Deaths." *Journal of the American Medical Association* 283:1159–66.

Falba, T., and M. B. McClellan. 2000. "The Costs of Illness in Middle Age." Manuscript.

GISSI Investigators. 1997. "A Comparison of Reteplase with Alteplase for Acute Myocardial Infarction." *New England Journal of Medicine* 337:1118–23.

Goldberg, R. J., J. M. Gore, J. S. Alpert, and J. E. Dalen. 1987. "Therapeutic Trends in the Management of Patients with Acute Myocardial Infarction (1975–1984): The Worcester Heart Attack Study." *Clinical Cardiology* 10, no. 1: 3–8.

Goldberg, R. J., J. M. Gore, J. S. Alpert, V. Osganian, J. de Groot, J. Bade, Z. Chen, D. Frid, and J. E. Dalen. 1991. "Cardiogenic Shock after Acute Myocardial Infarction. Incidence and Mortality from a Community-Wide Perspective, 1975 to 1988." *New England Journal of Medicine* 325, no. 16: 1117–22.

Gurwitz, J. H., R. J. Goldberg, Z. Chen, J. M. Gore, and J. S. Alpert. 1994. "Recent Trends in Hospital Mortality of Acute Myocardial Infarction: The Worcester Heart Attack Study. Have Improvements Been Realized for All Age Groups?" *Archives of Internal Medicine* 154, no. 19: 2202–8.

Health Care Financing Review: Medicare and Medicaid Statistical Supplement. 1999. U.S. Department of Health and Human Services, Health Care Financing Administration.

Heidenreich, P., and M. B. McClellan. 2001. "Trends in Treatment and Outcomes for Acute Myocardial Infarction: 1975–1995." *American Journal of Medicine* 110, no. 3: 165–74.

Hunink, M. G., L. Goldman, A. N. Tosteson, M. A. Mittleman, P. A. Goldman, L. W. Williams, J. Tsevat, and M. C. Weinstein. "The Recent Decline in Mortality from Coronary Heart Disease." *Journal of the American Medical Association* 277, no. 7: 535–42.

Kessler, D. P., and M. B. McClellan. 1996. "Do Doctors Practice Defensive Medicine?" *Quarterly Journal of Economics.* 111: 353–90.

———. 2000. "Is Hospital Competition Socially Wasteful?" *Quarterly Journal of Economics* 115: 577–615.

Kuttner, R. 1999. "The American Health Care System: Private Insurance." *New England Journal of Medicine* 340, no. 2: 163–68.

Laschober, M., 1997. *Health and Health Care of the Medicare Population: Data from the 1993 Medicare Current Beneficiary Survey.* Rockville, Md.: Westat.

Lau, J., E. M. Antman, S. J. Jimenez, B. Kupelnick, F. Mosteller, and T. C. Chalmers. 1992. "Cumulative Meta-analysis of Therapeutic Trials for Myocardial Infarction." *New England Journal of Medicine* 327, no. 4: 248–54.

Manton, K., L. Corder, and E. Stallard. 1997. "Chronic Disability Trends in Elderly United States Populations, 1982–1994." *Proceedings of the National Academy of Sciences* 94:2593–2598.

Mark, D. B., C. D. Naylor, M. A. Hlatky, R. M. Califf, E. J. Topol, C. B. Granger, J. D. Knight, C. L. Nelson, K. L. Lee, N. E. Clapp-Channing, W. Sutherland, L. Pilote, and P. W. Armstrong. 1994. "Use of Medical Resources and Quality of Life after Acute Myocardial Infarction in Canada and the United States." *New England Journal of Medicine* 331, no. 17: 1130–35.

McClellan, M. B. 1997a. "Hospital Reimbursement and the Dynamics of Medical Treatment Intensity." In *Topics in the Economics of Aging,* ed. D. Wise. Chicago: University of Chicago Press.

McClellan M. B. 1997b. "Hospital Reimbursement Incentives: An Empirical Analysis." *Journal of Economics and Management Strategy* 6, no. 1: 91–128.

McClellan, M. B., B. J. McNeil, and J. P. Newhouse. 1994. "Does More Intensive Treatment of Acute Myocardial Infarction Reduce Mortality? Analysis Using Instrumental Variables." *Journal of the American Medical Association* 272, no. 11: 859–66.

McClellan M. B., and J. P. Newhouse. 1997. "The Marginal Cost-Effectiveness of Medical Technology: A Panel Instrumental-Variables Approach." *Journal of Econometrics* 77, no. 1: 39–64.

McClellan M. B., and H. Noguchi. 1998. "Technological Change in Heart Disease Treatment: Does High Tech Mean Low Value?" *American Economic Review.* 88, no. 2: 90–96.

McGovern, P. G., A. R. Folsom, J. M. Sprafka, G. L. Burke, K. M. Doliszny,

J. Demirovic, J. D. Naylor, and H. Blackburn. 1992. "Trends in Survival of Hospitalized Myocardial Infarction Patients between 1970 and 1985: The Minnesota Heart Survey." *Circulation* 85, no. 1: 172–79.

McGovern, P. G., J. S. Pankow, E. Shahar, K. M. Doliszny, A. R. Folsom, H. Blackburn, and R. V. Luepker. 1996. "Recent Trends in Acute Coronary Heart Disease—Mortality, Morbidity, Medical Care, and Risk Factors: The Minnesota Heart Survey Investigators." *New England Journal of Medicine* 334, no. 14: 884–90.

McLaughlin, T. J., S. B. Soumerai, D. J. Willison, J. H. Gurwitz, C. Borbas, E. Guadagnoli, B. McLaughlin, N. Morris, S. C. Cheng, P. J. Hauptman, E. Antman, L. Casey, R. Asinger, and F. Gobel. 1996. "Adherence to National Guidelines for Drug Treatment of Suspected Acute Myocardial Infarction: Evidence for Undertreatment in Women and the Elderly." *Archives of Internal Medicine* 156, no. 7: 799–805.

National Center for Health Statistics. 1999. "Deaths: Final Data for 1999." <www.cdc.gov/nchs/data/nvsr/nvsr49/nvsr49_08.pdf>.

Rogers, W. J., L. J. Bowlby, N. C. Chandra, W. J. French, J. M. Gore, C. T. Lambrew, R. M. Rubison, A. J. Tiefenbrunn, and W. O. Weaver. 1994. "Treatment of Myocardial Infarction in the United States (1990 to 1993): Observations from the National Registry of Myocardial Infarction." *Circulation* 90, no. 4: 2103–14.

Rogers, W., N. Chandra, W. French, J. Gore, C. Lambrew, and A. Tiefenbrunn. 1996. "Trends in the Use of Reperfusion Therapy: Experience from the Second National Registry of Myocardial Infarction (NRMI 2)." *Circulation* 194, no. 8: Abstract.

Rouleau, J. L., L. A. Moye, M. A. Pfeffer, J. M. Arnold, V. Bernstein, T. E. Cuddy, G. R. Dagenais, E. M. Geltman, S. Goldman, D. Gordon, et al. 1993. "Comparison of Management Patterns after Acute Myocardial Infarction in Canada and the United States." *New England Journal of Medicine* 328, no. 11: 779–84.

Tu, J. V., C. L. Pashos, C. D. Naylor, E. Chen, S. L. Normand, J. P. Newhouse, and B. J. McNeil. 1997. "Use of Cardiac Procedures and Outcomes in Elderly Patients with Myocardial Infarction in the United States and Canada." *New England Journal of Medicine* 336:1500–1505.

U.S. Congress. 1994. Office of Technology Assessment. *Defensive Medicine and Medical Malpractice.* OTA-H-602. Washington, D.C.: U.S. Government Printing Office.

Yarzebski, J., R. J. Goldberg, J. M. Gore, and J. S. Alpert. 1994. "Temporal Trends and Factors Associated with Extent of Delay to Hospital Arrival in Patients with Acute Myocardial Infarction: The Worcester Heart Attack Study." *American Heart Journal* 128, no. 2: 255–63.

Introduction to the Canadian Chapters

A textbook description of the Canadian health care system would suggest that medical care for elderly patients with cardiac disease would be roughly similar across provinces.[1] Health care in Canada is financed by a set of 10 provincial and 2 territorial health insurance plans. The individual provinces or territories have jurisdiction over most health care issues, subject to their compliance with national requirements, as set forth by the Canada Health Act. The system is financed primarily through tax revenues. Services in Canada are provided by privately (largely self-) employed physicians, and by hospitals which are non-profit organizations governed by community boards. The system generally reimburses physicians on a fee-for-service basis (with some limitations, such as individual salary caps) and hospitals on the basis of prospective payment.

Yet, in Canada—as in the United States—there are substantial variations in cardiac health and care for AMI across geographic areas. Table I.1 summarizes some selected health statistics for the four provinces studied in this book: Ontario, Quebec, Alberta, and Manitoba. Both the incidence of and the population mortality from AMI differ dramatically across provinces. The incidence of AMI in Manitoba was more than twice the incidence in Alberta, with Ontario and Quebec occupying a wide middle range. Population mortality from AMI was lowest in Alberta, and highest in Quebec.

Care for AMI also differs substantially in the four provinces we study. A patient with AMI was more than twice as likely to be admitted to a hospital with a catheterization laboratory in Alberta as in Ontario, and this difference in technology availability was reflected in the differences in the share of AMI patients receiving catheterization after the onset of their illness. As is well-known, differences in catheterization are associated with differences in revascularization. In addition, the provinces exhibit important differences in the type of revascularization provided. PTCA is much more widely used than CABG in Alberta and Quebec, equally used in Ontario, and less widely used in Manitoba.

If the financing, coverage, and incentives provided by the Canadian health care system are similar across provinces, what accounts for the differences in care? And, do these differences in care lead to differences in health outcomes across provinces? As is the case with geographic differences in care in the United States, there are no simple answers. The following chapters highlight for four provinces some of the distinctive institutional features of their health care delivery systems, the differences in care for AMI supplied, and the possible connections between incentives, institutions, and technological change in health care.

Note

1. Health Canada (1996) provides an excellent and comprehensive description of the Canadian Health Care system.

References

Health Canada. 1996. "Canada Health Act Annual Report—1996." <http://www.hc-sc.gc.ca/medicare/documents/cha9596e.pdf>.

Reeder B., A. Choickalingam, G. Dagenais, D. MacLean, C. Nair, A. Petrasovits, A. Shuaib, D. Skwarchuk, G. Taylor, A. Wielgosz, and E. Wilson.

TABLE I.1. Comparison of Populations and Care for AMI, Selected Canadian Provinces, 1995

	Ontario	Quebec	Alberta	Manitoba
Population characteristics				
Population (millions)	10.96	7.24	2.74	1.13
% over 65[a]	12.4%	12.4%	9.9%	13.6%
Selected AMI statistics				
AMI rate per 100,000	172	137	109	224
AMI mortality per 100,000 (M)	76	95	61	85
AMI mortality per 100,000 (F)	57	69	48	65
AMI patients admitted to hospitals with catheterization laboratory	15.4%	23.2%	37.4%	27.6%
Number of hospitals with catheterization lab	13	16	4	2
Number of hospitals with revascularization lab	9	12	3	2
Length of stay (days)	8.7	11.4	10.1	14.7
AMI patients receiving catheterization	27%	31%	57%	32%
AMI patients receiving PTCA	7%	15%	26%	10%
AMI patients receiving CABG	7%	8%	9%	12%

Source: Statistics Canada 1997, 1998; Reeder et al. 1997; and chapters 3–6 in the present volume.
Note: All the procedure rates are one year, except Ontario's, which are six-month procedure rates.
[a]Figures are for 1998.

1997. *Heart Disease and Stroke in Canada, 1997.* Ottawa: Heart and Stroke Foundation of Canada.

Statistics Canada. 1997. "Annual Demographic Statistics." <http://www.statcan.ca/english/IPS/Data/91–213-XPB.htm>.

———. 1998. "Health and Social Services Institutions Revenue and Expenditure, by Province and Territory." <http://www.statcan.ca/english /Pgdb /State/Government/govt32.htm>.

CHAPTER 3

Technological Change in Heart Attack Care in Ontario, Canada, 1981–1995

Jack V. Tu, Peter C. Austin, and C. David Naylor

Canada's health system is characterized by the five principles of the Canada Health Act: "Universality, accessibility, comprehensiveness, portability, and public administration." Each province administers its own health insurance system under these national principles, with financing from the federal government and provincial governments through general tax revenues. All citizens are covered under the system with insured services including physician care, dental surgery, and all medically necessary hospital services. These services are generally provided to patients with no direct out-of-pocket charges. Outpatient drug coverage is also provided to elderly citizens and recipients of social assistance in each province, although the level of coverage varies and copayments are the norm. In Ontario, the Ontario Drug Benefit (ODB) plan covers a comprehensive formulary of drugs for the elderly aged 65 and older.

Like most other developed countries, Canada has experienced both substantial growth in medical expenditures and improvements in health outcomes. Aggregate health care expenditures in Canada gradually rose throughout the 1970s and 1980s, although there was a leveling off during the mid-1990s. In fiscal 1994, the Ontario government spent a total of Can.$17.55 billion (approximately U.S.$11.7 billion at current exchange rates) on the health care system with Can.$7.28 billion devoted to the hospital sector, Can.$4.95 billion to physicians services under the Ontario Health Insurance Plan (OHIP), Can.$0.91 billion to the ODB program, and Can.$4.55 billion to other health care services (Goel et al. 1996.) This annual spending translates to a per capita expenditure of Can.$2,614 per Ontario resident, or 9.5 percent of the gross domestic product. Correspondingly, overall life expectancy in Canada has increased to 75.0 years for men and 81.2 years for women.

How have technological changes in care for cardiovascular disease, particularly care for heart attack (AMI), affected trends in treatment decisions, health care costs, and life expectancy in Canada? And, to what extent have financial and regulatory incentives affected technological change? In Canada, cardiovascular disease is both an important component of health expenditures and a prevalent cause of mortality. Cardiovascular disease accounted for a total of Can.$8.3 billion dollars in direct costs and another Can.$12.4 billion in indirect costs in 1993 (Reeder et al. 1995). A total of 79,117 Canadians died from cardiovascular causes in 1995, representing 37 percent of all-cause mortality. The purpose of this chapter is to explore these questions by analyzing hospital discharge data from 1981 through 1995 from the Canadian Institute for Health Information (CIHI) administrative database. We examine several key medical treatment decisions for all AMI patients from Canada's largest province, Ontario—approximately one-third of all Canadians live in Ontario, with a population of 11 million. We also examine an important measure of health outcomes, in-hospital mortality.

This chapter proceeds as follows. Section 1 outlines some of the incentives for technological change in care for AMI provided by the OHIP. Section 2 begins with a detailed description of our data sources, and then discusses trends in the use of key treatments for heart attack. Section 3 demonstrates how changes in treatments over time may have affected patient health outcomes, and section 4 concludes.

1. Incentives for Technological Change in Ontario, Canada

Financing of Care for Heart Disease

Under the Canadian health care financing system, care is universally available to all Canadian citizens, regardless of income or "ability to pay." Patients do not pay anything directly out of pocket for hospital treatment of AMI, with all services including thrombolytic drug treatment and revascularization procedures covered under the provincial health care system. Thus, financial incentives for patients have not played a role in changes in AMI treatment over the past two decades.

All Ontario hospitals are funded with an annual global budget that is used to pay most of the costs (e.g. drugs, nursing, etc.) associated with treating AMI patients. The amount of this global budget is determined by the government. Expensive acute drug therapies such as tissue plasminogen activator (tPA) are funded from this global budget, creating economic incentives for Ontario hospitals to use cheaper agents such as streptokinase preferentially. At present, most hospitals in Ontario are believed to be using streptokinase predominantly with tPA reserved for certain patient subgroups, such as young patients with large anterior infarcts (personal communication, Dr. Toni Basinski). Unfortunately, there are no population-based data available on the use of these two agents in Ontario hospitals.

The vast majority of Ontario physicians continue to be reimbursed under a "fee-for-service" system, in which physicians are directly reimbursed for all insured services rendered. For example, cardiologists who perform coronary angiography and PTCA receive a minimum of Can.$246 per angiogram and Can.$400 per angioplasty (approximately U.S.$164 and U.S.$267 at current exchange rates, respectively), with the actual fee depending on the complexity of the procedure. However, the government sets overall limits on the number of invasive cardiac procedures that can be performed in the province as a whole. Hospitals in Ontario that offer these invasive procedures cover most of the costs out of their global budgets, but they also receive supplemental funding for these procedures in a separate envelope. Hospitals that perform more than their allotted quota of procedures must fund the additional procedures out of their own budgets unless they receive authorization from the Ministry of Health (MOH), while hospitals that perform less than their quota have their funding reduced in subsequent years. As a result, most institutions performing revascularization procedures meet but do not exceed their annual funded target procedure rate.

Technology Regulation

The availability of revascularization procedures has been restricted by the government to only 9 hospitals in Ontario throughout the 1990s with another 4 hospitals having a stand-alone cardiac catheterization lab, out of a total of 193 acute care hospitals in the province. The overall rate of cardiac procedures and the number of procedures per institution are determined by government policymakers. Because the demand for these procedures has exceeded the supply, significant waiting lists for coronary angiography, percutaneous transluminal coronary angioplasty (PTCA), and coronary artery bypass graft (CABG) surgery emerged in the late 1980s in Ontario. At that time, there were several highly publicized deaths of patients waiting for cardiac surgery at Toronto-area hospitals (Naylor 1991). Government policymakers responded to the crisis by increasing the amount of cardiac surgery funded and a central provincewide cardiac surgery waiting list registry was established. This registry eventually became known as the Cardiac Care Network (CCN) of Ontario. Data from the registry have subsequently been used to plan additional increments in the annual amount of CABG surgery done in the province (Naylor et al. 1997). Cases have been preferentially allocated to centers servicing regions with historically lower procedure rates. Data from the CCN registry indicate a 0.4 percent mortality rate on the waiting list and a median wait of 17 days for CABG surgery in 1991–93 (Naylor et al. 1995).

The recent publication of several studies that suggest that American patients have better quality of life after an acute myocardial infarction than Canadian patients has also increased the pressure on the Ontario government to increase its funding for cardiac procedures (Rouleau et al. 1993; Mark et al. 1994). The CCN, Institute for Clinical Evaluative Sciences, and the Ontario MOH have agreed on a minimum target rate of 100 CABGs (and also 100 PTCAs) per 100,000 adult population as an appropriate benchmark for cardiac procedure use in Ontario, in light of the currently available evidence on the marginal benefits of coronary revascularization. This rate lies approximately midway in between the 1993 CABG rate of 67 per 100 000 adults in Ontario and 120 per 100,000 adults in New York state (Tu et al. 1997).

Other Incentives for Technology Adoption and Use

Drug and Device Regulation and Pricing

With the exception of invasive cardiac procedures and a few other high-ticket items (e.g., stents), there are no other major restrictions on the availability or use of other commonly used MI treatments such as beta-blockers, calcium channel blockers, Swan-Ganz catheters, and continuous ECG monitors. Cost effectiveness analyses are required before new drugs are approved for inclusion on the Ontario Drug Benefit Plan, which covers outpatient drugs for the elderly (Detsky 1993). However, the plan is fairly comprehensive and covers nearly all cardiac drugs of proven benefit in treating cardiac disease.

Microregulation of Provider Decisions

There is very little explicit micromanagement of Canadian physicians in the Ontario health care system. Utilization review and other cost-containment mechanisms are not used at the individual provider level. Rather, the control on the diffusion of technology occurs at a macro level with global limits placed by the government on the availability of certain high-tech procedures. However, the health system uses a relatively detailed clinical evaluation system to prioritize waiting lists for some high-tech procedures. Otherwise, individual physicians have complete autonomy in selecting patients who they feel will benefit from these procedures.

Malpractice Liability

It is unclear the extent to which malpractice liability concerns have contributed to technological change in the management of AMI in Ontario. There has been a steady rise in the total number of malpractice claims against Canadian physicians, although the rate of claims is still much below that in United States. Most Canadian physicians are insured by the Canadian Medical Protective Association with fees being determined by specialty. The most recent annual fee for cardiologists was Can.$3,036 and Can.$17,688 for cardiac surgeons (approximately U.S.$2,024 and U.S.$11,792 at current exchange rates, respectively), as compared to Can.$2,976 for internists and Can.$1,932 for family doctors.

Regulation of Physician Supply

Government policymakers have a major impact on the supply of physicians, as they fund all five medical schools in Ontario and most residency training programs. The number of specialists (e.g., cardiologists, cardiac surgeons) is determined by the government in consultation with university program directors. Most cardiovascular specialists are extremely busy because the demand for their services exceeds the supply. For example, there are essentially no low-volume cardiac surgeons in Ontario (e.g., who perform less than 50 CABG cases per year) (Tu and Naylor 1996). Similarly, most invasive cardiologists are extremely busy because of the long waiting lists for these procedures. It is anticipated that Ontario may have a significant shortage of invasive cardiac specialists in the future as the population ages and many of the currently practicing specialists retire.

2. Technological Change in Heart Attack Care in Ontario

Data Sources

For this part of the chapter, we focus on trends in the acute hospital treatment of AMI patients in Ontario between 1981 and 1995. We obtained hospital discharge data on all AMI patients discharged between 1981 and 1995 from the Canadian Institute for Health Information (CIHI) administrative database. All patients in Ontario with a most-responsible admitting diagnosis of AMI (International Classification of Diseases, 9th revision, Clinical Modification [ICD9-CM] code 410) in alternate years between 1981 and 1995 were identified for possible inclusion in the analysis (Naylor and Chen 1994). The accuracy of ICD9-CM coding of AMI in the Ontario CIHI database has been established through multicenter chart audits (Cox et al. 1997). Several exclusion criteria were applied in order to increase the specificity for the diagnosis of AMI. We excluded patients who were discharged alive with a length of stay of less than three days under the assumption that these patients represented miscoded or ruled-out AMIs rather than true AMIs. We also excluded patients admitted to hospital in Ontario within the past year to ensure that our cohort consisted of only new AMIs. This avoids the problem noted in other studies where some patients admitted with a coded AMI were actually admitted for a cardiac procedure related to a recent AMI. We also excluded patients who were not residents of Ontario.

Basic demographic data on patient's age, gender, length of stay, and in-hospital mortality were obtained from the CIHI database. Information on the use of cardiac catheterization, percutaneous transluminal angioplasty (PTCA), and coronary artery bypass graft (CABG) surgery during the acute admission were also obtained using the appropriate Canadian Classification of Procedures (CCP) code from the CIHI database. Six-month rates of cardiac procedure use from 1992 to 1995 were obtained by linking uniquely identified anonymous patient records across the CIHI database. Complete linked data were not available prior to 1992. The Charlson comorbidity index score was calculated for all patients based on the 15 secondary diagnosis fields for each patient in the CIHI database (Deyo, Cherkin, and Ciol 1992; Charlson et al. 1987).

Changes in High-Tech Care

A summary of the demographic characteristics of the AMI cohorts is shown in table 3.1. This table shows a steady rise in the mean age of

TABLE 3.1. Demographic Characteristics of Acute Myocardial Infarction Cohorts in Ontario, Canada, 1981 to 1995

	1981	1983	1985	1987	1989	1991	1993	1995
Number of patients	15,528	15,066	16,510	16,526	15,248	16,880	18,504	18,841
Mean age	64.8	65.3	66.0	66.4	66.2	66.8	67.0	67.4
Age ≥ 65 (%)	52.2	53.4	56.7	57.8	57.5	59.6	60.7	61.5
Female (%)	34.8	35.1	36.0	36.4	36.0	35.7	36.0	37.0
Charlson comorbidity index 1 (%)	24.1	25.0	26.9	26.2	26.8	28.7	29.5	30.1
Charlson comorbidity index ≥ 2 (%)	10.0	11.2	12.6	14.3	14.8	17.3	18.9	19.3

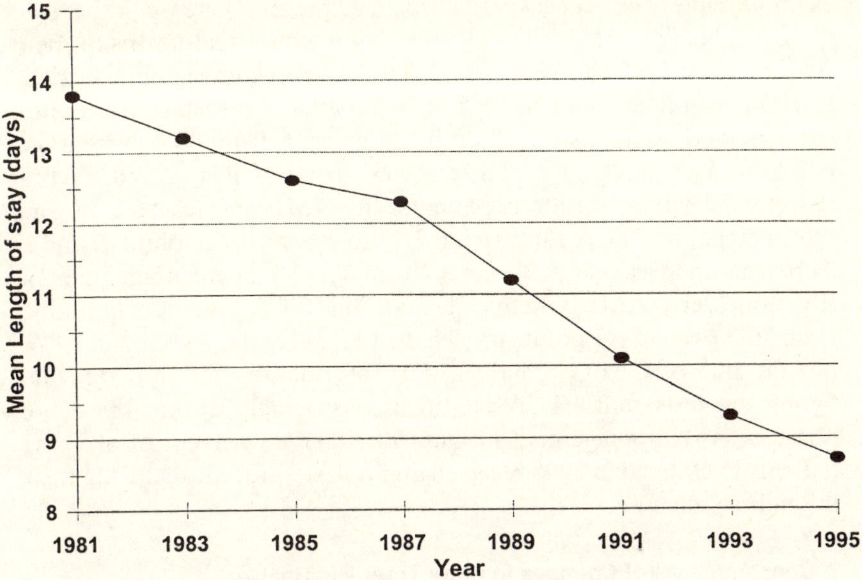

Fig. 3.1. Length of stay after an AMI, 1981–95

patients having an AMI in Ontario from 64.8 years in 1981 to 67.4 years in 1995. It also shows that the proportion of female patients in Ontario has increased over time. The number of patients with significant comorbidity as defined using the Charlson comorbidity index has increased over the past 15 years. The mean length of stay for AMI patients in Ontario has declined a total of five days during this time period, as shown in figure 3.1.

Trends over the 1992 to 1995 period in the use of three key invasive cardiac procedures—cardiac catheterization, PTCA, and CABG—during the six months after admission for an initial AMI are shown in figures 3.2–3.4. Overall, there have been relatively low rates of use of cardiac catheterization, percutaneous transluminal coronary angioplasty, and coronary artery bypass grafting in Ontario during this time period, although procedure use has increased modestly. The greatest increase in the use of procedures in percentage terms has occurred among elderly patients (i.e., those aged 65 or older). However, for PTCA and CABG, this is due to the fact that elderly patients began the period at a much lower baseline level of intervention. For example, elderly patients experienced an 37 percent increase in the likelihood of being treated with catheterization within six months of their AMI over the 1992 to 1995 period, from 12.5 percentage points in 1992 to 17.1 percentage points in 1995. By comparison, catheterization rates for nonelderly patients increased by 10 percent, from 39.6 percentage points to 43.5 percentage points. Rates of use of PTCA and CABG reflect similar trends. Elderly patients with AMI experienced a 47 percent increase in PTCA rates (from 2.73 to 4 percentage points), and a 24 percent increase in CABG rates (from 4.2 to 5.2 percentage points). For nonelderly AMI patients, the rate of PTCA rose substantially, from 10.3 percentage points in 1992 to 12.3 percentage points in 1995, but the rate of CABG remained flat. Information not shown in the figures suggests that PTCA is still used sparingly during the acute phase of AMI management in Ontario. Only 1.8 percent of all AMI patients in Ontario in 1995 received angioplasty procedure during their initial hospital stay.

3. Consequences of Changes in Care: Trends in Health Outcomes for AMI Patients

In-hospital mortality rates after an AMI in Ontario are shown, for various periods and demographic groups, in figures 3.5–3.7. These figures show dramatic improvements in overall in-hospital post-AMI survival in all patient subgroups including the elderly and nonelderly, and male and female patients. The overall mortality rate has declined from 19.0 percent in 1981 to 13.6 percent in 1995, with most of this decline occurring in the late 1980s. Although figure 3.5 suggests that this may not be an artifact of declining length of stay (because 7-day and 14-day in-hospital mortality rates declined in a parallel manner), these figures do not rule out this possibility; both a substantial fraction of AMI mortality and of the aggregate decline in length-of-stay may occur in the first 7 days after patients' initial admission. Figure 3.6 shows that elderly patients have had the greatest absolute decline in in-hospital mortality, from 27.8 percent in 1981 to 18.8 percent in 1995. Males and females have experienced similar declines in in-hospital mortality, as shown in figure 3.7. Unfortunately, we do not have more detailed data on the reasons for this decline (e.g. thrombolytics, beta-blockers, etc.) although it seems unlikely to be due to invasive cardiac procedures since the rate of procedure use in Ontario remains very low. However, without more extensive historical data on treatment of AMI, this conclusion is also necessarily tentative.

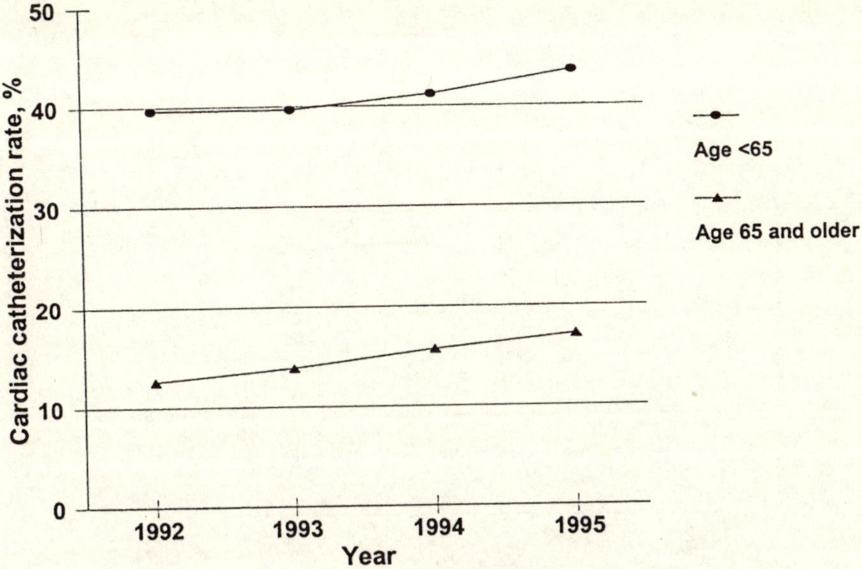

Fig. 3.2. Six-month rates of cardiac catheterization after an AMI, elderly and nonelderly, 1992–95

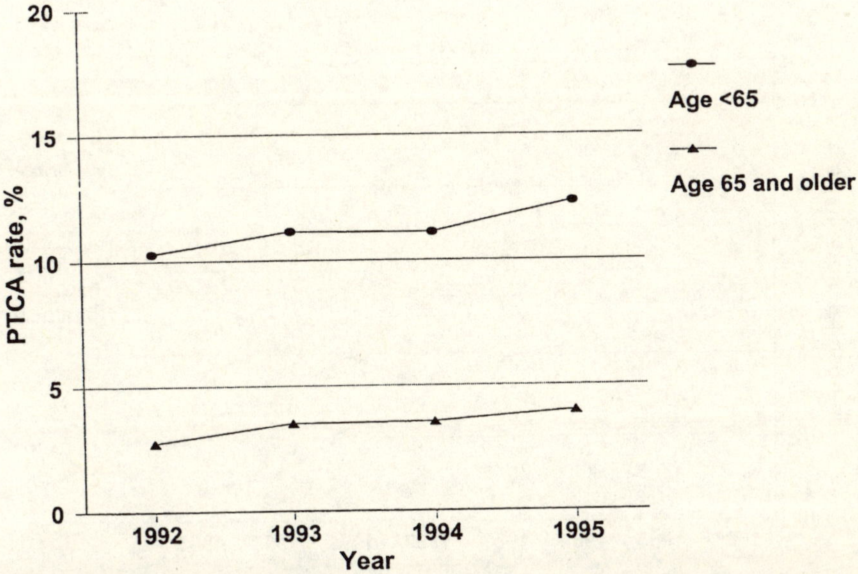

Fig. 3.3. Six-month rates of PTCA after an AMI, elderly and nonelderly,1992–95

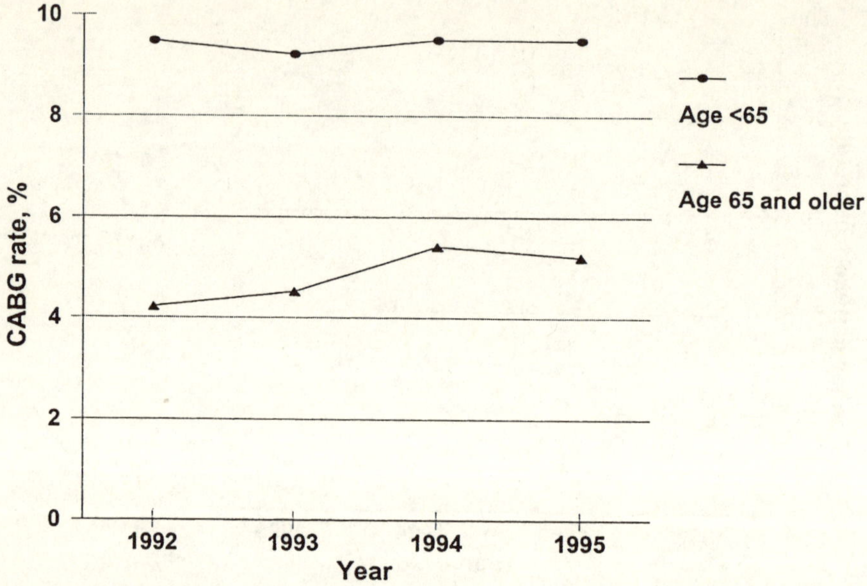

Fig. 3.4. Six-month rates of CABG after an AMI, elderly and nonelderly,1992–95

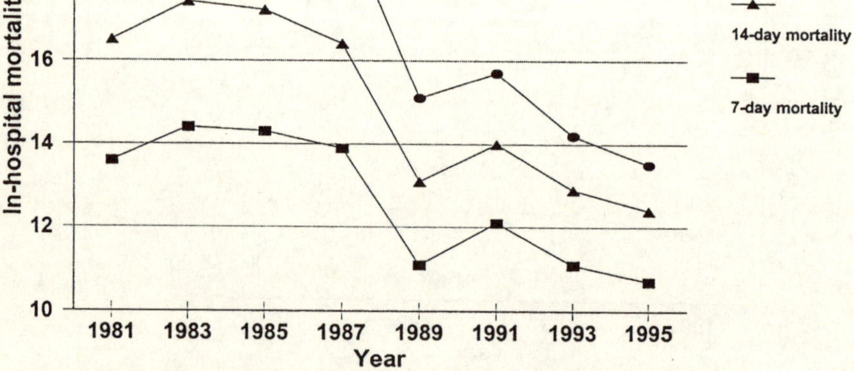

Fig. 3.5. In-hospital mortality rates after an AMI, at 7 days, 14 days, and total, 1981–95

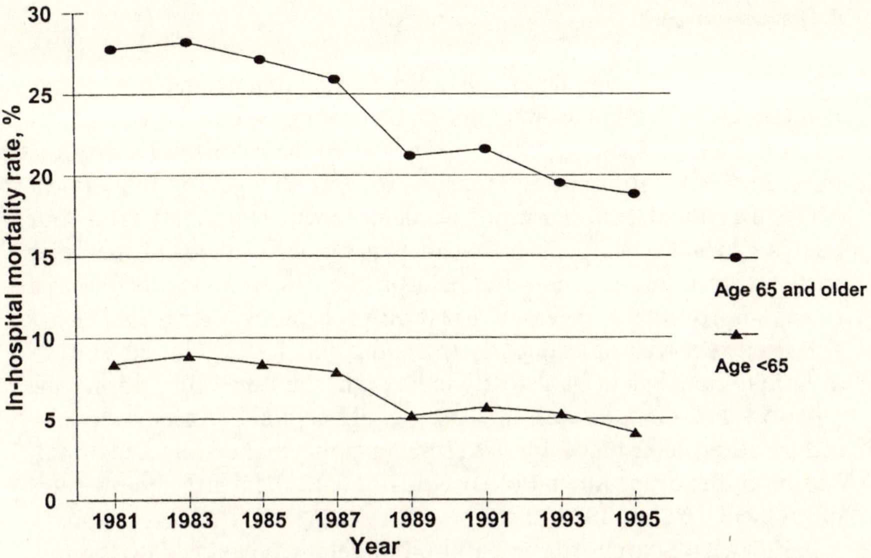

Fig. 3.6. In-hospital mortality rates after an AMI, elderly and nonelderly, 1981–95

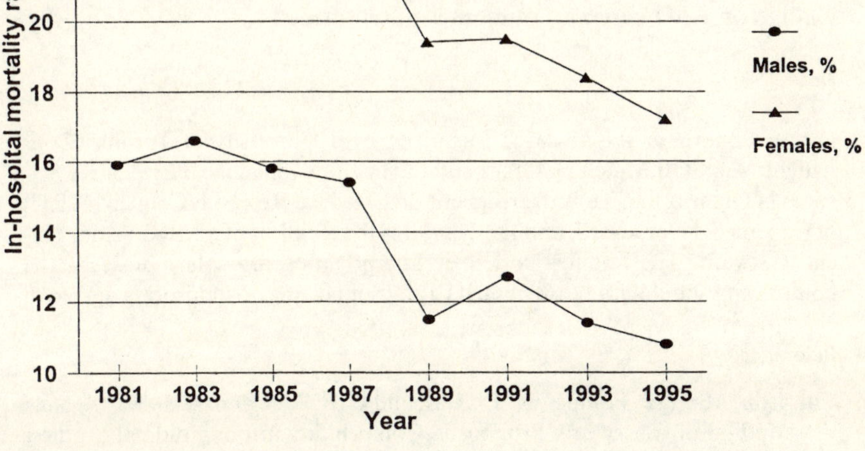

Fig. 3.7. In-hospital mortality rates after an AMI, by gender, 1981–95

4. Discussion

There have been significant changes in the management of acute myocardial infarction in patients in Ontario, Canada, between 1981 and 1995. Short-term outcomes, as measured by in-hospital mortality, have improved, although the reasons for this change and its implications for patient health cannot be determined definitively from our analysis to date. We believe that increasing use of medical therapies such as thrombolytic agents and beta-blockers likely accounts for most of the improvement. Revascularization procedures after an AMI are still used relatively infrequently (as compared to the United States), although there has been a steady increase in the rate of use during the past 15 years. Lengthy waiting lists, global hospital budgets, fixed procedure rates determined by government policymakers, and regionalization of the procedure all likely contribute to the relatively low rates of revascularization in Ontario.

Further research will be required to definitively elucidate the factors contributing to the apparent improvement in post-AMI survival in Ontario, and to determine the relative contribution of changes in patient risk factors, improved medical management, and use of invasive cardiac procedures. These objectives could be accomplished in part by detailed retrospective chart audits of a random sample of AMI patients in Ontario over this time period. We plan to conduct such a study in the near future. Creation of more comprehensive linked databases of AMI patients is also under way. Comparison of trends in procedure use, medical therapy, and long-term survival with other countries would help us to better understand the impact of technological change on AMI care and outcomes in Ontario.

Note

Grant support for this research was given by a University of Toronto Connaught New Staff Matching Grant and the Institute for Clinical Evaluative Sciences in Ontario. Dr. Tu is the recipient of a Medical Research Council (MRC) of Canada Scholar award, and Dr. Naylor is the recipient of a MRC Senior Scientist Award. The findings and their interpretation are solely those of the authors and should not be attributed to any supporting or sponsoring agency.

References

Charlson, M. E., P. Pompei, K. L. Ales, and C. R. MacKenzie. 1987. "A New Method of Classifying Prognostic Comorbidity in Longitudinal Studies: Development and Validation." *Journal of Chronic Diseases* 40, no. 5: 373–83.

Cox, J. L., M. P. Melady, E. Chen, and C. D. Naylor. 1997. "Towards Improved Coding of Acute Myocardial Infarction in Hospital Discharge Abstracts: A Pilot Project." *Canadian Journal of Cardiology* 13, no. 4: 351–58.

Detsky, A. S. 1993. "Guidelines for Economic Analysis of Pharmaceutical Products." *Pharmacoeconomics* 3, no. 5: 354–61.

Deyo, R. A., C. D. Cherkin, and M. A. Ciol. 1992. "Adapting a Clinical Comorbidity Index for Use with ICD-9 CM Administrative Databases." *Journal of Clinical Epidemiology* 45, no. 6: 613–19.

Goel, V., G. M. Anderson, P. Blackstien-Hirsch, C. Fooks, and C. D. Naylor, eds. 1996. *Patterns of Health Care in Ontario: The ICES Practice Atlas.* 2d ed. Ottawa: Canadian Medical Association.

Mark, D. B., C. D. Naylor, M. A. Hlatky, R. M. Califf, E. J. Topol, C. B. Granger, J. D. Knight, C. L. Nelson, K. L. Lee, N. E. Clapp-Channing, W. Sutherland, L. Pilote, and P. W. Armstrong. 1994. "Use of Medical Resources and Quality of Life after Acute Myocardial Infarction in Canada and the United States." *New England Journal of Medicine* 331, no. 17: 1130–35.

Naylor, C. D. 1991. "A Different View of Queues in Ontario." *Health Affairs* 10, no. 3: 110–28.

Naylor, C. D., and E. Chen. 1994. "Population-Wide Mortality Trends among Patients Hospitalized for Acute Myocardial Infarction: The Ontario Experience, 1981 to 1991." *Journal of the American College of Cardiology* 24, no. 6: 1431–38.

Naylor, C. D., P. Slaughter, K. Sykora, and W. Young. 1997. *Waits and Rates: The 1997 ICES Report on Coronary Surgery Capacity for Ontario.* North York, Ontario: Institute for Clinical Evaluative Sciences.

Naylor, C. D., K. Sykora, S. B. Jaglal, and S. Jefferson. 1995. "Waiting for Coronary Artery Bypass Surgery: Population-Based Study of 8,517 Consecutive Patients in Ontario, Canada." *Lancet* 346, no. 8990: 1605–9.

Reeder, B. A., A. Chockalingam, G. R. Dagenais, D. MacLean, Y. Mao, C. Nair, A. Petrasavits, A. Shuaib, A. T. Wielgosz, and E. Wilson. 1995. *Heart Disease and Stroke in Canada, 1995.* Ottawa: Heart and Stroke Foundation of Canada.

Rouleau, J. L., L. A. Moye, M. A. Pfeffer, J. M. Arnold, V. Bernstein, T. E. Cuddy, G. R. Dagenais, E. M. Geltman, S. Goldman, and D. Gordon. 1993. "A Comparison of Management Patterns after Acute Myocardial Infarction in Canada and the United States." *New England Journal of Medicine* 328, no. 11: 779–84.

Tu, J. V., and C. D. Naylor. 1996. "Coronary Artery Bypass Mortality Rates in Ontario: A Canadian Approach to Quality Assurance in Cardiac Surgery." *Circulation* 94, no. 10: 2429–33.

Tu, J. V., C. D. Naylor, D. Kumar, B. A. DeBuono, B. J. McNeil, and E. L. Hannan. 1997. "Coronary Artery Bypass Graft Surgery in Ontario and New York State: Which Rate Is Right?" *Annals of Internal Medicine* 126, no. 1: 13–19.

CHAPTER 4

Technological Change in Heart Attack Care in Quebec, Canada

Louise Pilote, Frédéric Lavoie, Vivian Ho, and Mark J. Eisenberg

Marked international and regional variations in the treatment of acute myocardial infarction (AMI) have been observed (Mark et al. 1994; Pilote, Califf, et al. 1995). The reasons and consequences related to these differences in the treatment of AMI have remained the topic of intensive investigation (Pilote, Racine, and Hlatky 1994; Pilote et al. 1996). Whether a more aggressive use of expensive technologies is cost-effective and whether these technologies are under- or overutilized remain unanswered questions (Pilote, Granger, et al. 1995; Pilote, Bourassa, et al. 1995).

Using detailed longitudinal microdata on individual patients, this chapter analyzes recent changes in medical treatment patterns and patient health outcomes for individuals with AMI from the Canadian province of Quebec. The main purpose of this chapter is to document how the care and consequences of AMI changed in Quebec over the period from 1988 to 1995, and to suggest some possible determinants of these trends.

Over the last decade, the age- and gender-adjusted rate of AMIs in the Quebec population has declined from 148 per 100,000 population in 1988 to 137 in 1995 (fig. 4.1). The decline is apparent in both males and females. Despite the lower rate of AMIs, the mean age and gender distribution of AMI patients has remained constant over time (table 4.1). In addition, both in-hospital and all-cause mortality among AMI patients declined during the study period. Accompanying this change in health outcomes was a marked change in treatment: intensive procedure use increased, and hospital length of stay decreased.

To what extent were these trends driven by exogenous technological change, and to what extent were they driven by changes in technol-

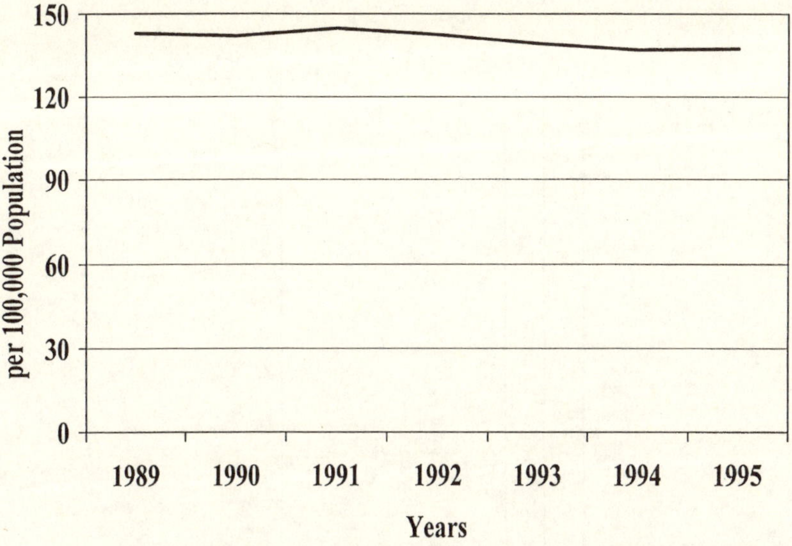

Fig. 4.1. Age- and gender-adjusted rate of AMI in Quebec

ogy attributable to financial and regulatory incentives? Although any conclusions of this sort are necessarily speculative, our results suggest that both factors play an important role. We first describe some of the financial and regulatory incentives in the province that may have affected treatment for AMI. Then we discuss the implications of these incentives for treatment decision-making processes. Finally, we demonstrate how changes in treatments of AMI over time may have affected patient health outcomes.

Incentives for Technological Change in Quebec

Financing of Care for Heart Disease

Quebec is the second most populous of the 10 Canadian provinces with a population of 7.3 million people. The organization of the health care system in each province in Canada is based on the principles of the Canada Health Act: universality, accessibility, comprehensiveness, portability, and public administration. The provincial government covers the cost of health care for all citizens and legal residents. Federal and provincial tax revenues finance the Canadian health care system.

TABLE 4.1. Characteristics of the Quebec AMI Cohort

	Index Year								
	1988	1989	1990	1991	1992	1993	1994	1995	Total
N	8,995	8,995	9,143	9,594	9,688	9,728	9,790	10,079	76,012
Age at index									
Mean	64.0	64.1	64.3	64.7	65.0	64.9	64.8	64.7	
Median	65	65	65	66	66	66	66	66	
Proportion of males	66.5	66.4	66.2	65.7	65.6	65.5	65.9	65.7	
LOS at index									
Mean	13.3	13.8	13.7	12.9	13.2	12.4	12.0	11.4	
Median	11	11	10	10	10	10	9	9	

The health care budget is administered at the provincial level. Each provincial government determines health care delivery and provider reimbursement. For inpatient health care, each hospital is allocated an annual budget by the provincial government. This budget finances all in-hospital services (including drugs, tests, and nursing care) except for physicians' services. Physicians are paid fee-for-service directly by a governmental agency called la Régie de l'Assurance Maladie du Québec (RAMQ). All physicians have an annual salary cap, which varies according to specialty. For outpatient health care, physician's services and diagnostic tests are paid fee-for-service by the government.

During the study period, the government covered the cost of outpatient drugs for individuals older than 65 years and individuals on welfare. Only drugs on the government formulary are paid for. The government is advised by a group of experts on which drugs to include on the formulary, and there is an important lobbying process from drug companies who have interest in seeing their product on the provincial formulary. Nonformulary drugs are either paid out of pocket or through private insurance coverage. The extent of private insurance coverage is limited, by law, to certain services such as dental plans, drug plans, private rooms, and private nursing. Finally, there are minor differences between provinces, which may become greater with time. For example, in Quebec, hospital-based physicians may become salaried in the near future.

Thus, at the macroeconomic level, the government has control over technological growth by limiting the availability of cardiac medications and procedures (see below). At the microeconomic level, hospitals and physicians also influence growth of technology. Because hospitals are on a fixed global budget, there is a financial incentive to limit rather than to encourage the use of invasive, costly technology. In contrast, physicians who are paid fee-for-service have a financial incentive to provide more services. Physicians can increase their revenue by increasing the number of procedures they perform. This might contribute to technology growth. However, salary caps per individual physician, per procedure, and per specialty have been instituted by the government to limit the ability of physicians to increase their reimbursement by performing more (or more lucrative) procedures. Thus, although there are conflicting incentives at the hospital level between hospital administrators and physicians, there are mechanisms in place to limit growth of technology.

Technology Regulation

As seen in the previous section, except for drug coverage, the government maintains exclusive responsibility for health care financing. Consequently, the government has the final say on the distribution of health care resources and more specifically the availability of cardiac procedures. For example, the government decides on the number of angiography laboratories in the province. We speculate that such control has been a major regulatory disincentive for growth in the use of cardiac technology in Quebec.

One of the most striking facts about AMI treatment in Quebec compared to the United States is the small proportion of patients with AMI that were admitted at a site with availability of angiography and coronary revascularization procedures. Only 18 percent of AMI patients are admitted at sites with angioplasty or bypass surgery and 23 percent at sites where only angiography is available. In 1995, there were 16 sites that provided angiography and 12 sites that provided both angioplasty and bypass surgery (fig. 4.2). These sites served a population of 7.3 million with approximately 10,000 AMIs per year. The availability of these services changed little over the seven years of observation with the exception of 1991, when 3 new sites started providing angiography, 1 additional site started offering angioplasty, and 2 additional sites started performing bypass surgery.

Similar to most changes in the distribution of health care resources, the change in procedure availability in 1991 was a politically driven decision made by the provincial government. It most likely contributed to the modest increase in resource utilization after 1991, as discussed below. Figures 4.3 and 4.4 show the increase over time in the proportion of patients who were admitted to a hospital that did not provide angiography or revascularization procedures, but were transferred to a site capable of providing these procedures. For example, among patients who were admitted at a site without availability of angiography, 25 percent of them were transferred in 1988, for treatment during or immediately after their index stay, whereas this proportion increased to 30 percent in 1995. For angioplasty, the proportion of transfers increased from 7 percent to 12 percent; for bypass surgery, from 7 percent to 9 percent. Thus, both increased availability and frequency of transfers partly explain the change.

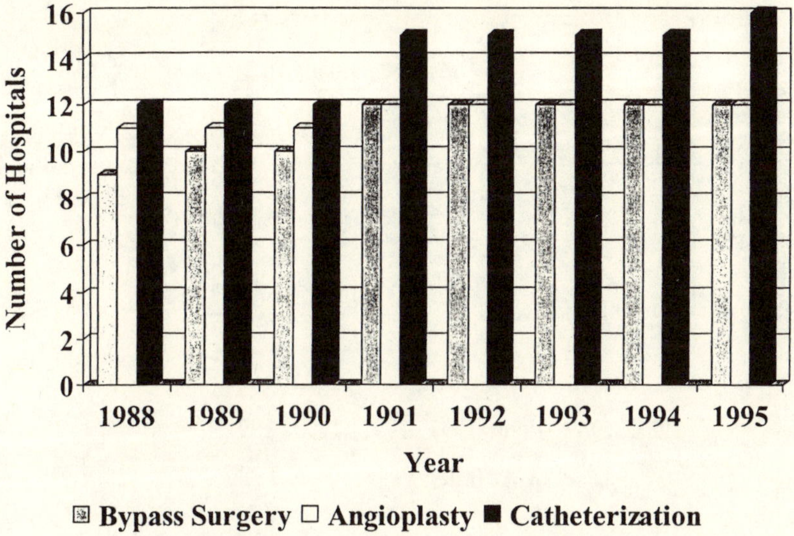

Fig. 4.2. Number of hospitals providing specific procedures in Quebec

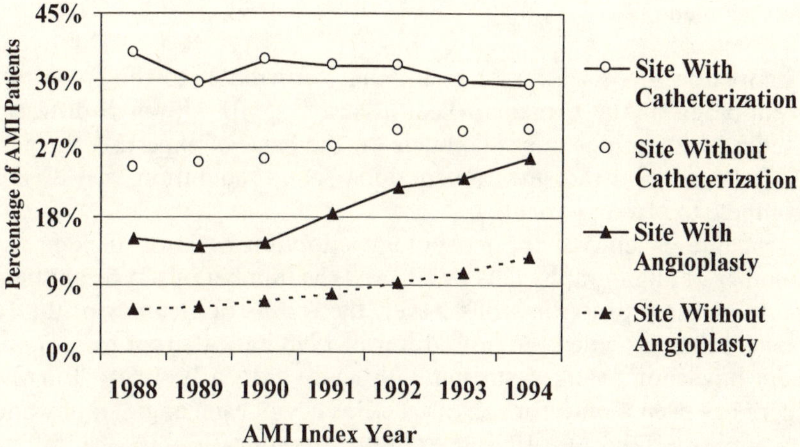

Fig. 4.3. One-year use of catheterization or angioplasty by on-site availability of procedures

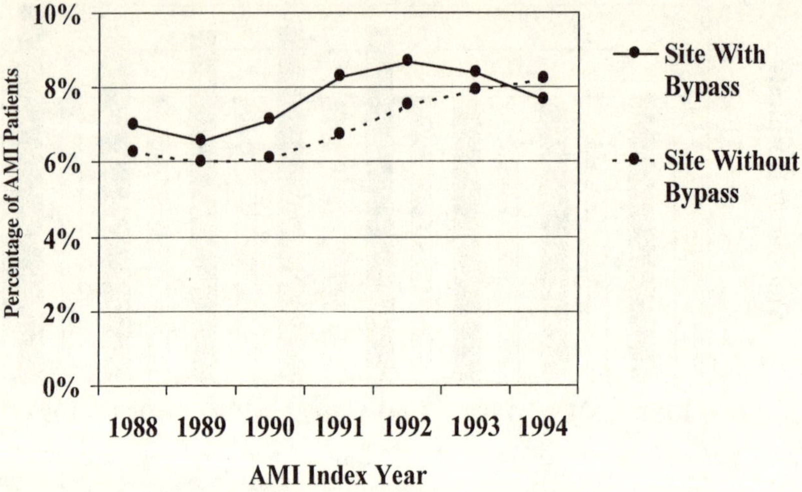

Fig. 4.4. One-year bypass surgery rate by on-site availability of procedure

Competition and Other Incentives for Technology Adoption and Use

Competition is not a major factor that contributes to the growth of technology in the Canadian health care system. Although different medical institutions might compete on the basis of expertise, the perceived need to attract government dollars, and reputation, they do not compete to attract patients.

Other incentives for technology adoption and use include the number of angiography labs by site and the number of physicians who perform these procedures. However, the results of a survey of the 16 centers that provided the procedures in 1998 indicate that these numbers have not changed substantially since the early 1980s. Finally, there has been a push for increased efficiency of each angiography and angioplasty laboratory. For example, modification in the billing process has given an incentive for physicians to perform angiography and angioplasty during the same session. Resources have been invested to upgrade the existing facilities. As a result, the number of procedures per laboratory has increased dramatically during the study period (e.g., for patients with a first AMI, from an average of 69 angioplasties per site in 1988 to 228 in 1995).

Technological Change in AMI Care in Quebec

The data on AMI care were obtained from government administrative databases in Quebec. Annual cohorts of AMI patients were constructed using longitudinal data files of hospital admissions in the province of Quebec from January 1, 1985, to December 31, 1995. The hospital discharge summary database in Quebec is called Med-Echo. Med-Echo records provide universal information on hospital admissions, because all citizens and legal residents in the province of Quebec benefit from full coverage health insurance. Using the Med-Echo data, we identified patients for inclusion in the AMI cohort on the basis of a hospitalization for a main diagnosis of AMI (ICD9 code 410).

We also used Med-Echo data to identify admissions that followed the index AMI for diagnoses such as recurrent AMI, old AMI, ischemic heart disease, ventricular arrhythmia and congestive heart failure, unspecified cardiovascular disease, atrial fibrillation, and conduction disorders. For each of the above diagnoses, we chronologically ordered the related admissions and recorded their duration. We excluded admissions within 30 days after initial AMI, because they were likely to represent the consequences of treatment of the AMI itself, rather than later complications.

To describe the pattern of treatment in the AMI patients, we used the Quebec Medicare database (compiled by RAMQ). This administrative database contains records on all diagnostic or therapeutic procedures that are performed in Quebec. This database also contains records on drug prescriptions for all individuals 65 years of age and older and for welfare recipients. Quebec physicians are remunerated on the basis of the services they declare to RAMQ. Therefore, there is a great incentive for physicians to fully report their professional activities. We have all the RAMQ records for our AMI cohort from January 1, 1987, to December 31, 1995. We report the use of angiography only, angiography and angioplasty, and angiography and bypass surgery and of cardiac medications following AMI.

Information on in-hospital drug use is not available because the global hospital budget absorbs their cost and the latter is not itemized. For example, information on use of different thrombolytic agents is not available. However, information on drug use after discharge is available because it is reimbursed to the patient by the provincial government. The data on drug use is available from January 1, 1991, to December 31, 1995.

We created a variable for hospital transfer by comparing the site of hospitalization at the time of the index AMI to the hospital where procedures were performed during or immediately after the index hospital stay. The date and the site of treatment are available in our data, allowing the evaluation of transfers. For instance, among individuals who received angiography and who were hospitalized with an index AMI at a site where this procedure was not available, we distinguished between the ones transferred for catheterization during the index hospital stay and the ones readmitted later on for catheterization. The same data manipulations were done for angioplasty and bypass surgery.

The one-year cumulative incidence rate of angiography was 28 percent in 1988 and 31 percent in 1994 (fig. 4.5). The increase in the catheterization rate over time was greater, in both absolute and relative terms, in the time period shortly after the index AMI (data not shown). For example, the proportion of patients undergoing angiography within 7 days increased from less than 8 percent before 1991 to 12 percent in 1995. Along these lines, by 1994, over 71 percent of angiographies performed within the first year were done within the first 30 days after the index AMI. Thus, intensive procedure use was growing, and occurring earlier, in the Quebec AMI population. Rates of revascularization followed similar trends. The one-year cumulative incidence of angioplasty rose from 8 percent in 1988 to 15 percent in 1994 and that of bypass surgery from 6 percent to 8 percent.

These trends in procedure utilization occurred in most age and gender groups (figs. 4.6–4.8). For angiography and for bypass surgery, the increment was greatest in females and in individuals at least 65 years of age (figs. 4.6, 4.8). For angioplasty, increments were seen across all age and gender groups but were greatest among the nonelderly (under 65 years of age) (fig. 4.7). The use of primary angioplasty increased very slowly during that period from .3 to 1.8 percent.

Cardiac medication use also changed during the study period (fig. 4.9). Prescriptions for aspirin, beta-blockers, lipid-lowering drugs, and ACE inhibitors increased, whereas prescriptions for nitrates, calcium channel blockers, and ionotropes decreased.

The Consequences of Changes in AMI Care in Quebec

To assess the vital status of the AMI patients, we used both Med-Echo and RAMQ data. The all-cause mortality variable in Med-Echo is coded if and only if a patient died within the hospital setting, while the RAMQ mortality variable is built on death certification that can occur

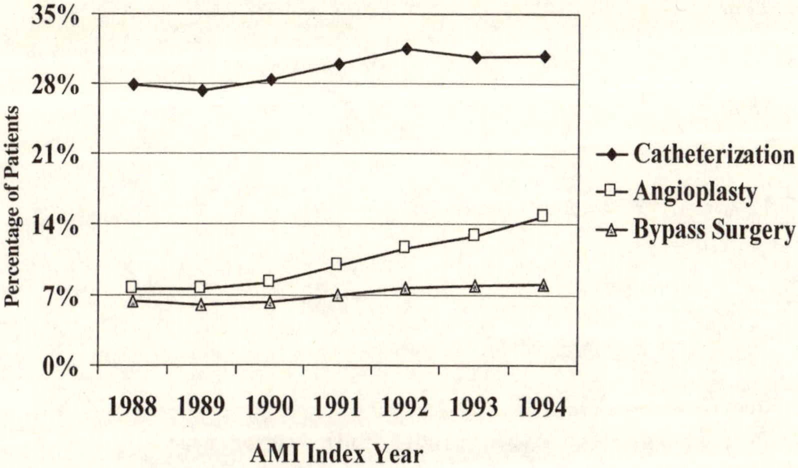

Fig. 4.5. One-year catheterization, angioplasty, and bypass surgery rate

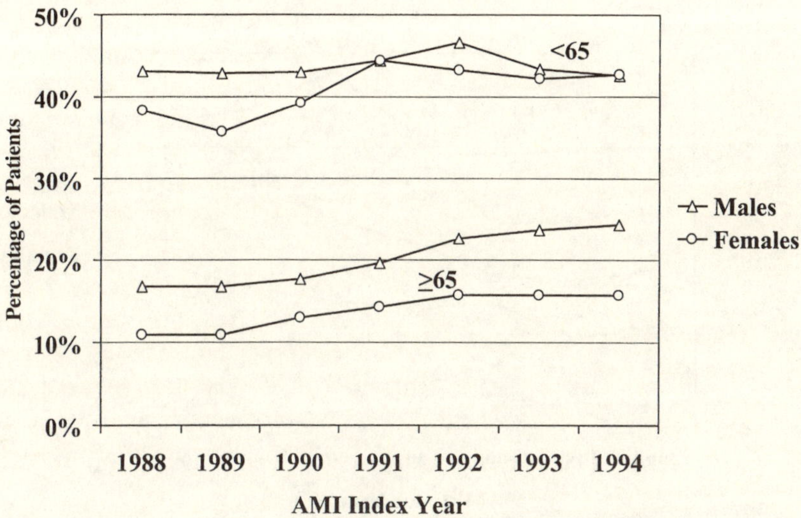

Fig. 4.6. One-year catheterization rate by age and sex

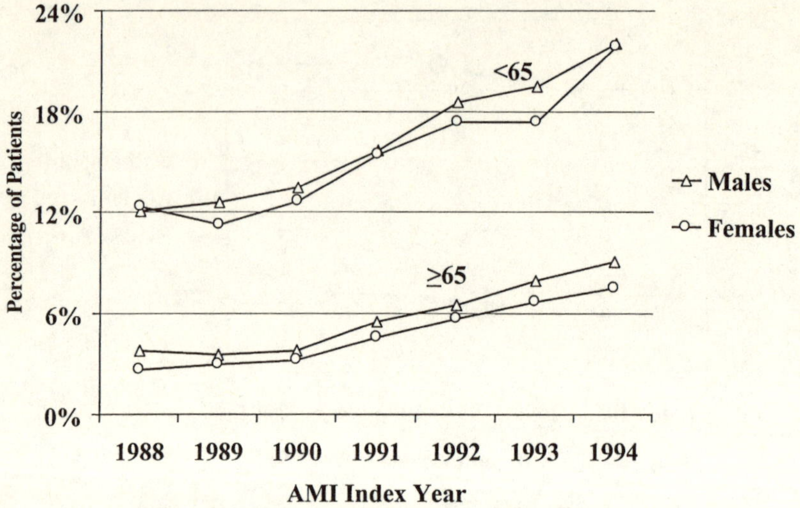

Fig. 4.7. One-year angioplasty rate by age and sex

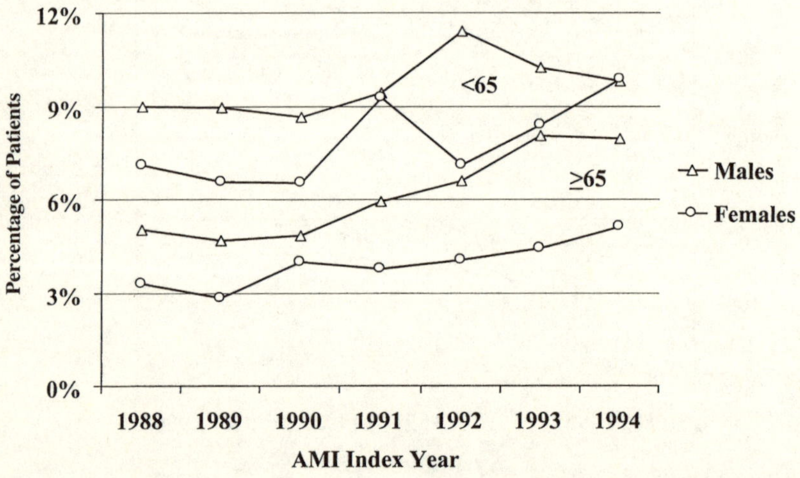

Fig. 4.8. One-year bypass surgery rate by age and sex

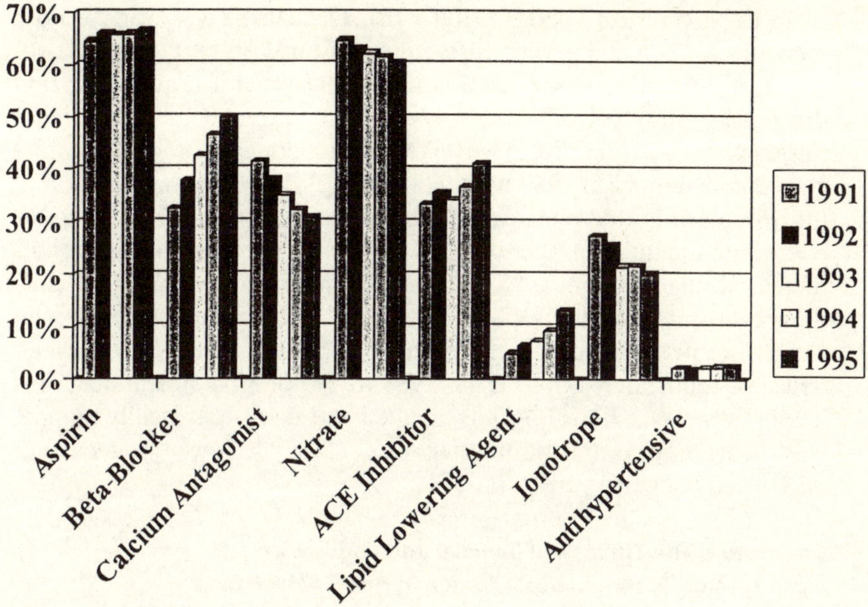

Fig. 4.9. Medications at discharge

out of hospital. This latter variable is constructed by RAMQ by comparing vital status information provided by the Quebec institutions that manage pensions and car insurance. Therefore, a date of death exists in the RAMQ data if and only if those two institutions agreed on mortality of one individual. In addition to these mortality variables, there is a RAMQ code for death certification and the date of the latest treatment received. Using every source of information in order to document mortality in our data, we built an algorithm intended to maximize the reliability of the vital status variable. Through this algorithm, we ascertained the vital status in 99.75 percent of the AMI patients in our database.

The increase in average procedure use over the 1988–94 period was paralleled by a dramatic decrease in average age- and gender-adjusted mortality rate (for the 1995 population). All-cause one-year mortality decreased between 1988 and 1994 (23 percent in 1988 to 19 percent in 1994). From 1988 to 1995, in-hospital mortality rate declined from 14 percent to 11 percent, and 30-day mortality declined from 15 percent to 12 percent (fig. 4.10). The decline was seen for both men and women and across different age groups (fig. 4.11).

The incidence of post-AMI readmissions remained quite constant during the study period. The one-year cumulative incidence of readmissions for angina, recurrent AMI, and congestive heart failure stayed constant from 1988 to 1994 (fig. 4.12). While the proportion of individuals admitted one year after AMI for complications was stable over time, the total number of hospitalizations for these complications increased steadily from 1988 to 1994. A similar proportion of patients were rehospitalized after their first AMI, but among the ones who experienced complications, there was a 25 percent increase in the incidence of rehospitalizations from 1988 to 1994 (3,072 hospitalizations in 1988 versus 3,837 in 1994). Ischemic heart disease, typically angina, was the leading complication after AMI, closely followed by recurrent AMIs and congestive heart failure.

Discussion: The Effects of Financial and Regulatory Incentives on Technological Change in Heart Attack Care

From 1988 to 1995, mortality from AMI in Quebec decreased, while the distributions of patients' age and gender at index AMI remained constant. During the same period, the use of angiography, angioplasty, and

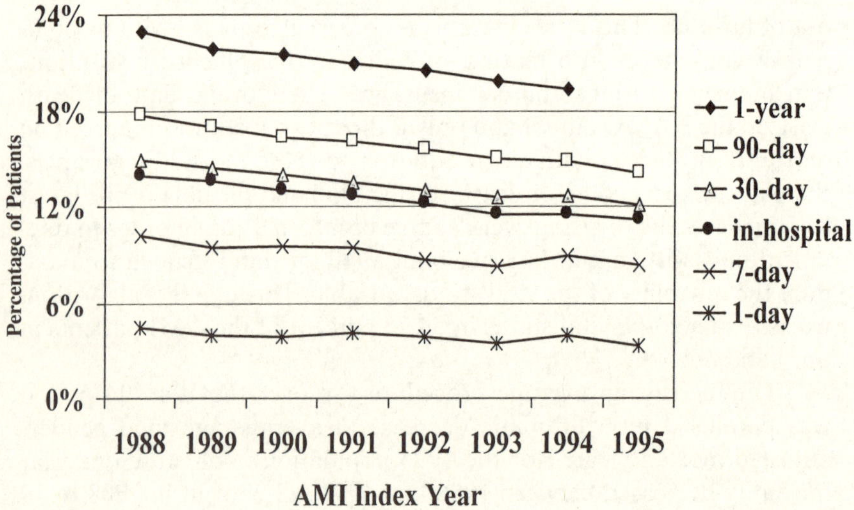

Fig. 4.10. Mortality rate by timing after AMI

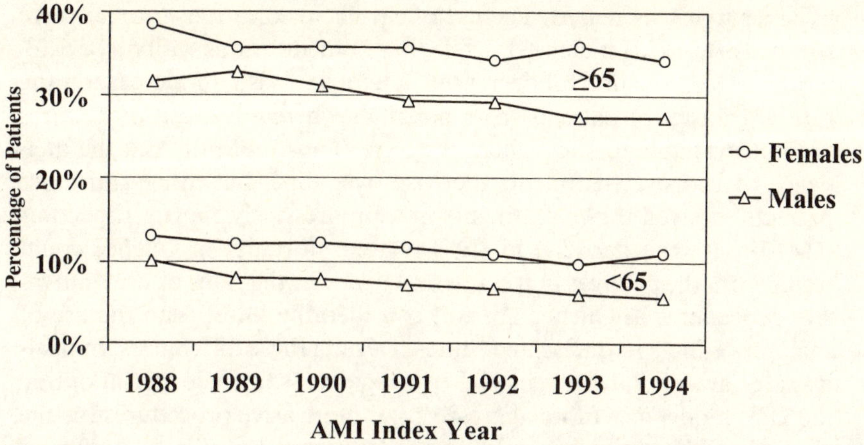

Fig. 4.11. One-year mortality rate by age and sex

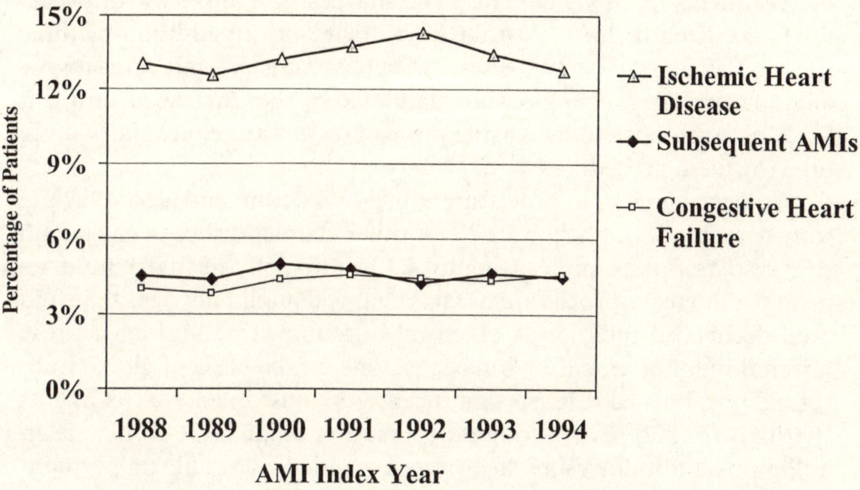

Fig. 4.12. Proportion of patients admitted for selected diagnoses within one year of AMI

bypass surgery increased. The use of cardiac medications that improve survival after AMI increased, while that of medications with no or deleterious effect on survival decreased. There was also an increase in the rate of transfer of patients from hospitals where advanced procedures are not available to sites where they are. Thus, not only did the incidence of invasive treatments increase over time, but more and more patients received these treatments in a progressively shorter time after AMI onset. The decrease in AMI-related mortality in Quebec could result from the changes in treatment. However, the rates of use of invasive procedures in Quebec are still considerably lower than the use of such procedures in the United States. Despite these differences, mortality rates are similar between the two regions. Thus, whether adopting the U.S. model of a more aggressive use of invasive procedures for the care of AMI patients would have additional benefits in terms of decreased mortality remains an open question.

There is evidence that the financial and regulatory incentives particular to the health care system in Quebec have had important effects on treatments for AMI patients. The sharpest rise in the use of procedures occurred in 1991. At that time, there was an addition of three sites for angiography, two sites for bypass surgery, and one site for angioplasty. These changes were mandated by the Quebec government likely as a response to increasing public pressure to reduce the waiting time for these procedures.

Indeed, changes in procedure utilization before and after 1991 are somewhat modest, likely because of other characteristics of the health care system. For example, as figure 4.13 shows, physicians' reimbursement for intensive procedure use has changed minimally over time and even declined if inflation is taken into account. In addition, because hospital reimbursement in Quebec is done on the basis of global budgeting, hospitals have important incentives to use intensive treatments sparingly. Finally, even though the diffusion of intensive cardiac technology to additional sites has been expanded, it is still tightly controlled, relative to the United States.

References

Mark, D. B., C. D. Naylor, M. A. Hlatky, R. M. Califf, E. J. Topol, C. B. Granger, J. D. Knight, C. L. Nelson, K. L. Lee, N. E. Clapp-Channing, W. Sutherland, L. Pilote, and P. W. Armstrong. 1994. "Use of Medical Resources and Quality of Life after Acute Myocardial Infarction in Canada and the United States." *New England Journal of Medicine* 331, no. 17: 1130–35.

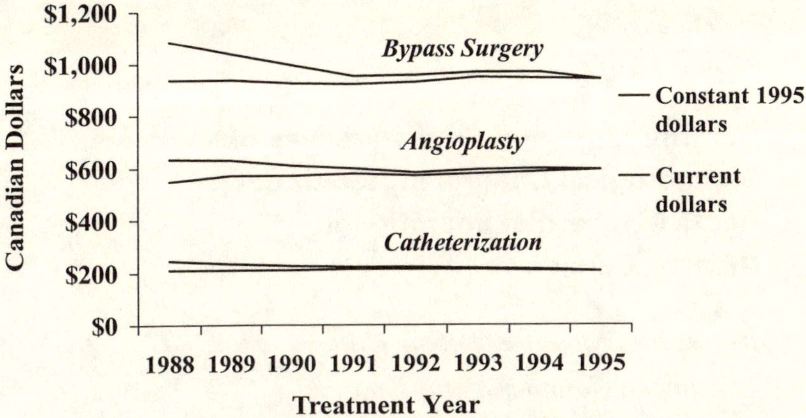

Fig. 4.13. Proportion of patients admitted for selected diagnoses within one year of AMI

Pilote, L., M. G. Bourassa, C. Bacon, J. Bost, K. Detre, D. B. Mark, B. Pitt, G. Reeder, W. J. Rogers, T. Ryan, and M. A. Hlatky. 1995. "Better Functional Status in American Than in Canadian Patients after Myocardial Infarction: An Effect of Medical Care?" *Journal of the American College of Cardiology* 26, no. 5: 1115–20.

Pilote, L., R. M. Califf, S. Sapp, D. P. Miller, D. B. Mark, W. D. Weaver, J. M. Gore, P. W. Armstrong, E. M. Ohman, and E. J. Topol. 1995. "Regional Variation across the United States in the Management of Acute Myocardial Infarction." *New England Journal of Medicine* 333, no. 9: 565–72.

Pilote, L., C. Granger, P. W. Armstrong, D. B. Mark, and M. A. Hlatky. 1995. "Differences in the Treatment of Acute Myocardial Infarction in the United States and Canada: A Physician's Survey." *Medical Care* 33, no. 6: 598–610.

Pilote, L., D. P. Miller, R. M. Califf, J. S. Rao, W. D. Weaver, and E. J. Topol. 1996. "Determinants of Use of Coronary Angiography and Revascularization after Thrombolysis for Acute Myocardial Infarction in the United States." *New England Journal of Medicine* 335, no. 16: 1198–205.

Pilote, L., N. Racine, and M. A. Hlatky. 1994. "Treatment of Acute Myocardial Infarction in the United States and Canada: A Comparison of Two University Hospitals." *Archives of Internal Medicine* 154, no. 10: 1090–96.

CHAPTER 5

Determinants and Consequences of Technological Change in Health Care: Acute Myocardial Infarction in Alberta, Canada

Konrad Fassbender, David Hailey, L. Duncan Saunders, and Koon K. Teo

Cardiovascular disease (CVD)[1] is a significant cause of morbidity and mortality in Canada. Although Canada's mortality rate for cardiovascular disease is low when compared to 20 other countries in the mid-1990s (Heart and Stroke Foundation of Canada 1997), cardiovascular disease is the leading cause of death in Canada, contributing to 37 percent of all deaths in 1995 (*Statistics Canada* 1997).

Consumption of resources as a result of CVD is substantial. Patients with cardiovascular disease were hospitalized for a total of 6,522,117 days for an average length of stay of 12 days (1994/95).[2] Retail pharmacies dispensed 29,994 (12.8 percent of all) prescriptions for patients with CVD in 1996 (IMS 1996). It has been estimated that CVD accounts for 26 million, or 9.9 percent, of all physicians visits (IMS 1994).[3] Together, these direct costs total C$7.354 billion (U.S.$4.758 billion, at current exchange rates), or 16.7 percent of all costs. Economic consequences due to loss of future earnings and productivity arising from premature mortality and disability have been estimated at a further C$12.367 billion (U.S.$8.001 billion) (*Statistics Canada* 1997).

Alberta provides an interesting case study with which to examine the relationships between incentives, health care costs, and patient health outcomes. As table 5.1 shows, despite spending less than the Canadian average on health care, residents of Alberta have among the lowest rates of mortality from CVD in Canada. This chapter seeks to explore the causes and consequences of technological changes in care for CVD in general, and heart attack (AMI) in particular, in Alberta. To what extent have the incentives provided by the system of health care finance in Alberta and in Canada generally affected technological change? And, how in turn has technological change in care for AMI patients affected treatment decisions, health care costs, and patient health outcomes?

This chapter proceeds as follows. Section 1 outlines some of the incentives for technological change in care for AMI provided by the Alberta Health Insurance System. Section 2 begins with a detailed discussion of our data sources, and discusses trends in the use of key intensive treatments for heart attack. Section 3 examines some of the consequences of these changes in treatment decisions for medical expenditures, the use of other health care resources, and ultimately patient health outcomes, and Section 4 concludes.

1. Incentives for Technological Change in Alberta

Financing of Care for Heart Disease

The Government of Alberta administers health care on a not-for-profit basis through the Hospitalization Benefits Plan and the Health Care Insurance Plan. All residents of Alberta, with minor exceptions, receive insurance coverage. Alberta residents pay a premium that may be subsidized or waived depending on income. However, no resident may be denied services if the premiums have not been paid. Seniors are

TABLE 5.1. Age-Standardized Mortality Rates by Gender per 100,000 Population and Expenditures per Capita, Selected Canadian Provinces, 1995

	AMI		IHD		CVD		Expenditures per capita (C$)
	Male	Female	Male	Female	Male	Female	
Newfoundland	103	70	201	147	317	294	2,288
Prince Edward Isl.	99	76	181	141	312	255	2,373
Nova Scotia	84	62	167	118	278	253	2,285
New Brunswick	86	51	151	110	280	245	2,388
Quebec	95	69	163	125	260	235	2,342
Ontario	76	57	160	128	252	243	2,632
Manitoba	85	65	165	131	283	259	2,632
Saskatchewan	82	50	148	99	258	222	2,433
Alberta	**61**	**48**	**139**	**109**	**240**	**243**	**2,290**
British Columbia	74	53	128	94	226	219	2,668
Canada	81	59	155	120	254	239	2,496

subject to premiums but these may be subsidized under the Alberta Seniors Benefit Program. Registered residents, on the other hand, may opt out of the program. To date only 200 residents have opted out.

Both plans require a minimum residency of three months and provide for temporary absences. Services received outside Alberta but within Canada are reimbursed according to rates agreed upon by the provinces. Only insured services received outside Canada at a hospital are reimbursed (to a maximum of C$100 [U.S.$65] per day). Full payment of treatment costs outside Canada may be provided when required services are not available within Canada or when the treatment expense could not be avoided.

The Health Care Insurance Plan covers all medically required services provided by a physician or dental surgeon. Furthermore, these services must be listed under the Medical Benefits Regulations. With respect to cardiac procedures this includes specialized services like pacemakers, valve implants, and other technologies approved by the minister. In addition, the province funds air ambulance service when ordered by a physician. Notably, uninsured services include ambulance care (during transport to hospital); drugs that are to be taken at home; and services typically required by third parties such as medical reports or certificates. Other services not covered include those deemed "experimental" or treatment received outside the province or country without prior ministerial approval. Residents aged 65 and over are entitled to additional services under the Extended Benefits Program that includes premium-free Blue Cross coverage.

Funding for these health care services is illustrated in figure 5.1. Each arrow represents a particular flow of funds from the individual and employer to the government and from third-party insurers to the providers. The type of payment is summarized in the textual description above each arrow. For example, physicians are primarily paid on a fee-for-service basis. They may bill the plan or the patients, but extra-billing (physician assignment of direct, out-of-pocket costs) was terminated in October 1986. However, pure fee-for-service reimbursement for physicians has gradually been subjected to funding constraints. In 1991, the agreement between the plan and the physicians was renegotiated to include a cap on the total medical care budget. And in 1995–96, physician services were capped at C$758,950,000 (U.S.$491,040,000) under an agreement plus another C$28,796,000 (U.S.$18,631,000) for out-of-country and salaried physician services.

Funding for hospitals is provided by 17 regional health authorities. Hospital reimbursement changed from global budgeting to case-

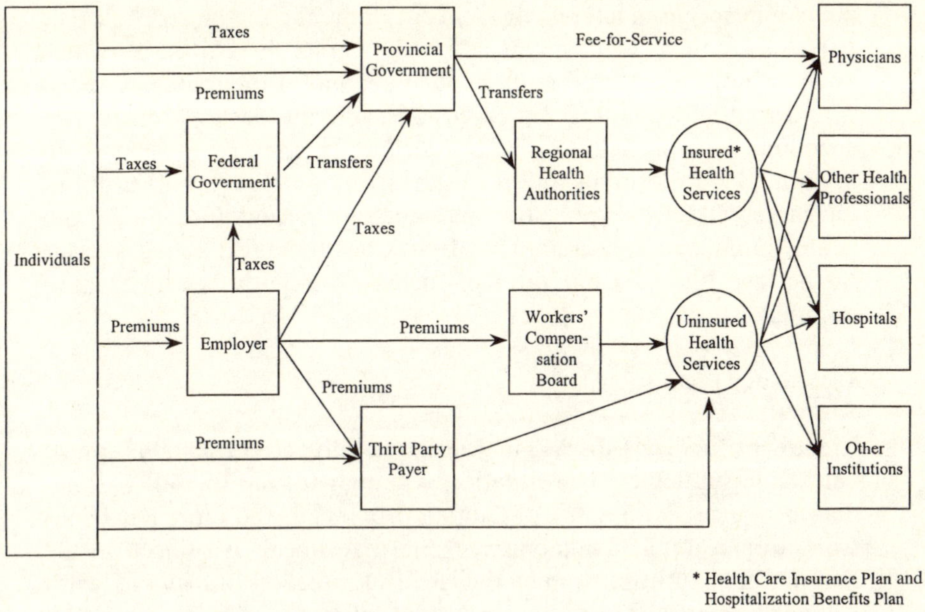

Fig. 5.1. Funding of health care services in Alberta

mix funding in the second quarter of 1990 (closely following Ontario). Alberta uses a system based on diagnosis-related groups, including severity overlays to the diagnosis groupings to classify patients. Case weights were determined from the original Ontario weights that in turn were based on New York per diem costs and Canadian lengths of stay. The Alberta Acute Care Funding System comprises a system of incentives that essentially redistributes money from hospitals with relatively high costs per weighted case to those with low costs. The system was complex and included an adjustment factor that changed annually and was a function of teaching status, number of beds, and the number of separate diagnostic categories treated at the hospital.

Table 5.2 shows the relative importance of each of these sources and uses of funds, and how they have changed over time in Alberta. Total health expenditures per capita in Alberta increased by approximately 1.7 percent annually in real terms from 1975 to 1995. However, health reforms introduced in the late 1980s have caused this trend to reverse with annual declines in per capita spending of approximately 2 percent annually between 1990 and 1995. Most of the recent declines in per capita spending have come from cuts in public-sector expenditures, particularly those to hospitals and other capital expenditures, which includes not only construction of facilities but also equipment necessary for high-technology interventions. Private sector increases in spending have partially offset this decline. In contrast to the cuts to investments in hospitals and facilities, spending on other institutions has increased by 4 percent over the same time period. Growth in both professional care and drug expenditures has remained above average in the last 20 years, but rates of increase for both categories have declined.

Technology Regulation

Treatment for heart disease in Alberta is influenced by regulation of various technologies. The situation is similar to that for other Canadian provinces, with a mix of federal, provincial, and more local controls. For example, availability of pharmaceuticals is subject, in the first place, to authorization by the Health Protection Branch of Health Canada with regard to demonstration of safety and efficacy. Availability within Alberta is a matter for determination by the Health Ministry as to whether and under what conditions a pharmaceutical product

TABLE 5.2. Sources and Uses of Health Care Expenditures, 1995, and Trends over Time, 1970–95 and 1990–95

	% of Total in 1995	Average Annual % Change, 1970–95	Average Annual % Change, 1990–95
By source of funds			
Public sector	72.7	3.2	–2.1
Private sector	27.3	3.8	3.4
Per capita public	72.7	1.5	–3.5
Per capita private	27.3	2.1	1.9
By use of funds			
Hospitals	36.2	3.2	–2.1
Other institutions	8.6	1.8	4.0
Physicians	14.1	3.7	1.2
Other professionals	13.2	4.9	1.3
Drugs	11.0	6.1	2.0
Capital	2.4	0.4	–16.6
Other health spending	14.5	5.1	4.9
Total	100.0	3.3	–0.8

should be included in the provincial formulary. As in other provinces, there has been much debate and negotiation with industry on fair prices for products within the provincial system.

For the period covered by the available data, major drug categories required in the treatment and prevention of AMI have generally been made available to the province without major delays. The dominant factor influencing deployment has been the length of the product development cycle, which would apply to the rest of the nation and to other countries. Only some drugs are considered in the model presented here.

As is the case in other provinces, regulatory controls on devices and procedures are less well developed than for those for pharmaceuticals. The major technologies considered in this chapter—coronary artery bypass grafting (CABG), percutaneous transluminal coronary angioplasty (PTCA), and associated cardiac catheterization facilities—were well established in the province by 1992. Limitations on approval and introduction of some diagnostic technologies are thought by many to be relatively minor. Furthermore, regional influence on overall costs is likewise probably minor.

Alberta has its own health technology assessment programs, operated by the Alberta Heritage Foundation for Medical Research and the Institute for Pharmaco-Economics. These initiatives are quite recent and have not been concerned with technologies included in the analysis. The influence of out-of-province assessments on use of technologies, for example PTCA, has probably been minor.

Other Incentives for Technology Adoption and Use

Availability of these technologies, however, has in practice been subject to various constraints imposed at a local level by individual hospitals or health authorities, with a primary aim of protecting budgets. There have been restrictions on investment in catheterization laboratories, both in respect to numbers established and hours of operation of existing facilities. As table 5.2 shows, the reduction in capital expenditures over the last five years has averaged almost 17 percent.

In recent years there has been substantial reorganization of health care in Alberta, with the creation of 17 regional health authorities that have been given broad responsibilities for the delivery of health care. Initial operation of the authorities has been associated with closure of some health care facilities and changes in roles and levels of activity for others. Although the period in question is relatively recent, it is possible that these changes had an influence on the final year included in this analysis.

Nonfinancial incentives are an important consideration for patients in Alberta, as waiting lists are prevalent for many of the cardiac procedures. As in other Canadian jurisdictions, substantial waiting lists for cardiac surgery and catheterization procedures have been a reality over the period in question.

2. Technological Change in Heart Attack Care in Alberta

The sources of data used for this study are the morbidity file and the discharge abstracts from inpatient hospitalizations and Vital statistics. Vital statistics death data have been used to calculate total rates of mortality. There is an Alberta Health initiative under way to refine the linkage between these two files. A more extensive analysis, which includes physician and outpatient services plus drug utilization data, is currently in progress.[4]

Hospitalization data used in this analysis covers the fiscal years 1991–92 to 1995–96.[5] In order to include only patients with a new AMI in our analysis (see below), and to obtain one-year follow-up information on patients, we report results from fiscal years 1992–93 through 1994–95.

An index AMI admission is the unit of observation for this analysis. It is defined as a hospital admission of an individual with ICD9-CM Code 410.xx and diagnosis type M (most responsible) or 1 (preadmit comorbidity). We exclude patients who meet any of the three following criteria: ICD9-CM Code 410.x2 (fifth digit = 2 means AMI within 90 days); ICD9-CM Code 412 (e.g., old AMI); those patients with length of stay of three days or less who neither died nor were transferred; and any patient admitted with an AMI within the previous 365 days. Combined, these exclusion criteria have resulted in the loss of 10.9 percent of potential admissions. As there is no apparent trend in this figure over the three years, the loss is considered acceptable. There are some characteristics of the Canadian coding system that have been exploited. Since the fifth digit is 100 percent complete, it has been used as an exclusion criterion where codes of 2 mean subsequent care for a previous AMI (within three months). Diagnosis type is the second criterion, limited to a type M, meaning most responsible for the hospitalization, or type 1, signifying a preadmission comorbidity. Postadmission comorbidities and complications were not considered.

Exclusion of AMI cases with lengths of stay less than or equal to three days without death or transfer was performed but needs further study. It is important to understand the nature of these admissions. In Alberta, there have been acute bed shortages. Physicians are under intense pressure to release patients. Perhaps limited chart reviews of these cases are warranted. Alternatively, a formal model incorporating hospital capacity utilization could be used to determine whether nonfinancial aggregate demand factors influence discharge decisions.

Procedural definitions are defined on the basis of the ICD9-CM procedure codes. Bypass surgery (CABG) is defined as 36.1x or 36.03. Angioplasty (PTCA) is defined as any of the following codes: 36.0, 36.00, 36.01, 36.02, or 36.05. Finally the following ranges of codes define catheterization: 37.21–37.23 or 88.52–88.58. The coding system in Alberta allows for up to 16 diagnoses and 10 procedure codes per hospital admission.

Changes in High-Tech Care

Catheterization, angioplasty (PTCA), and coronary artery bypass graft surgery (CABG) are the high-technology treatments for AMI considered in this analysis. Table 5.3 presents cardiac catheterization rates within 7, 30, 90, and 365 days of admission for patients' index AMI for men and women for the fiscal years 1992–93, 1993–94, and 1994–95. Catheterization rates are higher for males than females by 10 percentage points at 7 and 30 days, growing to approximately 15 percentage points at one year. The growth rates for females, however, are about double that for males. For example, within one year of initial admission, the catheterization rate for females rose 15.1 percent, whereas the rate for males rose only 8.2 percent. The one-year rates are 50 percent higher than the 7-day rates, indicating that AMI patients are most likely to receive catheterization during the initial visit.

Table 5.4 presents PTCA rates for AMI patients for an analogous time period. Utilization of angioplasties is increasing more rapidly within 7 days (40.1 percent increase over the study period) than within 365 days (22.9 percent increase). Not only have rates increased overall, but it is more likely that PTCA will be done on an emergency basis. This trend is likely, as the 7-day and 1-day rates (not presented in the table) do not differ greatly. The rates are slightly higher for males than for females, but again the rate of increase for females is twice that of males, even over the very short time period under analysis.

Table 5.5 presents the analogous CABG utilization rates. These rates have actually declined within 7 and within 30 days of index AMI

TABLE 5.3. Catheterization Rates for AMI Patients, by Gender, Fiscal Years 1992–93 through 1994–95

	Male				Female				All Patients			
	7 Days	30 Days	90 Days	365 Days	7 Days	30 Days	90 Days	365 Days	7 Days	30 Days	90 Days	365 Days
1992–93	35.4	43.2	49.0	57.3	26.2	31.0	34.5	40.3	32.3	39.1	44.1	51.6
1993–94	37.8	44.5	49.9	58.3	23.2	27.8	33.0	39.7	32.9	38.8	44.2	52.0
1994–95	39.3	46.8	52.7	62.0	30.5	37.6	40.6	46.4	36.3	43.7	48.6	56.7

TABLE 5.4. Angioplasty (PTCA) Rates for AMI Patients, by Gender, Fiscal Years 1992–93 through 1994–95

	Male				Female				All Patients			
	7 Days	30 Days	90 Days	365 Days	7 Days	30 Days	90 Days	365 Days	7 Days	30 Days	90 Days	365 Days
1992–93	11.5	16.3	19.8	23.9	7.8	11.2	12.8	15.2	10.2	14.6	17.5	21.0
1993–94	12.7	16.7	19.1	23.6	8.7	11.6	13.7	17.1	11.3	15.0	17.3	21.4
1994–95	15.2	20.2	23.2	28.1	12.6	17.0	18.6	21.2	14.3	19.1	21.6	25.8

TABLE 5.5. Coronary Artery Bypass Grafts (CABG) Rates for AMI Patients, by Gender, Fiscal Years 1992–93 through 1994–95

	Male				Female				All Patients			
	7 Days	30 Days	90 Days	365 Days	7 Days	30 Days	90 Days	365 Days	7 Days	30 Days	90 Days	365 Days
1992–93	3.4	5.5	6.7	9.7	2.7	4.1	5.1	7.0	3.2	5.0	6.2	8.8
1993–94	3.1	5.1	7.4	11.5	2.0	3.2	4.4	6.3	2.7	4.4	6.4	9.7
1994–95	3.5	5.7	7.4	10.6	1.9	3.7	4.7	6.4	2.9	5.0	6.5	9.2

while increasing within 90 and 365 days. This pattern may be explained by the shift toward longer waiting lists over this time period. Like catheterization, utilization of CABG is greater in males than females. Unlike the other procedures, the rates decline or remain flat in females over the three-year time period.

To summarize, angioplasty rates have increased most dramatically over the study time period, while catheterization rates have increased more moderately. CABG rates declined at 7 and 30 days but increased slightly at 90 and 365 days, reflecting the shift to longer waiting times. These results are curious in that physician fees are capped and capital expenditures have decreased by 16 percent per year over this time period. Furthermore, declines in hospital spending have translated into fewer nurses, which would also be expected to reduce procedure rates.

Changes in Low-Tech Care

Low-tech treatments for AMI primarily refer to drug treatment. Low-tech treatments generally considered efficacious during the initial admission for AMI include the following: thrombolytic drugs, aspirin and other antiplatelet agents, beta-blockers, calcium channel blockers, nitrates, ACE inhibitors, and lidocaine. Low-tech treatments typically used at or after discharge include aspirin, beta-blockers, calcium channel blockers, nitrates, ACE inhibitors, and statins or other cholesterol-reducing drugs.

Data for the comprehensive evaluation of drug utilization are not available from one source. In-hospital medication is provided in an acute setting (emergency or the coronary care unit) or a subacute setting (stepdown units or general wards). Tertiary care hospitals in Alberta maintain electronic medication records for subacute care. Information for acute care medication is only available from patient charts. Postacute or out-of-hospital medication data are available electronically for elderly patients (Blue Cross data) and for selected employed individuals (private insurance). Plans to link and systematically analyze these data are under way.

Several studies have nonetheless been undertaken to assess utilization of medications in selected hospitals (CQIN Investigators 1996; Fassbender et al. 1996; Montague et al. 1991, 1992, 1996; Teo et al. 1994; Teo, Martin, Tsuyuki, Warnica, Greenwood, Morris, et al. 1996; Tsuyuki et al. 1994). The primary source of data in these studies has been chart review. For example, Montague et al. (1992) report that in-hospital thrombolytic usage is 43 percent for patients under 70 years of age but only 20 percent otherwise. Beta-blocker use by patients under 70 years of age is 62 percent, versus 41 percent for those who are 70 years or over. Aspirin use is 87 percent and 71 percent, respectively. Finally, use of nitrates is very high at 97 percent for the under-70 group and 86 percent for older patients. The other studies cited also demonstrate that the utilization has increased over the time period in this study. These other studies, however, demonstrate some evidence that age and gender gaps persist for low-tech utilization.

Hindle, Norheim, and Renger (1995) examined the use of thrombolytic therapy in rural hospitals. They found thrombolytic therapy is available in 80.8 percent of hospitals. Of physicians in these hospitals, 71.4 percent used streptokinase. Hospitals that did not provide thrombolytic therapy were smaller with an average of 21.9 beds and 2.4 medical staff. The primary barrier to the use of this therapy is inadequate nursing support (particularly availability of nurses holding Advanced Cardiac Life Support certification).

Montague et al. (1991) find that unexplained age differences in the utilization of other low-tech procedures exist. For example, postacute exercise testing, ejection fraction measurements, and coronary angiography are performed more frequently on patients under the age of 70 years (i.e. rates are higher).

Changes in Expertise or Appropriateness of Care

As discussed above, practice variations differ between selected hospitals in the utilization of low-tech care (Montague et al. 1995; Teo, Martin, Tsuyuki, Warnica, Greenwood, Imrie, et al. 1996; Teo, Warnica, et al. 1996). However, this observed difference may not be as great as that between young and aged patients or between males and females. The most important finding of these studies is that unexplained variations in practice patterns in Alberta are declining over time and can be successfully altered.

In particular, some recent studies have shown that the introduction of a critical path order sheet has resulted in more appropriate care (Fassbender et al. 1996; Teo, Warnica, et al. 1996). It is important to note that the definition of appropriateness is also expanded to include documentation of the decision-making process. (This process takes into account the existence of contraindications for generally efficacious therapies like beta-blockers and indications for therapies like calcium channel blockers). This important area of research that is currently being addressed by the Clinical Quality Improvement Network (CQIN) with centers in Alberta and some other provinces.

3. The Consequences of Changes in Heart Attack Care in Alberta

Changes in Health Outcomes for AMI Patients

There are limits to the use of administrative data in providing outcomes for analysis. The outcome measures that are available must be interpreted with caution. The most common outcome measures include in-hospital mortality and readmission to hospital. How is in-hospital mortality to be interpreted while hospital lengths of stay are also changing? What if out-of-hospital mortality has increased?

In-hospital death rates can be interpreted with some consistency if the same unit of time is compared across years. For men, in-hospital death rates have remained stable at one day, but declined slightly at seven days (table 5.6). For women, in contrast, in-hospital mortality rates have risen slightly at both one and seven days. Higher one-day rates for women may be explained by increased severity at admission. However, explanations of outcomes on the basis of hospital and procedural utilization would be premature and require more detailed study.

Data on aggregate mortality from AMI can supplement this analysis of administrative hospital records. Table 5.7 shows that total mortality from AMI per unit population declined by 8.1 percent in Alberta between 1992–93 and 1994–95 (information not in the table shows that age- and gender-adjusted mortality declined by slightly more, by 9.7 percent). However, according to table 5.7, the rate of new AMI admissions per unit population declined contemporaneously by almost as much, by 6.7 percent (or 9.0 percent in age-adjusted terms). Thus, although there is some evidence that mortality from AMI

TABLE 5.6. Inpatient Mortality from AMI, by Gender, Fiscal Years 1992–93 through 1994–95

	Male		Female		All Patients	
	1 Day	7 Days	1 Day	7 Days	1 Day	7 Days
1992–93	4.9	10.5	7.0	14.6	5.6	11.9
1993–94	5.0	10.4	7.3	14.8	5.8	11.9
1994–95	4.9	9.5	7.4	15.1	5.8	11.4

declined over our study period, this issue remains one for further analysis.

Changes in Medical Expenditures and Resource Use

Table 5.8 summarizes five measures of how medical expenditures and resource use for treatment for Alberta's AMI patients have changed from 1992–93 to 1994–95: average length of stay (LOS) for a typical AMI admission (excluding admissions ending in death, transfers, discharge without approval, and long-stay outliers)[6]; average number of hospital visits per year; average total number of hospital days per year; the average expenditures for an initial AMI admission (in 1995 purchasing power parity [PPP] U.S.$); and the average expenditures per year for a new AMI patient (also in 1995 PPP U.S.$).

Even as procedure rates were rising rapidly over the study period, lengths of stay and the total number of days in hospital per year were falling. For example, the average LOS for a typical AMI admission declined by approximately 9 percent, from 10.9 days in 1992–93 to 9.5 days in 1994–95. Hospital expenditures declined even more dramatically, a product of the public-sector cuts in spending detailed in table 5.2. Indeed, spending on cardiovascular treatment has been targeted, as hospital expenditures in aggregate have only declined 2.1 percent over this time period. Decreases in expenditures are comparable for both males and females.

However, these results should be interpreted with caution, because of the several changes in the financing of health care in Alberta that took place over the study period. To begin with, it is possible that these three years constitute too short a time period to make any conclusions. Furthermore, the average severity of admissions—which affects reimbursement to providers, and therefore measured expenditures—had started to decline at the beginning of the study period.[7] Thus, it is difficult to determine whether the decrease in costs reflects real

TABLE 5.7. Number of New Admissions for AMI and AMI Mortality (per 100,000 population), by Gender, Fiscal Years 1992–93 through 1994–95

	Male		Female		All Patients	
	Admissions	Mortality	Admissions	Mortality	Admissions	Mortality
1992–93	192.0	66.0	97.3	44.1	144.7	55.0
1993–94	193.2	67.6	98.4	42.8	145.8	55.2
1994–95	178.6	58.6	91.5	42.3	135.0	50.5

TABLE 5.8. Resource Use in the Treatment of AMI Patients, by Gender, Fiscal Years 1992–93 through 1994–95

	Length of Stay Typical Admission (days)			Visits per Year			Inpatient Hospital Days per Year			Expenditures for Initial Admission[a] (U.S.$)			Expenditures per Year[a] (U.S.$)		
	Male	Female	All	Male	Female	All	Male	Female	All	Male	Female	All	Male	Female	All
1992–93	10.9	12.1	11.3	1.7	1.8	1.8	18.6	24.0	20.4	5,933	5,929	5,932	10,662	10,898	10,741
1993–94	10.0	11.9	10.7	1.7	1.9	1.8	18.2	23.9	20.1	5,293	5,523	5,370	9,740	10,154	9,880
1994–95	9.5	11.4	10.1	1.7	1.8	1.7	16.1	20.0	17.4	5,055	5,052	5,054	9,032	8,940	9,001

[a]Converted at PPP exchange rate to 1995 U.S. dollars.

decreases in resource consumption or is a product of the hospital's reaction to the new funding system and method of assigning case weights.

4. Discussion

Despite funding cutbacks, increases in high-technology utilization have occurred in Alberta. Angioplasty rates have increased dramatically over the study time period. Catheterization rates have increased more moderately despite cuts in hospital funding, though this trend is due in part to decreased admissions. CABG rates decreased initially but increased at one year, reflecting longer waiting times for surgery.

Part of the reconciliation of these seemingly inconsistent facts lies in the fact that overall AMI admissions have fallen. As catheterization labs operated at capacity during this time, more procedures per AMI patient resulted. Furthermore, cost containment resulted in shortened lengths of stay and fewer days per year for each AMI patient, as well as lower payments to providers conditional on treatment. Together, these factors may have resulted in a decrease in the cost of an episode, even though the use of specific intensive procedures has risen.

In part, the high and growing rates of procedure use may account for the fact that population rates of AMI mortality are lowest in Western Canada, and declining over our study period. These low rates, referred to as the East-West gradient, may be partly due to lifestyle and socioeconomic characteristics of the population. Economically speaking, Alberta has lower unemployment and higher per capita income than other provinces, which may translate into healthier behavior. Albertans do, in fact, exhibit lower blood pressure and cholesterol. However, they are average in smoking, obesity, and sedentary lifestyle (Canadian Heart Health 1995).

As discussed above, however, the decline in population mortality from AMI has been accompanied by a decline in AMI admissions rates. In addition, there has not been nearly as substantial of a decline in short-term in-hospital mortality rates. On the other hand, the decline in AMI admissions rates may be a result of the additional intensive treatment, which could result in a decrease in subsequent reinfarctions. Successful treatment of initial AMI may be followed by subsequent deaths from other disorders of the circulatory system. In fact, a hypothesis has been developed that links successful treatment of Q-wave infarctions and the incidence of subsequent non-Q-wave infarctions (Montague et al. 1996). For these reasons, measured decreases in population mortality due to AMI must be interpreted cautiously.

Notes

The authors gratefully acknowledge comments from Unto Häkkinen and Devidas Menon. This study is based in part on data provided by Alberta Health. Interpretations and conclusions contained herein are those of the researchers and do not necessarily represent the views of the Government of Alberta.

1. Disease classification in this document will refer to the World Health Organization's (WHO) International Classification of Diseases (ICD9) coding system. Cardiovascular disease refers to ICD9 codes 390–459 inclusive, while ischemic heart disease consists of codes 410–414. Health Canada data (including the Heart and Stroke Foundation) includes 429.2 in ischemic heart disease. Acute myocardial infarction consists of the single code, 410.

2. Length of stay based on 1992/93 Hospital Morbidity Data.

3. Cardiovascular disease is actually second only to respiratory disease, ICD9 460–519.

4. Project HEAT (Health Expenditure and Technology) is a joint initiative between the Institute of Pharmaco-Economics, and the Alberta Heritage Foundation for Medical Research.

5. The registration numbers were assigned on the basis of family units prior to 1992 and individuals' numbers were available thereafter. Alberta Health has recoded registration numbers for the year 1991. Fiscal years cover the April 1–March 31 period.

6. A long-stay outlier is defined by the following formula: *LOS 3QR* + 2 × *IR,* where *LOS* refers to length of stay, *3QR* is the third quartile, and *IR* is the interquartile range.

7. This is based on data for all hospitalizations of Albertans during the time period 1987 to 1993.

References

Canadian Heart Health Surveys. 1995. *Canadian Heart Health: Reducing the Risks.* Health Canada.

Clinical Quality Improvement Network (CQIN) Investigators. 1996. "Cardiovascular Risk Management among 1806 Low Risk Patients in a Primary Care Setting." *Canadian Journal of Cardiology* 12, no. 9: 797–801.

Fassbender, K., P. Montague, K. K. Teo, W. Tymchak, and T. Montague. 1996. Abstract. "Role of Critical Path Order Sheets in Process-Based Performance Review of Use of Beta-Blockers and Calcium Antagonists in Acute Myocardial Infarction." *Canadian Journal of Cardiology* 12 (suppl. E): 162E.

Heart and Stroke Foundation of Canada. 1997. *Heart Disease and Stroke in Canada.* Ottawa: HSFC.

Hindle, H., J. K. Norheim, and R. Renger. 1995. "Rural Alberta Thrombolysis Study: Survey of Practice Patterns for Managing Acute Myocardial Infarction." *Canadian Family Physician* 41:1180–87.

Intercontinental Medical Statistics, Canada (IMS). 1994. *Canadian Disease and Therapeutic Index, Year Ending 1994.*

———. 1996. *Compuscript.*

Jacobs, P., K. Fassbender, K. Bay, and J. R. Lave. 1995. "The Impact of Case Mix Funding in Ontario and Alberta, 1989–1993." Paper presented at the Australian Case-Mix Conference, September.

Jacobs, P., E. M. Hall, J. R. Lave, and M. Glendining. 1992. "Alberta's Acute Care Funding Project." *Healthcare Management Forum* 5, no. 3: 4–20.

Jacobs, P., E. M. Hall, and R. H. Plain. 1995. "Alberta's Acute Care Funding Plan: Update to December 1994." *Healthcare Management Forum* 8, no. 2: 17–22.

Montague, T. J., R. M. Ikuta, R. Y. Wong, K. S. Bay, K. K. Teo, and N. J. Davies. 1991. "Comparison of Risk and Patterns of Practice in Patients Older and Younger Than 70 Years with Acute Myocardial Infarction in a Two-Year Period (1987–1989)." *American Journal of Cardiology* 68, no. 9: 843–47.

Montague, T., P. Montague, M. Barnes, L. Taylor, L. Wowk, K. Fassbender, M. Ackman, S. Martin, and K. K. Teo. 1996. "Acute Myocardial Infarction in Canada: New Epidemiologic Insights on Incidence, Therapy, and Risk." *Journal of Thrombosis and Thrombolysis* 3:101–5.

Montague, T., L. Taylor, M. Barnes, M. Ackman, R. Tsuyuki, R. Wensel, R. Williams, D. Catellier, and K. K. Teo. 1995. "Can Practice Patterns and Outcomes Be Successfully Altered? Examples from Cardiovascular Medicine." *Canadian Journal of Cardiology* 11, no. 6: 487–92.

Montague, T. J., R. Y. Wong, J. R. Burton, K. S. Bay, D. J. Catellier, and K. K. Teo. 1992. "Changes in Acute Myocardial Infarction Risk and Patterns of Practice for Patients Older and Younger Than 70 Years, 1987–90." *Canadian Journal of Cardiology* 8, no. 6: 596–600.

Statistics Canada. 1997. Laboratory Centre for Disease Control.

Teo, K. K. 1994. Abstract. "The Relative Contribution of Age, Sex, and Medical Therapy to Mortality in 3896 Patients with Acute Myocardial Infarction, 1987–93." *Circulation* 90 (suppl. 2):1–527.

Teo, K. K., S. Martin, R. Tsuyuki, J. W. Warnica, P. V. Greenwood, J. Imrie, T. H. Ashton, A. Morris, J. Kornder, D. McLeod, and T. Montague. 1996. Abstract. "Contemporary Medical Therapy and Mortality Risk in 6724 Patients with Acute Myocardial Infarction, 1987 to 1996." *Canadian Journal of Cardiology* 12 (suppl. E): 81E.

Teo, K. K., S. Martin, R. T. Tsuyuki, J. W. Warnica, P. V. Greenwood, A. L. Morris, T. H. Ashton, J. R. Imrie, J. M. Kornder, D. McLeod, and

T. Montague. 1996. Abstract. "Influence of a Critical Path Management Process in Myocardial Infarction." *Circulation* 94 (suppl. I): 1–10.

Teo, K. K., J. W. Warnica, J. Imrie, P. V. Greenwood, T. Ashton, R. Tsuyuki, A. Morris, D. McLeod, and T. Montague. 1996. Abstract. "Patient Care Enhancement with Continuous Quality Improvement Techniques." *European Heart Journal* 17 (abs. suppl.): 233.

Tsuyuki, R. T., K. K. Teo, R. M. Ikuta, K. S. Bay, P. V. Greenwood, and T. J. Montague. 1994. "Mortality Risk and Patterns of Practice in 2070 Patients with Acute Myocardial Infarction, 1987–92." *Chest* 105:1687–92.

Wen, C. P., and S. P. Tsai. 1982. "Anatomy of the Healthy Worker Effect—a Critique of Summary Statistics Employed in Occupational Epidemiology." *Scandinavian Journal of Work, Environment, and Health* 8 (suppl. 1): 48–52.

CHAPTER 6

Health Reform and Technological Change in Manitoba: Treatment of Acute Myocardial Infarction

Leslie L. Roos, Randy Walld, Ruth-Ann Soodeen, and Noralou P. Roos

The Canadian health care system, with its universal coverage and a single payer, has been characterized by a relatively high degree of vertical equity. Over the past several years, Canadian health reform has been at the center of much debate, the primary concerns being the cost of care and the impact of budgetary constraints on access, quality, and equity (Roos et al. 1998). Excessive waiting times for common diagnostic and therapeutic procedures have been a source of particular criticism (Roos et al. 1998; Bell et al. 1998). A downward trend in Canadian hospital spending began in 1991; by 1994 such spending had declined 9.2 percent (Tully and Saint-Pierre 1997). However, despite continuing challenges of cost containment and health reform, the single-payer Canadian system has been widely praised for providing coverage to the entire population more cheaply than the American system.

Manitoba typically ranks in the middle of all the Canadian provinces on measures of health care expenditures, mortality, and health status indicators (Shanahan and Gousseau 1998). The health care sector in Manitoba, which accounted for 33 percent of Manitoba's total budget, has experienced significant shrinkage, comparable to, but perhaps less than, the other Canadian provinces. Hospital expenditures per capita dropped by 11 percent between 1990 and 1995, from Can.$727 to Can.$648 (Brownell, Roos, and Burchill 1999). These reductions have had direct effects upon bed supply. In 1990, the two teaching hospitals (which perform all cardiac catheterization and revascularization in the province) accounted for 55 percent of the total beds in Winnipeg, the provincial capital. By 1996, budget cuts forced the closure of 28 percent of these beds as well as 20 percent of beds in the city's urban community hospitals. Changes in health care outside Winnipeg were much smaller during this period.

Despite the downsizing of hospital resources, aggregate measures of access to care did not appear to decline. For Winnipeg hospitals, the number of separations (combined rate of discharge for both inpatient and outpatient services) per 1,000 residents ranged from 132 in 1990 to 136 in 1995. This was accomplished through reductions in surgical lengths of stay, while outpatient surgery increased by 69 percent (Brownell, Roos, and Burchill 1999). By way of comparison, the growth of outpatient surgery in the United States from the late 1980s to the early 1990s facilitated a 1.8 percent decrease in inpatient discharge rates and a 3 percent drop in average length of stay (Centers for Disease Control and Prevention 1996).

The Manitoba government was particularly sensitive to public concern that the most severely ill patients might not receive necessary treatment after health reform. However, hospitalization rates for patients with three or more conditions known to increase the risk of death remained stable over the five-year period, while hospitalizations for patients with less serious conditions declined by 7 percent, from 736 to 687 per 10,000.

This brief review of health care and health reform in Manitoba provides the context for a survey of trends and variations in treatment of acute myocardial infarction (AMI). We first describe Canada's approach of late adoption of costly new technology. Next, we highlight the effects of technological change upon post-AMI care in Manitoba. Finally, we analyze how technological change has affected the outcome of heart attack patients, closing with a discussion of key issues that need to be addressed by health care decision-makers.

Incentives for Technological Change in Manitoba

Canada has emphasized the regulation of technology and cost containment through global budgets and tightly negotiated fee schedules for physicians. In conjunction with these fiscal restraints, Canadian provinces have adopted strategies to manage the health care system through regulation of the supply of specialists, operating rooms, hospital beds, and equipment (Mullan 1998; Saltman and Figueras 1998). Because of the need to contain health care costs, treatments with high fixed costs of adoption or high costs associated with each use of the technology (high-tech treatments) are particular candidates for management.

A strategy of limited adoption of such technologies may not affect quality of care, especially when the availability of expensive new technologies is restricted to a few hospitals. Such centralization generally leads to a higher volume in each hospital performing the given procedure, which is often associated with better outcomes (Grumbach et al. 1995). Moreover, "limited adoption" may be the wrong term to describe the Canadian experience. Although procedure rates are low by U.S. standards, Canadian rates of cardiovascular procedures are comparable to many other developed countries. Understanding the health and cost consequences of different strategies for technology adoption and regulation may permit countries to learn from diverse experiences and generate better policies for improving quality of care.

While delayed adoption may have potential long-run advantages, serious problems can also occur when new technologies have clear and important consequences for public health. Special efforts need to be made to prevent public health catastrophes, as tight cost containment through strict limits on new technologies can go too far, leading to almost automatic postponement of requests for funding major new programs. A limited adoption strategy must deal with the possibility of "doing too little." The challenge for Canadian planners is to be smart adopters of cost-effective technology. With these considerations in mind, we turn to a more detailed review of the Manitoba experience of changes in heart attack treatment.

Technological Change in Heart Attack Care in Manitoba

Data sources

The annual cohorts of AMI patients were defined on the basis of hospital discharges during each fiscal year from 1989 to 1996 (fiscal years run from April 1 of a given year to March 31 of the next year). Essentially all individual residents in the province of Manitoba are covered by the universal public health insurance system. Information on mortality is provided by the Manitoba research registry, a unique longitudinal resource built from Vital Statistics data and Manitoba Health registry information (Roos and Nicol 1999). Extensive information is available on the quality of these administrative data (Roos, Nicol, and Cageorge 1987; Roos, Sharp, and Wadja 1989; Roos et al. 1993).

The starting point for defining the AMI cohort was all inpatient discharges with an ICD9-CM diagnosis of 410 in any position on the discharge abstract among Manitoba residents aged 40 and over at the time of the AMI. The very small number of obstetrical patients was excluded, as were questionable AMI cases (defined as AMI patients discharged alive with index hospital lengths of stay less than 5 days). All AMI inpatient admissions that were transferred to another hospital were included. Patients who died in hospital or within 30 days of hospital discharge were included, even when the length of stay was less than 5 days. A patient was only counted once in a given fiscal year, but the same patient could be counted twice if an AMI diagnosis was recorded twice in two different fiscal years.[1]

The demographic characteristics of AMI patients in Manitoba are presented in table 6.1. Compared with other provinces, the onset of AMI may be delayed in Manitoba (although our use of data only from those 40 and over may skew comparisons). The small increase in the number of AMI patients and trends in the Charlson index (as a measure of comorbidity accompanying AMI) seem in line with what might be expected in an aging population (Charlson et al. 1987; Romano, Roos, and Jollis 1993).

Changes in High-Tech Care

Certain high-profile treatments, including CABG and PTCA, seem to have enjoyed a special status in the health reform process, in part because of the widespread publicity about Canadian waiting lists. With little formal queue management in Manitoba, as compared with the situation in Ontario, the reasons for trends and fluctuations are unclear. Although Roos and Sharp (1989) found a steady increase in CABG between 1977 and 1983, the utilization of angiography, CABG, and PTCA appeared to grow more rapidly with the recruitment of a new director for the provincial cardiovascular surgery program in the early 1990s. The director did have a clear mandate to increase revascularization and to reduce waiting times, especially among the elderly population. During the 1989–96 period, age- and sex-adjusted rates among those 40 and over were up 29 percent for coronary angiography (from 43.74 to 56.53 per 10,000), 69 percent for coronary artery bypass graft surgery (from 9.81 to 16.54 per 10,000), and 67 percent for percutaneous transluminal angioplasty (from 8.94 to 14.97 per 10,000). Angiography and PTCA rates for women increased substantially more than those for men (46 percent versus 21 percent and 106 percent versus 53 percent, respectively). As table 6.2 indicates, the probability of having CABG within one year of index AMI increased between 1989

TABLE 6.1. Demographic Characteristics of AMI Cohorts in Manitoba

	Fiscal Year								Absolute	Relative
	1989	1990	1991	1992	1993	1994	1995	1996	Change	Change (%)
Number of AMIs	2,428	2,362	2,442	2,370	2,419	2,431	2,527	2,454	26	1.1
Mean age	69.6	70.0	70.0	69.9	70.0	70.4	70.7	70.5	0.9	1.3
Age ≥ 65 (%)	69.2	69.8	70.3	68.8	69.8	70.3	71.4	70.5	1.3	1.9
Female (%)	38.6	40.1	38.4	38.5	39.4	38.8	38.1	38.6	0.0	0.0
Charlson index[a] score 1 (%)	22.9	21.1	23.1	22.4	22.9	22.5	23.8	25.8	2.9	12.7
Charlson index[a] score ≥ 2 (%)	14.6	14.6	15.3	14.5	15.3	15.5	16.4	16.3	1.7	11.6
Length of stay (Index hospitalization)	16.1	17.5	17.9	15.3	14.3	14.7	14.7	14.1	–2.0	–12.4
Episode[b] length of stay	19.8	20.8	22.3	18.8	18.8	18.2	18.3	17.2	–2.6	–13.1

Note: Only patients 40 years of age and older at the time of the AMI are included.

[a]The Charlson index score was based on the Dartmouth-Manitoba version of the index (Charlson et al. 1989; Romano et al. 1994).

[b]Episode includes transfers to and from hospital of index admission.

(7.8 percent) and 1995 (11.6 percent). Similarly, PTCA within one year of AMI grew from 7.0 percent in 1989 to 10.4 percent in 1995.

Manitoba's rates of angiography and revascularization seem sensitive to two factors: the centralization of these procedures at the two teaching hospitals in Winnipeg and local practice patterns vis-à-vis referring patients to Winnipeg. Higher utilization rates for angiography, CABG, and PTCA have consistently been found for residents of Winnipeg, compared to those in other regions (Hartford, Roos, and Walld 1998; Roos and Sharp 1989).

Brandon is a referral center for western Manitoba and the province's second largest city. Its physicians have traditionally been reluctant to refer patients out of region to Winnipeg (Roos and Sharp 1989). The western region has had higher age- and sex-adjusted rates of AMI and thus a greater percentage of patients potentially available for revascularization. However, this region actually had lower rates for CABG and PTCA because of a "funnel effect" (table 6.3): the fewer patients from a particular area referred for a screening procedure (in this case, angiography), the fewer patients from the same area who undergo therapeutic procedures (i.e., CABG, PTCA). Analyses of age and sex differences and of comorbidities associated with index angiography, CABG, and PTCA failed to change the findings. Trend analyses within a province are complicated by the relatively small numbers

TABLE 6.2. Probability of Angiography, CABG, or PTCA in the Year following AMI

Procedure within One Year of Index AMI	Fiscal Year of Acute Myocardial Infarction (AMI)						
	1989	1990	1991	1992	1993	1994	1995
Angiography (%)	26.3	26.6	25.0	31.2	32.0	31.8	31.7
Coronary artery bypass graft surgery (CABG) (%)	7.8	7.7	8.2	10.6	9.4	11.2	11.6
Percutaneous transluminal coronary angioplasty (PTCA) (%)	7.0	7.6	6.4	8.3	10.5	10.1	10.4
Number of individuals with acute myocardial infarction	2,428	2,362	2,442	2,370	2,419	2,431	2,527

Note: Analyses were based on adults 40 years and older. Unadjusted probabilities were used. Differences among years were significant at the .001 level for angiography ($X^2 = 68.7$, $df = 6$), for CABG ($X^2 = 45.6$, $df = 6$), and for PTCA ($X^2 = 54.9$, $df = 6$). Index AMI cases were defined as the first AMI per person in a given fiscal year. Multiple AMIs for the same individual in one fiscal year were not counted.

of cases in any given year, but the western region's funnel effect appears to have endured through 1996.

Manitoba has had no registry to record waiting times and no field in the hospital abstracts or physicians' claims to indicate when a patient started to wait for surgery. Using a "best available" marker from administrative data, DeCoster, Carriere, and Peterson (1999) defined waiting time as the time between the date of surgery and the date of the patient's visit to the operating surgeon beforehand. Various analyses looked at scheduled patients, excluding those who waited three days or less and delayed surgery (when patients wait more than three months). For bypass surgery, the waits decreased between 1990 and 1996, while the waits for coronary angioplasty fluctuated considerably from year to year.

Changes in Low-Tech Care

Relatively little Manitoba data are available on low-technology treatments for myocardial infarction. Little change in postinfarction physician visits and hospital readmissions has been recorded over the 1990–95 period (Brownell, Roos, and Burchill 1999). Longitudinal

TABLE 6.3. Procedure Rates in Manitoba by Region (1989–1996)

	Rates (95% confidence interval)		
Region	Number	Unadjusted	Adjusted[a]
	Angiography		
Other rural	4,594	48.9 (47.5–50.3)	49.9 (48.2–51.6)
Western	2,137	37.6 (36.0–39.2)	36.6 (34.5–38.9)
Winnipeg	11,713	57.1 (56.1–58.1)	58.1 (57.0–59.2)
	CABG		
Other rural	1,101	11.7 (11.0–12.4)	11.8 (11.0–12.7)
Western	580	10.2 (9.4–11.1)	9.9 (8.8–11.1)
Winnipeg	2,750	13.4 (12.9–13.9)	13.4 (12.9–14.0)
	PTCA		
Other rural	927	9.9 (9.3–10.5)	10.3 (9.6–11.2)
Western	471	8.3 (7.6–9.1)	8.7 (7.6–9.9)
Winnipeg	2,710	13.2 (12.7–13.7)	13.4 (12.9–13.9)

Note: Rates were based on adults 40 years and older.

[a]Direct age/sex/income-adjusted rates (per 10,000 population) using 1992 Manitoba population as the standard.

administrative data on cardiac medications have not been readily accessible, but this is changing (Metge, Black, and Kozyrskyj 1999). One analysis of primary data on a 1991–92 cohort of Manitoba residents found overall rates of aspirin use similar to rates reported in the United States and in England (Schwartz et al. 1997). Women reported more angina, had more physician visits, and received more nitrates (both short-acting and long-acting). Less diagnostic testing, "less aggressive treatment of coronary artery disease, and less use of aspirin" were found among women than among men in the first year after AMI (Schwartz et al. 1997). After appropriate controls, "women with coronary artery disease experienced a more rapid decline in physical health status than did men" during the one-year follow-up. Given the likelihood that low-tech treatments (aspirin and thrombolytic use) may be very important in acute survival after AMI, more attention should be paid to practice patterns and outcomes associated with such treatments (McClellan et al. 2002).

Consequences of Changes in AMI Care in Manitoba

Changes in Health Outcomes

An examination of unadjusted mortality rates at different intervals after AMI and revascularization found no consistent trends over time. Analyses of overall post-AMI mortality accord with the general Manitoba picture of slow or no change. Figures 6.1 and 6.2 show 30-day and one-year post-AMI mortality for men and women ages 40–64 and age 65 or older. A similar lack of trends was found for 90-day mortality. Age and sex adjustment of the AMI mortality rates made only very minor differences; differences due to adjustment of 30-day and one-year mortality rates were always less than 1 percent.

Changes in Resource Use

Manitoba health reform has had a definite impact on the length of stay of AMI patients (table 6.1). Between 1989 and 1996, length of stay for the index AMI hospitalization dropped two days, while the number of hospital days for the episode of care associated with AMI fell 2.6 days. The most dramatic declines in length of stay were found among women aged 65 and older. The median lengths of stay decreased considerably less than the means, indicating that much of the decline was due to a drop in long lengths of stay. In contrast to the declines in overall length

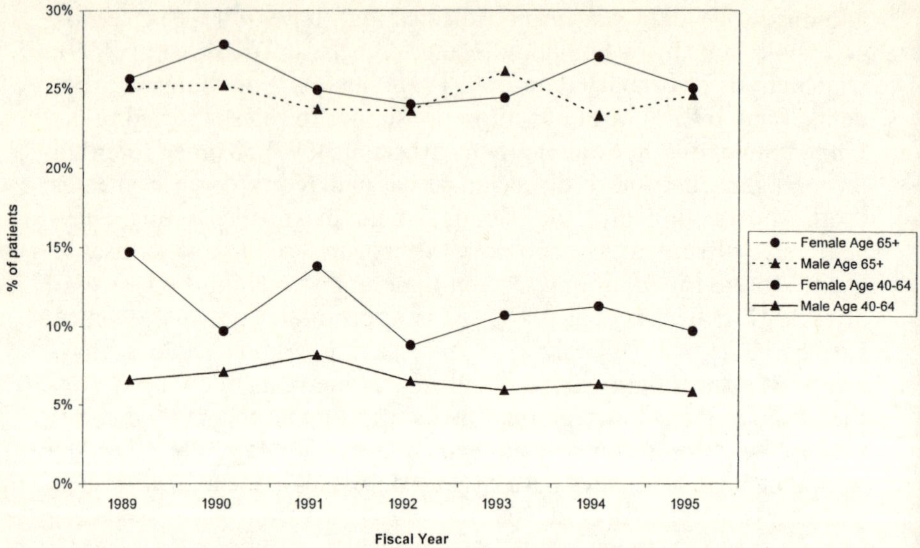

Fig. 6.1. Thirty-day mortality after AMI in Manitoba (by sex and age)

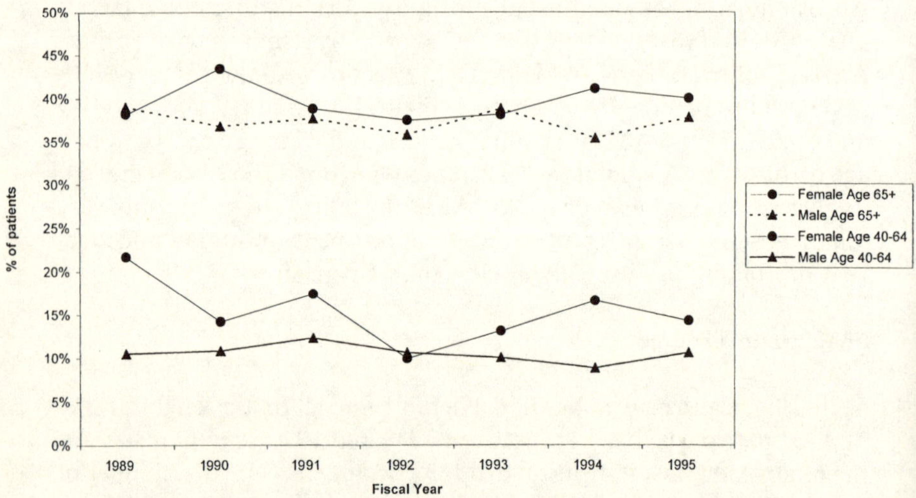

Fig. 6.2. One-year mortality after AMI in Manitoba (by sex and age)

of stay, the mean number of days elderly AMI patients spent in intensive care units showed little or no change.

Conclusion

The data presented in this volume suggest considerable improvement in post-AMI mortality in the United States but a more mixed picture in Canada. However, there is a disconnect between AMI findings and those regarding all-cause mortality that raises fascinating issues. All-cause mortality differences across and within societies seem related to disease-specific findings in ways that are not well understood. The rate of adoption of new technology is only one factor that affects population health. Indeed, comparative data on the treatment of AMI must be placed in the context of the level of U.S. health, often "in the bottom quartile among the twenty-nine industrialized countries" in measures of health (Anderson 1997). The gap in life expectancy at birth between Canada and the United States widened between 1990 and 1995. This is truly remarkable, given Canadian health reform with its accompanying controversy about a possibly deteriorating system. The gap for males was 2.0 years (73.8 versus 71.8 years) in 1990 and 2.8 years (75.3 versus 72.5 years) in 1995; for females, the gap increased from 1.6 years (80.4 versus 78.8 years) in 1990 to 1.9 years (81.2 versus 79.2 years) in 1995 (Anderson 1997). Canadian life expectancy at birth continued to rise in 1996 (from 78.3 years to 78.7 years for both sexes combined) (Statistics Canada 1998).[2] With the United States ranking third on life expectancy at age 80, Canada and Iceland have ranked first and second on this measure across OECD countries (Anderson 1998; Brody and Lie 1993; Schieber, Poullier, and Greenwald 1993).

Within Canada, lower levels of income inequality and intergovernmental transfers to the poorer provinces appear to have moderated life expectancy differences. A recent Canadian study found a range of only 1.7 years between the province with the longest life-expectancy (British Columbia at 79.0 years) and the province with the shortest (Newfoundland at 77.3 years) (Nault 1997). Shorter life expectancies were found in Canada's two northern territories with small, primarily aboriginal populations. In contrast, American states varied greatly in life expectancy, with over a 5.3 year difference among states in the 1979–86 period (U.S. Bureau of the Census 1986, 1990); similar variations for age-adjusted mortality rates were found for the 1990s (Ventura et al. 1997).

If improvements in life expectancy at older ages can be attributed to better treatment of AMI (Braunwald 1997), it is important to look at cancer, where progress has been very slow (Bailar and Gornick 1997). Specifically, Canadians, as compared with Americans, appear both to be at lower risk for cancer and to survive longer after diagnosis (North American Association of Central Cancer Registries 1998).[3] The relationships among stage at which cancer is detected, social class, and mortality are currently being explored within a comparative framework (Gorey et al. 1997, 1998).

Comparative research could provide useful insights into the relationship between health insurance, ability to pay, and utilization. Among 29 industrialized countries "only the United States had less than half of its population eligible for publicly mandated health insurance in 1995. The United States appears to be comparable to the other G7 countries in terms of access to physicians, inpatient hospital services, and pharmaceuticals" (Anderson 1997). In countries (such as Canada) with 100 percent population coverage, the poor (who are at higher risk for almost all conditions) may be more likely to receive preventive services, to have problems detected earlier, and to get more timely treatment than in countries where complete population coverage is lacking. Moreover, although nursing home stays and nonmedical services associated with home care often involve copayments in Canada, charges are more likely to be income-based and affordable in Canada than in the United States (OECD 1988; Canadian Home Care Association 1998).

Because insurance coverage (albeit with copayments) under the American Medicare programs typically begins at 65, this watershed should be reflected in utilization, particularly by those of lower socioeconomic status. With no such age-related watershed in the Canadian public insurance system (and some other OECD countries), appropriate comparisons of utilization and mortality should help isolate the effects of insurance in adult populations. In the United States utilization by those aged 65 and 66 should be substantially greater than those aged 63 and 64. In Canada, increases in utilization at age 65 should be much less. Mortality comparisons might show similar results.

The interrelationships among health, health care, and societal factors are receiving increasing attention (Evans, Barer, and Marmor 1994; Roos and Shapiro 1995b; Kindig 1997). The relative importance for average life expectancy of income distribution and the social environment, as compared with individual interventions, needs to be studied (Marmot 1998; Wilkinson 1992; Kaplan et al. 1996). In Canada, explicit discussions about trade-offs among investments in health care (particularly end-of-life care) and other strategies for improving health are beginning (Lavis and Stoddart 1994). Tensions between efforts to provide more rapid coronary artery bypass surgery for patients for whom the operation seems necessary (Fox, O'Dea, and Parfrey 1998; Naylor 1998) and other needs for public expenditures will continue. Although the treatment of AMI and other high-profile conditions will evolve, the competition for alternative uses of public funds has historically led to the relatively late adoption of new technologies in Canada.

Notes

This work was supported by the National Health Research and Development Program (NHRDP 6607–1766–012), the Medical Research Council (Grant MA-13703), and the Manitoba Centre for Health Policy and Evaluation. The interpretations and conclusions contained herein are those of the researchers and do not necessarily represent the views of Manitoba Health. The authors gratefully acknowledge the assistance of Phyllis Jivan and Jo-Anne Baribeau with preparation of the manuscript.

1. These case definitions differ slightly from those used by the other research teams; in particular, other investigators only included patients with a primary diagnosis of AMI and patients with short initial stays who were discharged dead. Our algorithm was developed by investigators at Dartmouth Medical School to determine total length of stay as an inpatient and efficiently identify AMIs without having to link records longitudinally. The transfer patients accounted for only a small share of total cases (6.8 percent); thus, it is unlikely that their exclusion would substantively change results.

2. See also <http://www.statcan.ca/Daily/English/980416/d980416.htm#ART1>.

3. See also <http://www.naaccr.org/cinap/index.htm>.

References

Anderson, G. F. 1997. "In Search of Value: An International Comparison of Cost, Access, and Outcomes." *Health Affairs* (Millwood) 16, no. 6: 163–71.

———. 1998. *Multinational Comparisons of Health Care: Expenditures, Coverage, and Outcomes.* New York: Commonwealth Fund.

Bailar, J. C., and H. L. Gornick. 1997. "Cancer Undefeated." *New England Journal of Medicine* 336, no. 22: 1569–74.

Bell, C. M., M. Crystal, A. S. Detsky, and D. A. Redelmeier. 1998. "Report: Shopping Around for Hospital Services: A Comparison of the United States and Canada." *Journal of the American Medical Association* 279, no. 13: 1015–17.

Braunwald, E. 1997. "Shattuck Lecture—Cardiovascular Medicine at the Turn of the Millennium: Triumphs, Concerns, and Opportunities." *New England Journal of Medicine* 337, no. 19: 1360–69.

Brody, B. A., and R. K. Lie. 1993. "Methodological and Conceptual Issues in Health Care System Comparisons: Canada, Norway, and the United States." *Journal of Medical Philosophy* 18, no. 5: 437–63.

Brownell, M. D., N. P. Roos, and C. Burchill. 1999. "Monitoring the Impact of Hospital Downsizing on Access to Care, Quality of Care, and the Health of the Population." *Medical Care* 37 (suppl.), no. 6: JS135–50.

Canadian Home Care Association in Collaboration with L'Association des CLSC et CHSLD du Quebec. 1998. "Portrait of Canada: An Overview of Public Home Care Programs." Presented at the National Conference on Home Care, March 8–10.

Centers for Disease Control and Prevention. 1996. *Vital and Health Statistics: Trends in Hospital Utilization: United States, 1988–92.* Hyattsville, Md.: U.S. Department of Health and Human Services.

Charlson, M. E., P. Pompei, K. L. Ales, and C. R. McKenzie. 1987. "A New Method of Classifying Prognostic Comorbidity in Longitudinal Studies: Development and Validation." *Journal of Chronic Disease* 40, no. 5: 373–83.

DeCoster, C., K. C. Carriere, S. Peterson, R. Walld, and L. MacWilliam. 1999. "Waiting Times for Surgical Procedures." *Medical Care* 37 (suppl.), no. 6: JS187–JS205.

Evans, R. G., M. L. Barer, and T. R. Marmor. 1994. *Why Are Some People Healthy and Others Not? The Determinants of Health of Populations.* New York: Aldine de Gruyter.

Fox, G. A., J. O'Dea, and P. S. Parfrey. 1998. "Coronary Artery Bypass Graft Surgery in Newfoundland and Labrador." *Canadian Medical Association Journal* 158, no. 9: 1137–42.

Gorey, K. M., E. J. Holowaty, G. Fehringer, E. Laukkanen, A. Moskowitz, D. J. Webster, and N. L. Richter. 1997. "An International Comparison of Cancer Survival: Toronto, Ontario, and Detroit, Michigan, Metropolitan Areas." *American Journal of Public Health* 87, no. 7: 1156–63.

Gorey, K. M., E. J. Holowaty, E. Laukkanen, G. Fehringer, and N. L. Richter. 1998. "Association between Socioeconomic Status and Cancer Incidence in Toronto, Ontario: Possible Confounding of Cancer Mortality by Incidence and Survival." *Cancer Prevention and Control* 2, no. 5: 236–41.

Grumbach, K., G. M. Anderson, H. S. Luft, L. L. Roos, and R. H. Brook. 1995. "Regionalization of Cardiac Surgery in the United States and Canada: Geographic Access, Choice, and Outcomes." *Journal of the American Medical Association* 274, no. 16: 1282–88.

Hartford, K., L. L. Roos, and R. Walld. 1998. "Regional Variation in Angiography, Coronary Artery Bypass Surgery, and Percutaneous Transluminal Coronary Angioplasty in Manitoba, 1987 to 1992: The Funnel Effect." *Medical Care* 36, no. 7: 1022–32.

Kaplan, G. A., E. R. Pamuk, J. W. Lynch, R. D. Cohen, and J. L. Balfour. 1996. "Inequality in Income and Mortality in the United States: Analysis of Mortality and Potential Pathways." *British Medical Journal* 312, no. 7037: 999–1003.

Kindig, D. A. 1997. *Purchasing Population Health: Paying for Results.* Ann Arbor: University of Michigan Press.

Lavis, J. N., and G. L. Stoddart. 1994. "Can We Have Too Much Health Care?" *Daedalus* 123, no. 4: 43–60.

Marmot, M. G. 1998. "Improvement of Social Environment to Improve Health." *Lancet* 351, no. 9095: 57–60.

McClellan, M. B., N. Every, A. Garber, P. Heidenreich, M. Hlatky, D. P. Kessler, J. Newhouse, and O. Saynina. 2002. "Technological Change in Heart Attack Care in the United States." In this volume.

Metge, C., C. Black, and A. Kozyrskyj. 1999. "The Population's Use of Pharmaceuticals." *Medical Care* 37 (suppl.), no. 6: JS42–JS59.

Mullan, F. 1998. "The 'Mona Lisa' of Health Policy: Primary Care at Home and Abroad." *Health Affairs* (Millwood) 17, no. 2: 118–26.

Nault, F. 1997. "Narrowing Mortality Gaps, 1978 to 1995." *Health Reports* 9, no. 1: 35–41.

Naylor, C. D. 1998. "Benchmarking the Provision of Coronary Artery Surgery." *Canadian Medical Association Journal* 158, no. 9: 1151–53.

North American Association of Central Cancer Registries. 1998. *Highlights of Cancer in North America, 1990–1994.* North American Association of Central Cancer Registries.

Organisation for Economic Cooperation and Development (OECD). 1988. *Aging Populations: The Social Policy Implications.* Paris: OECD.

Roberts, D. 1998. "Inquest into 12 Baby Deaths Leaves Parents Wondering." *Globe and Mail* (Toronto), September 30, A4.

Romano, P. S., L. L. Roos, and J. Jollis. 1993. "Adapting a Clinical Comorbidity Index for Use with ICD-9-CM Administrative Data: Differing Perspectives." *Journal of Clinical Epidemiology* 46, no. 10: 1075–79.

Roos, L. L., C. A. Mustard, J. P. Nicol, D. F. McLerran, D. J. Malenka, T. K. Young, and M. M. Cohen. 1993. "Registries and Administrative Data: Organization and Accuracy." *Medical Care* 31, no. 3: 201–12.

Roos, L. L., and J. P. Nicol. 1999. "A Research Registry: Uses, Development, and Accuracy." *Journal of Clinical Epidemiology* 52, no. 1: 39–47.

Roos, L. L., J. P. Nicol, and S. M. Cageorge. 1987. "Using Administrative Data for Longitudinal Research: Comparisons with Primary Data Collection." *Journal of Chronic Disease* 40, no. 1: 41–49.

Roos, L. L., and S. M. Sharp. 1989. "Innovation, Centralization, and Growth: Coronary Artery Bypass Surgery in Manitoba." *Medical Care* 27, no. 5: 441–52.

Roos, L. L., S. M. Sharp, and A. Wajda. 1989. "Assessing Data Quality: A Computerized Approach." *Social Science and Medicine* 28, no. 2: 175–82.

Roos, N. P., M. D. Brownell, E. Shapiro, and L. L. Roos. 1998. "Good News about Difficult Decisions: Why the Canadian Approach to Hospital Cost Control Appears to Work." *Health Affairs* (Millwood) 17, no. 5: 239–46.

Roos, N. P., and E. Shapiro. 1995a. "A Productive Experiment with Administrative Data." *Medical Care* 33 (suppl.), no. 12: DS7–DS12.

———, eds. 1995b. "Health and Health Care: Experience with a Population-Based Health Information System." *Medical Care* (suppl.) 33, no. 12: DS1–DS146.

Saltman, R. B., and J. Figueras. 1998. "Analyzing the Evidence on European Health Care Reforms." *Health Affairs* (Millwood) 17, no. 2: 85–108.

Schieber, G. J., J. P. Poullier, and L. M. Greenwald. 1993. "Health Spending, Delivery, and Outcomes in OECD Countries." *Health Affairs* (Millwood) 12, no. 2: 120–29.

Schwartz, L. M., E. S. Fisher, A. N. A. Tosteson, S. Woloshin, C. H. Chang, B. A. Virnig, J. Plohman, and B. Wright. 1997. "Treatment and Health Outcomes of Women and Men in a Cohort with Coronary Artery Disease." *Archives of Internal Medicine* 157, no. 14: 1545–51.

Shanahan, M., and C. Gousseau. 1999. "Using the POPULIS Framework for Interprovincial Comparisons of Expenditures on Health Care." *Medical Care* (suppl.) 37, no. 6: JS83–100.

Statistics Canada. 1988. *Postal Code Conversion File: Detailed User Guide.* Ottawa, Ontario: Geography Division, Statistics Canada.

———. 1998. "Deaths 1996." *The Daily,* April 16.

Tully, P., and E. Saint-Pierre. 1997. "Downsizing Canada's Hospitals, 1986/87 to 1994/95." *Health Reports* 8, no. 4: 33–39.

U.S. Bureau of the Census. 1986. *State and Metropolitan Area Data Book.* Washington, D.C.: U.S. Government Printing Office.

———. 1990. *Statistical Abstract of the United States.* Washington, D.C.: U.S. Government Printing Office.

Ventura, S. J., K. D. Peters, J. A. Martin, and J. D. Maurer. 1997. "Births and Deaths: United States, 1996." Monthly vital statistics report, vol. 46, no. 1, suppl. 2. Hyattsville, Md.: National Center for Health Statistics.

Wilkinson, R. G. B. 1992. "Income Distribution and Life Expectancy." *British Medical Journal* 304, no. 6820: 165–68.

CHAPTER 7

The Impact of New Technology on the Treatment and Outcomes of Acute Myocardial Infarction in Australia:

Incentives for Technological Change and Their Consequences for Treatment Decision-Making

Jeff Richardson, Iain K. Robertson, Michael Hobbs, and Diana Edwards

Changes in Medical Treatment and Their Consequences for Patient Health Outcomes

Michael Hobbs, Brenden Bertuola, Elizabeth Geelhoed, and Richard Hockey

Along with most Western countries, health expenditures in Australia rose rapidly in the 1960s but were stabilized in the mid-1970s at about 7.5 percent of GDP. Since then, expenditures have risen incrementally. By 1996, expenditures reached 8.5 percent of GDP, which is almost exactly what would be "expected" on the basis of its GDP and the direct relationship between GDP and health spending (AIHW 1996). Australia's growth in health spending has been controlled through a variety of mechanisms tailored to its health care financing system. Most important among these efforts have been the use of direct budget caps on public hospitals, which dominate the health sector. However, budget caps were less useful at controlling growing expenditures on physicians' services, because physicians' services were supplied largely through private markets. As a result, Australia sought effectively to control doctor supply; and in 1996, zero growth in the general practitioner (GP) supply was achieved, and accompanied by zero growth in the use of GP services.

As the example above indicates, Australia has an idiosyncratic health system, and the pattern of incentives that it generates for its publicly and privately insured populations is unique in the world. The main purpose of this chapter is to document how the care and consequences of a prevalent and costly illness—heart attack, or AMI—have changed in Australia over the 1982 to 1995 period, and to suggest some possible determinants of these trends. Specifically, we seek to explore the impact of the Australian health care financing system on incentives for technological change, and the consequences of those incentives for medical treatment decisions and health outcomes.

After briefly describing the health system, its regulation, and the resulting incentives, we outline the data sources that have been used in this study. We examine data on treatments and outcomes from Perth, Western Australia, because the Perth MONICA project has resulted in high-quality linked-record longitudinal databases that enable us to assess comprehensively the use and consequences of technology on AMI treatment. In addition, we analyze data from Victoria to explore the possibility of regional treatment differences and to investigate the impact of hospital ownership and patient insurance status on treatment decision-making. We describe how these data sources can be used to identify changes in both "high-tech" and "low-tech" treatment of AMI over the last two decades. We disaggregate differential trends by age and by sex, to detect how these factors have interacted with incentives to affect the use of technology in medical treatment, and ultimately how changes in treatment have affected health outcomes. Our chapter concludes with a discussion of the possible implications of our findings for the treatment decision-making process, and suggestions for future research.

Incentives for Technological Change in Australia

In the Australian Federation, the regulation, ownership, and control of the health sector are divided between the federal "Commonwealth" Government, the governments of the six states and two territories, and the private sector. Public hospitals are generally owned, regulated, and directly financed by the state governments. However, as these hospitals receive the overwhelming majority of their revenues from federal grants, the Commonwealth government can exert considerable influence over the states. Primary care in Australia is provided by GPs who constitute about 46 percent of the medical workforce and by the outpatient departments of public hospitals. Specialists constitute about 35 percent of the medical workforce and are divided between the salaried staff of public hospitals (who normally have limited rights to private practice) and fully private specialists who may see private patients in either public or private hospitals but who may also provide care to public patients in exchange for a negotiated payment. Health clinics are unusual and both GP and out of hospital specialists generally work in solo or small group practices. About two thirds of hospital beds are in public hospitals with the remainder divided between for profit and not for profit private hospitals. In 1995–96, private patients in private hospitals accounted for 31 percent of discharges. Private patients treated in public hospitals accounted for 12 percent of discharges, and public patients in public hospitals accounted for the remaining 57 percent.

Medical and pharmaceutical insurance are Commonwealth responsibilities, administered through the Medicare program. While there has been some experimentation with Commonwealth/state "coordinated care"/managed care for chronic and complex procedures there is little prospect of an early rationalization of this division of authority. As a result, there is a piecemeal approach to the adoption and diffusion of medical technologies. Australia was the first country in the world to require the economic evaluation of drugs included in its health scheme and it may soon extend this requirement to services covered by medical insurance. By contrast, there is no systematic regulation of hospital based technologies. Limited evaluation is carried out by the Commonwealth Department of Health but each hospital is free to propose the purchase of capital equipment that is then subjected to review by the hospital, state health department and state governments capital works committees. There is no state control over individual procedures.

By contrast with public hospitals, private hospitals have no formal constraint upon their use of medical technologies. Despite this fact, until recently the vast majority of private hospitals concentrated upon the delivery of simple interventions. Private hospitals are in competition with public hospitals and, as these have historically adopted arbitrary but below cost fees for private patients, doctors generally carried out complex procedures on private patients in the public hospitals that usually met the cost of theater use, nursing, and disposables.

Australia's Medicare scheme provides universal insurance for the costs of public hospitalization, private GPs and, upon referral, private specialists. The scheme is financed from general taxation and a 1.5 percent levy upon personal income.[1] While public hospital services are free, patients must accept care from the hospitals' salaried doctors. Partly for this reason, about one third of the population take out supplementary private health insurance to cover the cost of private hospital care or private medical care in a public hospital provided by a private doctor of their choice. Private health insurance also covers a number of relatively small expenses arising from auxiliary services and 'gap insurance' against the difference between the 'standard fee' in the Commonwealth's medical benefit schedule (CMBS) and the Medicare rebate of 75 percent of the CMBS for hospital services. Private insurance may not cover out of hospital fees above the rebate of 85 percent of the CMBS. Since 1996 insurance funds have been permitted to offer complete insurance against private hospital fees but only when private doctors have a contract with the hospital or insurance company to limit the patient's out-of-pocket expenses. The proportion of the population with private insurance has been declining by about 1 1/2 percentage points per annum since 1986 and the system is in a clear disequilibrium.

As there is a constitutional prohibition against any Commonwealth action that constitutes the 'civil conscription' of medical practitioners, the Commonwealth government does not believe it can regulate medical fees and, consequently, private patients are often left with significant out-of-pocket expenses and the extra billing by private practitioners represents a significant part of the net income of many specialists. Total private expenditures (private health insurance and out-of-pocket expenses) constitute about 32 percent of national health expenditure, which is the third highest private component in the OECD after Turkey, the United States, and Austria.

The result of this system and its operation has been a set of incentives that are unique to Australia. First, and arising from the division of responsibilities, there is an incentive for cost shifting between the two levels of government. Early discharge from state public hospitals, privatization of hospital outpatient care and the decreased provision of hospital drugs all pass costs back to the Commonwealth and, in recent years, these practices have become increasingly common. Second, and most perversely, patients with private insurance are charged fees and face copayments that are not imposed on uninsured public patients in public hospitals. Private insurance is primarily a means of insuring doctor of choice when this is possible and avoiding the public hospital queues, which have significantly increased in recent years as budget caps on public hospitals have been tightened.

In sum, there is no financial and little geographic barrier to the admission of most patients for emergency AMI or other emergency care. Tightening budget caps have given the public sector an increasing incentive to discharge patients quickly. There is an additional incentive to discharge private patients, as states that do not achieve a predetermined proportion of public patients are now financially penalized, and, unlike public patients, discharged private patients will not face a queue if and when a readmission for an elective procedure becomes necessary. Readmission as a private patient is also highly profitable for doctors, who receive significantly more from private than from public work. Private status also transfers costs from the state to the Commonwealth government. Unsurprisingly, both doctors and state governments have urged the Commonwealth government to introduce incentives to increase private insurance. Modest budget measures in 1997 appear to have slowed but not reversed the steady decline in private insurance.[2] For private elective procedures, lower fees give patients an incentive to seek public hospital care. However, because of queuing, the desire to select their own doctor, and the influence of their private doctor, patients may prefer private hospitals, which have retained and increased their share of the market.

Technological Change in AMI Care in Australia

As discussed above, we focus on trends in treatment and outcomes of AMI for the residents of Perth, Western Australia. The incidence of acute myocardial infarction (AMI) in residents of Perth under the age of 65 years has been extensively studied since 1971 through myocardial infarction registers (the Perth Coronary Register 1970–71 and the Perth MONICA Study 1984–93) and the linkage of routinely collected hospital statistical and mortality data.

Western Australia is the largest of the Australian states, occupying one-third of the landmass but containing only one-tenth of the population (1.7 million in 1996). Perth, the capital city, has a rapidly growing population (1.3 million persons in 1991) and loss from emigration is low. It is thus ideally suited for long-term studies of the epidemiology and hospital management of cardiovascular disease.

Studying AMI in Perth has other advantages. No other city in Western Australia has a population greater than 30,000 persons, so that virtually all medical care for the resident population of Perth is provided locally. And, although mortality from AMI and other ischemic heart disease (IHD) in Western Australia is lower than in other Australian states, downward trends are essentially the same as for Australia as a whole (which in turn are similar to trends seen in the United States, Canada, and New Zealand).

We also examine data from Victoria. The Victorian database does not include linked information on patient health outcomes. However, it does offer other advantages. Most important, it contains information on the ownership status of each hospital (public or private) and the insurance status of each individual patient (public or private). In addition, because the Victorian data are not comparable to the Western Australian database used in the rest of the chapter, we construct comparable Victorian–Western Australian cohorts to validate our results.

Trends in the incidence of AMI in Perth, based on persons admitted to hospital once in any 12-month period, are shown in table 7.1. Rates of AMI declined by about one-third in all age groups, with the greatest decrease being in the age group 55–64 in both males and females. However over most age groups the differences in the rate of decline were not great. In males, rates of decline were clearly greater in the second half of the period under study (25 percent compared with 7 percent), but in females there was no difference.

Changes in High-Tech Care: Intensive Cardiac Procedures and Hospital Use

Patients from Perth

A linked file of hospital and deaths records relating to all residents of Perth admitted to hospital or with evidence of any IHD in the period 1980 to 1995 inclusive was selected from the Western Australian Centre of Health Services Research linked database. The database, which is supported jointly by the University of Western Australia and the Health Department of Western Australia, includes electronic abstracts of all hospital separations and deaths since 1980. Records contain standard demographic and service data and diagnoses.

TABLE 7.1. Trends in Hospital Admissions for AMI, Perth, Western Australia, 1981–95 (rate per 100,000 person-years)

	35–54	55–64	65–69	70–74	75–79	Age Standardized
Males Rate 1981	187	781	1118	1358	1547	510.1
% decline 1981–1988	11.8	16.1	13.1	3.5	**0.3**[b]	7.1
% decline 1988–1995	20.0	31.5	19.2	31.4	34.2	25.0
% decline 1981–1995	29.4	42.5	29.8	33.8	34.0	30.3
Females Rate 1981	32	245	516	777	1070	205.4
% decline 1981–1988	34.4	27.3	16.7	23.3	18.8	18.4
% decline 1988–1995	**9.5**[b]	36.5	23.5	22.1	11.3	17.4
% decline 1981–1995	28.1	53.9	36.2	40.3	27.9	32.6

[a]Age standardized to world population.
[b]Bold type denotes percentage increase.

Record linkage is based on probabilistic methods using name and other identifiers. A unique personal number generated in the linkage process is added to the records of individual admissions, enabling the aggregation of a number of admissions to define a single episode of care incorporating the records of the initial admission, all subsequent readmissions, and deaths when relevant.

The interval from initial admission to admissions for selected procedures, complications, and survival were consequently calculated for each AMI event. Cumulative bed-days for all relevant admissions were also determined. First (or index) admissions for AMI were defined as those that were not preceded by an admission for AMI in the previous 12 months. Cases of recurrent AMI were defined as those occurring at least 28 days but less than one year following the initial admission. Cases of AMI occurring more than one year after the initial event were considered as separate events. Nonfatal readmissions were further defined as being of at least three days duration *and* coded as unbooked cases. To avoid double counting of the number of admissions and the number of bed-days in readmissions in which there was more than one procedure or diagnosis of interest, a hierarchical classification was established consisting of procedures in the following order: CABG; PTCA not associated with CABG in the same admission; and angiography not associated with either CABG of PTCA in the same admission. All remaining readmissions were then classified as shown in appendix table A7.1.

The cumulative frequency for each of the coronary procedures was independently determined for intervals of 30, 90, 180, and 365 days from the date of initial admission by age, sex, and calendar year. Cumulative mortality (case fatality) was determined at 30 days and one year. Post-acute-case fatality (defined as death within 12 months of AMI in cases alive at 30 days) was also estimated.

Age- and sex-specific rates for IHD mortality and hospital admissions for AMI and for coronary artery procedures (CARPs) were derived using estimates of the usually resident populations obtained from the Australian Bureau of Statistics (ABS). Age-standardized rates were determined by the direct method using weights from the World Standard population of Sergi.

The cumulative frequency (percentage) of persons who have undergone coronary artery revascularization procedures within 12 months from admission to hospital for AMI are shown in figures 7.1–7.3. This is shown separately for coronary angiography, CABG, and CABG and PTCA combined. The estimates are based on procedures performed during the index admission for AMI and all subsequent readmissions. If more than one type of procedure was performed during a particular admission, each has been recorded. The percentages are based on all cases of AMI and do not take into account deaths that occur within the first year. While procedures following AMI shown in the figures that follow represent only a minority of the total number of procedures, these data have the marked advantage of being related to a clearly defined clinical population. They thus provide valid comparisons of the frequency of procedures by age, gender, and calendar year.

The percentage of persons undergoing all types of procedure has increased progressively throughout the period of study and varies inversely with age. Within this population, coronary angiography was performed in 23 percent of males aged 35–69 years in 1982, rising to 72 percent in 1994. The increase is even more dramatic in the elderly. For example, among male AMI patients aged 70–79, approximately 3 percent received angiography in 1982; however, by 1994, fully 41 percent were treated with angiography. In females, the pattern is essentially the same although at a slightly lower level. However, the relative gap between men and women has shrunk over time.

By 1982, 17 percent of males in the age group 35–69 years having had an admission for AMI had undergone CABG within 12 months of the index admission (fig. 7.2). Information not in the figure shows that the frequency declined with increasing age, being 7 percent in males 65–69 years and less than 5 percent in the older age groups. Thereafter the frequency increased progressively with calendar year in the older age groups but actually declined in those aged 35–54 years. In females there was variability in the trends due to small numbers. The proportion of cases that received CABG in all age groups increased. In all age groups the proportions of females who received CABG was less compared with males.

Of particular note is that rates of CABG have tended to stabilize in younger age groups, which may be due the fact that treatment of younger patients has probably been pursued more vigorously in the past. Increasing use in older patients (despite evidence of declining incidence of AMI at all ages) suggests that this trend is spreading into older age groups and that as a consequence total requirements for CABG will continue to increase. On the other hand, the decline in CABG in younger ages may be due partially to substitution of PTCA for CABG. With improved angioplastic techniques including stenting and routine postoperative use of antiplatelet treatment, this trend may continue and extend into older age groups and thus moderate the demand for CABG.

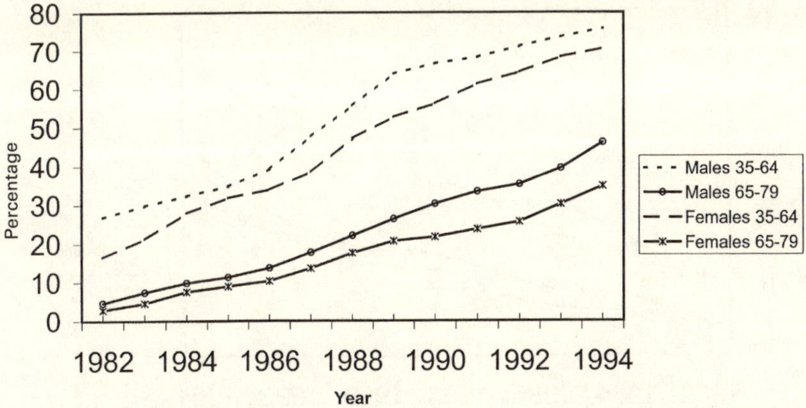

Fig. 7.1. Cumulative angiogram rates within 12 months of AMI (three-year moving average)

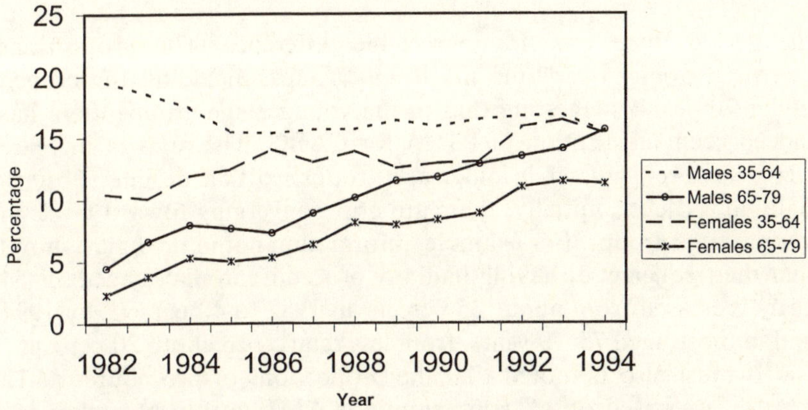

Fig. 7.2. Cumulative CABG rates within 12 months of AMI (three-year moving average)

Figure 7.3 begins our investigation of PTCA use, presenting the frequency of having either procedure occurring within 12 months of the index AMI. PTCA was introduced in 1981 and increased continuously thereafter in all age groups under the age of 70 years. In all years, there is a marked inverse relationship between PTCA and age. Initially the proportions were higher in males than in females, but at the end of

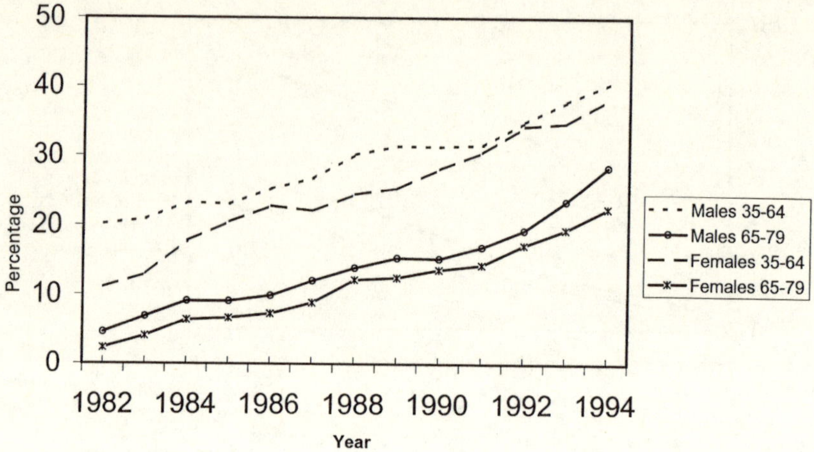

Fig. 7.3. Cumulative CABG or PTCA rates within 12 months of AMI (three-year moving average)

the period there was no appreciable difference. The proportions increased evenly over time in all age groups, including those aged under 70 years, suggesting that in the younger age groups there has indeed been substitution of PTCA for CABG. The rates of increase were, however, greater in older age groups, so that despite substantially lower levels initially, these are now converging toward levels in younger age groups. For example, information not in the figure shows that the frequency of having had any procedure in males aged 35–54 years increased from about 25 percent in 1982 to 40 percent by 1994 and in those aged 75–79 years, from less than 5 percent to 20 percent.

It must also be noted that the proportions of procedures at 12 months are based on all admissions for AMI and do not take into account the effects of survival on the probability of having a procedure. As case fatality varies directly with age and is substantial in older age groups, we would expect that the differences in prevalence of procedures at 12 months by age shown in the figures would be much less in survivors. This will be examined formally in a subsequent analysis.

The cumulative frequencies of CARPs by time from admission for AMI up to one year in 1995 are shown in table 7.2. In the case of angiography and PTCA, virtually all persons who undergo procedures do so within three months. As might be expected, the time intervals from AMI to CABG are longer, but nevertheless nearly all procedures within one year have occurred within six months. These results suggest that the follow up interval of 12 months chosen for this study of procedures related to AMI is adequate and that a period of six months would probably be sufficient to illustrate trends in coronary artery procedures in situations where opportunities for record linkage are limited.

As CARPs are frequently performed for angina in persons who have not had a previous AMI, it is important to consider what proportion of the resources utilized for CARPs is attributable to the investigation and management of AMI. It is also important to consider the extent to which CARPs performed for reasons other than post-AMI management may have contributed to the decline in IHD deaths and hospital admissions for AMI.

Table 7.3 demonstrates the distribution of all CARPs performed in Perth in the period 1993–95 by previous history and time from previous MI when relevant. Approximately 30 percent of procedures in males and females were performed in persons who had a previous MI since 1981. However only half of these (or 15 percent of the total) were performed within one year of the most recent MI. On the other hand nearly 30 percent of all procedures were performed within one year in persons who had an admission to hospital for an unbooked ischemic episode, some of whom would have been admitted for suspected AMI or unstable angina. These findings were the same for all age groups.

From Perth data not presented here, it is apparent that there are many similarities in both the acute and longer-term care between cases with a discharge diagnosis of AMI and many cases diagnosed as unstable angina. This applies particularly to the proportions undergoing coronary angiography and subsequent revascularization procedures.

TABLE 7.2. Cumulative Frequency of Procedures by Time from AMI, Perth, Western Australia, 1995 (%)

	Days from admission for AMI			
	30	90	180	365
Angiography				
Males	43	49	51	52
Females	32	37	39	40
Angioplasty				
Males	13	15	16	17
Females	13	17	17	18
CABG				
Males	6	12	14	14
Females	6	8	9	9

As the numbers of cases admitted to hospital because of unstable angina appear similar to those admitted for AMI, future studies will need to consider the impact of investigation and treatment of unstable angina.

Patients from Victoria

The second source of information was the minimum data set for the state of Victoria from 1986 to 1997. Admissions with a length of stay less than three days were deleted. Emergency AMI was identified from the fifth digit of the ICD code. When the corresponding separation was because of a transfer, the record was deleted, as an emergency admission would be recorded in the second hospital. The rate of "total" admissions was calculated as emergency plus readmissions within an eight-week period. (The Victorian database did not enable us to calculate one-year procedure rates.) As transfers between hospitals following a readmission were not subtracted from these latter data, they will have a small upward bias that should, however, remain consistent throughout the time period analyzed.

Finally, information was obtained from the Western Australia Minimum Data Set. In this, emergency admissions are defined as those where there has been no AMI related admission for at least 12 months, where there was no hospital booking, and where the subsequent records indicate that the admission was for AMI. "Total" admissions

TABLE 7.3. The Distribution of CARPs Performed in 1993–95 by Previous History and Time from Previous Admission[a]

	Time from Last Admission		
Previous History	Less than One Year	One Year and Over	All Periods
Males (N = 5,726)			
AMI	14.7	15.5	30.2
Other unbooked ischemic episode	28.4	9.7	38.1
Other IHD	8.8	6.6	15.4
No previous admission for IHD	16.3	0	16.3
All cases	68.2	31.8	100
Females (N = 1,734)			
AMI	15.7	11.1	26.8
Other unbooked ischemic episode	27.6	9.8	37.4
Other IHD	12.7	6.5	19.2
No previous admission for IHD	16.6	0	16.6
All cases	72.7	27.3	100

[a]Hierarchical classification of previous history of IHD.

are defined as emergency plus readmissions. From the data linkage these are calculated for a 12-month period but, for comparability with the Victorian data, estimated for an eight-week period.

The likelihood of angiography or any coronary artery revascularization procedure after admission for residents of Victoria and Western Australia is shown in figure 7.4. The figure reveals a number of interesting patterns. The rate of angiography in Western Australia significantly exceeded the Victorian rate for both men and women until 1994, when the rates converged. By contrast, the likelihood of a subsequent revascularization procedure has been significantly higher for most years in Western Australia for both men and women. A breakdown of revascularization into angioplasty and CABG, shown in figure 7.5, reveals that this pattern was entirely attributable to the greater rates of angioplasty in Western Australia. Rates of CABG have been, in fact, significantly higher in Victoria for both men and women. These data also reveal that the exponential increase in angioplasty, which occurred after 1991 in both states, was not accompanied by a decline in bypass surgery. To the contrary, CABG rates also accelerated in these years. The rapid growth of coronary artery stenting, after 1994, appears to have ended this trend and was accompanied by a modest decline for men and a static level for women in the number of "all admissions" for angioplasty in Victoria, although it should be noted that coronary artery stenting is a technological extension of coronary angioplasty. It did not, however, reduce the likelihood of bypass surgery. In sum, there is very limited evidence of the substitution of newer for older procedures. This could be a result of the substitution effect being obscured by the rapid increase in total revascularization.

The data are consistent with the hypothesis that there is a 12- to 18-month time lag between Victorian and West Australian practices, supporting the nationwide validity of our Perth database used in the remainder of the chapter. The likelihood of different procedures in Victoria is similar to the likelihood in Western Australia in the previous year.

As noted earlier, one of the unique features of the Australian system is its division into a public and private hospital sector in which financial incentives for both patients and doctors are different. In the private, but not in the public, sector, patients face an often significant copayment. Doctors receive a fee for service in the private sector and are either salaried or work at a sessional rate in the public sector. The same doctors often work in both sectors, but receive a much greater

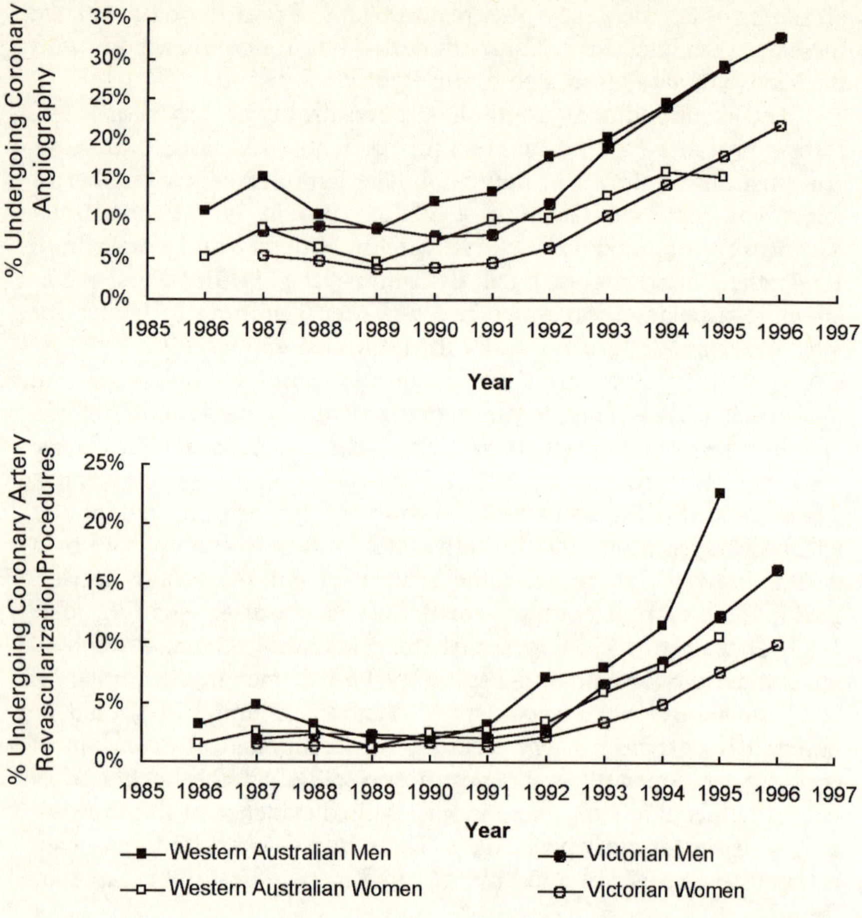

Fig. 7.4. Likelihood of coronary angiography and any coronary artery revascularization procedure, Victoria and Western Australia, 1986–96. Shown are the number of treatments as a percentage of total admission episodes. ICD9-CM coding for AMI, allowing distinction of initial admission episode and subsequent admissions within eight weeks, was implemented in 1990 in Victoria. This distinction is made by record linkage in WA. Victorian data refer to the financial year starting six months after the start of the calendar year of the WA data

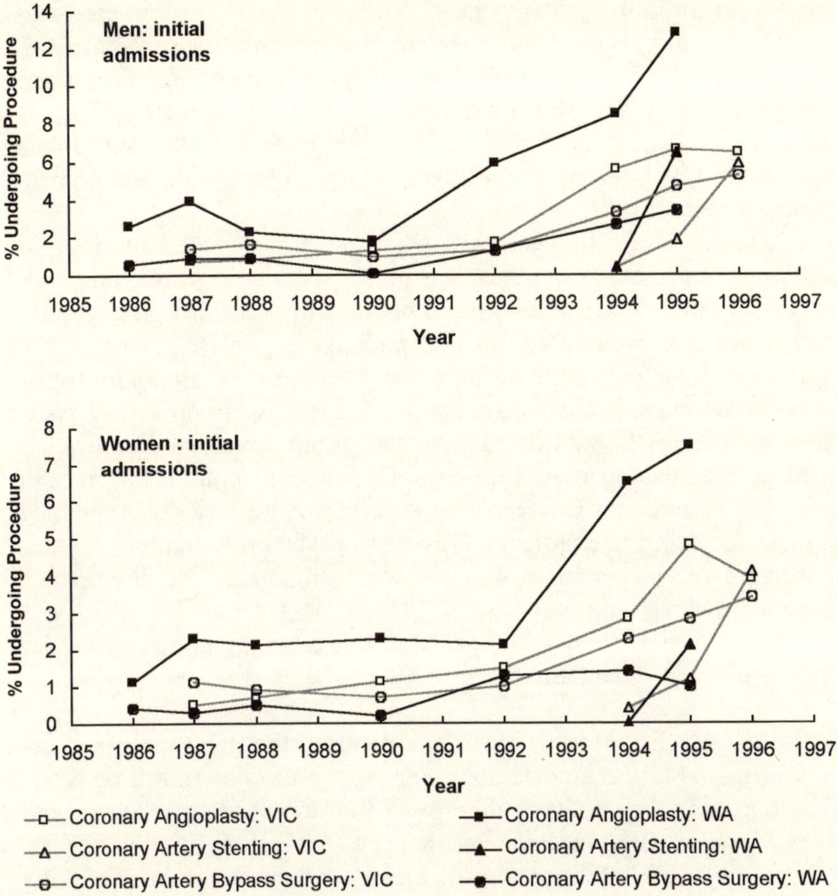

Fig. 7.5. Likelihood of different types of revascularization procedure, Victoria and Western Australia, 1986–96. Shown are the number of treatments as a percentage of total admission episodes. ICD9-CM, allowing distinction of initial admission episode and subsequent admissions within eight weeks, was implemented in 1990 in Victoria. This distinction is made by record linkage in WA. ICD9-CM code for coronary artery stenting was not fully implemented until 1995 in Victoria. Victorian data refer to the financial year starting six months after the start of the calendar year of the WA data.

rate of return in the private sector. While the pattern in Western Australia is somewhat obscured by the small numbers in the private sector, it is clear that this sector carries out a disproportionate number of the procedures. In 1996, private admissions in Victoria represented 27 percent of the total for both men and women. However, they led to 45.8 percent and 54.1 percent of the angiography and revascularization procedures, respectively.

The reason for this is clearer when we consider the likelihood of different treatments for publicly insured patients in public hospitals ("public/public"), privately insured patients in public hospitals ("public/private"), and privately insured patients in private hospitals (fig. 7.6). For both men and women, the likelihood of angiography or revascularization in Victoria in most years is between 50 and 120 percent greater in the private than in the pubic sector, and somewhat greater in a private patient than a public patient in a public hospital. In part, the discrepancy between a public and private patient is explained by the age of private patients. However, as shown in figure 7.5, standardizing for age reduces, but does not eliminate, the discrepancy between the two sectors.

Changes in Low-Tech Care

Randomized clinical trials have demonstrated the effectiveness of several drugs in reducing mortality or recurrent infarction following AMI. These include thrombolytic therapy (TT) during the acute event, and beta-blockers (BBs), antiplatelet therapy (APT), intravenous nitrates (IVN), and ACE inhibitors during and after the acute event. Smoking cessation remains one of the most important preventive measures following AMI, and recent trials have demonstrated strong protective effects of lipid-lowering agents (LLA) following AMI and in other chronic IHD (irrespective of initial levels of cholesterol).

The widespread uptake of these interventions in relation to key publications can be traced through the recording of drugs used during AMI in the MONICA project, the findings of which in this regard are fairly typical for MONICA centers in Australasia, Europe, and North America.

The use of these drugs during hospital admission for AMI in Perth is shown in table 7.4. In persons under the age of 65 years, BBs were used in 1984 in 55 percent of cases. This use increased progressively to 81 percent in 1989 and then continued at about that level. APT was used in 24 percent of cases in the same age group in 1984, but its use

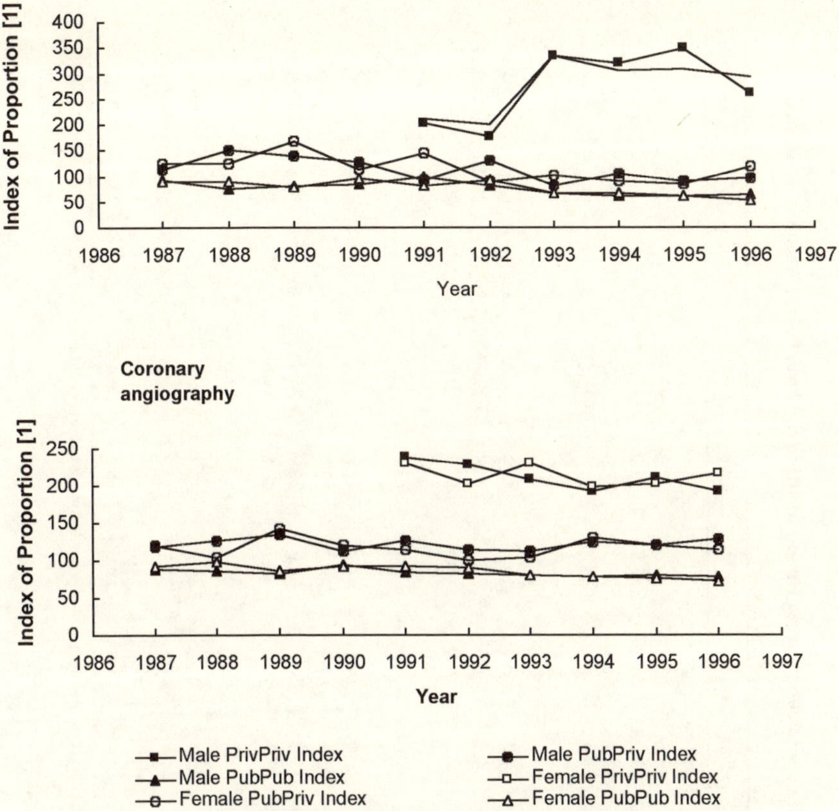

Fig. 7.6. Likelihood of procedures for public and private patients, standardized for age, in Victoria. Shown is the proportion of patients admitted with AMI who underwent any coronary artery revascularization procedure, according to private/public status: age-standardized index compared to all Victorians for men and women (all Victoria = 100). The financial year starts from July of the calendar year listed. Private hospital data were not included before 1991–92, with complete information after 1993–94.

increased dramatically to over 90 percent in 1989. In 1984, thrombolysis (TT) was used in only 3 percent of patients under age 65, but use then increased steadily to nearly 50 percent in 1993. While this increase appears to be much less than for BBs and APT, we found that by 1993, over 90 percent of cases with time to care of less than four hours and with ST elevation on the admission ECG, received TT. Thus when two of the main criteria for use of TT were present, most cases received

TABLE 7.4. Percentage of Cases Treated with Selected Drugs during Hospitalization for AMI, Perth, Western Australia, 1984–93

Age	All Years	1984	1985	1986	1987	1988	1989	1990	1991	1992	1993
Antiplatelet agents											
< 65	73.7	23.6	46.5	49.9	63.2	83.9	92.2	93.7	95.6	95.2	95.5
65–69	73.7	23.6	46.5	49.9	63.2	83.9	92.2	93.7	95.6	95.2	95.5
70–74	66.3	21.2	41.8	44.9	56.9	75.5	82.9	84.3	86.0	85.7	86.0
75–79	53.0	18.8	37.2	39.9	50.6	67.1	73.7	75.0	76.5	76.2	76.4
Thrombolysis											
< 65	27.9	2.5	7.6	14.2	20.1	29.3	34.9	39.0	44.9	40.6	47.9
65–69	15.1	0.8	2.3	4.2	6.0	20.5	24.4	27.3	31.4	28.4	33.6
70–74	11.2	0.8	2.3	4.2	6.0	14.6	17.4	19.5	22.5	20.3	24.0
75–79	5.6	0.5	1.5	2.8	4.0	5.9	7.0	7.8	9.0	8.1	9.6
Beta-blockers											
< 65	73.8	54.7	58.7	66.5	68.1	75.6	81.0	82.6	85.0	82.9	84.0
65–69	66.4	49.2	52.8	59.9	61.3	68.0	72.9	74.4	76.5	74.6	75.6
70–74	63.5	43.7	46.9	53.2	54.5	68.0	72.9	74.4	76.5	74.6	75.6
75–79	44.3	32.8	35.2	39.9	40.8	45.3	48.6	49.6	51.0	49.7	50.4
IV Nitrates											
< 65	51.5	47.7	50.4	44.4	43.6	40.8	47.1	51.6	56.7	60.0	73.9
65–69	46.4	47.7	50.4	44.4	43.6	32.7	37.7	41.3	45.4	48.0	59.1
70–74	43.8	42.9	45.4	40.0	39.2	32.7	37.7	41.3	45.4	48.0	59.1
75–79	23.2	23.8	25.2	22.2	21.8	16.3	18.8	20.6	22.7	24.0	29.6

Sources: Estimates based on Perth MONICA data (ages under 65 years) and a sample of records for admissions in older age groups.

treatment. Further increase in the use of TT is thus likely to depend on patients seeking medical care sooner after the onset of symptoms. ACE inhibitors were not recorded separately in the Perth study until 1989, when they were used in 8 percent of cases. Use then increased rapidly to 40 percent in 1993.

Prescribed use for persons in older age groups (shown in italics) has been determined from a smaller sample of records examined in the same time period. In general use declined with age, with the greatest trend seen in use of thrombolysis and the least in the use of antiplatelet agents.

The use of selected drugs after discharge following hospitalization for AMI, as recorded in the Perth MONICA Study (ages less than 65 years), is shown in table 7.5. Increases in prescribing of BBs, APT, and ACE inhibitors up to 1993 followed the same pattern as their use during hospital treatment. By that time, use had risen to 80 percent for BBs, 85 percent for APT, and 35 percent for ACE inhibitors. In addition, prescription of hypo-lipidemic agents increased from less than 1 percent in 1984 to 8 percent in 1993. A follow-up study of cases recorded in the Perth MONICA Study has shown that treatment with these drugs is sustained in a majority of cases for at least two years. Levels of use of these drugs before admission of recurrent cases of AMI is also consistent with continuing high levels of compliance with treatment.

Tables 7.4 and 7.5 indicate marked increases in the use of selected, effective cardiac drugs since the mid-1980s, of which the massive uptake of APT both during and after AMI is particularly notable. The timing of these increases suggests that clinicians have been influenced by publication of clinical trials, meta-analyses, and overviews. Several of these drugs are also widely used for other vascular reasons, such as chronic IHD, hypertension, following CARPs, and after stroke, where they have comparable protective benefits against coronary death and recurrent AMI. Hence the collective and increasing use of "low technology" interventions measures may well be equally or more important as "high technology" interventions in the treatment and prevention of AMI.

The Consequences of Changes in AMI Care in Australia

Changes in Health Outcomes for AMI Patients

We examine both mortality and the rate of cardiac complications as measures of health outcomes from AMI. We begin with case fatality at 30 days and one year, shown in figures 7.7 and 7.8. In addition we show

TABLE 7.5. Percentage of Cases Treated with Selected Drugs after Discharge following Hospitalization for AMI, Perth, Western Australia, 1984–93

Age	All Years	1984	1985	1986	1987	1988	1989	1990	1991	1992	1993
Antiplatelet agents											
< 65	65.6	14.6	33.2	42.4	56.2	75.5	85.6	87.8	86.8	87.8	84.2
65–69	59.0	13.1	29.9	38.2	50.6	67.9	77.0	79.0	78.2	79.0	75.8
70–74	52.5	11.7	26.6	33.9	44.9	60.4	68.4	70.2	69.5	70.2	67.4
75–79	49.2	11.0	24.9	31.8	42.1	56.6	64.2	65.8	65.1	65.8	63.2
Beta-blockers											
< 65	67.2	49.9	51.1	60.6	61.8	65.6	74.0	72.8	78.1	77.7	79.5
65–69	57.1	42.4	43.4	51.5	52.6	55.8	62.9	61.9	66.4	66.0	67.6
70–74	47.0	34.9	35.8	42.4	43.3	45.9	51.8	51.0	54.7	54.4	55.7
75–79	33.6	25.0	25.6	30.3	30.9	32.8	37.0	36.4	39.1	38.8	39.8
Hypolipidemic drugs											
< 65	4.0						3.4	2.4	6.6	7.3	8.3
ACE inhibitors											
< 65	19.5						5.5	12.9	21.7	24.2	35.6

Sources: Estimates based on Perth MONICA data (ages under 65 years) and a sample of records for admissions in older age groups.

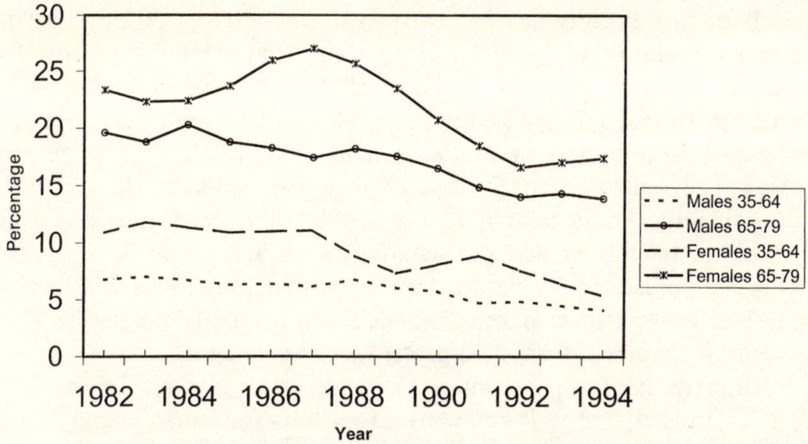

Fig. 7.7. Cumulative mortality at 30 days following AMI (three-year moving average)

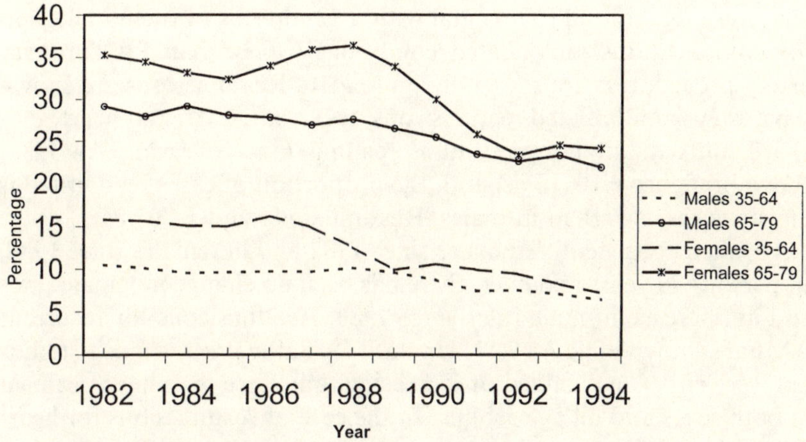

Fig. 7.8. Cumulative mortality at one year following AMI (three-year moving average)

trends in case fatality at one year in subjects alive at 30 days (post-acute-case fatality) in figure 7.9. It is notable that most of the improvement in these indices has occurred since 1988. In general the improvement since 1988, summarized in table 7.6, has been more pronounced in females, although case fatality in females was initially greater than in males. The improvement in case fatality also tends to decline with increasing age. In the case of 30-day case fatality, the decline was over 40 percent in both males and females in the age group 35–69 years (from 8.5 percent to 5.0 percent) but approximately 24 percent in the older age group (for men, mortality declined from 20.7 percent to 15.7 percent; for women, from 23.5 percent to 17.8 percent).

Improvement in post-acute-case fatality was greatest for younger females; indeed, one-year cumulative mortality for females aged 35–69 declined by almost half, from 19.3 percent to 10.4 percent. Information not in the figures indicates that in males the greatest improvement was seen in those aged 55–64 years, as compared to approximately 41 percent in the younger age group as a whole. With one-year as with 30-day case fatality, this benefit has occurred mainly from 1988 onward.

The proportions of cases of AMI who were alive at 30 days and who were readmitted to hospital within 12 months of the initial event for complications and related conditions (other than for coronary artery procedures) are shown in figure 7.10. Readmissions are shown separately for all related readmissions, recurrent AMI, and heart.

Trends in all nonprocedural readmissions following AMI are shown in figure 7.10. In general, the proportion of cases readmitted is higher in females than in males. Readmissions under 70 years of age have fallen consistently in males since 1982 and in females since 1988. In persons 70 years and over, there has been no change in female rates and an increase in male rates since 1986. Readmissions for recurrent AMI are shown in figure 7.11. Up until 1988, the proportions readmitted were either unchanged or increasing, but since then have declined in both sexes and all age groups. In the case of readmissions for heart failure (fig. 7.12), there has been considerable fluctuation over time, but overall there are clear increases in older males and females and younger males. Readmissions for heart failure are in general higher in females than males.

Changes in Medical Expenditures and Resource Use

In this section we show the extent to which the costs of treatment of AMI have changed as the result of increased use of procedures during the initial admission and through changes in the frequency of readmis-

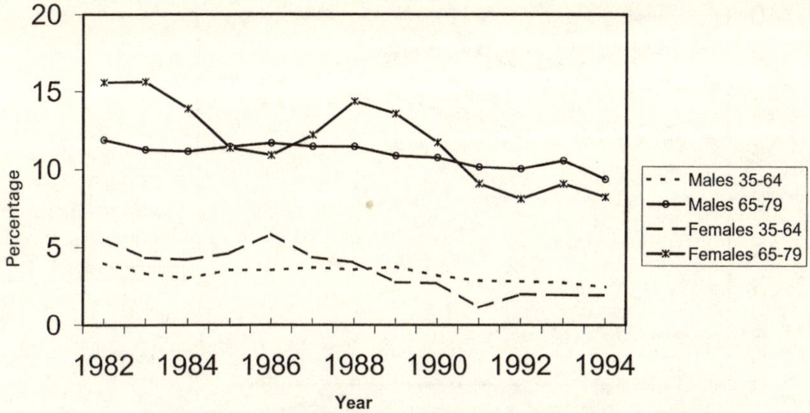

Fig. 7.9. Cumulative mortality at one year for survivors to 30 days (three-year moving average)

TABLE 7.6. Percentage Decline in Cumulative Mortality from AMI in Australia, by Age and Sex, 1988–1995

	30 Days	365 Days	30–365 Days
Males			
35–54	35.4	33.3	32.0
55–64	41.2	36.5	28.9
65–69	33.6	24.1	4.7
70–74	17.0	16.9	19.0
75–79	24.1	23.4	28.6
Females			
35–54	0.0	34.7	77.1
55–64	43.8	43.0	45.2
65–69	29.3	30.7	38.2
70–74	29.9	33.7	47.2
75–79	34.7	34.8	43.8

sions either for coronary artery procedures or for complications or associated comorbidity. Rather than describing exact costs, the figures reflect the extent of change according to changes in procedure use and readmissions.

Costs are based on the cost weights contained in the third edition of the Australian DRG classification. DRG codes had previously been assigned to hospital admissions for the period 1993–95 by HDWA and

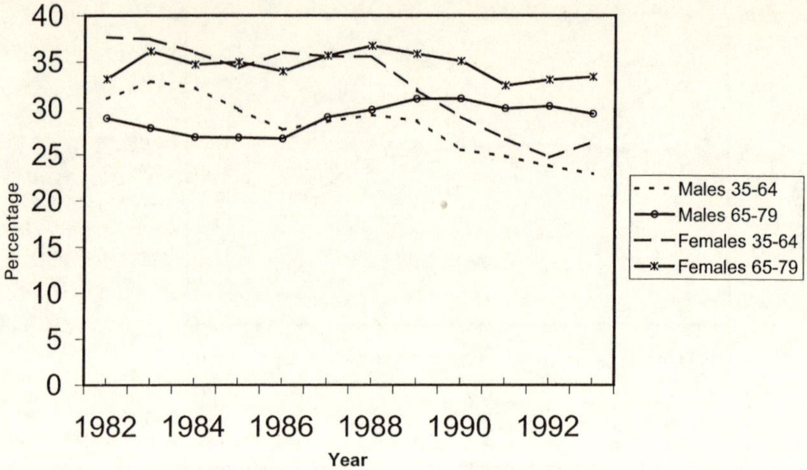

Fig. 7.10. Trends in readmission for nonprocedural related conditions (three-year moving average)

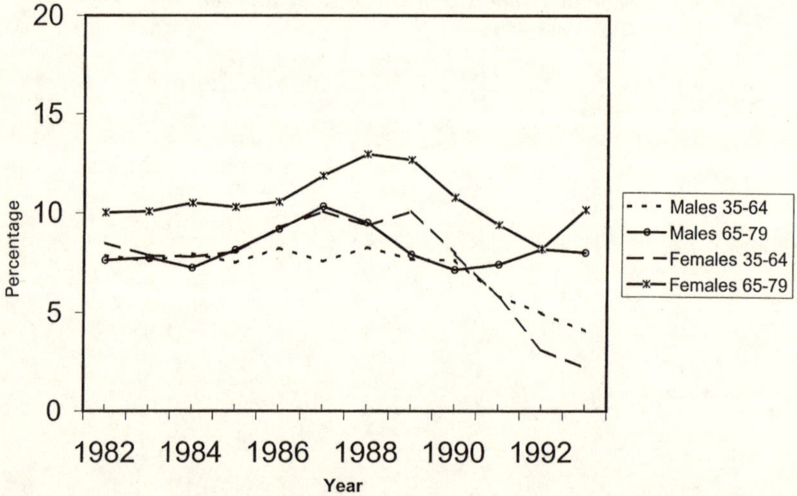

Fig. 7.11. Trends in readmission for recurrent AMI (three-year moving average)

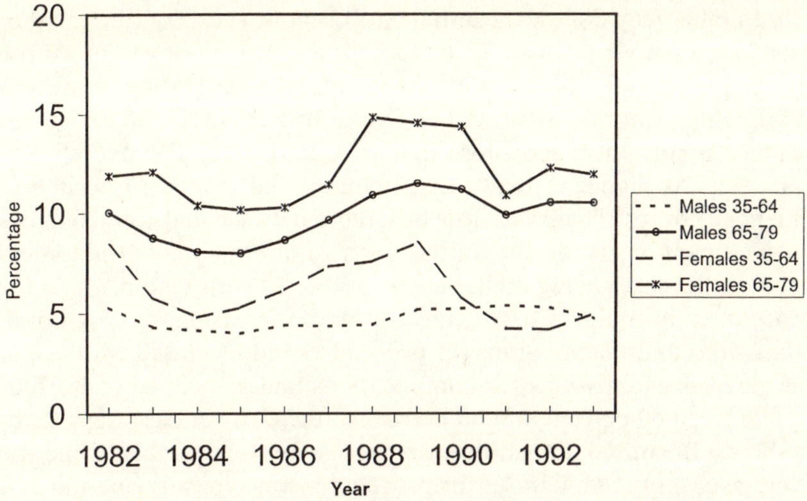

Fig. 7.12. Trends in readmission for heart failure (three-year moving average)

were present in the records used in this study. Ideally we would have assigned equivalent DRG codes to hospital admissions for the entire period, but the grouping software was not immediately accessible to us. We therefore classified all initial admissions for AMI and subsequent readmissions cases for all years to 12 principal procedure or diagnostic groups following the general logic of the DRG coding system, which assigns codes hierarchically on the basis of diminishing cost, first for major operative procedures and then on the basis of selected diagnostic codes and investigative procedures. Our classification is shown in appendix table A7.2.

All initial admissions and subsequent readmissions in the period 1993–95 were tabulated by disease group and DRG code. From this it was possible to determine an average DRG cost per case of AMI during this period for initial admissions and readmissions in each diagnostic group. These were then multiplied by the number of cases in each age and sex group in the equivalent diagnostic group for each year. For the purpose of presentation here, we have grouped readmissions into those for: procedures; recurrent AMI; heart failure or other complications; other readmissions related to AMI or IHD; and readmissions that were not directly related to admissions for AMI or IHD.

In table 7.7 we show the initial and 12-month costs of treatment of each case of AMI in 1994. Readmissions are broken down into those for major procedures and elective coronary angiography, recurrent AMI, complications attributable to the initial AMI and those for related comorbidity, and those that were unrelated. The overall cost per case was higher in males than females and tended to decline in older age groups. There was little difference between males and females in treatment costs in the initial admission, the main differences between the sexes being higher costs associated with readmissions for procedures in males. Costs decreased with increasing age for initial admissions and readmissions for procedures but increased with age in the case of readmissions for complications and associated comorbidity. Between 50 percent and 60 percent of the cost per case was attributable to the initial admission in most age and sex groups, while the average cost of readmissions for procedures was typically one-third of the total cost per case. This, however, declined with age and was greater in males than females. Conversely the proportion of the total cost attributable to other readmissions increased with age.

The increase in each component of the total cost per case from 1981 to 1994 is shown in table 7.8. In both males and females the increase in total cost per case rose with age (although not monotonically) and then declined. This was due principally to marked relative increases in the readmissions for procedures with only modest increases in costs of the initial admission and in other readmissions.

Discussion: The Effects of Financial and Regulatory Incentives on Technological Change in Heart Attack Care

Mortality from IHD in Perth has improved dramatically and consistently over a period of three decades. The magnitude of these changes are so great as to suggest that they are due mainly to changes in the incidence of acute coronary events or the natural history of IHD, rather than improved survival following admission to hospital for AMI. This is supported by declines in hospital admission rates for AMI reported here.

From previous studies in Perth of trends in the incidence of AMI and IHD deaths in persons under the age of 65 years, we have been able to apportion absolute declines in mortality since 1971 between first and recurrent events and between declining incidence and improved survival. In general, falls in mortality have both preceded

TABLE 7.7. Cost of Treatment and Aftercare of AMI in 1994, Perth, Western Australia

		Readmissions				
	Index Admission	Procedures	Recurrent MI and Heart Failure	Complications and Comorbidities	Total Readmissions	All Admissions
Males						
35–54	5.5	3.8	0.3	0.6	4.8	10.3
55–64	5.4	3.8	0.5	0.7	5.0	10.3
65–69	5.1	3.8	0.4	1.5	5.7	10.7
70–74	4.9	2.7	0.8	0.7	4.3	9.1
75–79	4.7	1.0	0.9	0.7	2.6	7.3
Females						
35–54	5.2	2.8	0.0	0.7	3.5	8.7
55–64	5.3	3.5	0.6	1.1	5.2	10.5
65–69	4.8	1.8	1.5	1.0	4.3	9.0
70–74	4.9	1.8	1.0	1.0	3.7	8.7
75–79	4.6	1.6	0.9	0.9	3.4	8.0

Note: Figures are per admission in thousands of dollars Australian, based on current DRG weighting.

TABLE 7.8. The Increase in 12-Month Costs of Treatment for AMI, Perth, Western Australia, 1981–94

		Readmissions				
	Index Admission	Procedures	Recurrent MI and Heart Failure	Complications and Comorbidities	Total Readmissions	All Admissions
Males						
35–54	1.3	1.3	0.4	0.6	1.0	1.1
55–64	1.2	2.1	0.7	0.9	1.5	1.3
65–69	1.2	5.4	0.8	1.9	2.8	1.7
70–74	1.1	14.7	0.9	1.0	2.4	1.5
75–79	1.1	7.0	1.8	0.8	1.8	1.3
Females						
35–54	1.1	1.2	0.0	0.5	0.7	0.9
55–64	1.2	3.6	0.8	1.1	1.9	1.5
65–69	1.1	3.5	1.3	1.3	1.8	1.3
70–74	1.1	9.1	1.3	2.1	3.0	1.6
75–79	1.1	28.2	1.2	1.2	2.2	1.4

Note: Figures represent percentage increases in costs per admission.

and exceeded declines in incidence of nonfatal AMI, so that population-wide case fatality (IHD deaths / [IHD deaths + nonfatal AMI]) has also declined. However most of the improvement in mortality associated with lower case fatality has occurred in cases not admitted to hospital and particularly in first events. This suggests that as incidence has fallen, so too has the severity of disease.

At least 70 percent of IHD deaths occur in cases not admitted to hospital during the fatal event. This ratio has remained fairly constant, indicating that deaths in hospital cases have declined at the same rate as out-of-hospital deaths. Most of this is, however, due to falling rates of hospital admission. Simple arithmetic indicates that improved case fatality in cases admitted to hospital due to improved acute coronary care can have accounted for no more that 5–10 percent of the total decline in IHD mortality. On the other hand, in males aged less than 65 years alive at one month after AMI, cumulative five-year mortality following AMI halved in the period from 1971 to 1991. Nonfatal recurrent AMI declined by a similar amount. In females the gains were much less. This improved longer-term survival following AMI could have contributed significantly to the decline in mortality in males at least.

In contrast to these long-standing trends in incidence and mortality, the widespread diffusion of clinical interventions shown in clinical trials to be effective in reducing mortality or nonfatal AMI has been relatively recent. Coronary revascularization procedures were introduced in the late 1970s, but it is probable that the cumulative incidence (or prevalence) of such procedures has only reached levels sufficient to have a measurable population impact on mortality in the last 10 years. Similarly, the widespread uptake of effective medications such as antiplatelet agents, beta-blockers, thrombolytics, ACE inhibitors, and lipid-lowering agents dates from the late 1980s. It is therefore reasonable to believe that "effective" medical treatment can have played an important role in falling mortality and rates of AMI only in the past decade. Determination of the extent of this, in the face of falling incidence and probable changes in the natural history of disease, however, is almost impossible, particularly if the factors that initiated the decline, including those related to behavior and lifestyle, have continue to operate.

In support of a contribution of new technology to declining mortality is the evidence that since 1988, the decline in both mortality and incidence of AMI seems to have accelerated since 1988 and that case fatality and recurrent AMI at 12 months have also fallen. Moreover, the greatest improvements in these various measures have occurred in younger age groups in whom interventions have been most intense. Further improvements in outcomes in older age groups might therefore be expected as aggressive treatment is extended to higher ages.

Our comparison of the Victorian and Western Australian data suggests that our analysis of the residents of Perth has nationwide validity. Our Victorian analysis also points out another striking result: the discrepancy in the treatment rates between privately and publicly insured patients, particularly privately insured patients in privately owned hospitals. There are several possible reasons for this. First, it is possible that those who purchase private insurance have a preferences for more aggressive therapies. There is no independent data to support this hypothesis, and it appears improbable that following an emergency heart attack patients would have such clear and different preferences. Second, it is possible that doctors face excess demand; that they treat the insured and uninsured equally during normal hours and give extra treatments to the insured by extending their working week. However, an explanation in terms of queuing appears inconsistent with the observation that readmission for intensive procedures is also greater among the insured. The explanation implies that public patients never reach the end of the queue. A third possible explanation is that doctors may treat aggressively those with whom they have the greatest empathy and that this would favor the higher socioeconomic status private population. Fourth, and consistent with supplier induced demand, doctors may determine treatment patterns on the basis of self interest. In Australia, private patients will usually be treated by a private visiting specialist, who receives a significant part of the direct fee. If a salaried hospital doctor is employed, then the fee is commonly placed in a tax exempt account for expenditure on overseas travel and other professional related activities. While these arrangements vary between hospitals, there is a financial incentive to favor the insured. Fifth, in some hospitals a proportion of the private fees is retained by the hospital and used for the purchase of equipment for the treatment of public patients. This factor may also influence the doctor's choice of patient.

This study has focused on changes in treatment during AMI and the following 12 months. This provides a convenient model for examining relative changes in technology in a well-defined clinical population. It must, however, be born in mind that this will account for only a minority of deaths from IHD and new cases of AMI. Similarly, only about one-fifth of all revascularization procedures occur within one year of AMI and about one-third in persons who have ever had a myocardial infarct. It is therefore likely that medical interventions in the remainder of the population with clinically defined IHD have had a greater impact on both incidence and mortality. The costs will obviously also have been greater.

A further limitation of the study is that outcomes are expressed only in terms of death, recurrent AMI, or heart failure. Further study is required of the extent to which CARPs following AMI are undertaken for relief of angina, as opposed to vascular obstruction demonstrated at angiography. In this regard it is notable that up to 80 percent of younger patients receive angiography within one year and that the rate is rising rapidly in older patients as well. Apart from the trend to urgent angioplasty (which in fact has not been great in Perth) it would seem that this form of investigation has become almost routine compared with earlier regimes, when, in the absence of symptoms, it was performed as the result of postacute exercise stress testing.

Our study is of interest in that rates of CABG in both the general population and following AMI have declined in younger age groups, whereas PTCA has continued to increase. As PTCA is most frequently performed for single-vessel disease, in which CABG provides only marginal survival benefits, the proportion of younger cases undergoing CABG presumably reflects the number of cases with major obstruction or multiple-vessel disease. Beyond this, it is likely that further increases in CARPs in the form of PTCA would have only marginal benefits with regard to further acute coronary events. Further studies are therefore required to assess the efficacy of "urgent" PTCA, and the extent to which delayed PTCA is undertaken for symptoms or because of disordered anatomy. For any assessment of the likely impact of CARPs on event rates, detailed information is required on the distribution of site and severity of coronary artery obstruction obtained at angiography. Finally, in the absence of adequate evidence from clinical trials, careful observational studies of survival following stenting for coronary artery obstruction are required.

The uptake of selected drugs shown through clinical trials to reduce fatal and nonfatal outcomes during and following AMI increased dramatically in the late 1980s from the mid-1980s. It seems that this was to a large extent related to publications of the results of major trials or overviews of trials. The uptake of antiplatelet agents in particular represents a massive therapeutic change. Given that these agents, mainly in the form of aspirin, which is cheap, have benefits in all forms of arterial vascular disease, it is likely that they have had a measurable impact on disease rates. Recent trials of antiplatelet agents in persons with chronic IHD irrespective of initial cholesterol levels have shown marked benefits in relation to both fatal and nonfatal endpoints. It can be anticipated that with the publications of the results of recently conducted trials, these drugs will also be used eventually in the majority of cases. A question to be answered is the extent to which the benefits of various medical and surgical interventions are additive, and from this what are the average marginal benefits of different combinations.

Further extensions of the present study will be to determine longer-term survival and complication rates following AMI and the extent to which this is associated with revascularization procedures and varying intervals after the initial event. Models of the incidence and prevalence of IHD will also be developed using record linkage to determine the putative benefits of various treatment regimes.

TABLE A7.1. Classification Scheme for Readmissions following AMI Not Associated with Coronary Artery Procedures

Group	Main Reason for Readmission	Condition	ICD Code
A	Recurrent AMI	AMI	410
A1	Other conditions probably related to index admission for AMI or subsequent CARPs	Anemia	280-285
		Coagulation and bleeding disorders	286, 287
		Valve disorders	424
		Conduction disorders, dysrhythmias	426, 427
		Heart failure	428
		Cerebral embolus and thrombosis	434
		Venous embolism and thrombosis	453
		Other cardiac symptoms and chest pain	785, 786.5
		Other general symptoms, abnormal tests	Remainder 780–799
		Mechanical complications of vascular grafts	9960, 9961
		Cardiac complications	9971
		PV complications	9972
		After care	V01–V82
B	Associated conditions possibly related to readmission	Diabetes	250
		Hypertensive disease	401–405
		Angina	411.1, 413
		Other IHD	412, 414
		Pericardial disease	423
		Other cardiac	Remainder 390–429
		Other cerebral vascular disease	430–433, 435–438
		Peripheral vascular disease	440–449
C	Other conditions not related to AMI	All other conditions	All other codes

TABLE A7.2. Classification of Index and Readmissions Used for Allocation of Costs

Group Number	Procedure or Diagnosis
1	Insertion of pacemaker
2	CABG with angiogram or PTCA or both
3	CABG without angiogram or PTCA or both
4	AMI (code 410) + PTCA
5	AMI (code 410) + angiogram
6	AMI without procedure
7	Other PTCA
8	Other angiogram
9	Heart failure
10	Other complications[a]
11	Other comorbidity[b]
12	Unrelated conditions[c]

[a]See group A1, table A7.1.
[b]See group B, table A7.1.
[c]See group C, table A7.1.

Notes

This work was performed with financial assistance of the Commonwealth Government of Australia. The Australian Institute for Health and Welfare supplied data for admissions and procedures performed in patients in Australia who suffered acute myocardial infarctions, with the permission of the States and Territory Governments of Australia. The Victorian Department of Human Services supplied data from the Victorian Inpatient Minimum Dataset.

1. From 1997 there has been a surcharge of 1 percent on households with an income above $100,000 or single-person households with an income above $50,000.

2. In 1997 the federal government introduced limited subsidies for private health insurance and an income tax surcharge on households above $A100,000 who have no private health insurance. Another perversity of the Australian system is that the net cost of private health insurance for many wealthy families is negative as the price of private health insurance may be less than the income surcharge avoided by purchasing the insurance.

References

Australian Institute of Health and Welfare (AIHW). 1996. *Australia's Health.* Canberra: Australian Government Publishing Service.

———. 1997. "Health Expenditure." *Health Expenditure Bulletin 13*. Canberra: Australian Institute of Health and Welfare.

Private Health Insurance Administration Council. 1998. *Quarterly Statistics, December 1997.*

Richardson, J. 1988a. "The Healthcare Financing Debate." In *The Economics of Australian Health Policy,* ed. G. Mooney and R. Scotton. Sydney: Allen and Unwin.

———. 1988b. "Medical Technology and Its Diffusion in Australia." *International Journal of Technology Assessment and Health Care* 4, no. 3: 407–31.

CHAPTER 8

The Causes and Consequences of Technological Change in the Treatment of Acute Myocardial Infarction in Japan

Aki Yoshikawa, Haruko Noguchi, Saburo Ide, Akihiro Koike, Toru Maruyama, Naoto Uemura, and Akinori Urae, with Tsuruhiko Nambu

Estimating effects of both medical treatments and changes in medical technology on patient outcomes is important for guiding treatment and policy decisions of medical doctors and patients. In this chapter, we focus on a specific disease, heart attack, which is an important health problem in the aging society in Japan as well as in other countries. Japan provides a perspective on the question of treatment and outcomes for heart attack care very different from the United States and most European countries. The rate of AMI and other ischemic heart diseases (IHD) is dramatically lower in Japan. As table 8.1 shows, in 1990, there were 41.9 deaths per 100,000 population in Japan from ischemic heart diseases. The rate is much lower than other nations, for instance, 161.2 in Canada (1991), 196.7 in the United States (1990), 226.2 in Germany (1991), 287.5 in England (1992) (WHO 1993). Similarly, death from AMI per 100,000 in Japan was 25.9 in 1991 (table 8.2). Compared with the United States, where the rate was 99.5 in 1991, death from AMI is much less common in Japan.

Tables 8.1 and 8.2 also point out another striking fact: cardiac illness and death from cardiac illness have been increasing rapidly in Japan. The crude IHD incidence rate in Japan increased rapidly, by about 300 percent, during 1950–93. The IHD incidence rates of males and females per 100,000 population increased by approximately 258 percent, from 13 to 45, and 425 percent, from 7 to 39, respectively, during 1950–93. Death rates from AMI have also been rising in Japan, as table 8.2 indicates. (The dramatic increase between 1994 and 1995 may

TABLE 8.1. Trends in Death Rates from Ischemic Heart Disease in Japan, by Sex, 1950–93 (per 100,000)

	1950	1955	1960	1965	1970	1975	1980	1985	1990	1993
Crude rate										
Total	9.9	11.6	21.3	28.5	37.9	39.4	41.6	41.1	41.9	41.9
Male	12.6	14.3	26.0	34.1	44.3	44.0	47.0	45.5	45.4	45.1
Female	7.4	9.0	16.7	23.1	31.7	34.9	36.3	36.9	38.6	38.9
Age-adjusted										
Male	24.6	26.9	48.7	61.7	75.7	70.4	65.5	54.7	46.3	41.9
Female	13.0	14.8	26.4	35.0	43.7	42.8	37.4	30.9	25.6	22.6

Source: Ministry of Health and Welfare, Jinko Dotai Tokei (Vital statistics in Japan).

be a result of changes in Japan's death certificate and the switch from ICD9 to ICD10 in 1995.)

These trends in health outcomes have occurred despite the provision of guaranteed, uninhibited access to comprehensive medical care for virtually the entire country's population. Japan's 120 million residents enjoy complete freedom to choose medical care under its extensive health insurance coverage. Anyone who is insured can walk into any hospital or clinic in the country and expect to receive care of comparable quality for a small cost-sharing fee. In addition, the rate of diffusion of expensive high-technology medical equipment in Japan is among the highest in the world (Yoshikawa, Bhattacharya, and Vogt 1996). The purpose of this chapter is to investigate the consequences of the incentives provided by the Japanese health care system for treatments and outcomes of heart attack care, focusing on the role of technological change. The chapter begins by describing the Japanese health care system in general and the medical technology for treatment of cardiovascular diseases in Japan. Then, the chapter analyzes "microlevel" case study data of seven hospitals from Fukuoka Prefecture that collaborated with this study. Unfortunately, no preexisting microlevel database on treatments and outcomes exists in Japan. For this reason, we are constructing our own database, on a hospital-by-hospital basis. Sections 2 and 3 of this chapter represent the first report from our investigation of the impact of medical technology on the treatments and outcomes of AMI, respectively. Section 4 concludes and suggests some avenues for future development of our microdata collection efforts.

TABLE 8.2. AMI Deaths per 100,000, All of Japan and Fukuoka Prefecture, 1985–95

	Japan	Fukuoka
1985	25.4	23.8
1990	26.0	24.0
1991	25.9	23.4
1992	25.4	22.7
1993	26.3	26.1
1994	32.1	30.8
1995	42.3	37.5

Source: Ministry of Health and Welfare, *Kokumin Eisei no Doko* (Trends in people's health status in Japan) 1996.

1. Incentives for Technological Change in Japan

Under the Japanese universal health insurance system, all medical facilities are reimbursed on a fee-for-service basis according to an official fee schedule *(shinryo hoshu)*. There is a separate reimbursement schedule for pharmaceuticals. Patients are responsible only for a small copayment at the point of service, and hospitals and clinics send the bills to intermediary clearing organizations for reimbursement once every month. Over 900 million claims are submitted annually. The review process is rather primitive because the system is not computerized. The average time spent reviewing each bill is less than 10 seconds.

Physician visits, pharmaceuticals, and intensive surgical procedures are reimbursed separately. Providers' bills itemize each procedure, including the dispensing of drugs, for which a predetermined number of "points" is assigned according to the fee schedule. Currently each point is worth 10 yen. The fee schedule is a very detailed form of pricing control, listing more than 3,000 medical procedures for physicians alone. For example, according to the 1997 fee schedule, a body CT scan is worth 1,045 points. Table 8.3 shows the points for several other procedures according to the 1997 fee schedule.

Manipulation of the fee schedule serves as one of the primary mechanisms by which the Ministry of Health and Welfare (Koseisho) regulates the supply of medical services, utilization rates, and aggregate health care expenditures. Lower health care expenditures have not been realized accidentally; systemic manipulation of the fee schedule has been a cost containment tool. However, with growing concern over its increasing health care costs and its rapidly aging society, a few years ago the Japanese government introduced a fixed payment system for its long-term geriatric care hospitals. The new payment system provides a daily fixed amount of reimbursement for each inpatient day regardless of a patient's disease or his/her severity.

When a new medical device or procedure is proposed in Japan, Koseisho decides whether to include it in the fee schedule and at what level its use should be reimbursed. Understandably, the diffusion of any medical device is very slow until it is added to the fee schedule. Thus in Japan, the key to selling any medical device or drug is to have the associated procedure listed on the government's fee schedule, which then enables the national health insurance system to pay for it.

Perhaps as a result of this virtually unrestricted fee-for-service reimbursement system, more high-technology medical devices are available per capita in Japan than in the United States (see, e.g.,

Yoshikawa et al. 1993 and Yoshikawa, Bhattachary, and Vogt 1996 for discussion of the case of CT scanner diffusion and evidence on this point). Table 8.4 presents trends in reimbursements (measured in points for PTCA and CABG, and in number of yen for drugs) for various treatments of cardiac illness over the 1985–97 period. Reimbursement for PTCA has grown the most over this period, with some growth in CABG reimbursement as well. Strikingly, reimbursement for thrombolytic drugs has actually shrunk.

The upward trend in reimbursement for intensive cardiac treatment has translated into increased availability of the procedures. Table 8.5 details the diffusion of available intensive cardiology treatment over the 1987–93 period. According to the National Facility Survey

TABLE 8.3. 1997 Fee Schedule for Reimbursement, Ministry of Health and Welfare

Procedure	Number of Points[a]
Initial consultation	
At hospital	230
At clinic	250
Second and subsequent consultation	
At hospital	59
At clinic	70
Imaging	
CT scan	
Head	760
Body	1,045
MRI scan	
Head	1,900
Other part	2,000
Surgery	
Appendectomy	6,900
C-section	
Elective	8,500
Emergency	10,800
Cardiac treatments	
Implantation of pacemaker	13,600
PTCA	15,500
Stent	15,600
Intracoronary thrombolytic therapy	7,800
CABG	
Single	37,100
Double or more	60,500

Source: Ministry of Health and Welfare, *Shinryo Hoshu Tensu Hayamihyo* (Quick reference table of fee schedules) 1997.

[a]Currently, one point is worth 10 yen.

TABLE 8.4. Trends in Reimbursement Rates for Treatment of Cardiac Illness, 1986–97

	1985	1986	1988	1989	1990	1992	1993	1994	1996	1997
PTCA	6,600	6,600	8,500	8,500	8,500	13,800	13,800	15,500	15,500	15,500
Stent								15,500	15,600	15,600
CABG										
1	26,000	26,000	26,000	26,000	26,000	32,000	32,000	34,000	37,100	37,100
2 or more	41,000	41,000	43,000	43,000	43,000	52,000	52,000	56,000	60,500	60,500
Urokinase										
6 (10_4IU)				8,089		6,076	6,076	5,545	5,095	4,861
12 (10_4IU)				15,046		12,280	12,280	11,280	10,120	9,581
24 (10_4IU)				23,840		17,060	17,060	15,690	14,440	13,861
Alteplase (Activacin)										
600 (10_4IU)						82,670	82,670	81,000	77,840	76,505
1,200 (10_4IU)						161,870	161,870	158,500	152,800	149,270
2,440 (10_4IU)						316,940	316,940	316,940	307,820	297,500
Tisokinase (Hapase)										
160 (10_4IU)						82,670	82,670	79,280	75,730	75,645
340 (10_4IU)							84,350	83,000	78,760	78,672
1440 (10_4IU)									304,500	297,440

Source: Ministry of Health and Welfare, *Shinryo Hoshu Tensu Hayamihyo* (Quick reference table of fee schedules) 1997.

Note: Reimbursement rates for procedures are measured in points (1 point = 10 yen); reimbursement rates for drugs are measured in yen.

TABLE 8.5. Availability of Cardiology-Related Departments

	Number of Hospitals			Internal Cardiology			Cardiological Surgery		
	1987	1990	1993	1987	1990	1993	1987	1990	1993
Total	8,749	9,006	8,752	2,713	3,104	3,235	322	407	472
Public									
MHW	239	236	231	127	131	124	38	40	44
Prefectural	266	307	310	57	61	69	40	45	52
Municipal	747	772	773	119	142	166	31	43	51
Private									
Iryo-hojin	3,069	4,235	4,550	1,130	1,443	1,615	66	101	130
Individual	3,088	3,081	2,530	872	863	754	43	48	51
Teaching hospital	162	163	168	30	31	38	31	38	39

Source: Ministry of Health and Welfare, *Iryo Shisetsu Chosa* (Medical faculty survey).

Note: Iryo-hojin translates literally to "juridical person," meaning a corporation in the medical industry.

(Iryo Shisetsu Chosa), a comprehensive data set of medical facilities in Japan collected by Koseisho, in 1993 there were 8,752 ordinary hospitals in Japan. Of these hospitals, 3,235 had an internal cardiovascular medicine department, and 472 had a cardiovascular surgery department. Whereas the total number of hospitals stayed almost the same between 1987 and 1993, the number of hospitals with these departments has increased by 522 (19.2 percent) and 150 (46.4 percent), respectively. Private sector hospitals account for the most of such dramatic increase. We explore the implications of this trend in technology use in the remainder of the chapter.

To attempt to constrain the diffusion of new technologies placed on the fee schedule, Koseisho has encouraged hospitals and clinics to specialize in the provision of specific intensive treatments *(kinobunka)*. In addition, it has established a subsidiary fee category for some new devices, "the Highly Advanced Medical Treatment System." However, despite these new policies, proliferation of many "big ticket" items has continued almost exponentially in Japan.

2. Technological Change in Heart Attack Care in Japan

We use two surveys for our "microlevel" empirical analyses in Japan: the 1989–95 Social Medical Treatment Survey and our seven-hospital case study.

The Social Medical Treatment Survey includes patient demographic and geographic characteristics, the number of treatments, treatment days, and points for both inpatients and outpatients who got any kind of medical treatments within a specific month of each survey year. This is the only nationwide survey that contains information on medical expenditures by treatment. However, this survey is of limited utility for investigating AMI in Japan for the following reasons: (1) the survey classifies all patients with cardiovascular disease into one category. Therefore, patients with new AMIs cannot be distinguished from patients with other heart diseases such as old or remote AMI, ischemic heart diseases, or chronic heart failure (CHF); (2) the survey contains no information on patient health outcomes such as mortality or readmission caused by AMI complications; (3) the survey period includes treatment information from one calendar month only, and so does not provide complete information on a given medical episode for each patient (for example, a patient who admitted to a hospital on June 30 and underwent intensive treatment July 1 would be coded as not having undergone treatment); (4) the survey uses neither the ICD9 coding system, nor any other coding system that is consistent over time. So, for example, we could not trace the trend in PTCA over the study period; (5) the survey does not record the date of intensive treatment. Therefore, we cannot estimate the number of days between hospital admission and treatment; and (6) the survey contains no detailed information on patient severity.

Since no appropriate national surveys are currently available to investigate technological change in AMI care in Japan other than the Social Medical Treatment Survey, we asked five hospitals in the southern part of Japan and two hospitals located near Tokyo to collaborate with our study and collect microlevel data on their AMI patients. Table 8.2 shows the AMI death rate per 100,000 population in Japan and in Fukuoka Prefecture, where our case study took place. Although Fukuoka exhibits consistently lower AMI death than the Japanese average, trends over time in AMI mortality are similar.

Of the seven hospitals in this case study, three are regional main hospitals. One is a 900-bed governmental hospital with a cardiac center; the other two are 1,400-bed (one of the largest and most profitable hospitals in the country) and 500-bed private hospitals. (In Japan, only 0.8 percent of hospitals have more than 900 beds.) The remaining four hospitals are smaller private hospitals with less than 300 beds. They are a hospital specializing only in cardiology, a general hospital with a specialized cardiology department, and two typical long-term geriatric hospitals. The last two may resemble a skilled nursing home rather than a hospital in the United States. We refer to hospitals anonymously by number in the text below.

The total number of AMI patients in these hospitals is 151 in 1992, 185 in 1994, and 186 in 1996. Out of seven hospitals, only three have time-trend data in all survey years during 1992–96, although we are hoping to accomplish a more detailed and complete study on AMI patients in Japan in the near future.

Figure 8.1 shows the age/sex decomposition of our sample of AMI patients. The number of younger males (under 65) admitted with AMI has increased, and the number of the oldest males (85 and older) has decreased during the study period. On the other hand, the number of oldest females admitted with AMI has increased. As a whole, the proportion of females admitted has increased. (Complete descriptive statistics appear in appendix table A8.1.)

Figure 8.2 shows the share of patients treated in 1996 with "high tech" intensive cardiac procedures (PTCA and CABG) and thrombolytic drugs at each of the five hospitals for which detailed data are

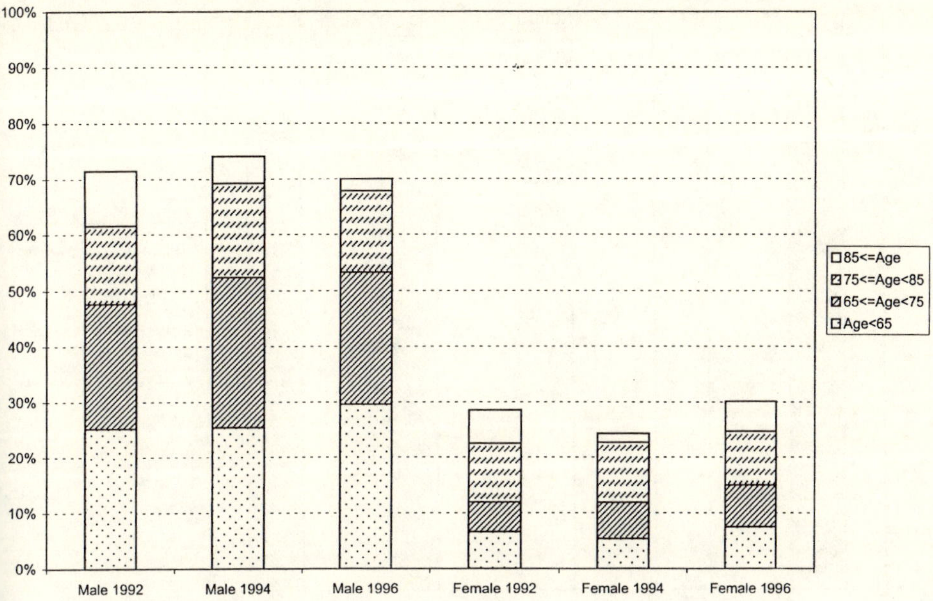

Fig. 8.1. Age/sex decomposition of the seven-hospital case study, 1992–96. Total patients number 151 in 1992, 185 in 1994, and 186 in 1996.

available. Data are from 1996 only due to the lack of sufficient information on treatments in the earlier study years.

In general, in treating AMI patients, these five hospitals have relied heavily on thrombolytics and PTCA, rather than CABG. The total patient share of three treatment groups, thrombolytics only, PTCA only, and thrombolytics plus PTCA only, is more than 70 percent for all hospitals. We also observe wide variation among these five hospitals in their use of PTCA and thrombolytics. The use of PTCA is much more intensive in hospitals 4 and 5. There are *no* patients who are treated only with thrombolytics at hospitals 4 and 5. In interviews, physicians at these hospitals stated that they treat patients with PTCA at first, and if they decide that further intervention is necessary, then they use thrombolytics. In contrast, the use of thrombolytics is much more extensive at hospital 3 than other hospitals. About 50 percent of patients are treated with thrombolytic drugs at hospital 3, with 33 percent of patients treated *exclusively* with thrombolytic drugs. Physicians at hospital 3 mentioned that they provide thrombolytics routinely at

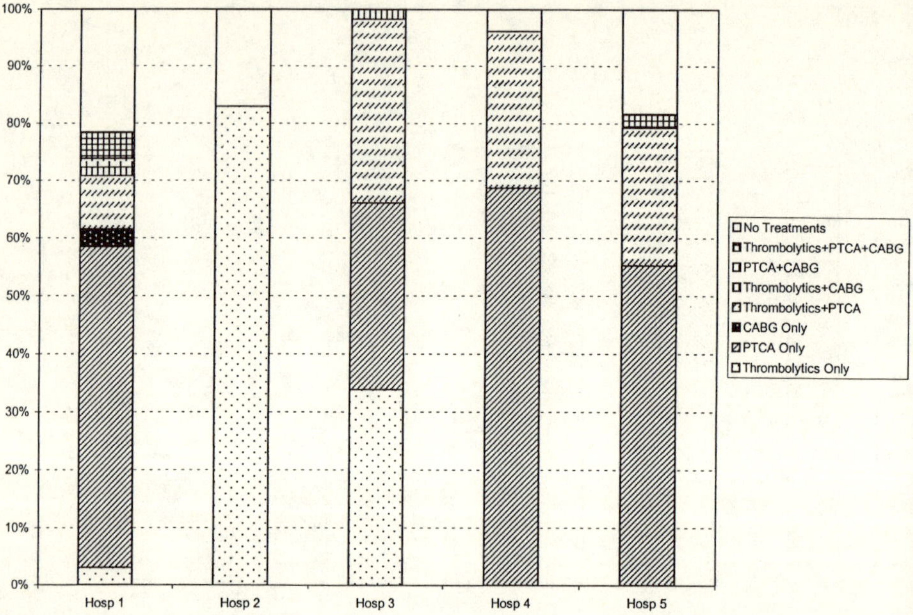

Fig. 8.2. Treatment share rate, five-hospital case study, 1996

first and then wait to see whether PTCA is needed. Hospital 2 exhibits a very different style; hospital 2 is a typical small private hospital in Japan that provides long-term care for its elderly patients. Very few acute-care patients are taken to the hospital. When such an occasion does happen, the only available treatment is intravenous coronary thrombolytics.

Changes in High-Tech Care: Intensive Cardiac Procedures and Hospital Use

Figures 8.3, 8.4, and 8.5 show the change from 1992 to 1996 in the use of major intensive cardiac procedures within 90 days after the first hospital AMI admission in the three hospitals (hospitals 1, 3, and 5) from which trend data is available. In particular, the utilization of both CATH and PTCA has grown rapidly. At hospital 1, CATH increased from 65 percent in 1992 to 90 percent in 1996. Using the combined data from the three hospitals, less than 50 percent of AMI patients underwent catheterization in 1992, compared with almost 75 percent in 1996.

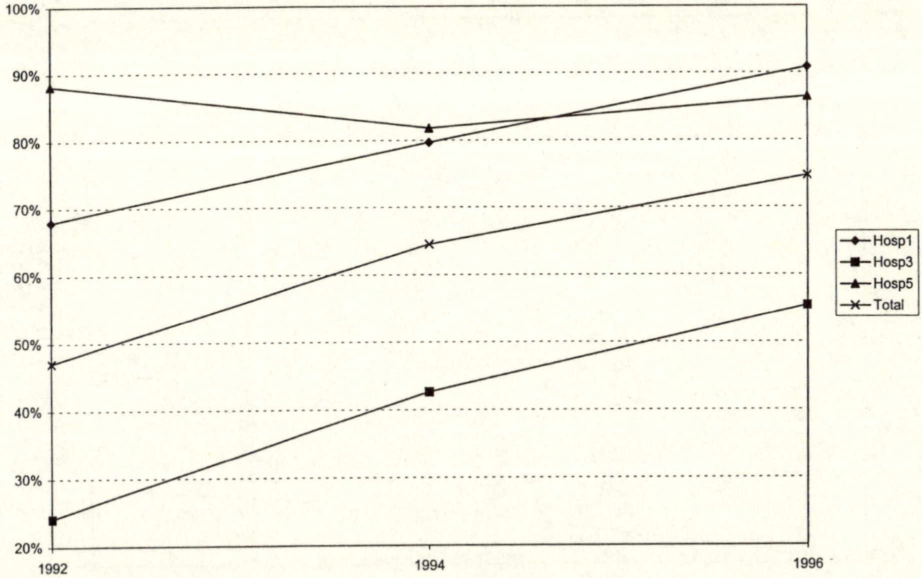

Fig. 8.3. Ninety-day cath rate, three-hospital case study in Japan. Total patients are 148 in 1992, 183 in 1994, and 168 in 1996.

CABG

The first CABG in a Japanese hospital was performed in 1970 (Sezai 1970; Hayashi 1970; and Asada 1970). In the early history of CABG in Japan, the mortality rate was alarmingly high. According to a 1976 survey of 112 hospitals, there were 523 CABG cases and 100 deaths (a mortality of 19.1 percent) (Sakae and Asada). However, the mortality rate for CABG in Japan has been decreasing and is currently on the same order as the United States (Endo and Koyanagi 1994). Perhaps because of the historical mortality from CABG, relatively few CABG procedures were performed in our sample of hospitals, and this rate has been stable over the 1992–96 period. As figure 8.4 indicates, 90-day CABG rates were roughly constant at about 4 percent.

PTCA

The first PTCA was performed in 1980 in Japan. Since then the use of PTCA has spread in Japan like a "rapid wildfire" (Sasakuri et al. 1997).

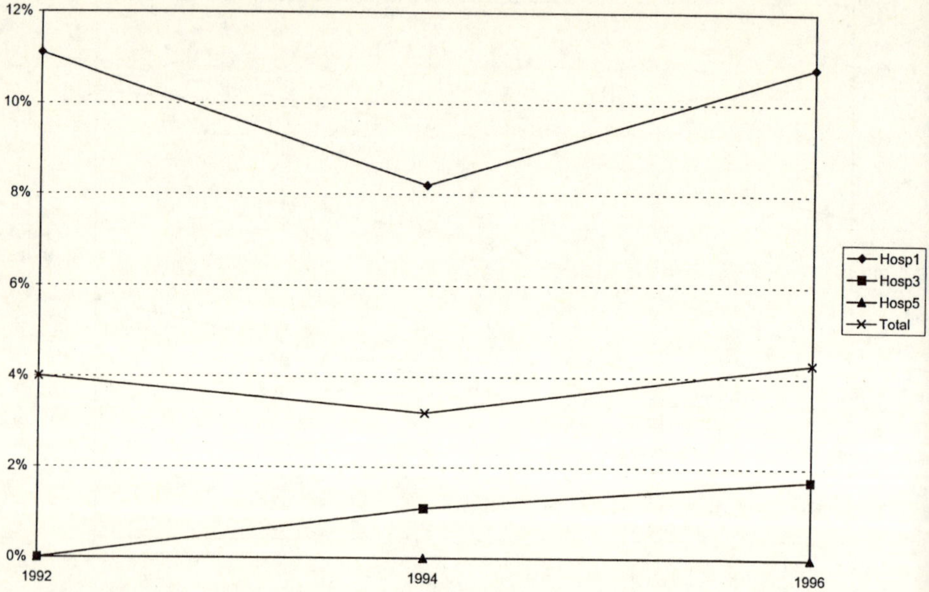

Fig. 8.4. Ninety-day CABG rate, three-hospital case study in Japan. Total patients are 148 in 1992, 183 in 1994, and 168 in 1996.

According to one estimate, about 80,000 PTCAs are performed at 600 facilities annually in Japan (Aoki 1997). In our sample of hospitals, about 25 percent of patients underwent PTCA in 1992, compared with more than 55 percent in 1996. Indeed, the growth rate of PTCA is higher than in the United States.

Figure 8.6 shows that the timing of PTCA differs among hospitals. Figure 8.6 shows the average number of days between the patient admission and the PTCA procedure for those who underwent the procedure at three hospitals in 1992, 1994, and 1996. For hospitals 1 and 5, the average is about 8 days, whereas for hospital 3, it is more than 16 days. The difference between hospital 3 and others is shown more dramatically in figure 8.6. About 85–90 percent of patients at hospitals 1 and 5 are treated with PTCA on the day of admission. At hospital 3, the number is about 15 percent; most patients at that hospital waited for 30–90 days.

Figure 8.6 also shows time trends in the timing of PTCA across hospitals. Hospital 1 dramatically shortened its time duration between

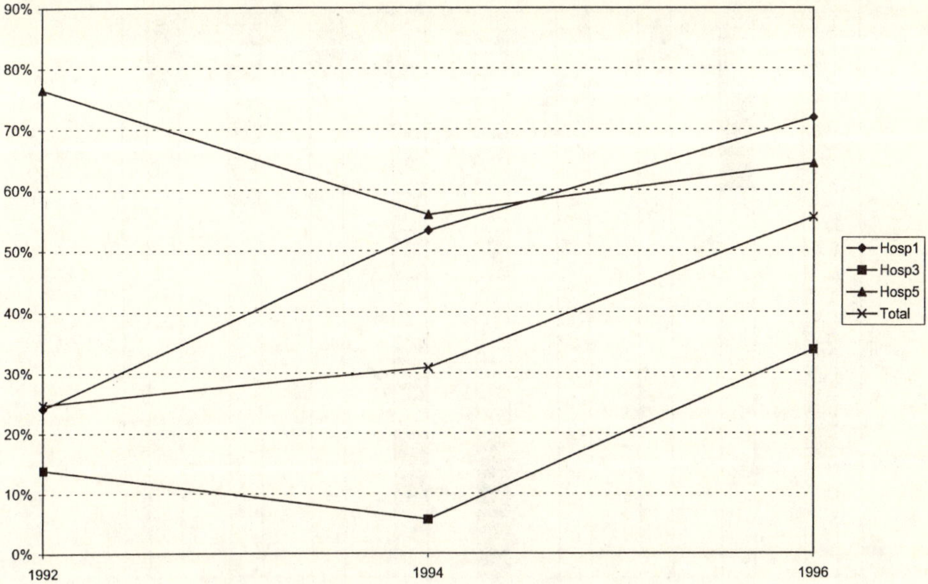

Fig. 8.5. Ninety-day PTCA rate, three-hospital case study in Japan. Total patients are 148 in 1992, 183 in 1994, and 168 in 1996.

admission and the PTCA procedure for its AMI patients. At hospital 1, less than 20 percent of patients underwent angioplasty on the first day of the inpatient admission in 1992. More than 50 percent waited more than 30 days. In 1996, more than 90 percent of patients underwent PTCA within a day. There are very few patients who had to wait for more than 30 days before undergoing PTCA. The average pre-PTCA inpatient stay has dropped from 40 days in 1992, the highest among the three hospitals, to less than 10 days in 1996. On the other hand, both hospital 3 and hospital 5 increased the average waiting time between 1992 and 1996.

Changes in Low-Tech Care

The trend of drug use for AMI patients among the hospitals in our case study is very similar to the United States except for thrombolytic and calcium channel blocker use. Among the hospitals in our case study, use of ACE inhibitors has increased by approximately a factor of four,

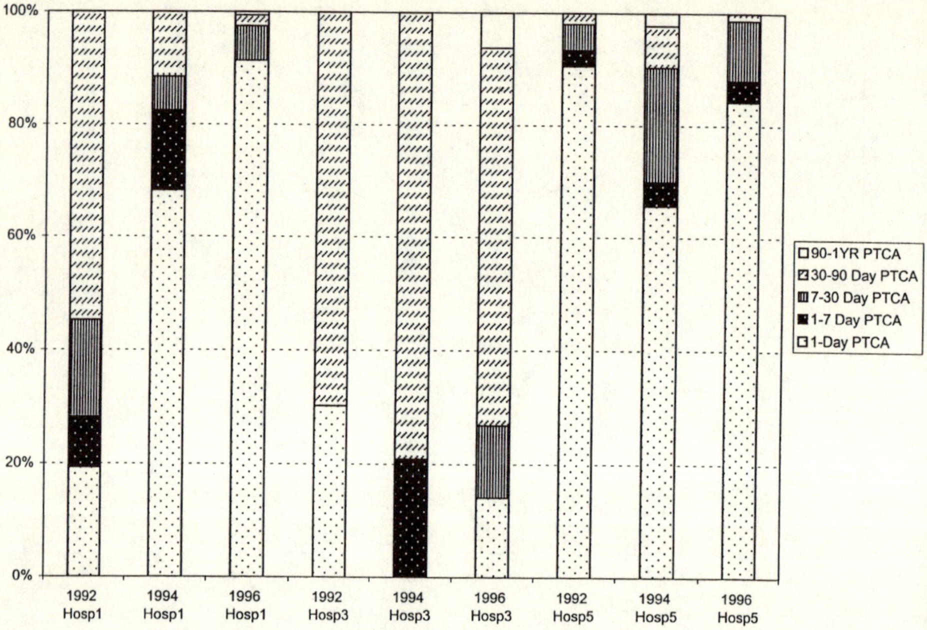

Fig. 8.6. Timing of PTCA, three-hospital case study, 1992, 1994, and 1996

from 8 percent of patients in 1992 to 31 percent of patients in 1996. Likewise, the use of beta-blockers (from 5 percent to 18 percent); aspirin (from 39 percent to 72 percent); calcium channel blockers (from 35 percent to 60 percent); IV nitroglycerin (from 57 percent to 95 percent); and heparin (from 53 percent to 81 percent) has also increased during the study period (appendix table A8.1). In the United States, the use of these drugs has increased from the 1980s through the 1990s (Goldberg et al. 1987; Gurwitz et al. 1994; McGovern et al. 1996; McLaughlin et al. 1996; Rogers et al. 1994), except for calcium channel blocker use, which decreased from 64 percent in the 1980s to 31 percent in 1993 (Rogers et al. 1994).

However, while the rate of thrombolytic use in Japan has decreased from 50 percent of patients (1992) to 35 percent of patients (1996), the rate in the United States has increased from 24 percent to 31 percent during the same period (Rogers et al. 1994; Chandra et al. 1997). This trend may be related to the rapid growth of performing angioplasty in Japan. The patients who were admitted to hospitals that have the capability for catheterization and revascularization are more likely to undergo angioplasty (PTCA) directly without thrombolytic drug use, or to undergo both treatments (fig. 8.2). In addition, the falling reimbursement rate for thrombolytics may act as a disincentive for their use relative to PTCA.

Changes in Appropriateness of Care

PTCA is much more frequently used in Japan than in other developed countries. Other researchers have also found this result. For example, Endo and Koyanagi (1994) and Nippon Shinkekkan Intervention Gakkai Gakujutsu Iinkai (1993) maintain that the ratio of PTCA to CABG is much higher in Japan, almost five to one. This average ratio masks even more substantial regional differences in treatment. The PTCA to CABG ratio is four to one in the eastern region of Japan, whereas it is eight to one in the western region.

The historically high mortality from CABG may be one source of this difference, as may be the reimbursement for PTCA over CABG, relative to the procedures' costs. In addition, there may be institutional factors that explain this unique treatment pattern. The PTCA procedure is, in general, in the domain of internal medicine cardiologists, whereas CABG is in the domain of cardiovascular surgeons. These two specialties—internal medicine and surgery—are almost completely separated in Japan in terms of both education and career path. Many expressed their concerns over a serious lack of communication and coordination between the two parties. Some surgeons find that internal cardiologists perform unnecessary, inappropriate angioplasties (Sasakuri et al. 1997; Nishida, Endo, and Koyanagi 1997). On the other hand, internal medicine specialists question the high mortality rate for CABG, though many cardiovascular surgeons insist that their performance has improved to the level of Western nations.

3. The Consequences of Changes in AMI Care in Japan

Changes in Health Outcomes for AMI Patients

Figure 8.7 shows trends in 30-day mortality for those patients who we know were not transferred from another hospital. Surprisingly, even though both high-tech care and drug use in AMI cases increased, the 30-day mortality rate increased on average among the three hospitals

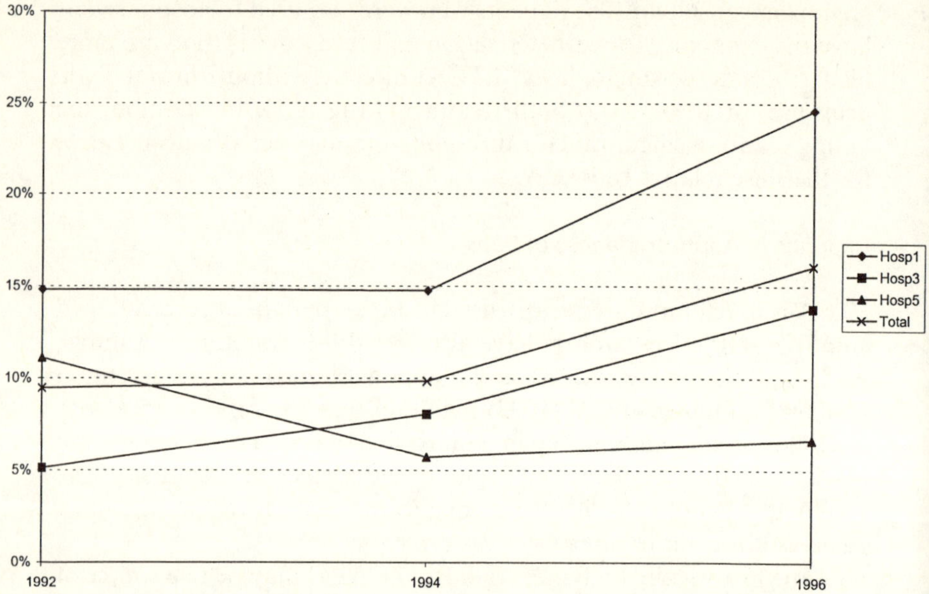

Fig. 8.7. Thirty-day mortality rate, three-hospital case study in Japan. Total patients are 148 in 1992, 183 in 1994, and 168 in 1996.

from 10 percent in 1992 to 16 percent in 1996. Only hospital 5 showed an improvement in the mortality rate.

However, this result may not be a reliable representation of the overall trend of AMI patient outcomes in Japan. First, since this survey traced patients only until they were discharged from hospital, deaths that occurred after discharge were unobservable. However, due to extraordinarily long average lengths of stay (e.g., exceeding 30 days), this may not be a serious limitation. Second, this survey does not include only patients admitted to the hospital with a new AMI. Third and most important, even though our study tried to control for patients who were transferred in from other acute care hospitals, most observations were missing information on this variable. Because of data limitations, we included these observations in our calculation of mortality statistics. This approach has the potential to induce a serious bias because patients who are transferred in from other acute care hospitals may be more ill than new AMI patients. Specifically, because hospitals 1, 3, and 5 all have the ability to perform intensive cardiac procedures, it is likely that their patient populations include a substantial and increasing number of transfer patients, which would make their patient populations look increasingly sicker over time, even if their quality or an adjusted mortality rate measure were improving.

Changes in Medical Expenditures

The nature and quality of care as well as the ownership of hospitals appears to be highly correlated with the level of medical expenditures. For AMI patients, higher expenditures appear to be attributable to more intensive high-tech care and private hospitals. Figure 8.8 shows the share of actual reimbursement points per patient by treatment in 1996. Each point is worth 10 yen (about 13–14 cents at current exchange rates). Total points per patient in the three hospitals (hospitals 1, 4, and 5) where CATH, PTCA, and CABG rates were relatively high in 1996 are much higher than hospital 2, where no high-tech procedures were performed; and, in the three high-expenditure hospitals, expenses related to the surgical category are the most significant. Hospitals 1 and 4, which are private hospitals, show higher points for AMI treatment than hospital 5, which is a public hospital. (Note that data on expenditures are not available from hospital 3.)

Length of Stay

Although length of stay (LOS) for AMI patients has been falling in Japan, it is still substantially higher than that of most other developed countries. On average, the total length of hospital stay has decreased from 54 to 44 days over the observed time period, 1992–96 (appendix table A8.1). However, as figure 8.9 shows, focusing on averages masks important differences across hospitals. The average LOS at hospital 1 decreased from 58 to 40 days. Hospital 5's LOS actually went up from 27 to 39 days on average. In addition, figures 8.8 and 8.9 together suggest that high lengths of stay, potentially due to Japan's fee-for-service reimbursement system, are an important cause of high expenditure levels. Length of hospital stay is significantly correlated with total medical expenditure. Indeed, hospitalization in all hospitals appears to account for the second-highest share of total expenditure (fig. 8.8).

The overall trend of LOS is consistent with the hypothesis that LOS may decline as a result of improved treatment methods over time. In addition, in order to contain its health care expenditures, the Japanese government has recently introduced various measures to shorten

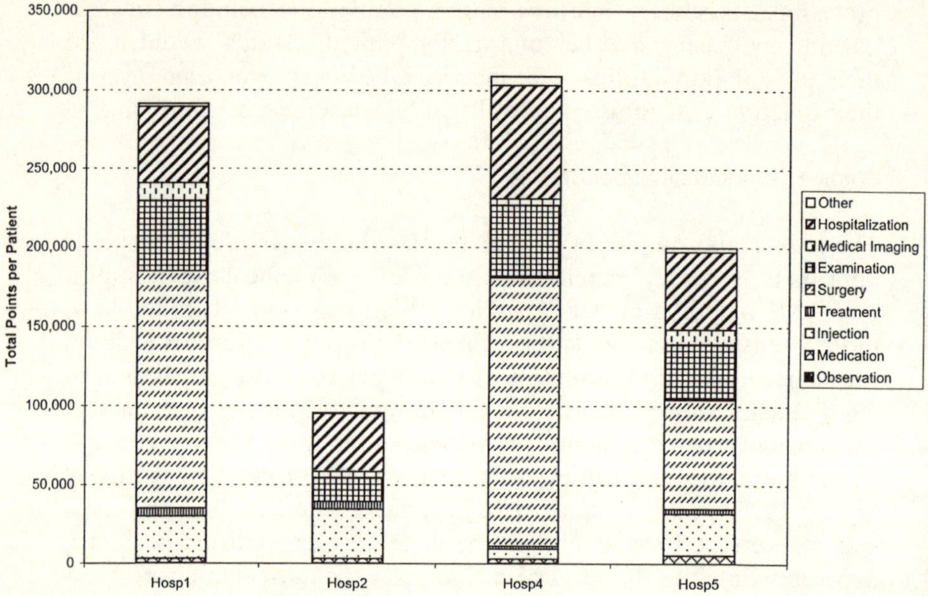

Fig. 8.8. Share of actual total points per patient by treatment, four-hospital case study, 1996

inpatient lengths of stay, by offering relatively higher per diem reimbursement for shorter hospitalization. The possibility of introducing a prospective payment system is currently being discussed in Japan. Nevertheless, the fundamental incentives provided by the current fee-for-service reimbursement system provides Japanese hospitals with weak incentives for cost containment.

As in the United States, the increase in medical expenditures over time has been caused mainly by changes in the nature and quality of care such as technological change, rather than by real growth in medical care prices (Cutler et al. 1996; Cutler and McClellan 1998). Figure 8.10 represents changes in total points per patient by treatment form 1992 through 1996. (Only data from hospitals 1 and 5 are available for this analysis.) The growth rates of 90-day CATH and PTCA are the highest in hospital 1, as is the growth of medical expenditures.

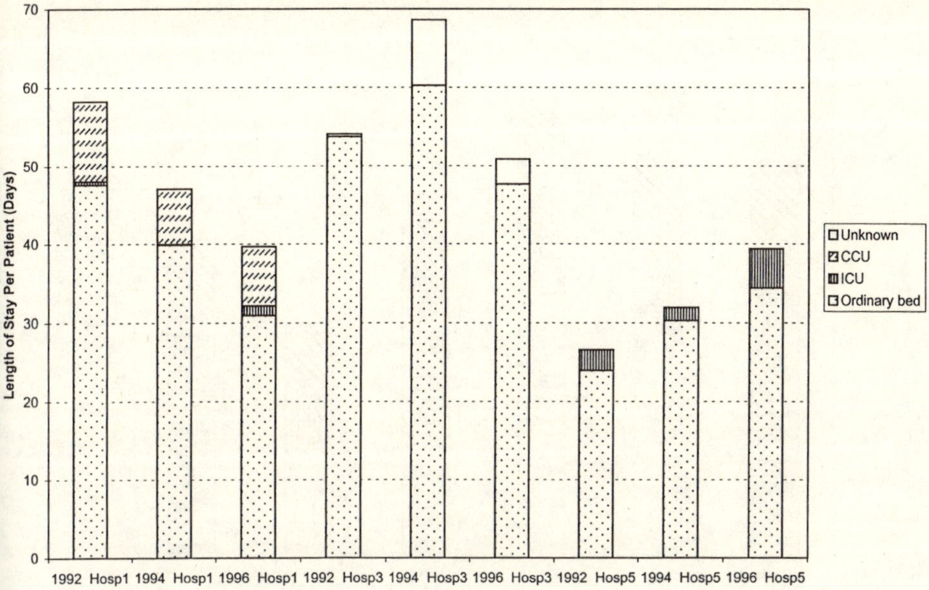

Fig. 8.9. Trend of length of hospital stay, five-hospital case study, 1992, 1994, and 1996

4. Conclusions and Future Development of Hospital Case Study in Japan

The empirical results based on the hospital case study provide evidence consistent with previous studies of the Japanese health care system. Among AMI patients, the hospitals in our case study have relied heavily on thrombolytic drugs and angioplasty rather than bypass surgery.

Both catheterization and angioplasty rates increased rapidly, from 47 percent to 75 percent, and from 25 percent to 57 percent, respectively, during 1992–96, while the rate of bypass surgery remained almost the same (4–5 percent). This is undoubtedly a reflection of the fact that there are 476 facilities that have a capability to perform catheterization and revascularization in Japan, while the number of facilities that perform bypass surgeries still remains lower than other

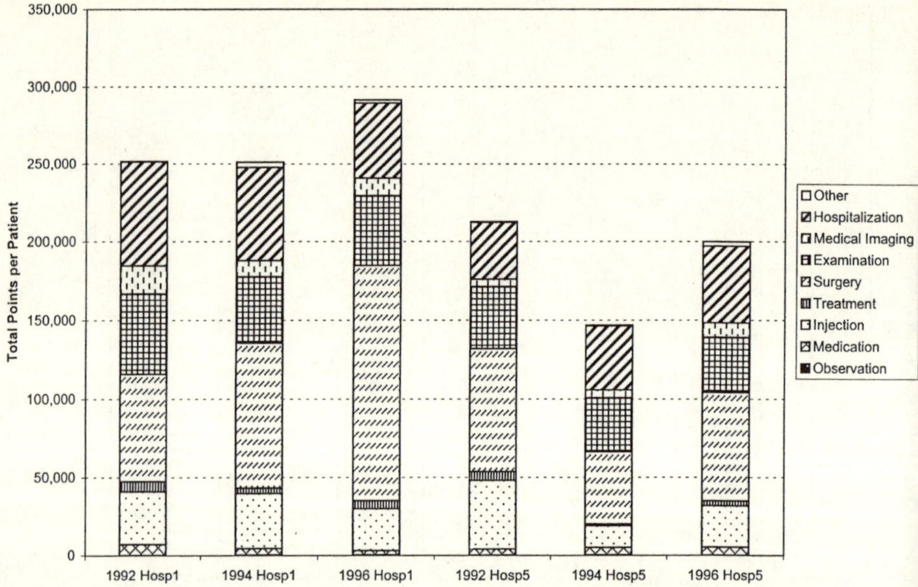

Fig. 8.10. Trend of actual total points per patient by treatment, two-hospital case study, 1992, 1994, and 1996

countries (Endo and Koyanagi 1994). Use of several drug treatments (e.g., aspirin, beta-blockers, IV NTG, ACE inhibitors, and calcium channel blockers) has increased, while use of thrombolytic drugs has decreased.

This pattern of treatments may be due to one or more of three factors: (1) changes in reimbursement rates over time; (2) the historically high mortality from CABG; and (3) institutional features of the Japanese health care system. First, reimbursement for thrombolytic drugs has declined over time; reimbursement for PTCA and CABG has increased. Second, mortality among AMI patients treated with CABG in Japan has been historically quite high (although the mortality rates for patients treated with this procedure has become similar recently to the mortality rate in most other developed countries). Third, there may be institutional factors that explain this unique treatment pattern. The PTCA procedure is, in general, in the domain of internal medicine cardiologists, whereas CABG is in the domain of cardiovascular surgeons. The two specialties are almost completely separated in Japan in terms of both education and career path.

As in other countries, the increase in medical expenditures over time has been caused mainly by changes in the nature and quality of care, such as technological change, not by real growth in medical care prices. Our time-trend analyses did not find evidence that overall mortality rate from AMI has been decreasing, in contrast to changes that have occurred in most other developed countries. However, our mortality results may not be reliable for several reasons. Most important, even though our study tried to control for the share of patients who were transferred in from other acute care hospitals, most patients were missing information on this variable. Because of data limitations, we included these patients in our calculation of mortality statistics. For this reason, the mortality rates of patients at our large "high tech" hospitals may not be representative of the population mortality rate from AMI in Japan; because patients admitted to high-tech hospitals include a substantial and increasing number of transfer patients, their patient populations would look increasingly sicker over time, even if hospital quality was improving.

The above simple statistical analyses reveal the shortcomings of the current data. In order to overcome these shortcomings, our goal is to expand the hospitals (and patients) covered by our study in the future.

TABLE A8.1. Definitions and Descriptive Statistics for AMI Patients: The Seven-Hospital Case Study in Japan

Rate (%)	Full Cohorts				Hospital 1 Means			Hospital 2 Means		Hospital 3 Means				Hospital 4 Means		Hospital 5 Means				Hospital 6 Means	Hospital 7 Means
	1992 (N = 151)	1994 (N = 185)	1996 (N = 186)	1998 (N = 204)	1992 (N = 54)	1994 (N = 61)	1996 (N = 65)	1996 (N = 8)	1998 (N = 1)	1992 (N = 79)	1994 (N = 89)	1996 (N = 58)	1998 (N = 10)	1996 (N = 9)	1998 (N = 3)	1992 (N = 18)	1994 (N = 35)	1996 (N = 46)	1998 (N = 4)	1998 (N = 10)	1998 (N = 176)
Patient Characteristics																					
Age in Years	67.1	66.4	68.5	68.7	66.4	66.9	67.9	65.5	57.0	67.4	66.4	67.9	70.4	68.2	64.3	67.9	65.3	70.5	69.3	70.0	67.2
Female = 1	28.5	24.3	30.1	34.5	27.8	26.2	30.8	25.0	0.0	25.3	28.1	24.1	30.0	22.2	33.3	44.4	11.4	39.1	25.0		34.7
Comorbidity (Top 5 Second <= Diagnoses)																					
IHD	6.6	6.5	21.5	2.9	16.7	13.1	15.4	50.0	100.0	1.3	0.0	8.6	30.0	11.1	0.0	0.0	11.4	43.5	25.0	0.0	5.7
CHF	9.9	3.8	9.1	3.9	24.1	9.8	13.8	12.5	100.0	2.5	0.0	1.7	40.0	0.0	33.3	0.0	2.9	13.0	50.0	0.0	0.0
Diabetes/Mellitus	17.9	9.7	33.9	3.9	22.2	6.6	24.6	25.0	100.0	13.9	6.7	36.2	60.0	0.0	33.3	22.2	22.9	52.2	0.0	0.0	0.0
Hypertension	16.6	24.3	37.6	4.4	11.1	19.7	32.3	37.5	0.0	15.2	15.7	32.8	50.0	0.0	33.3	38.9	54.3	58.7	75.0	0.0	0.0
Old MI	4.6	4.3	4.3	3.4	1.9	4.9	0.0	0.0	0.0	6.3	0.0	5.2	0.0	11.1	0.0	5.6	14.3	8.7	25.0	0.0	3.4
Pneumonia	4.0	1.1	4.3	1.0	7.4	1.6	6.2	0.0	0.0	1.3	0.0	0.0	0.0	0.0	0.0	5.6	2.9	8.7	0.0	0.0	1.1
Treatments																					
Cath	47.3	67.6	75.3	55.6	68.5	80.3	90.8	0.0	0.0	24.1	52.8	56.9	30.0	88.9	100.0	88.2	82.9	87.0	100.0		9.2
PTCA	24.7	32.4	56.5	22.2	24.1	54.1	72.3	0.0	0.0	13.9	7.9	36.2	10.0	77.8	33.3	76.5	57.1	65.2	50.0		
CABG	4.0	3.2	4.8	0.0	11.1	8.2	10.8	0.0	0.0	0.0	1.1	1.7	0.0	0.0	0.0	0.0	0.0	2.2	0.0		4.5
Timing of cath in Days	19.5	28.9	9.6	0.0	19.5	38.2	4.9			27.8	36.9	15.6		1.1	0.0	9.1	1.9	13.2			
Timing of PTCA in Days	18.0	23.6	9.7	0.0	39.8	34.2	8.1			11.9	42.6	16.4		8.9	0.0	1.4	1.4	7.7	0.0		
Timing of CABG in Days	24.5	22.5	13.6		24.5	11.2	14.7				79.0	6.0									
1-day cath	14.1	36.8	57.8	27.3	22.7	63.6	87.2	0.0	0.0	3.2	6.7	7.4	0.0	85.7	100.0	75.0	64.7	70.0	0.0		
7-day cath	20.2	42.9	64.3	27.3	39.3	70.7	89.3	0.0	0.0	3.2	8.7	16.7	0.0	88.9	100.0	77.8	66.7	76.9	0.0		
30-day cath	34.2	58.0	71.1	27.3	59.5	78.2	90.2	0.0	0.0	6.3	25.0	37.5	0.0	88.9	100.0	85.7	81.3	85.4	0.0		
90-day cath	47.0	64.5	74.7	27.3	67.9	79.7	90.8	0.0	0.0	24.1	45.5	55.4	0.0	88.9	100.0	88.2	81.8	86.4	0.0		
1-day PTCA	11.0	16.7	42.6	17.6	4.7	36.4	66.0	0.0	0.0	4.2	0.0	5.1	0.0	66.7	33.3	69.2	37.5	54.3	50.0		
7-day PTCA	12.4	20.9	43.4	17.6	6.8	44.0	66.0	0.0	0.0	4.2	1.2	5.1	0.0	66.7	33.3	71.4	40.0	56.8	50.0		
30-day PTCA	15.0	25.1	50.3	17.6	10.9	47.2	70.5	0.0	0.0	4.2	1.2	9.8	0.0	77.8	33.3	75.0	51.6	63.6	50.0		
90-day PTCA	24.7	30.9	55.5	17.6	24.1	53.3	71.9	0.0	0.0	13.9	5.7	33.9	0.0	77.8	33.3	76.5	55.9	64.4	50.0		
1-day CABG	0.7	1.1	1.1		2.0	3.4	3.3	0.0	0.0	0.0	0.0	0.0	0.0	0.0	0.0	0.0	0.0		0.0		
7-day CABG	1.4	1.6	3.3		4.0	5.1	7.9	0.0	0.0	0.0	0.0	1.7	0.0	0.0	0.0	0.0	0.0		0.0		
30-day CABG	3.4	2.2	3.8		9.4	6.7	9.4	0.0	0.0	0.0	0.0	1.7	0.0	0.0	0.0	0.0	0.0		0.0		
90-day CABG	4.0	3.2	4.3		11.1	8.2	10.8	0.0	0.0	0.0	1.1	1.7	0.0	0.0	0.0	0.0	0.0		0.0		
Thrombolytics	50.0	31.9	34.9	50.0	46.3	57.4	12.3	37.5	100.0	55.7	20.2	81.0	70.0	22.2	33.3	35.3	17.1	10.9	0.0		
Heparin	52.7	54.6	81.2	22.2	85.2	93.4	93.8	62.5	100.0	20.3	13.5	55.2	0.0	88.9	100.0	100.0	91.4	97.8	0.0		
Inotropic agents	22.7	29.7	42.5	38.9	48.1	68.9	63.1	50.0	100.0	3.8	0.0	12.1	30.0	66.7	100.0	29.4	37.1	45.7	0.0		
Beta-blocker	5.3	15.7	18.3	0.0	9.3	21.3	29.2	12.5	0.0	0.0	0.0	1.7	0.0	0.0	0.0	17.6	45.7	28.3	0.0		
Warfarin	7.3	19.5	12.4	0.0	20.4	36.1	13.8	0.0	0.0	0.0	2.2	6.9	0.0	0.0	0.0	0.0	34.3	21.7	0.0		
Aspirin	39.3	46.5	71.5	33.3	51.9	70.5	83.1	12.5	100.0	24.1	14.6	60.3	30.0	88.9	66.7	70.6	85.7	76.1	0.0		
Ca+ blocker	34.7	37.3	59.7	11.1	77.8	59.0	70.8	12.5	0.0	7.6	13.5	67.2	20.0	88.9	0.0	23.5	60.0	37.0	0.0		
IV ntg	56.7	57.3	95.2	33.3	81.5	91.8	96.9	87.5	100.0	32.9	19.1	93.1	30.0	100.0	66.7	88.2	94.3	95.7	0.0		
ACE inhibitors	8.0	13.0	30.6	16.7	22.2	21.3	44.6	0.0	100.0	0.0	2.2	13.8	0.0	11.1	66.7	0.0	25.7	41.3	0.0		
Ticlopidine	14.7	8.6	22.0	0.0	14.8	6.6	16.9	0.0	0.0	8.9	3.4	34.5	0.0	22.2	0.0	41.2	25.7	17.4	0.0		

Outcomes																					
1-day mortality	2.0	2.7	3.8	10.5	1.9	3.3	1.5	25.0	0.0	2.6	3.4	6.9	30.0	0.0	33.3	0.0	0.0	0.0	0.0		5.1
7-day mortality	7.4	8.2	9.7	14.1	11.1	11.5	12.3	37.5	0.0	3.9	8.0	10.3	30.0	0.0	33.3	11.1	2.9	2.2	0.0		11.4
30-day mortality	9.5	9.8	16.1	18.2	14.8	14.8	24.6	37.5	0.0	5.3	8.0	13.8	30.0	0.0	33.3	11.1	5.7	6.5	0.0		15.9
90-day mortality	10.8	10.3	17.7	18.7	16.7	16.4	26.2	37.5	0.0	5.3	8.0	13.8	30.0	0.0	33.3	16.7	5.7	10.9	0.0		16.5
1-year mortality	12.6	11.4	19.4	18.7	16.7	16.4	26.2	50.0	0.0	8.9	10.1	17.2	30.0	0.0	33.3	16.7	5.7	10.9	0.0		
Length of stay in days	53.7	45.3	44.0	19.2	58.3	47.0	39.7	39.7	12.0	54.1	68.6	50.9	17.0	27.1	15.3	26.6	31.9	39.4	27.5	32.0	14.7
Ordinary bed	45.3	41.1	37.5	18.2	47.6	39.9	31.0	38.4	11.0	54.1	60.3	49.3	17.3	24.1	13.0	23.9	30.3	34.4	26.3		
ICU	1.0	0.5	2.5	0.2	0.5	0.1	1.2	1.3	2.0				0.0	0.0	0.0	2.6	1.6	5.0	0.0		
CCU	7.5	3.7	4.0	0.8	10.2	7.1	7.5	0.0	0.0				0.0	3.0	3.3	0.0	0.0	0.0	0.0		
Total points	243,690	213,023	243,018	104,076	251,740	251,337	291,631	95,113	60,194				94,679	242,857	173,321	200,217	144,283	200,079	115,842	45,606	
per patient																					
Observation	235	279	229	400	248	329	317	236	480				327	239	950	162	190	101	153		
Medication	6,632	4,455	3,671	2,688	7,093	4,214	2,763	2,865	1,133				2,660	2,740	1,002	3,862	4,887	5,277	4,409		
Injection	35,225	27,657	25,661	8,779	33,738	35,243	26,984	31,591	31,595				8,913	6,497	4,347	44,143	14,048	26,509	6,063		
Treatment	4,633	1,437	2,453	2,169	4,716	1,919	2,818	3,093	279				3,007	1,124	2,611	4,132	574	2,086	212		
Treatment (drug)	1,689	1,201	1,710	1,782	1,742	1,541	2,300	1,752	481				3,030	589	0	1,368	590	1,088	323		
Surgery (anesthesia)	20,929	22,948	30,095	22,912	22,472	29,914	43,595	0	0				7,822	36,291	101,065	11,671	10,448	15,040	7,750		
Surgery (drug)	48,877	52,782	82,691	19,155	45,935	62,353	106,066	0	0				25,593	133,513	0	66,528	35,610	54,099	22,216		
Examination	34,165	24,989	27,328	18,105	35,728	27,308	29,604	13,965	8,993				12,546	45,959	36,114	25,723	20,829	22,791	20,773		
Examination (drug)	15,161	14,541	12,056	4,603	15,397	14,971	14,941	1,086	0				3,591	29	0	13,883	13,770	12,238	11,739		
Medical imaging	7,612	4,190	5,312	1,456	8,560	5,426	6,422	2,843	840				1,229	3,989	1,553	2,494	1,974	4,432	2,103		
Medical imaging (drug)	8,087	4,145	4,252	607	9,189	4,837	4,911	1,018	0				0	8	0	2,135	2,904	4,714	2,732		
Hospitalization	61,847	52,890	49,781	27,713	66,545	59,655	48,897	36,878	16,393				25,737	72,479	25,678	36,477	40,754	48,833	37,009		
Others	299	2,393	2,385	205	346	3,595	1,978	281	0				225	5,617	0	45	237	2,695	360		

Note

We would like to thank Ms. Atsuko Morofuji, Mr. Takuma Sugahara, and Fumito Kurosawa for outstanding research assistance. We appreciate the valuable support from the Institute for Health Economics and Policy in Japan, in particular, Mr. Nobuaki Tanaka and Mr. Hideki Sumiyoshi. Most of all, we appreciate the efforts of seven hospitals to provide us their precious medical information. All errors are our own.

References

Aoki, H. 1997. "PTCA no Kozai to PTCA no Chiryo no Genzai." *Mebio* 14, no. 12: 117.

Aoki, H., and K. Hiramori. 1992. "Relationship between Unstable Angina and Acute Myocardial Infarction." *Nippon Naika Gakkai Zasshi 10* 81, no. 8: 1164–68.

Asada, S. 1970. "Shinkinkosoku Setsujo no Ichirei—Sobo Benchikan Shijutsu ga Dojini Shinko Sareta Chikenrei ni tsuite." *Kyobugeka* 23:115.

Bhattacharya, J., W. B. Vogt, A. Yoshikawa, and T. Nakahara. 1995. "The Utilization of Outpatient Medical Services in Japan." *Journal of Human Resources* 31, no. 2: 450–76.

Chandra, H., J. Yarzebski, R. J. Goldberg, J. Savageau, C. Singleton, J. H. Gurwitz, and J. M. Gore. 1997. "Age-Related Trends (1986–1993) in the Use of Thrombolytics Agents in Patients with Acute Myocardial Infarction: The Worcester Heart Attack Study." *Archives of Internal Medicine* 157, no. 7: 741–46.

Cutler, D. M., and M. B. McClellan. 1998. "Technological Change in Medicare." In *Topics in the Economics of Aging,* ed. D. Wise. Chicago: University of Chicago Press.

Cutler, D. M., M. B. McClellan, J. Newhouse, and D. Remler. 1996. "Are Medical Prices Declining?" NBER Working Paper 5750.

Endo, M., and H. Koyanagi. 1994. "CABG: Sekai no Doko to Honpo no Jittai." *Nihon Rinsho* 52:961–69.

Endo, M., H. Nishida, and H. Koyanagi. 1997. "Nihonno Genkyouwo Domiruka." *Mebio* 14, no. 12: 25–34.

Garber, A. M., V. R. Fuchs, and J. F. Silverman. 1984. "Case-Mix, Costs, and Outcomes: Differences between Faculty and Community Services in a University Hospital." *New England Journal of Medicine* 310, no. 19: 1231–37.

Goldberg, R. J., J. M. Gore, J. S. Alpert, and J. E. Dalen. 1987. "Therapeutic Trends in the Management of Patients with Acute Myocardial Infarction (1975–1984): The Worcester Heart Attack Study." *Clinical Cardiology* 10, no. 1:3–8.

Gurwitz, J. H., R. J. Goldberg, Z. Chen, J. M. Gore, and J. S. Alpert. 1994. "Recent Trends in Hospital Mortality of Acute Myocardial Infarction:

The Worcester Heart Attack Study. Have Improvements Been Realized for All Age Groups?" *Archives of Internal Medicine* 154, no. 19: 2202–8.

Hayashi, H. 1970. "Kyoshinsho ni Taisuru Kankekkan Chokusetsu Hogoho ni yoru ichi chikenrei." *Shinzo* 3:351.

Hiramori, K. 1990. "Shinkinkosoku-sho no Shoko." *Saishin Naikagaku Taikei* 34:37–55.

Igaku no Ayumi. 1995. Tokyo: Ishiyaku shuppan gaisha.

Iwasaka, K. 1996. "Kandomyaku Shikkan Chiryo-ho no Nippon to Sekai no Hikaku-naika Gawa." In *Kandomyaku Shikkan no Chiryo: Naika to Geka no Tachiba Karano Kangaekata,* ed. N. Kitamura and Y. Imamura. Osaka: Medica Shuppan.

Kamijima, G. 1996. "Wagakuni ni okeru Junkannki Kyukyu Iryo no Genjo: Kyukyu Kyumei-si seido." *Rinsho-i* 22, no. 10: 114.

Kenko Hoken Kumiai Rengo Kai. 1995. "A Report on the Structural Change in the Costs for the Elderly's Hospitalization and the Cause of the Change." Tokyo: Kenko Hoken Kumiai Rengo Kai.

Kitamura, N. 1996. "Kandomyaku Shikkan Chiryo-ho no Sentaku ni okeru Honpo no Tokuisei." In *Kandomyaku Shikkan no Chiryo: Naika to Geka no Tachiba Kararo Kangaekata,* ed. N. Kitamura and Y. Imamura. Osaka: Medica Shuppan.

McClellan, M. B. 1995. "Uncertainty, Health Care Technologies, and Health Care Choices." *American Economic Review* 85, no. 2: 38–44.

McClellan, M. B., and J. P. Newhouse. 1997. "The Marginal Costs and Benefits of Medical Technology: A Panel Instrumental Variable Approach." *Journal of Econometrics* 77, no. 1: 39–64.

McClellan, M. B., and H. Noguchi. 1998a. "Technological Change in Heart Disease Treatment: Does High Tech Mean Low Value?" *American Economic Review* 88, no. 2: 90–96.

———. 1998b. "Validity and Interpretation of Treatment Effect Estimates Using Observational Data: Treatment of Heart Attacks in the Elderly." Stanford University. Photocopy.

McGovern, P. G., J. G. Pankow, E. Shahar, K. M. Doliszny, A. R. Folsom, H. Blackburn, and R. V. Luepker. 1996. "Recent Trends in Acute Coronary Heart Disease: Mortality, Morbidity, Medical Care, and Risk Factors. The Minnesota Heart Survey Investigators." *New England Journal of Medicine* 334, no. 14: 884–90.

McLaughlin, T. J., S. B. Soumerai, D. J. Willison, J. H. Gurwitz, C. Borbas, E. Guadagnoli, B. McLaughlin, N. Morris, S. C. Cheng, P. J. Hauptman, E. Antman, L. Casey, R. Asinger, and F. Gobel. "Adherence to National Guidelines for Drug Treatment of Suspected Acute Myocardial Infarction: Evidence of Undertreatments in Women and the Elderly." 1996. *Archives of Internal Medicine* 156, no. 7: 799–805.

Ministry of Health and Welfare. 1991. *Jinko Dotai Tokei.* (Vital statistics in Japan). Tokyo: Health and Welfare Statistics Association.

———. 1993. *Kanja Chosa.* Tokyo: Health and Welfare Statistics Association.

———. 1996. *Kokumin Eisei no Doko.* (Trends in people's health status in Japan). Tokyo: Health and Welfare Statistics Association.

———. 1997. *Shinryo Hoshu Tensu Tayamihyo* (Quick reference table of fee schedules). Tokyo: Health and Welfare Statistics Association.

———. 1900. *Iryo Shisetsu Chosa* (Medical faculty survey). Tokyo: Health and Welfare Statistics Association.

Motomiya, T. 1996. "Kessen Yokai Ryo-ho." *Rinsho-i* 22, no. 10.

Nikkei Health. 1995. May, 14–18.

Nippon Shinkekkan Intervention Gakkai Gakujutsu Iinkai. 1993. *Shin Shikkan* 8:465.

———. 1996. "Dai Nikai Nippon Shinkekkan Intervention Gakkai Gakujutu I innkai anketo hokoko kekka ni tsuite." *Shinkekkan* 8:465.

Nishida, H., M. Endo, and H. Koyanagi. 1997. "Nippon no genjo wo do miruka." *Meibo* 14, no. 12: 25–34.

Rogers, W. J., L. J. Bowlby, N. C. Chandra, W. J. French, J. M. Gore, C. T. Lambrew, R. M. Rubison, A. J. Tienfenbrunn, and W. D. Weaver. 1994. "Treatment of Myocardial Infarction in the United States (1990 to 1993): Observations from the National Registry of Myocardial Infarction." *Circulation* 90, no. 4: 2103–14.

Sasakuri, S., Y. Hosoda, T. Watanabe, K. Takazawa, I. Hayashi, T. Yamamoto, K. Minami, H. Miyagawa, and T. Fukuda. 1997. "Graft Selection in Coronary Artery Bypass Surgery in the Aged." *Nippon Kyobu Geka Gakkai Zasshi* 45, no. 3: 384–86.

Sezai, Y. 1970. "Kandomyaku no Chokusetsu Shijutsu, Ditaidomyakuhen ni yoru Jokodaidomyaku—Kandomyaku bypassho no Ichi Shorei." *Kyobugeka* 23:888.

Shakai Hoken Kenkyu Jo. 1997. "Ykka Kisun Tensu Hayami Hyo." Tokyo: Shakai Hoken Kenkyu Jo.

Stertzer, S., and R. Myler. 1994. "Coronary and Peripheral Angioplasty: Historic Perspective." In *Textbook of International Cardiology.* 2d ed. Philadelphia: W. B. Saunders.

Suma, H. 1996. "Kandomyaku Bypass-jutsu." *Rinsho-i* 22, no. 10: 68.

Tanaka, H., C. Date, H. Chen, T. Nakayama, T. Yokoyama, N. Yoshiike, H. Iwaoka, M. Iwaya, M. M. Zaman, M. Yamaguchi, Y. Matsumura, M. Sugiyama, W. Kushiro, T. Ichimura, A. Noji, A. H. Chowdhury, I. S. Kim, T. B. Kwan, and B. M. Cho. 1996. "Research Activities of Epidemiology in Japan: Cardiovascular Disease—a Brief Review of Epidemiological Studies on Ischemic Heart Disease in Japan." *Journal of Epidemiology* 6 (suppl.), no. 3: S49–S59.

Ueda, T., and T. Sumiyoshi. 1995. "Coronary Thrombolysis." In *Igaku no Ayumi,* p. 364. Tokyo: Ishiyaku Shuppan Gaisha.

Vogt, W. B., J. Bhattacharya, S. Kupor, A. Yoshikawa, and T. Nakahara. 1996. "The Role of Diagnostic Technology in Competition among Japanese Hospitals." *International Journal of Technology Assessment in Health Care* 12, no. 1: 93–103.

Yoshikawa, A., J. Bhattacharya, and W. Vogt, eds. 1996. *Health Economics of Japan.* Tokyo: University of Tokyo Press.

Yoshikawa, A., M. Holt, K. Ishikawa, and W. Kasumi. 1993. "High Tech Fad: Medical Equipment Use in Japan." In *Japan's Health System: Efficiency and Effectiveness in Universal Care.* Washington, D.C.: Faulkner and Gray Health Care Information Center.

CHAPTER 9

Technological Change in the Treatment of Acute Myocardial Infarction in Korea

Bong-min Yang

Ischemic heart disease (IHD) generally and heart attack (AMI) specifically are emerging as major causes of death in Korea. Indeed, among the circulatory and cardiovascular diseases, AMI is noted as the principal cause of death. Table 9.1 shows that the number of deaths from IHD and AMI has increased dramatically over the past 12 years. Deaths from IHD have skyrocketed from 1,102 in 1984 (2.8 per 100,000 population) to 5,934 (13.1 per 100,000 population); trends in death from AMI have been similar, increasing from 2.4 to 10.6 per 100,000 over the same period. Prevalence of AMI is rising as well. Between 1992 and 1996, the number of AMI inpatient cases has increased by almost 50 percent, from 6,399 to 9,467 (National Federation of Medical Insurance 1992–96). This trend is expected to continue in the coming years, with some acceleration possible. The current trend implies that the total AMI cases will double every decade.

Along with this increase in incidence came a significant increase in medical expenditure per AMI inpatient case. Real expenditures per case, adjusted for the consumer price index, increased steadily over the 1992–96 period, with an annual compounded growth rate of 2.4 percent, from a 1992 baseline of 1.3 million won (approximately U.S.$1,000 at current exchange rates; National Federation of Medical Insurance 1992–96). With these increases in both incidence and real expenditure, both medical economists and public health specialists are increasingly concerned with AMI and the use of AMI-related medical technologies.

During this same period, the government launched a compulsory health insurance program. Although compulsory health insurance was essentially an expansion of existing programs, it fundamentally changed the pattern of health service provision and the composition of providers. Providers found that the many constraints inherent in the system limited their autonomy. Physicians' and hospitals' charges became contingent upon government-authorized fee schedules. The acquisition of certain equipment and expansion or establishment of hospitals in certain areas began to require the express approval of the Ministry of Health and Welfare.

To what extent has the Korean system of financing care for heart disease influenced the adoption of new technologies for treatment of heart attack? And how did the system of health care finance interact with the increasing prevalence of IHD and AMI to affect medical treatment decisions and expenditures during the 1980s and 1990s? This chapter investigates these two questions by analyzing data on two high-tech treatments for AMI—percutaneous transluminal coronary angioplasty (PTCA) and coronary artery bypass graft surgery (CABG)—from a sample of four hospitals during the 1980s and 1990s. Unfortunately, individual data on changes in treatment decisions, medical expenditures, and health outcomes for AMI are not available. Although our ability to examine trends in the causes and consequences of technological change for heart attack care is limited by this fact, our analysis suggests the ways in which health care finance in Korea may affect treatment decision making for heart attack care.

This chapter proceeds as follows. Section 1 outlines the incentives for technological change in treatment of heart attack care under the

TABLE 9.1. Deaths from Ischemic Heart Disease in Korea, 1984–96

Year	Deaths from All Ischemic Heart Disease	Deaths from Heart Attack (AMI) Only	IHD Deaths per 100,000 Population	AMI Deaths per 100,000 Population
1984	1,102	919	2.8	2.4
1985	1,374	1,133	3.9	3.2
1986	1,478	1,220	4.3	3.6
1987	2,104	1,807	6.1	5.3
1988	2,350	1,975	6.7	5.7
1989	3,133	2,712	9.0	7.8
1990	3,617	3,054	10.4	8.8
1991	4,229	3,498	11.6	9.6
1992	4,924	4,159	12.5	10.6
1993	5,596	4,221	13.5	10.1
1994	5,471	4,466	12.7	10.4
1995	5,922	4,844	13.2	10.8
1996	5,934	4,791	13.1	10.6

Source: Cause of Death, Bureau of Statistics, various years.

Korean system of health care finance. Section 2 describes our data on high-tech treatments for heart attack, and how care for heart attack has changed over the past decade. Section 3 concludes with some hypotheses about the impact of insurance incentives on technological change in Korea and suggestions for future research.

1. Incentives for Technological Change in Korea

Financing of Heart Disease Care

In 1989, the government launched a compulsory health insurance program (the National Health Insurance, or NHI) for the entire population. As of 1996, 95.6 percent of the Korean population were under health insurance plans; the remaining 4.4 percent were under the Korean Medicaid program, which provides health insurance to the poor. Health insurance is provided through one of approximately 375 private insurance funds.[1] Each fund is financially autonomous. The size of each insurance fund is small, covering 30,000 to 200,000 people.

Health service delivery in Korea has been basically a market-oriented, private-sector-dominated system, although providers are paid by fee-for-service for certain covered services.[2] The government plays a major role in setting the reimbursement rates, although fee schedules are negotiated at the national level by the relevant parties. Part of the cost of service provision is covered by the insurance funds, and part by patients' out-of-pocket payments. Two types of cost-sharing features are incorporated into the NHI. The first feature is a copayment applied to each unit of service. For example, a flat fee of about U.S.$4 has to be paid by a patient for each physician visit. On top of the deductible, a patient pays coinsurance rates of 30 percent for clinic outpatient services, and 50–55 percent for hospital outpatient services. The coinsurance rate for inpatient services is 20 percent across all types of providers.

Not all health services are covered by the NHI. Next to the high, uncapped coinsurance payments, this is the most controversial feature of the NHI. For example, although PTCA and CABG are covered, PTCA with intracoronary stents—that is, wire rims that are designed to help keep a blood vessel open after it has undergone angioplasty—is not covered. For uncovered services such as stents, providers charge unregulated market prices.

Other factors further limit the scope of the NHI. If a patient prefers to be treated by a board specialist in a general hospital, the patient has to pay a "special treatment charge" (STC) that is not covered by health insurance; otherwise, interns or residents are automatically assigned to their case. In addition, for people under 65 years old, there is an upper limit on the number of days of hospitalization and care (270 days).

Taken together, these limitations mean that only a fraction of total medical expenditures are covered by health insurance schemes in Korea. Out-of-pocket payments (STCs and payments for uncovered services) as a percentage of total treatment costs range from 50 percent to 70 percent (Yang 1997).

Although it would seem that the limited coverage of the NHI, combined with high coinsurance payments, would limit the use of costly high-tech treatments, two key features of the Korean health care system weaken such an effect. First, because of asymmetric consumer information and a lack of competition, the much greater potential profitability of relatively high-tech uncovered services may lead providers to adopt high-tech, intensive practice patterns. Second, the starting point for negotiations between the government and hospitals over reimbursement for covered services is based on each hospital's retrospective costs, including the hospital's expenditures on equipment and personnel used to produce uncovered services. By investing in new cost-inducing technologies whose services are not covered by insurance, increases in hospitals' costs are at least partially offset by allowed increases in the fee-for-service reimbursement schedule. Increased costs as a result of high-technology investments are spread over all other services in the form of higher fee levels, including covered services. Indeed, because the government sets fees for covered services on the basis of costs plus a profit margin, hospital profits may actually be *increasing* with the level of hospital costs. For this reason, the current cost-plus reimbursement mechanism may facilitate rather than discourage the rapid diffusion of new medical technology.

Other Incentives for Technology Adoption and Use

The role of the government has been limited primarily to the public health area. There has been very little regulation or monitoring of the ever-growing number of private providers on technology acquisition, provision of services, insurance claims, and prescription of drugs.

In most cases, patients are given a choice of providers: they can choose among various providers at multiple referral levels. Because there is no patient referral channel, they can go directly to the outpatient departments of general hospitals. In 1989, some regulatory provisions were enforced in the choice of providers under the NHI, requiring patients to visit local clinics and health centers first. However, most patients do not abide by the rules, and hospitals, for fear of losing revenue, do not enforce these rules. As a result, the provisions have become ineffective.

2. Technological Change in AMI Care in Korea: Trends in the Use of Technology across Hospitals

There are two basic high-technology approaches to treating AMI patients: CABG and PTCA. CABG and PTCA are the two major types of revascularization procedures to eliminate the blockage of blood flow into the heart. Of the two, PTCA is the more recently developed technology. Coronary artery stent is another recent technology that is used in conjunction with PTCA.

Unfortunately, only a limited amount of data on medical treatment decisions are available in Korea. This study examines hospital data on the use of PTCA and CABG at four different general hospitals in the Seoul metropolitan area: a public university hospital (hospital A), a private university hospital (hospital B), a private university hospital but owned by a corporate firm (hospital C), and a corporate hospital (hospital D). All of them are large hospitals with over 1,500 inpatient beds, except hospital D, which has 1,102 beds.

The number of PTCA and CABG per 100 AMI inpatients at the four sample hospitals is shown in tables 9.2 and 9.3. PTCA was introduced to hospital A in 1986 and hospital B in 1984. Hospitals C and D started providing PTCA services from the beginning of their operation, in 1989 and in 1994, respectively. For unknown reasons, hospital A no longer releases information on PTCA (or CABG) cases beyond 1991, although many cases of those procedures are still performed in that hospital. Data have been consistently made available from hospital B.

TABLE 9.2. Number of PTCA Procedures per 100 AMI Inpatients

Hospital	1984	1985	1986	1987	1988	1989	1990	1991	1992	1993	1994	1995
A	0.0	0.0	8.0	13.5	19.9	11.3	10.1	12.4				
B	3.9	5.2	6.3	10.0	9.6	8.2	11.7	11.6	12.0	13.2	13.1	16.4
C						11.2	12.1	14.2	19.3	19.0	25.8	23.8
D											18.4	25.1

TABLE 9.3. Number of CABG Procedures per 100 AMI Inpatients

Hospital	1981	1982	1983	1984	1985	1986	1987	1988	1989	1990	1991	1992	1993	1994	1995
A	0.5	1.8	0.5	0.0	1.5	1.5	0.0	0.3	0.5	0.0					
B	1.0	5.9	5.5	0.0	2.2	1.0	1.4	1.5	2.2	2.4	2.3	3.3	3.2	3.2	3.6
C									5.0	6.3	3.3	5.0	5.7	3.9	5.1
D														4.3	8.1

The use of PTCA has increased dramatically in our study hospitals over the past decade. For hospital B, the increase has been the most significant—a fourfold increase, from 3.9 procedures per 100 AMI inpatients in 1984 to 16.4 in 1995. During 1989 and 1995, the number of PTCA procedures per 100 AMI patients more than doubled for both hospital B and hospital C. PTCA is used much more frequently in the treatment of AMI at corporate hospitals (C and D) than at the university hospital B.

The CABG rate per 100 inpatients at the four sample hospitals is shown in table 9.3. CABG use has increased, although not as dramatically as have PTCA rates. And as with PTCA, there is a consistent difference in CABG procedures per AMI patient among different types of hospitals. Comparing data points among hospitals for certain years, for example, hospital A and hospital B for 1981–90, and hospital B and hospital C for 1989–95, and hospital C and hospital D for 1994–95, one can find that corporate hospitals record the highest rates, the private university hospital the next, and the public university hospital the lowest rate.

Strikingly, as in other Asian countries, PTCA is much more commonly used than CABG in treating AMI patients. This preference has become more apparent in recent years. Physicians argue that there are several reasons why PTCA use is increasing more rapidly than CABG use in Korea. First, hospitals and physicians try the less invasive procedure (i.e., PTCA) first. Second, in Korea, PTCA success rate is known to be higher than that of CABG. Third, there are more cardiologists than cardiac surgeons in Korea.

There also may be incentive-based reasons why PTCA is more commonly used. Stents are a relatively new technology used in conjunction with PTCA, beginning with some general hospitals in 1991. However, stent use is not covered by the NHI.[3] Yet, for the reasons described above, hospitals may have a strong incentive to adopt this technology. Information about using stents with PTCA is available only from hospitals B and C, where the rate of PTCA with stents is rising very rapidly. By 1995, in those two sample hospitals, more than half of the PTCA procedures were accompanied with stents. Indeed, conditional on PTCA, the rate of stent use rose to 75 percent in 1996 for AMI patients in hospital B. Even if stents are not covered by the NHI in the near future, it is apparent that they are becoming part of common practice in treating AMI cases in Korea.

3. Conclusion

Although the importance of medical technology in explaining growth in expenditures for health care is well known, little in-depth research in this area has been undertaken in Korea. Particularly for cardiac illness and AMI—which are skyrocketing in Korea—rigorous analysis is important. As a first step to respond to such a need, this study focused on CABG and PTCA, the increasingly used and highly demanded technologies that treat AMI patients.

There are several noticeable limitations of this study. The major weakness is the quality of data used in the analysis. The hospital-based data are far from complete. Most significantly, the lack of individual-level data precludes examining the health benefits of high-technology treatment for AMI. This limitation could be addressed with individual patient data in future research.

The chapter presents four key findings. First, the number of AMI patients is increasing and is likely to increase further with the aging of the population in Korea. Second, expenditures per AMI patient are rising and so could consume a dramatically larger chunk of health care resources over time. Third, even though the limited coverage of the NHI, combined with high coinsurance payments, would seem to constrain the use of costly high-tech treatments, two key features of the Korean health care system weaken such an effect: asymmetric consumer information combined with a lack of competition, and the incentives provided by cost-plus reimbursement through the NHI.

Finally, corporate general hospitals—which may have a more powerful incentive to earn profits—are more aggressive in performing costly high-tech procedures than are university or public general hospitals. Moreover, these high-intensity providers react more sensitively to economic incentives, such as those that may encourage the use of uncovered technologies such as stents. This factor is important because the proportion of corporate hospitals is very high, as high as 85 percent in some regions (Yang 1997). Our study shows that these hospitals are more likely to use expensive technologies when costs are recoverable.

Notes

1. Reform in the health insurance market, under way in 1998, seeks to consolidate the many small insurers in Korea into a single payer.

2. An experiment with a case-based, or DRG-like, payment structure began in 1997.

3. The price of 2.5 million Korean won per stent (approximately U.S.$2,000) is borne fully by the patient. When two stents are used in a PTCA operation, for example, an average patient has to pay at least 6 million won (U.S.$5,000)—5 million for two stents and 1 million for coinsurance—as a direct out-of-pocket payment.

References

Banta, D. H., and B. R. Luce. 1993. *Health Care Technology and Its Assessment—an International Perspective.* Oxford: Oxford University Press.

Bureau of Statistics, Government of Korea. 1995. *Annual Report on the Cause of Death.* Seoul, Korea.

———. 1996. *Future Population Projection.* Seoul, Korea.

Cutler, D. M., and M. B. McClellan. 1996. "The Determinants of Technological Change in Heart Attack Treatment." NBER Working Paper 5751, September.

Department of Health Policy and Management, School of Medicine, Seoul National University. 1997. *Efficiency, Efficacy, and Safety of Medical Technologies.*

Kim, J. S. 1996. "Coronary Heart Disease and Its Prevention Strategy: A Path to Health for All" (in Korean). *Korean Journal of Public Health* 33, no. 1: 1–26.

Lee, J. W. 1990. "Survey on New Medical Technology Equipment in Hospitals" (in Korean). *Health Insurance* 14, no. 6: 128–31.

National Federation of Medical Insurance. 1992–96. *Medical Insurance Statistical Yearbook.* Seoul, Korea.

Yang, B. M. 1993. "Medical Technology and Inequity in Health Care: The Case of Korea." *Health Policy and Planning* 8, no. 4: 385–93.

———. 1997. "The Role of Health Insurance in the Growth of the Private Health Sector in Korea." In *Private Health Sector Growth in Asia,* ed. W. Newbrander. New York: John Wiley and Sons.

CHAPTER 10

Technological Change in Heart Attack Care in Taiwan

Joan C. Lo and Mei-shu Lai

Taiwan is a small island, with a total land area of 36,000 square kilometers. In 1996, there were 21.5 million inhabitants, and among them 7.9 percent were over 65 years old. There were 773 hospitals and 114,923 beds, with private hospitals owning 64 percent of the beds. There were 24,745 physicians, 59 percent of whom worked in hospitals. Hospitals provided both inpatient and outpatient services. Though hospitals are not evenly distributed throughout Taiwan, convenient transportation has made care accessible to most people.

The Taiwanese system of health care finance underwent substantial changes in the 1990s. Health insurance coverage expanded steadily from 1990 to 1995 (DGBAS 1996). And on March 1, 1995, Taiwan adopted universal National Health Insurance (NHI). The NHI generally reimburses clinics and hospitals on a fee-for-service basis, although it does reimburse for a few procedures on a prospective, DRG-like basis. One important implication of this change is that financial accessibility of medical care ceased to be a problem for virtually all Taiwanese. (Prior to the NHI, health care financing in Taiwan was three-pillared, with out-of-pocket expenditures and NHI-precursor public insurance benefits each accounting for about 40 percent, with the remainder financed directly out of the government budget.)

Another implication of the expansion in health insurance coverage has been rising health care expenditures. As a percentage of GDP, total health care expenditures were rather steady prior to 1990 (fig. 10.1). However, expenditures rose dramatically after 1990 due to expansions of health insurance coverage, and by 1996 the share of GDP on health was 5.3 percent (DOH 1997b).

Heart disease is the fourth leading cause of death in Taiwan, staying there for almost four decades. The number of deaths attrib-

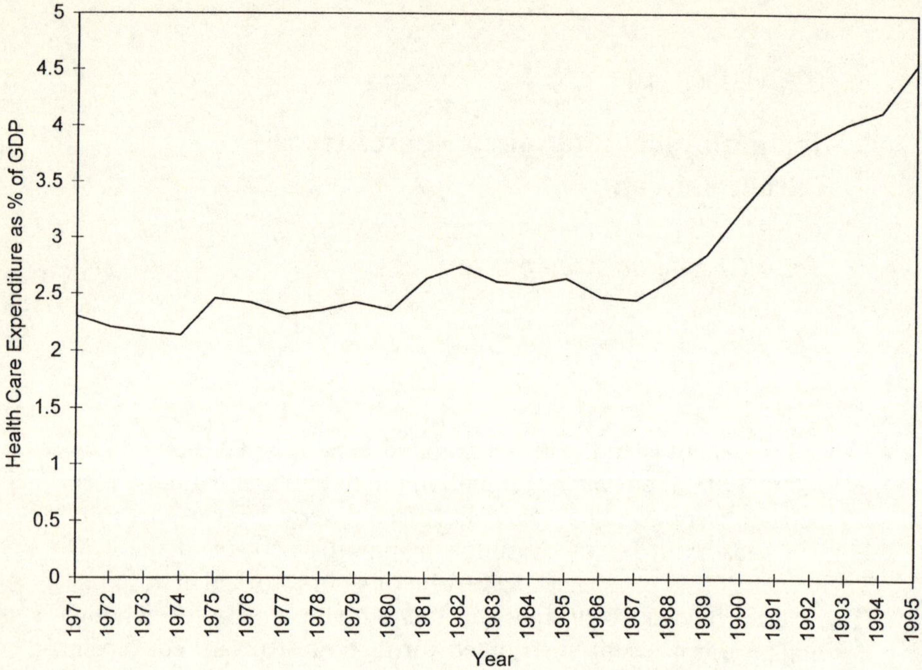

Fig. 10.1. Health care expenditure as percentage of GDP

uted to heart attack (or AMI) has increased, from 1,802 in 1984 to 4,058 in 1996 (a growth rate of 7 percent [DOH 1997a]). Similarly, the number of inpatients with AMI on any particular day was 55 in 1984, with an average growth rate of 9.5 percent; the corresponding figure for IHD was 286 in 1984, with the same growth rate (DOH 1997b) (fig. 10.2).

To what extent has the expansion in health insurance coverage in Taiwan over the 1990s, culminating in the adoption of universal NHI, affected the extent of technological change for care for heart disease? And what has been the impact of the use of new technologies on medical expenditures and patient health outcomes? This chapter explores these questions with the first analysis of longitudinal patient-level microdata that has been carried out in Taiwan since the adoption of the NHI. We use the Hospital Claim File collected by the NHI, matched with the Cause of Death Data File, compiled by the Department of Health. This database allows us to identify both the intensive

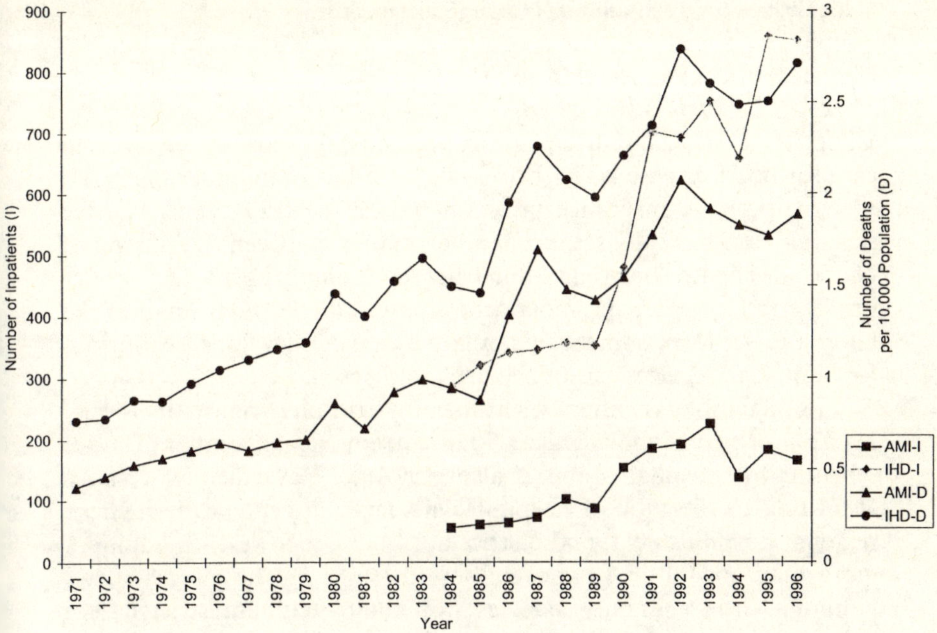

Fig. 10.2. Number of inpatients with, and number of deaths from, AMI and IHD

surgical and the nonintensive treatments that each individual hospitalized with AMI received, and also allows us to follow these individuals after their discharge from hospital.

Although our ability to examine trends in the causes and consequences of technological change for heart attack care is limited by the fact that the Hospital Claim File only contains information on treatments occurring after the adoption of the NHI, our analysis suggests how health care finance in Taiwan may affect treatment decision making for heart attack care. This chapter proceeds as follows. Section 1 outlines the incentives for technological change in treatment of heart attack care under the NHI. Section 2 describes how we constructed our cohorts of AMI patients and provides basic facts about treatment for heart attack care in Taiwan. Section 3 explores the consequences of this care for patient health, and section 4 concludes with some hypotheses about technological change in Taiwan and suggestions for future research.

1. Incentives for Technological Change in Taiwan

Financing of Care for Heart Disease

Under the NHI, reimbursement for both hospitals and doctors for all care for heart disease is fee-for-service, as it has been under the NHI-precursor public insurance program for the past 20 years. The fee schedules are basically set through negotiation between the Bureau of National Health Insurance and the representatives of the service providers. However, the monopsony power of the NHI enables the bureau to set low payment fees, relative to most developed countries, for almost all services except new technologies.

For example, reimbursement for inpatient physician visits is only NT$200, which is about U.S.$6.70 at current exchange rates. The fee schedule for hospital rooms is also very low. Nevertheless, it varies according to the type of hospital, with medical centers the highest, regional hospitals next, and district hospitals the lowest. In addition, more than 16,700 drugs are reimbursed based on the fee schedules, although drug reimbursement is not completely unrestricted (see below). Hospitals are allowed to bill the bureau separately for physician fees, hospital bed charges, laboratory fees, therapeutic treatment fees, dispensing fees, and many other itemized charges. Nursing and services provided by other supporting staffs are not allowed to be billed separately. No balance-billing of patients is allowed for either the medical services or drugs. However, hospitals are permitted to charge extra for private luxury rooms and for some expensive medical devices, such as a pacemaker.

Reimbursement for new technologies is based primarily upon analysis of the costs of those hospitals that adopt the technology. Since there are few hospitals in Taiwan that adopt any specific new technology, those hospitals that do adopt a technology have the incentive to report that its costs are high, thereby increasing their own reimbursement. Care for heart attack provides a textbook example. In 1990, when angioplasty (PTCA) was first listed on the fee schedule, the fees were NT$44,000 for one vessel, NT$60,000 for two vessels, NT$76,000 for three vessels (at current exchange rates, approximately U.S.$1,475, U.S.$2,010, and U.S.$2,545, respectively). The corresponding fees were NT$23,340, $28,500, and $32,940 for bypass surgery (CABG), which is not widely used in Taiwan (approximately U.S.$780, U.S.$955, and U.S.$1,100, respectively). The payment for CABG has changed three times since 1990, while the payment for PTCA has remained the same. The current fee schedule for CABG is NT$35,200 for one vessel, $42,970 for two vessels, and $49,680 for three vessels (approximately U.S.$1,180, U.S.$1,440, and U.S.$1,665, respectively). (The fees quoted above are for that particular procedure only. All other expenses such as room charges, surgical surcharges, physician fees, device charges, and drugs are allowed to be charged separately when necessary. Therefore, the difference in total expenditures between patients who receive PTCA and those who receive CABG is not known a priori.)

Other Incentives for Technology Adoption and Use

Technology Regulation

Generally speaking, "macro" technology regulation in Taiwan is rather limited; it is no exception in the treatment for heart disease. There are neither caps on cardiac procedure capacity nor strict medical device regulation, as is done by the U.S. Food and Drug Administration. In addition, there is minimal "microregulation" of technology. For example, utilization review is not widely implemented in Taiwan. However, expensive drugs are subject to tight control; thrombolytic drug use is reimbursed only if administered within 12 hours of an AMI.

Regulation of Physician Supply

Though the overall supply of physicians is subject to medical school capacity, there is no clear restriction as to how many of them can become cardiac surgeons, which is more influenced by the establishment and expansion of the hospitals' cardiac divisions. Since surgery appointments in Taiwan are generally higher paying and more prestigious, they have historically attracted the best medical students. However, the situation changed right after the implementation of NHI, which resulted in broadly lower reimbursement for surgical procedures. A shortage of surgeons may be a serious problem in the future.

Competition and Hospital Ownership

Since the Taiwanese health care delivery system is a closed one, and heart disease is generally a life-threatening disease, there is practically no competition between private clinicians and hospital physicians. All patients subject to heart problems will either visit doctors in the outpatient department or stay in the inpatient setting of the hospitals. Hospital ownership does not prove to be an influential factor in terms of incentives for procedure choice for care in Taiwan (Lo 1998).

2. Heart Attack Care in Taiwan

We use two versions of the Hospital Claim File collected by the NHI—the Summary Hospital Claim File and the Detailed Hospital Claim File. The Summary Hospital Claim File was available for patients admitted throughout 1996. This data set provides us with summary statistics for each patient's hospital stay with individual patient identifiers. It includes the patient's date of birth, gender, the hospital that filed the claim, the date of admission, the date of discharge, total length of stay, principal diagnosis (ICD9), secondary diagnosis, and 17 broad categories of expenditures. The Detailed Hospital Claim File was available only from January through June 1997 (at the time the analysis for this chapter was performed). This data set provides us with information on specific treatment decisions (i.e., cardiac catheterization only, versus catheterization plus PTCA, versus catheterization plus CABG), in addition to the information on the Summary Hospital Claim File.

From these two data sets, we constructed two cohorts—a "treatment analysis" cohort based on the Detailed Hospital Claim File, and an "outcome analysis" cohort based on the Summary Hospital Claim File. Unfortunately, one implication of the limited horizon of the Detailed Hospital Claim File is that no intermediate- or long-term outcome follow-up could be performed for our treatment analysis cohort. For this reason, we only matched the Summary Hospital Claim File data with the Cause of Death Data File, compiled by the Department of Health. Thus, our two databases allow us to identify both the intensive surgical and the nonintensive treatments that each individual with AMI received, but only allow us to describe in broader terms mortality from heart attack.

The treatment analysis cohort included only patients with a principal diagnosis of AMI (ICD9 code 410). We adopted four exclusion criteria for eliminating cases unlikely to represent a true new AMI: (1) Patients with a fifth-digit ICD9 code indicating subsequent or follow-up care for AMI (e.g., ICD9 410.02); (2) patients discharged alive, and not transferred, within three days of admission. Transfers are defined as admissions occurring within one day of discharge from the previous admission; (3) patients transferred from another hospital, unless the principal diagnosis upon previous hospitalization was also AMI; and (4) patients previously admitted for AMI within one year of the current admission.

High-Tech Care

Since detailed treatment data are only available for 1997, we cannot render any trend analysis in this regard. Nevertheless, the individual inpatient data allow us to perform a much more detailed analysis of invasive treatment for heart attack care in Taiwan than ever before.

Table 10.1 displays invasive treatment rates as a percentage of admissions during initial hospitalization for AMI by age for our treatment analysis cohort. Table 10.1 points out several interesting characteristics of heart attack care. First, CABG was performed on the middle range of the age distribution. PTCA was more likely to be performed on younger age groups than CABG, with the highest rate of 37 percent occurring at the age of 45 to 54, while the highest rate of CABG occurred at the age of 55 to 64. Second, patients with only the catheterization were distributed among even younger age groups than PTCA. Overall, patients of ages 45 to 54 had the highest proportion of some form of invasive treatment; the rate of intensive treatment declined with age. Fully 60 percent of those with AMI received no invasive treatment in their initial hospital stay.

TABLE 10.1. Invasive Treatments by Age, Treatment Analysis Cohort, January to June 1997

	Treatment									
	None		Catheterization Only		PTCA		CABG		Total	
Age	*N*	%	*N*	%	*N*	%	*N*	%	*N*	%
1–29	4	80.0	1	20.0					5	100.0
30–44	60	46.5	30	23.3	39	30.2			129	100.0
45–54	117	43.3	51	18.9	99	36.7	3	1.1	270	100.0
55–64	214	51.9	59	14.3	125	30.3	14	3.4	412	100.0
65–69	202	56.6	57	16.0	89	24.9	9	2.5	357	100.0
70–74	245	62.3	54	13.7	81	20.6	13	3.3	393	100.0
75–79	234	70.7	43	13.0	46	13.9	8	2.4	331	100.0
80–84	155	80.3	15	7.8	21	10.9	2	1.0	193	100.0
85+	98	81.7	13	10.8	9	7.5			120	100.0
Total	1,329	60.1	323	14.6	509	23.0	49	2.2	2,210	100.0

But perhaps the most striking fact presented in this table is the remarkably high ratio of PTCA to CABG performed in Taiwan. Angioplasty rates are roughly comparable to those in the United States and in other developed countries, but CABG rates are much lower. Indeed, the probability of receiving PTCA relative to CABG is more than *10 times* as great. A similar preference for PTCA over CABG is also present in other Asian countries, such as Japan; we explore some potential causes of this treatment difference below.

Low-Tech Care

Information from our treatment analysis cohort not presented in table 10.1 suggests that low-tech care in Taiwan is used much less than in other countries (compare to Rogers et al. 1994; Rouleau et al. 1993). In general, 12 percent of the AMI patients received thrombolytics during their hospital stay, and 42.7 percent received aspirin. Patients with CABG had a much lower percentage of thrombolytics use and a much higher percentage of aspirin use than those with PTCA. The corresponding figures were 9.5 percent versus 11.3 percent, and 58.1 percent versus 44.5 percent. The low percentage of thrombolytics use primarily results from the refusal of NHI to reimburse for such drugs unless administered within 12 hours of the AMI. In contrast, the low percentage of aspirin use is likely due to a miscoding or misidentification from the huge drug list.

3. The Consequences of Heart Attack Care in Taiwan

Health Outcomes for AMI Patients

Table 10.2 presents mortality rates at various time intervals after admission for AMI, as well as in-hospital mortality, by age and gender, from our outcome analysis cohort, based on the Summary Hospital Claim File Data for 1996. The in-hospital mortality rate is in general increasing with age; all-cause mortality rates at specific time intervals, such as the mortality rate for 1 day, 7 days, 30 days, and 90 days, showed a similar pattern. On average, one-fifth of deaths occurred within 30 days of initial admission for AMI. Interestingly, the mortality rate for women was generally greater than that for men; gender differences were most pronounced among middle-aged (45–64) and young elderly groups (65–74).

Medical Expenditures and Resource Use

Table 10.3 continues our investigation of the outcome analysis cohort with a decomposition of 1996 expenditures on AMI patients by broad expenditure category. As expected, the highest expenditure share is for the hospital room, consisting of 27 percent of total expenditures. Examination and laboratory fees ranked second, occupying one-fifth of the total. Drugs and medical devices ranked third and fourth, each

TABLE 10.2. Mortality Rates per 100 Patients at Various Time Intervals after Admission for AMI by Age and Sex, Outcome Analysis Cohort, 1996

Age	1 Day	7 Days	30 Days	90 Days	In-hospital
Male					
1–29	0	5.9	5.9	11.8	5.9
30–44	1.2	4.1	4.9	4.9	4.5
45–54	2.0	6.5	8.3	9.2	7.4
55–64	3.6	8.7	12.0	13.6	10.4
65–69	3.9	11.3	16.0	18.1	14.1
70–74	4.7	13.8	20.5	24.4	17.3
75–79	4.8	20.2	28.1	31.6	25.4
80–84	6.8	25.2	33.3	39.8	30.1
85+	10.3	28.6	40.5	45.2	37.3
Average	4.1	12.7	17.7	20.4	15.6
Female					
1–29	12.5	12.5	12.5	25.0	12.5
30–44	0	3.3	3.3	3.3	3.3
45–54	3.7	11.0	15.9	19.5	13.4
55–64	3.3	14.8	18.1	19.8	17.7
65–69	2.5	15.4	23.8	25.0	19.6
70–74	6.2	22.9	29.5	33.1	28.0
75–79	8.2	24.9	30.4	35.0	28.4
80–84	7.5	25.7	36.9	44.4	31.3
85+	5.7	29.5	41.8	47.5	36.9
Average	5.4	20.5	27.5	31.3	24.8
Total					
1–29	4.0	8.0	8.0	16.0	8.0
30–44	1.1	4.0	4.7	4.7	4.4
45–54	2.2	7.1	9.3	10.6	8.2
55–64	3.5	10.1	13.4	15.0	12.0
65–69	3.6	12.4	18.0	19.9	15.5
70–74	5.1	16.3	23.0	26.8	20.3
75–79	6.0	21.9	28.9	32.8	26.5
80–84	7.1	25.4	34.8	41.7	30.6
85+	8.1	29.0	41.1	46.4	37.1
Average	4.4	14.9	20.4	23.4	18.1

TABLE 10.3. Hospital Expenditures and Their Composition by Age, Outcome Analysis Cohort, 1996 (% unless otherwise indicated)

	Age									
	1–29	30–44	45–54	55–64	65–69	70–74	75–79	80–84	85+	Total or Average
Number of patients	25	276	623	1,073	929	992	713	523	248	5,402
Length of stay (days)	15.0	10.0	10.7	11.4	11.6	12.7	13.0	13.9	11.1	12.0
Expenditures (1995 U.S.$)	2,687.3	3,165.1	3,536.0	3,784.0	3,682.2	3,982.1	3,724.2	3,192.9	2,759.4	3,625.4
Share of expenditures, by type										
Physician	4.19	3.02	2.92	2.87	3.02	3.03	3.25	3.79	3.90	3.11
Room charges	25.98	25.21	24.99	25.09	26.26	26.67	29.34	31.71	34.67	27.10
Dietary	0.55	0.08	0.20	0.27	0.48	0.52	0.88	1.61	1.17	0.57
Examination and laboratory	24.44	25.92	22.23	21.92	21.25	19.74	18.53	18.31	19.33	20.71
Radiology	9.99	16.15	16.45	12.87	10.24	7.94	7.38	4.68	3.14	10.14
Therapeutic treatment	11.19	5.09	5.44	6.43	7.83	9.01	11.04	13.52	13.15	8.52
Surgical	1.27	0.14	1.82	1.91	1.99	3.07	1.80	0.97	0.57	1.93
Rehabilitation	0.57	0.05	0.12	0.11	0.22	0.29	0.23	0.22	0.12	0.19
Blood transfusion	3.33	0.04	0.21	0.28	0.20	0.20	0.25	0.70	0.14	0.27
Hemodialysis	0.06	0.02	0.56	0.67	0.69	1.20	1.10	1.02	1.21	0.85
Anesthesia	0.88	0.19	0.72	0.86	0.81	1.10	0.82	0.43	0.19	0.79
Medical devices	10.34	16.98	16.82	17.68	15.56	15.17	12.00	9.25	5.99	14.74
Drugs	11.04	14.44	14.09	15.00	16.32	14.97	16.82	18.15	20.87	15.81
Dispensing fees	1.04	0.67	0.64	0.63	0.67	0.66	0.70	0.80	0.78	0.68
Injection	1.36	1.55	1.47	1.45	1.60	1.66	1.78	1.98	2.21	1.64

consisting of about 15 percent of total expenditures. Radiology fees occupied around 10 percent, and surgical fees were 2 percent. In addition, the physician fee was 3 percent, while the dispensing fee was 0.7 percent; a low fee schedule for the physicians as well as pharmacists is the primary reason for such low percentages.

Table 10.3 shows that on average, the length of stay for AMI patients was 12 days, about 2 days longer than the average length of stay for all diseases in 1996. Except for the very young (under 30), and very old (over 85), length of stay increased with age. This pattern is true for both sexes. However, the length of stay for females is lower in all age groups, which is likely attributable to the higher female mortality rate. The length of stay for those who died within 7 days of admission was 2.8 days, while the corresponding figure for those who died within 30 days (90 days) was 5.6 days (7.9 days).

Table 10.4 shows that, in the treatment analysis cohort, there were 1,726 out of 2,210 patients who used the ICU facility. The youngest age group, under age 30 with a patient size of 5, had a 100 percent utilization rate. Even though those ages 80 to 84 had the lowest utilization rate, it was reasonably high with a rate of 72 percent. Generally speaking, the ICU utilization rate by age was very flat. The average rate was 78 percent.

Except for the youngest age group (under age 30) and the group between 70 and 74, the ICU days increased with age, ranging from 2.6 days to 5.1 days. Those who stayed in the medical centers had longer ICU stays than those in the regional hospitals, and those in the

TABLE 10.4. Length of Stay and ICU Utilization by Age, Treatment Analysis Cohort, January to June 1997

Age	Number of Patients	Patients with ICU Days	ICU Utilization Rate	Average LOS	Average ICU Days	Ratio of ICU Days to LOS
1–29	5	5	100.0	16.80	8.20	0.49
30–44	129	101	78.3	8.65	2.57	0.30
45–54	270	222	82.2	10.39	3.18	0.31
55–64	412	346	84.0	11.19	3.87	0.35
65–69	357	285	79.8	11.73	3.92	0.33
70–74	393	292	74.3	11.39	3.16	0.28
75–79	331	244	73.7	12.24	4.15	0.34
80–84	193	139	72.0	13.50	4.78	0.35
85+	120	92	76.7	13.76	5.11	0.37
Total	2,210	1,726	78.1	11.58	3.79	0.33

regional hospitals had much longer ICU stays than those in the district hospitals. Whether the patients admitted to the medical centers were sicker is yet to be studied; however, quite a few district hospitals had no ICU facilities, and the medical centers had more CABG cases. The average ratio of ICU days to LOS was 0.35 for those with PTCA, 0.37 for those with CABG, and 0.30 for those with catheterization but neither CABG nor PTCA. The corresponding ICU days for the above three cases were 4.5, 9.0, and 3.6, respectively.

Table 10.5 decomposes expenditures for the initial hospital admission into broad categories, by the treatment that the patient received. The major components of expenditures for those with PTCA were radiology fees, medical devices charges, examination and laboratory fees, and room charges. For those with CABG, they were special material charges, surgical fees, drugs, and examination and laboratory fees. Strikingly, expenditures for CABG patients were almost three times greater than expenditures for PTCA fees. Although this difference in expenditures may be due in part to differences in the *ex ante* health sta-

TABLE 10.5 Expenditures and Their Composition by Treatment, Treatment Analysis Cohort, January to June 1997 (% unless otherwise indicated)

	None	Catheterization Only	PTCA	CABG	Total
Number of patients	1,329	323	509	49	2,210
Length of stay (days)	10.6	12	12.6	24	11.6
Expenditures (1995 U.S.$)	2,510.3	3,625.2	7,095.0	20,658.1	4,131.6
Expenditures per day (in U.S.$)	236.8	302.1	563.1	860.8	356.2
Share of expenditures, by type					
Physician	3.8	3.2	1.8	1.2	2.6
Room charges	33.1	27.6	16.7	11.1	23.5
Dietary	1.0	0.2	0.1	0.2	0.5
Examination and laboratory	17.0	31.3	16.9	12.2	18.3
Radiology	1.6	1.7	28.2	3.1	12.3
Therapeutic treatment	13.3	6.0	3.8	6.3	7.9
Surgical	0.7	0.3	0.2	17.4	2.3
Rehabilitation	0.2	0.1	0.1	0.3	0.1
Blood transfusion	0.8	1.2	0.2	4.6	1.0
Hemodialysis	0.6	0.3	0.2	0.3	0.4
Anesthesia	0.2	0.1	0.1	5.0	0.7
Medical devices	4.8	11.8	23.5	23.6	15.2
Drugs	20.0	13.0	6.9	13.4	13.3
Dispensing fees	0.7	0.7	0.4	0.3	0.5
Injection	2.0	1.5	1.0	1.1	1.4

tus or the severity of illness in those patients receiving CABG versus PTCA, it certainly lends little support to the hypothesis that the relatively greater prevalence of PTCA is due to reimbursement rates. It is more likely that CABG is viewed as too risky and too skill-intensive, so that few physicians are willing or able to perform the procedure.

4. Discussion

The fee-for-service nature of the NHI has dominated health-care financing in Taiwan for many years. Though the incentive effects of the low-powered nature of fee-for-service reimbursement and health insurance are well known, it is unlikely that the system will be changed any time in the near future. Among both patients and providers, satisfaction levels with the current public health insurance is high—in surveys, more than 70 percent of respondents report satisfaction since the inception of the NHI.

Setting the fee schedule for medical services is a difficult task, due to the fact that providers want them to be as high as possible, while the Bureau of National Health Insurance wants them to be as low as possible at a given level of quality. Setting the fee schedule for new technologies is even harder. The reference prices are normally from the medically advanced countries, and they are known to have high quality of care, therefore high medical expenditures. On one hand, the Bureau of National Health Insurance cannot openly confess that our quality of care, or the qualification of the physicians, is not as good as those in the advanced countries; on the other hand, the bureau cannot deny the opportunity of adopting the new technologies. Both of these factors inevitably result in high fees for the new technologies relative to the existing ones.

Although heart disease is only the fourth leading cause of death in Taiwan, both the number of deaths attributed to heart disease and the number of inpatients with IHD have increased very rapidly, with an average annual growth rate of 7 and 9 percent, respectively. The fact that population mortality is growing more slowly than this rate is consistent with the hypothesis that technological change in Taiwan has led to improvements in the outcomes of heart attack care. However, because our data do not cover a broad time frame, we are unable to formally examine this hypothesis in the current chapter.

The Detailed Hospital Claim File of the NHI recently made available contains procedures being performed and drugs being prescribed. We therefore are able to provide some information regarding the treatments of AMI patients: whether PTCA or CABG or simply catheterization was performed and whether ICU and thrombolytics were utilized. With this kind of claim data, we can build up longitudinal data for tracing trends in treatment decisions, medical expenditures, and patient health outcomes. Only with this information can we begin to examine the causes and consequences of technological change in health care in Taiwan.

References

Assaf, A. R., K. L. Lapane, J. L. McKenney, and R. A. Carleton. 1993. "Possible Influence of the Prospective Payment System on the Assignment of Discharge Diagnoses for Coronary Heart Disease." *New England Journal of Medicine* 329, no. 13: 931–35.

Ayanian, J. Z., and A. M. Epstein. 1991. "Differences in the Use of Procedures between Women and Men Hospitalized for Coronary Heart Disease." *New England Journal of Medicine* 325, no. 4: 221–25.

Cutler, D. M., and M. B. McClellan. 1996. "The Determinants of Technological Change in Heart Attack Treatment." NBER Working Paper 5751.

Department of Health (DOH). 1997a. *Report on Patient Survey in Hospitals and Clinics: Taiwan Area, R.O.C.* Tapei, Taiwan: Department of Health.

———. 1997b. *Vital Statistics: Taiwan Area, R.O.C.* Tapei, Taiwan: Department of Health.

Director General of Budget, Accounting and Statistics (DGBAS). 1996. *National Income Account.* Tapei, Taiwan: Director General of Budget, Accounting and Statistics.

Ford, E., R. Cooper, A. Castaner, B. Simmons, and M. Mar. 1989. "Coronary Arteriography and Coronary Bypass Survey among Whites and Other Racial Groups Relative to Hospital-Based Incidence Rates for Coronary Artery Disease: Findings from NHDS." *American Journal of Public Health* 79, no. 4: 437–40.

Gillum, R. F. 1987. "Coronary Artery Bypass Surgery and Coronary Angiography in the United States, 1979–1983." *American Heart Journal* 113, no. 5: 1255–60.

———. 1993. "Trends in Acute Myocardial Infarction and Coronary Heart Disease Death in the United States." *Journal of American College of Cardiology* 23: 1273–77.

Gillum, R. F., A. Folsom, R. V. Luepker, D. R. Jacobs Jr., T. E. Kottke, O. Gomez-Marin, R. J. Prineas, H. L. Taylor, and H. Blackburn. 1983. "Sudden Death and Acute Myocardial Infarction in a Metropolitan Area, 1970–1980: The Minnesota Heart Survey." *New England Journal of Medicine* 309, no. 22: 1353–58.

Lo, J. C. 1998. "Treatment of Acute Myocardial Infarction in Taiwan." Paper presented at the Conference on Technological Change in Health Care: A

Global Analysis, Center for Economic Policy Research, Stanford University, February 26–28.

McGovern, P. G., A. R. Folsom, J. M. Sprafka, G. L. Burke, K. M. Doliszny, J. Demirovic, J. D. Naylor, and H. Blackburn. 1992. "Trends in Survival of Hospitalized Myocardial Infarction Patients between 1970 and 1985. The Minnesota Heart Survey." *Circulation* 85, no. 1: 172–79.

McGovern, P. G., J. S. Pankow, E. Shahar, K. M. Doliszny, A. R. Folsom, H. Blackburn, and R. V. Luepker. 1996. "Recent Trends in Acute Coronary Heart Disease—Mortality, Morbidity, Medical Care, and Risk Factors." *New England Journal of Medicine* 334, no. 14: 884–90.

Rogers, W. J., L. J. Bowlby, N. C. Chandra, W. J. French, J. M. Gore, C. T. Lambrew, R. M. Rubison, A. J. Tiefenbrunn, and W. D. Weaver. 1994. "Treatment of Myocardial Infarction in the United States (1990 to 1993): Observations from the National Registry of Myocardial Infarction." *Circulation* 90, no. 4: 2103–14.

Rouleau, J. L., L. A. Moye, M. A. Pfeffer, J. M. O. Arnold, V. Bernstein, T. E. Cuddy, G. R. Dagenais, E. M. Geltman, S. Goldman, D. Gordon, P. Hamm, M. Klein, G. A. Lamas, J. McCans, P. McEwan, F. J. Menapace, J. O. Parker, F. Sestier, B. Sussex, and E. Braunwald. 1993. "A Comparison of Management Patterns after Acute Myocardial Infarction in Canada and the United States." *New England Journal of Medicine* 328, no. 11: 779–84.

Whittle, J., J. Conigliaro, C. B. Good, and R. P. Lofgren. 1993. "Racial Differences in the Use of Invasive Cardiovascular Procedures in the Department of Veterans Affairs Medical System." *New England Journal of Medicine* 329, no. 9: 621–27.

CHAPTER 11

Technological Change in the Treatment of Acute Myocardial Infarction in Sweden

Alexander Dozet, Sören Höjgård, Anna Lindgren, Hans Öhlin, and Carl Hampus Lyttkens

The Swedish health care system is public and decentralized, with most decisions made at the level of 23 county councils (which are subdivided into health care districts) and 288 local municipalities. It is staffed by salaried physicians and nurses. All county councils and municipalities are governed by locally elected politicians and empowered to impose proportional income taxes for the financing of their activities. The central government has a more passive role. Apart from supervising the fulfillment of the overall objectives of the health care legislation, which has a strong emphasis on equity,[1] its influence is mainly manifested through indirect measures such as general and targeted subsidies. It can also impose a tax ceiling on the county councils to prevent excessive use of taxation. Finally, through the National Board of Health and Welfare, the government supervises health care personnel (both privately and publicly employed) and performs evaluations of Swedish health care and related social issues.

During the second half of the 1900s the Swedish health care sector expanded, and the responsibilities of the county councils grew.[2] From the 1970s to 1992, the county councils and three local municipalities were actually responsible for all health care services and planning in Sweden. Over this period, Swedish health care expenditures grew rapidly, from 4.7 percent of GDP in 1960 to a peak of 9.5 percent of GDP in 1981. By 1991, they had fallen to 8.6 percent of GDP, mainly because the care for mentally retarded was reclassified and excluded from the national health statistics. In 1992 long-term care (mainly nursing homes) for elderly became the responsibility of the municipalities. This so-called *ÄDEL-reform* also transferred U.S.$2.29 billion, or

21 percent of total county council health care expenditures, to the municipalities (Lindgren 1995). Since the nursing homes were reclassified as "units for special accommodation" and excluded from the health care sector (Paulsson 1995), the reform reduced health care expenditures by another 1.1 percentage points to 7.5 percent of GDP in 1993. Hence, contrary to beliefs in Sweden, there may not have been large *real* reductions in Swedish health care expenditures during the last 10 to 15 years (SOU 1996, 64).

To what extent has care for heart disease contributed to real growth in expenditures in Sweden? Heart disease is an important cause of mortality in Sweden. Of all registered deaths in Sweden in 1993, heart attack (AMI) accounted for about 16 percent (*Yearbook of Health and Medical Care* 1995, 49). Approximately 62 percent of the 39,831 AMI-cases in 1993 were men, while 38 percent were women.[3] From 1987 to 1994, the incidence of AMI declined at an average annual rate of 1.6 percent for men and 1.0 percent for women (fig. 11.1). Mortality followed an even greater downward trend, with an average annual decrease of 2.5 percent for men, and 2.0 percent for women.[4] Although the incidence of AMI is decreasing, the incidence of ischemic heart disease (IHD) is increasing. Age-adjusted (to 1970) figures confirm the increased incidence. In 1987, the incidence was 450 cases per 100,000 inhabitants for women and 982 cases per 100,000 inhabitants for men; by 1994, the incidence for women had increased to 568 cases per 100,000 and to 1,121 cases per 100,000 for men.[5] This chapter explores the open research question regarding the relative importance of the Swedish health care system, changes in medical technology, changes in lifestyle, and other factors in explaining changes in health expenditures and heart disease rates.

Incentives for Technological Change in Sweden

Financing of Care for Heart Disease

The main source of finance in the Swedish health care system is the proportional income tax. The tax rate increased from an average of 8 percent in 1970 to 13.6 percent in 1988 in order to finance the expansion of Swedish health care during these years. Sweden also has a compulsory social health insurance program.[6] In effect since 1954, the program is not a major component of financing of the health care sector. Instead, it has served mainly as a sickness and parental cash-benefit system (Lindgren 1995). Nevertheless, it has some impact on demand

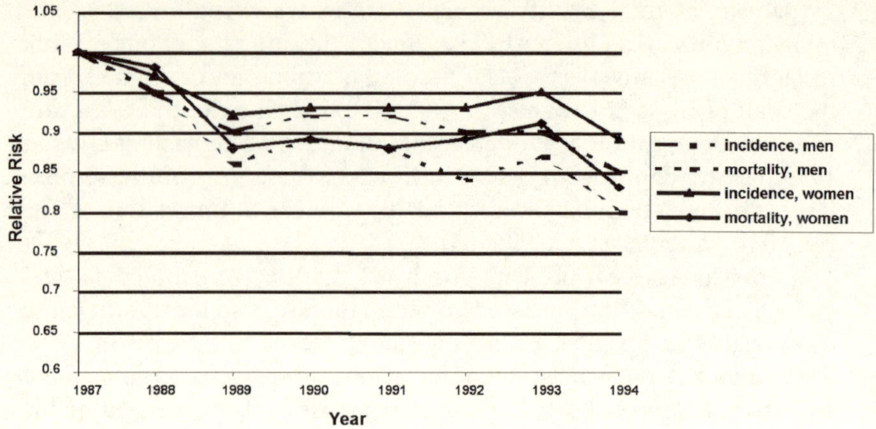

Fig. 11.1. The incidence of AMI in Sweden, 1987–94

for health care since the program reimburses patients' visits to private physicians and patients' purchases of prescription-drugs. As an example, in 1988, 59 percent of total health care expenditures were financed by the county councils, another 23 percent by social health insurance and central Government subsidies, 7 percent by local municipalities, and 11 percent by patients' out-of-pocket payments (Lindgren 1995).

Until the first half of the 1980s, the dominant reimbursement system to hospitals was based on historical costs, number of staff, and queues. The budget of the previous year was the starting point for the year to follow (Anell 1994). In practice, the system provided almost cost-plus reimbursement: soft budget restrictions allowed hospitals to exceed their budgets without risk of punishment.

In the late 1980s, however, the county councils began to experience difficulties in both the financing and the provision of care. The onset of these difficulties may have been due, inter alia, to a generally lower growth rate in the economy, a tax ceiling imposed by the government, an aging population, and cost-increasing technological change. As a result, some latent problems became visible. One such problem was that of queues. Patients needing coronary treatments such as PTCA, CABG, and coronary angiography were put on waiting lists in some cases for over six months (KRUS 1987). [7] Several studies also suggested that the productivity in Swedish health care was low (Lindgren and Roos 1985; Murray, Lundvall, and Hallerby 1994).

Low productivity, increasing queues, and high expenditures led to growing awareness about the need for boosting productivity in the health care sector. The role of the county councils also came under scrutiny (i.e., should they both provide and finance health care?). At the end of the 1980s, county councils implemented several important policy changes to enhance cost-effectiveness.[8] For example, some councils began to finance hospital care with global budgets, shifting detailed planning of resource allocation to districts and departments (Anell and Svarvar 1995). To further enhance cost-awareness, internal price setting was introduced for certain medical services (Anell and Svarvar 1995). Some hospitals, geriatric care facilities, psychiatric clinics, and outpatient clinics became production units. Patients were allowed to choose among health care facilities within their own county council, and their role as consumers was emphasized. Some councils also introduced DRG-like payment schemes. However, by 1993, only a few county councils reimbursed large parts of their health care sector through a DRG system (Anell 1994). Thus, conclusions concerning the outcome of the different reforms have been preliminary in nature.[9]

Throughout these reforms, though, patient out-of-pocket payments have remained low. Patient copayment rates were initially determined by the central government. However, in 1991 county councils acquired more freedom to determine copayments.[10] For hospital care, patients currently (1997) pay U.S.$7.70–8.20 per day, and for outpatient care U.S.$6.20–26.80 per visit.[11] The fee is the same regardless of implemented treatment. In addition, total patient copayments are capped at a low level by the central government: for example, in 1997, the maximum amount a patient had to pay annually for physician visits was U.S.$93 (*Yearbook of Health and Medical Care* 1997).

The county councils finance pharmaceuticals for inpatient care, and these expenditures are included in the budget of each clinic. Hence, hospitals have an incentive to be cost conscious in their use of pharmaceuticals, which is likely to have some impact also on the physicians' decisions (SOU 1995).[12] For prescribed drugs in outpatient care, the patient pays a copayment. Accordingly, 27 percent of the costs for prescribed drugs in 1994 were financed by the patients, 13 percent by the county councils, and 60 percent by the central government. For over-the-counter nonprescribed products, the patient pays full charges.

Despite these copayment policies, Sweden has had weak incentives for cost-effective use of outpatient prescription drugs. Although physicians neither bear the costs of, nor earn income from prescribing, drugs, the marginal cost of use of expensive drugs was borne almost entirely by the Social Health Insurance system instead of by individual patients or the county councils. There is no competition between pharmacies, which are all owned by the National Corporation of Pharmacies (a state monopoly). The main role of the corporation is to distribute pharmaceuticals; the company has no influence on products that are registered for sale. In 1995, a governmental committee suggested changes in the pharmaceutical reimbursement system designed to make prescription drug use more cost-effective. Implemented in 1998, these reforms transferred responsibility for pharmaceuticals reimbursement from the Social Health Insurance to the county councils, giving them larger incentives to control pharmaceutical expenditures. In addition, higher copayments for consumers had already been introduced in 1997.[13]

Technology Regulation

Regulation per se was not a major obstacle for the introduction of new technologies in Sweden until 1993 (Liedström 1995), as the county council and the health care staff were exclusively responsible for the safety of products. The change started in 1985 when the government appointed a committee to overlook the safety of medical equipment. Many new regulations and laws were harmonized with the directives from the EEC (Liedström 1995). The proposition was laid down for the parliament in the spring of 1993 (Svensk Författningssamling 1993). After 1995, Swedish regulation became similar to that of other EC countries. Thus, when a new device is introduced, full proof of its performance and full documentation of its potentially dangerous side effects must be submitted to the Swedish National Board of Health and Welfare. It should be carefully noted, however, that there is still no regulation on the use of new procedures, insofar as they do not require the use of new kinds of equipment. In addition, there is no "microregulation" of technology use similar to that used by HMOs in the United States. Patients can make appointments with the hospitals' outpatient departments without any referral from primary care or private physicians, implying that the "gatekeeper" role of primary care physicians is not very prominent (Lindgren 1995).

The approval process for pharmaceuticals in Sweden was until 1991 the responsibility of the National Board of Health and Welfare, and since then it has been the Medical Products Agency. The task of the agency is to scientifically evaluate pharmaceuticals that are used within the Swedish health care system, checking that the products are safe, effective, and adapted to their purpose.[14] Assessment times are now harmonized with those required by EC directives.[15]

Decisions concerning large investments, such as a new thoracic surgery department, rest with the county councils; under global budgets, this is likely to serve as an important mechanism for cost-control. Smaller investments are handled by the hospitals themselves.

Other Incentives for Technology Adoption and Use

Since 1970, all publicly employed physicians are paid fixed salaries (SOU 1993). Bonus systems are not usually used in the public health care sector. [16] The career development for publicly employed physicians depends on experience, research merits, and clinical skill. In Sweden there seems to be a tendency to emphasize research merits, which may promote early adoption of technologies. Public physicians have no personal financial interest, either in the kind of technology used, or in how many patients are treated. However, hospital clinics have faced sharper resource limits during the 1990s, and the incentives affecting them influence the physicians. The stricter budget constraints, therefore, ought to force physicians in the future to also focus on economic aspects of medical decision-making and thus promote the diffusion of cost-saving technologies.

During the 1970s and 1980s, it was very difficult for a patient to go to a primary care center or a hospital of his or her choice outside the designated district.[17] Patients were allowed to choose their own physician, although this was possible mainly in urban areas.[18] In 1989 the Federation of Swedish County Councils recommended its members make efforts to increase patients' freedom of choice. The same year, 17 out of 26 county councils allowed their inhabitants to choose a primary health care center freely within the county council; in 16 of them it was also possible to choose one's hospital within one's own county council. Since then, some county councils have made it possible for their patients to seek treatment in other county councils, provided there is an existing agreement between the councils.[19] By 1993, all county councils allowed patients to choose their primary health care center; in 17 county councils it was also possible to seek inpatient care at county hospitals in neighboring county councils without referral (SOU 1997, 150).[20]

Today, most patients still choose the nearest hospital or doctor. In practice, the possibility to choose is limited, particularly because there often is only one hospital reasonably close to the patient. Sweden is sparsely populated; inpatient resources are substantial but concentrated to large hospitals (Anell 1994). There is also lack of information on where the best service is offered.[21] Hence, there is a gap between theory and practice. Moreover, a 1995 survey found that although 17 county councils claimed to allow patients freely and without referral, in 9 of them the clinics demanded referral anyway.[22] As the knowledge about the freedom to choose spreads, incentives to compete for patients among both primary care units and hospitals will increase. One probable effect will be a faster diffusion of technology, as it is often regarded as quality enhancing.

Organizational structures within the hospital are also important for the diffusion of technologies. For example, PTCA is traditionally and still mainly performed by radiologists rather than cardiologists, although cardiologists increasingly are entering the field. Obviously, both the fact that PTCA has been performed at a clinic other than the one with primary responsibility for the AMI patient, and the process of changing boundaries of clinical departments, may affect the speed of technology diffusion. To this, one may add that there has been a relative lack of radiologists in Sweden for much of the relevant period.

There are two classifications of malpractice in Sweden: conscious deviation from the accepted rules, and unconscious or negligent deviation from the rules. There is also a large group of cases concerning omission of conducting specific diagnostic examination, failure to properly examine a patient, failure to use proper precautions, and omitted instructions or incomplete information given to the patient (Westerhäll 1992).[23] In 1975, a "patient insurance" system was introduced, with the purpose of (1) compensating the patient for direct and indirect damages, and (2) separating the question of compensation to patients from that of deterrence.[24] In 1993 there was a limit on compensation at U.S.$540,000 per individual (Sverne and Sverne 1993). Almost all patients are covered. For injuries caused by pharmaceuticals, there is a pharmaceutical insurance system that works in a similar way. The patient insurance is financed by premiums paid by county councils, private physicians, and other professionals (Danzon 1994), and a separate department controls the claim settlements to ensure a uniform judgment of claims compensation.[25] In consequence, individual health care producers do not risk any financial drawback from malpractice. The only time they would have to pay is if they were convicted by a court in accordance with the Tort Act. However, this seldom happens (Westerhäll 1994). Moreover, since malpractice is basically defined as deviation from "normal practice," the Swedish judicial system does not put substantial pressure on providers to use new technologies. The patient is not entitled to demand some particular type of treatment, although any treatment has to be given in consultation with the patient and with the patient's full consent. This also suggests that engagement in "defensive medicine" should not be a strong issue in Sweden, compared to countries like the United States.

Technological Change in Heart Attack Care in Sweden

Due to the lack of reliable aggregate time series data on treatments and drugs, it is not a straightforward matter to present a comprehensive picture of AMI care in Sweden. There are several different data sources, each covering one aspect of AMI treatment. Most of the nationwide registers began to operate in the early 1990s. For earlier periods, there are hospital-based data. However, these are often inaccessible by computer since they have not been converted into electronic databases.[26] Some nationwide registers are operated by individual hospitals, but these too are not easily accessible. For this survey, we have used databases that are described in what follows.

Sources of Data

The Swedish National Inpatient Register

This is a public register administered by the National Board of Health and Welfare. It has been operating since 1964, although its coverage was poor at the start. In 1983 it contained 85 percent of all discharged inpatients, and since 1987 participation by the county councils has been compulsory (private facilities are not included). It covers 1.7 million admissions per year and contains variables such as the age of the patient, sex, admission date, type of treatment, date of discharge, length of stay, diagnosis, at which hospital and clinic the patient was treated, if and when the patient died or was transferred to his or her home or some other clinic or hospital. It is possible to follow a patient over time through his or her social security number. The register has a good coverage of coronary artery bypass grafts (CABG), but not of coronary angioplasty (PTCA), and it does not contain any information on drug use, or the cost of treatment.

The Swedish National AMI Register

This is also a public register administered by the National Board of Health and Welfare. Primarily created for epidemiological research, it covers all AMI cases in Sweden between 1987 and 1995. It includes information on the date of the AMI, possible cause and date of death, and where the patient was treated. This register can be connected to the National Inpatient Register, thus enabling us to concentrate on treatment for AMI-patients in particular. It has a good coverage of all AMI cases in Sweden. However, the problems concerning data on the cost of treatment, use of thrombolytic drugs, and PTCA procedures still remain.

The Swedish Register for Coronary Angioplasty

This is a nationwide, nonpublic register administered by the Sahlgrenska Hospital, Gothenburg. It covers patients who have received PTCA treatment at both public and private hospitals. It contains data on diagnosis, whether thrombolytic drugs were used in connection with the PTCA, and the results of treatment. However, it does not include data on the costs of treatment. It started in 1991 and currently covers about 99 percent of all PTCA cases in Sweden.

In the future it may be possible to obtain data from the Swedish National Registry for Cardiac Intensive Care (RIKS-HIA): This is a nationwide, nonpublic register administrated by the county council of Uppsala that started in 1995. In 1997 it covered 50,000 patients per year treated with intensive care at 70 percent of all departments treating acute cardiac patients. Important variables included in this dataset are age, sex, risk factors, previous health problems, types of drugs used, types of invasive treatments, and outcomes. However, again no data on the costs of treatment are included. Finally, it may be possible and desirable to obtain data from specific hospitals and the Swedish MONICA project, although these data are regional and limited to certain age groups.

Changes in High-Tech Care

The first coronary care unit (*Hjärtinfarktavdelning,* HIA) was introduced in Sweden in 1966. Today there are such wards at every emergency hospital. The objective is to continuously monitor patients with specially trained personnel through ECG for the purpose of discovering and treating serious arrhythmias. Before the introduction of the HIAs, the in-hospital mortality rate for AMI in Sweden was as high as 35–40 percent. The introduction of HIAs led to a drop in the mortality rate after it became possible to detect ventricular fibrillation and perform defibrillation.[27]

The spread of coronary interventions is strongly correlated with the diffusion of diagnostic technologies like coronary angiography (CATH). Until the end of the 1980s, catheterization was mostly performed at the university clinics. Between 1990 and 1996 the number of procedures increased by over 100 percent (fig. 11.2), and presently they are performed at most large county hospitals. In 1995, there were 26 departments performing catheterization, compared to 11 in 1989.

Along these lines, after the first CABG treatment in the early 1960s, CABG was performed at a few university hospitals in the 1970s. Until 1992, the number of CABGs increased rapidly. Since then, it has remained fairly constant with a small decrease in 1995, probably due to the substitution of PTCA for CABG after 1991. By 1996, the total number of coronary interventions (PTCA and CABG) had increased to 12,021, of which 6,484 are CABG operations. Open-heart surgery is currently performed at 13 hospitals, 9 of them university hospitals.

CABG is most commonly performed as an elective procedure. However, there is a trend toward an earlier use after an AMI has occurred. Figure 11.3 shows that, in 1988, of those elderly (70 years and older) AMI patients who had a bypass operation, only 30 percent had their CABG within 90 days, while 11 percent were operated on within 30 days, and only a very small number within 7 days. By 1994 the fraction of patients that had received a bypass within 90 days had risen to 48 percent. It can also be seen that CABG is a more common procedure for older than for younger patients (under 69 years). In 1988, both the mean and the median time from the incident of AMI to the operation were approximately 180 days (table 11.1). Six years later, the mean decreased to 130 and the median time to 114 days. (The large decrease in 1995 is due to the fact that patients' receiving an AMI in late 1995 will not appear as treated until the next year.)

The first PTCA was performed in 1982 in Sweden. The rate of diffusion was slow until 1990 (when the annual number of procedures was 1,098). After 1990, the diffusion accelerated, and by 1996 the annual number of procedures was 5,537. The use of PTCA has been considered to be conditional on the presence of a thoracic surgery department at the treating hospital. This of course restricts the diffusion of the technology to large hospitals. Apart from elective PTCA, there is emergency PTCA, which can be divided into direct, rescue, and subacute PTCA.[28] Direct (or primary) PTCA is very rare in Sweden and is only performed at 10 regional hospitals (all but 1 are also university hospitals). The numbers of subacute PTCA are rising rapidly, but the majority of PTCA procedures is still elective (fig. 11.4).[29] The figure

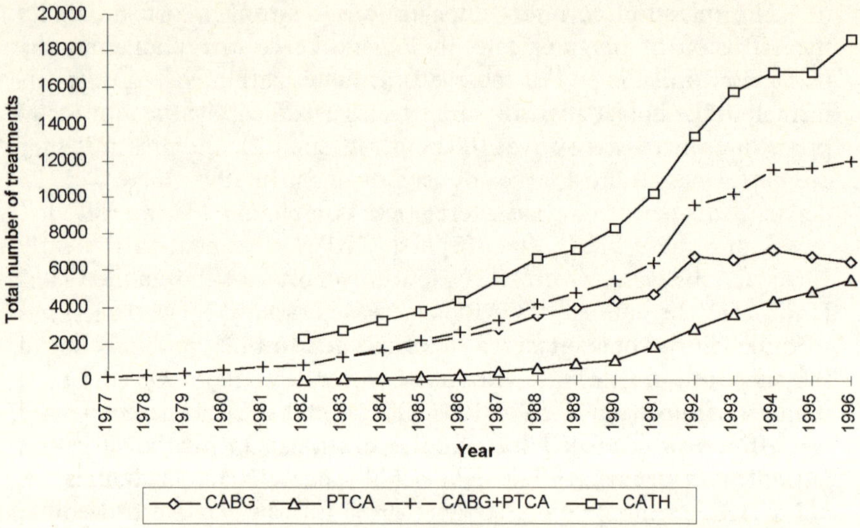

Fig. 11.2. Number of intensive cardiac procedures performed in Sweden, 1977–96. (Data from National Board and Health and Welfare and Federation of County Councils.)

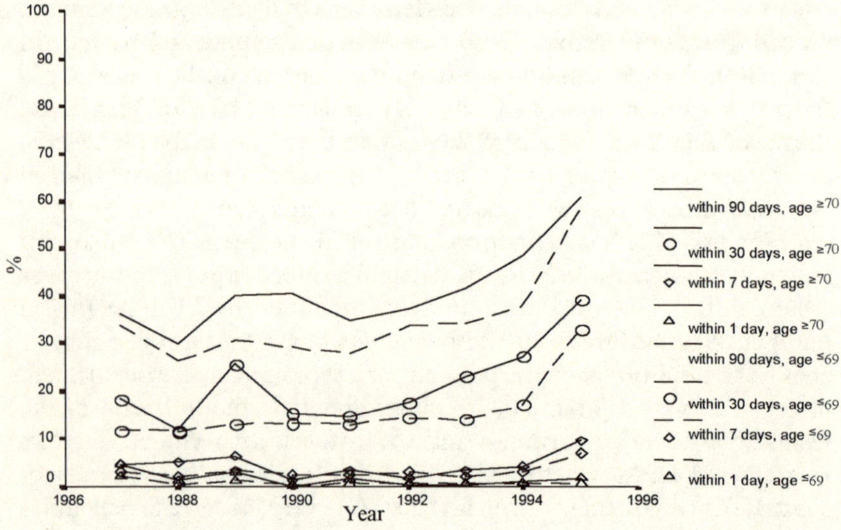

Fig. 11.3. Share of AMI patients treated with CABG, by age and time between admission and CABG, 1987–95

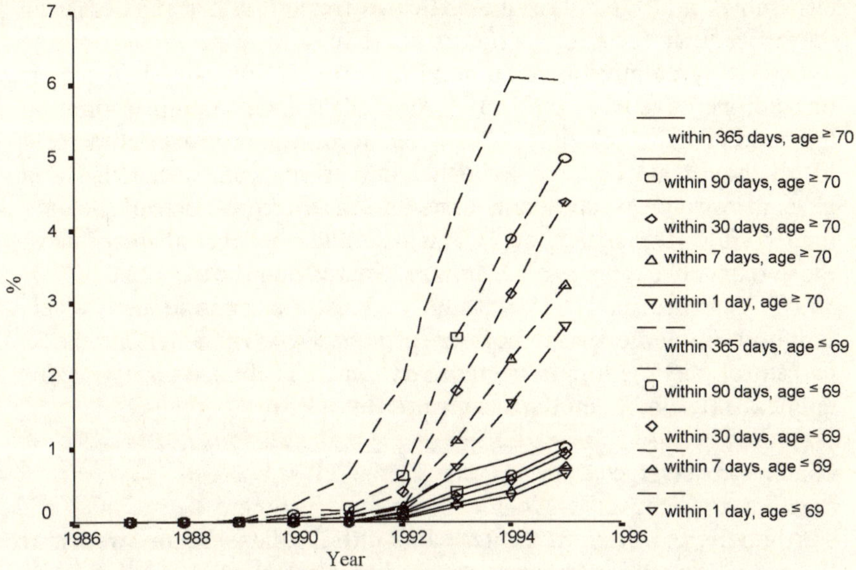

Fig. 11.4. Share of AMI patients treated with PTCA, by age and time between admission and PTCA, 1987–95

TABLE 11.1. Days between Admissions for AMI and CABG, 1987–95

Year of Admission	*N*	Mean	Std. Deviation	Percentiles 25	50	75
1987	432	170	108	69	166	267
1988	518	181	109	87	180	280
1989	638	169	110	63	172	262
1990	809	161	105	69	154	246
1991	998	167	107	68	164	257
1992	1,158	146	98	60	136	218
1993	1,301	137	95	52	129	205
1994	1,450	130	97	41	114	202
1995	804	84	76	17	60	133

also shows that the share of AMI cases treated with PTCA is rising more rapidly in the younger age group than in the older.

To differentiate further among the different types of PTCA performed, we have used the PTCA register. In this, the most common indication for a PTCA is stable angina, accounting for over 60 percent of all the 19,334 interventions that it represents between 1991 and 1996. However, one should be careful in the interpretation of the data for 1991 and 1992 since the PTCA register did not cover all hospitals in those years. The register also shows an increase in the use of stents. Of all PTCAs performed in 1994, stents were used in approximately 6 percent of the interventions in both age groups. Two years later, almost 38 percent of all PTCA patients received stents. There are no major differences in use between the age groups (fig. 11.5).

Changes in Low-Tech Care

Thrombolytic drugs and aspirin came into frequent use in Sweden at the end of the 1980s. The result was a significant drop in AMI mortality. For example, at a hospital in Gothenburg (Östra sjukhuset) 400 patients were treated annually for AMI between 1979 and 1990. During this period the hospital mortality fell from 18.5 percent to 11.8 percent. The decline was believed to depend on the use of intravenous treatments with beta-blockers, nitroglycerin, thrombolytics, and prophylactic low-dose aspirin (Hjalmarsson 1995, 97).

The data, supplied by the National Corporation of Pharmacies, show that the total use of thrombolytic agents, expressed as DDD (defined daily dose) per 1,000 inhabitant days, reached a peak in 1992 and since then has decreased significantly. The expansion from the mid 1980s is however still considerable (fig. 11.6). In 1986, there were 1,157 DDD units; eight years later, in 1994, this figure had risen to 11,093 DDD. Among other things, this change may have been caused by recommendations for thrombolytic use publicized by the Swedish National Board of Health and Welfare and the Medical Products Agency (Beermann 1995, 220). One reason for the decline since 1992 in the total use of thrombolytics could be the decrease in AMI incidence.

The Consequences of Changes in Heart Attack Care in Sweden

Changes in Health Outcomes for AMI Patients

Figure 11.7 shows the rate of heart failure as an outcome of AMI treatment between 1987 and 1995. The data are obtained through the AMI

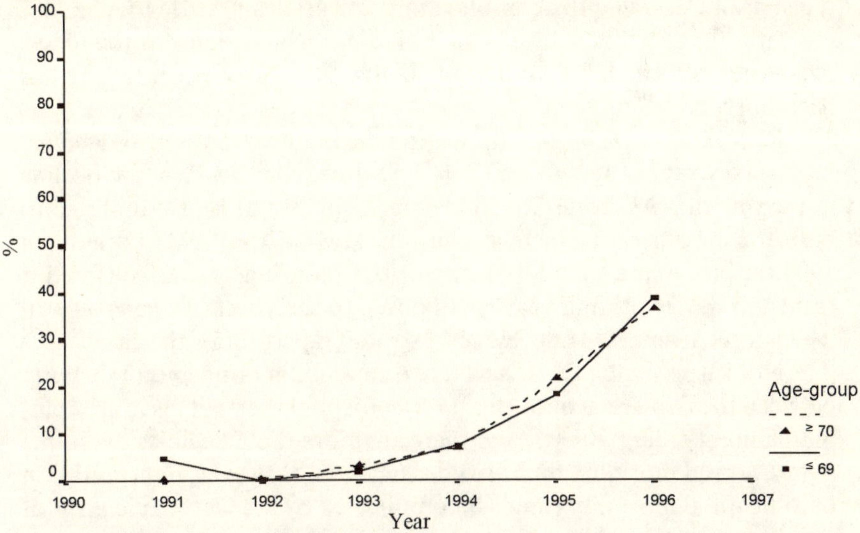

Fig. 11.5. Share of PTCA treatments involving stents, AMI patients, 1991–96

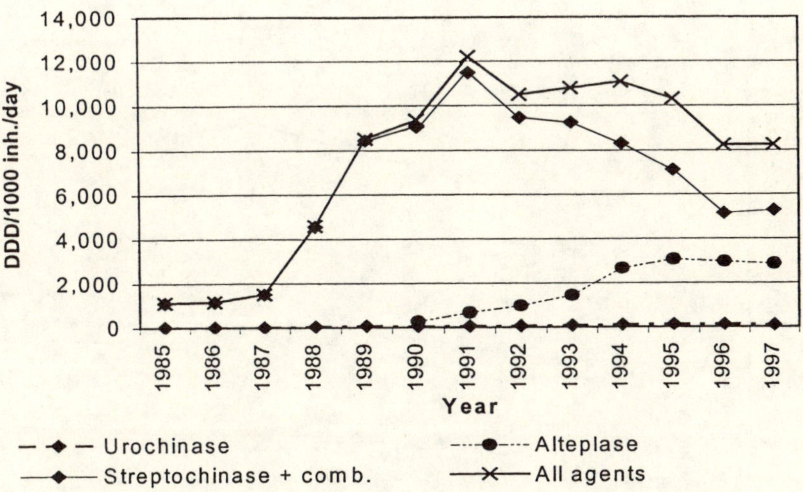

Fig. 11.6. Consumption of thrombolytic agents, 1985–97. Figure for 1997 is based on annualized data collected through November. (Data from National Corporation of Pharmacies.)

register and describe the complication rate after an AMI. Figure 11.7 indicates that there has been a slight increase for patients in the oldest age group, although for younger patients, the rate of heart failure has been fairly constant.

Recurrent AMI as a complication during 1987–95 is also decreasing in the younger age group (fig. 11.8). For older Swedes, the decline in the rate of AMI complication is much smaller. It is also more common for the elderly to have a recurrent AMI. Of all AMI patients in 1994, approximately 10.5 percent in the older age group suffered a recurrent AMI within a year, as opposed to the younger age group, in which a recurrent AMI developed in about 8 percent of the cases.

Not surprisingly, there is a large difference in in-hospital mortality between the two age groups (fig. 11.9). Hospital mortality is more common among older patients, and there are more rapid declines over time in in-hospital mortality among older patients. However, interpretation of in-hospital mortality trends is complicated by the fact that lengths of stay have also been decreasing over time (fig. 11.10) and may have been changing differentially across age groups.

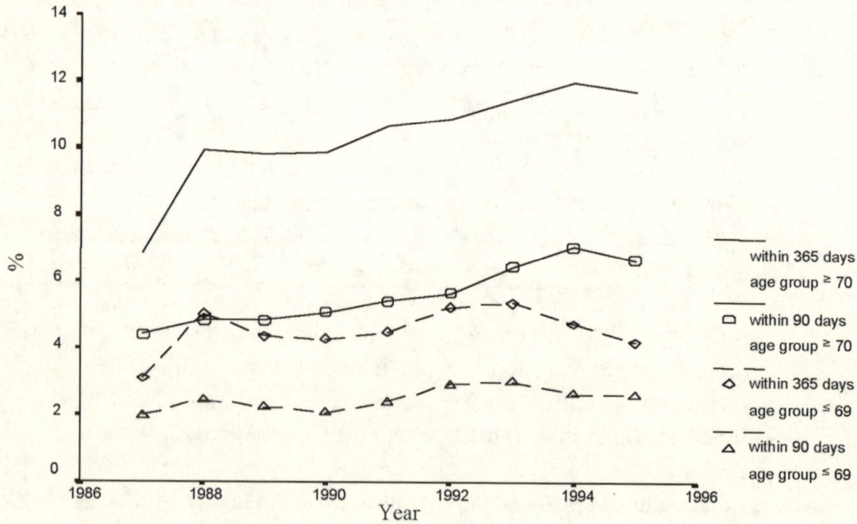

Fig. 11.7. Complication rates among AMI patients (heart failure), 1987–95

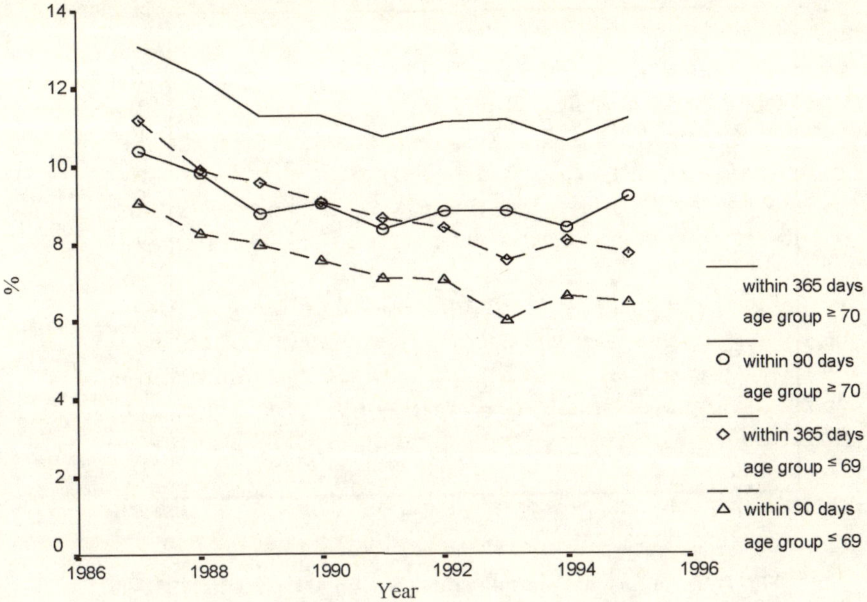

Fig. 11.8. Complication rates among AMI patients (recurrent AMI), 1987–95

Changes in Medical Expenditures and Resource Use

Because inpatient care in Sweden is financed in part with global hospital budgets, it is not easy to develop expenditure trends for heart attack care. However, most attempts to estimate trends in the cost of cardiac care in Sweden suggest that expenditures are growing relatively slowly. Although aggregate resource use for treating AMI patients more than doubled from 1960 to 1992, the number of cases treated has also increased dramatically. Indeed, in more recent years, real total expenditures on treatment for AMI have been flat. For example, the direct cost of AMI was estimated in 1975 at U.S.$132 million (in 1995 U.S. dollars, converted at PPP exchange rates); in 1995, the estimated direct costs of AMI were U.S.$134 million annually.[30] At the same time, the indirect cost for society decreased to U.S.$381 million, from U.S.$1.27 billion (Lindgren 1983, 61),[31] due to lower mortality (Murray, Lundvall, and Hallerby 1994, 80).

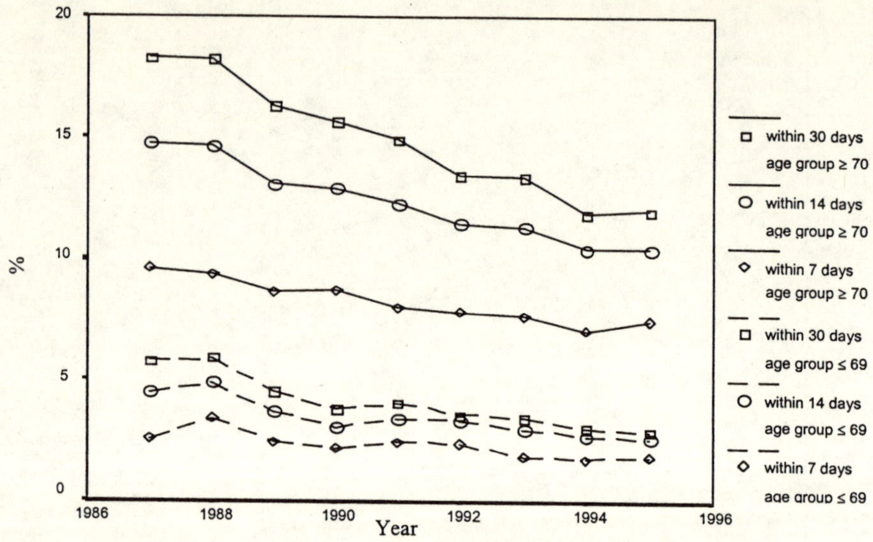

Fig. 11.9. In-hospital mortality rates among AMI patients, 1987–95

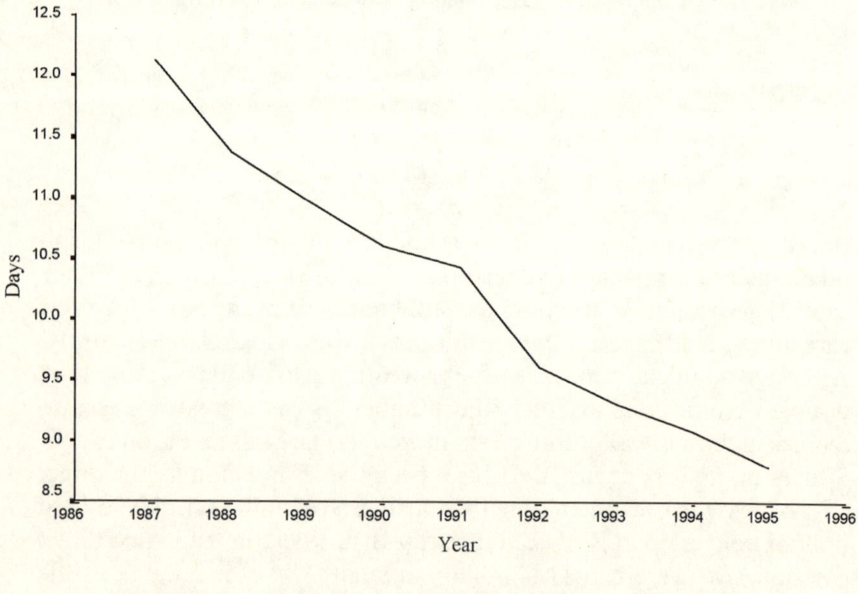

Fig. 11.10. Average length of stay for AMI patients, 1987–95

Other indicators, such as length of hospital stay and the aggregate number of hospital days treating AMI patients, reflect this phenomenon. The average length of hospital stay for AMI patients has fallen substantially (fig. 11.10): for example, from 1987 to 1991, there was a decline in the average length of stay from 12 days to 10.5 days. Length of stay has continued to fall after 1991, although the post-1991 change should be interpreted with caution because of the *ÄDEL-reform,* which may have shifted rehabilitation after AMI from hospitals to nursing homes. Along these lines, total hospital days for AMI patients (including all hospital days for the AMI itself, for all complications related to the AMI, and for performed invasive treatments) have declined as well (fig. 11.11). Although the decline for the older age-group is far greater than for the younger, this picture is moderated by excluding all individual cases with more than 100 hospital days, on the basis that this high level of total days probably represents comorbidity not related to AMI. After the exclusion, the difference between the two age groups still remained but was smaller.

Discussion

Effects on Technological Change

The effects of Sweden's health care financing system on technological change have been mixed. The ability of the county councils to finance an expansion of the health care sector by tax increases, and the resulting soft budgets for hospitals, clinics, and primary care centers from the 1960s to the early 1980s, suggest that a lack of financial restriction may have facilitated technology diffusion during this time. However, when intensive cardiac procedures began to become popular in the late 1980s, many county councils abandoned retrospective cost-based budgeting systems, substituting global budgets and DRG-type prospective reimbursement systems. These financial incentives would favor diffusion of cost-reducing technologies, but not necessarily cost-increasing technologies.

Other features of Sweden's health care system may also have worked to limit technology diffusion. Historically, patients have had only limited opportunities to choose where and how to be treated. First, except for acute cases, patients were traditionally assigned to a particular provider within their county council. Second, according to the Swedish judicial system, patients have no rights to demand a particular type of treatment. Third, competition from private hospitals

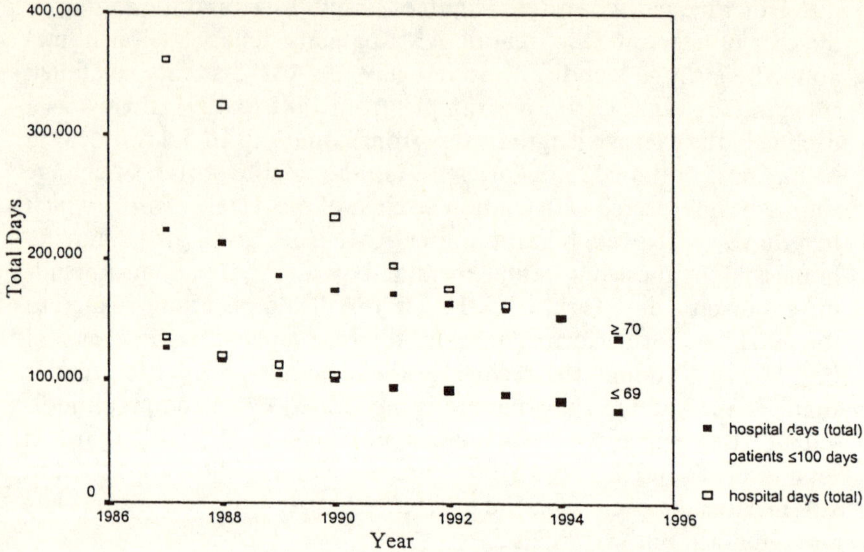

Fig. 11.11. Total hospital days for AMI patients, including complications

has been very limited, and the county councils have in fact a geographical monopoly on health care (although this situation has been changing in recent years).

On the other hand, there is strong political support for "equity" in health care, which might be exploited by hospital/clinical management or individual physicians. This could possibly put pressure on policymakers to provide similar treatments for cardiac patients nationwide and stimulate diffusion of technologies already in use (regardless of their relative cost-effectiveness). Although salaried physicians run hospitals and other health care facilities and have no financial incentives as to the type of treatment to use or how many patients to treat, for career development there is an emphasis on research merits, which may promote early introduction of new technologies. And, because patients' out-of-pocket payments are low, the patients' main incentives when choosing among technologies would be the quality rather than cost or cost-effectiveness.

As a preliminary observation, this view of the incentives for diffusion of medical technology in Sweden seems mirrored in the diffusion of high-tech procedures such as CABG and PTCA. From a relatively early date of introduction, the use of these procedures continue to increase at a moderate pace over an extended period. The stagnation in the use of CABG (although at a high level) coincides with an accelerated use of PTCA in the early 1990s (i.e. when the financial difficulties of the county councils became acute). Moreover, this is preceded by a rapid increase in thrombolytic treatment in the late 1980s. Most of the PTCAs performed have been elective, but the use of subacute PTCA is rapidly rising. The use of PTCA is restricted to hospitals with thoracic surgical departments, which limits the diffusion of nonelective PTCA. Notably, the use of direct (or primary) PTCA is very rare in Sweden. The dominant treatment for AMI is thrombolytic agents.

Implications for Changes in Expenditures and Outcomes

Most estimates of trends in the cost of cardiac care in Sweden suggest that expenditures are growing relatively slowly. There has been a decline in the length of stay for AMI patients. During the same period there was a decline in AMI incidence and in-hospital mortality in the Swedish population, but also an increase in the incidence of IHD and in the cases of heart failure as a complication to AMI treatment. It is likely that surplus funds from organizational reforms and successful treatment of AMI patients are increasingly available to treat other heart diseases. The occurrence of these illnesses could perhaps be attributed to the advances in the treatment of AMI, which expose patients to increasing probability of complications.

Notes

This research project has received financial support from the Swedish Council for Social Research, the Swedish Medical Research Council, and the Swedish Research Foundation of the National Corporation of Pharmacies. Helpful contributions by Per Albertsson at the Swedish Register for PTCA, Leif Forsberg at the Swedish National Board of Health and Welfare, and Lars Nyberg at the Swedish National Board of Health and Welfare (Division HS) are gratefully acknowledged.

1. The target of the Swedish health care system is to provide “good health and health care on equal terms for the entire population regardless of where a patient lives, or his/her income” (Swedish Health Care Act 1982).

2. The county councils were created in 1862. In the 1860s, central government transferred ownership of acute-care somatic hospitals to the county councils. In 1928, they became responsible for the provision of hospital care to

their inhabitants. During the 1950s their responsibilities widened to include the mentally retarded, mental patients, centers of convalescence, and outpatient care at hospitals. In the 1960s, the responsibility for primary care was transferred to the county councils, partly from central government and partly from local municipalities. During this time the mental hospitals were also transferred to the county councils (Lindgren 1995, 247).

3. See the electronic publication "Hjärtinfarktregistret" at the website <http://www.sos.se/epc/hjartreg/info.htm> of the National Board of Health and Welfare.

4. The Swedish AMI register operated by the National Board of Health and Welfare.

5. The data is taken from the database Sjukvårdsdata i fokus at <www.lf.se> administrated by Federation of Swedish County Councils.

6. The Social Health Insurance is financed by a proportional payroll tax, supplemented with government grants and controlled by the central government through the National Social Insurance Board.

7. In response to the queues and growing public pressure, the government issued in 1991 a "care guarantee" that ensured patients treatment within three months for 12 diagnoses; otherwise the county councils had to pay for treatment with another provider. This "care guarantee" was the result of an agreement between the government and the Federation of County Councils, and it lasted to 1996. Currently, queues have emerged again, probably due to bottleneck factors, and there is a discussion of whether to reestablish the "care guarantee."

8. Cf. Lyttkens and Borgquist 1995a, 1995b for an analysis of the mechanisms behind these changes, and of the diversity of applied solutions.

9. Some studies suggest, though, that productivity in somatic short-term treatment grew by 13.5 percent in the county council of Stockholm after the introduction of DRGs and more detailed statements of account (Svensson and Nordling 1995). The study looked at the productivity growth and cost development between 1991 and 1993. It is particularly interesting because Stockholm is the largest county council with a population of 1.1 million.

10. The fee schedule is not completely free, however, since the public sector cannot charge more than the average cost of the service (Lindgren 1995).

11. For visits to a physician at a primary care center, the patient pays U.S.$6.20–14.40. The fee for a visit to a specialist is slightly higher, U.S.$10.30–26.80.

12. The hospitals' share of total pharmaceutical cost has been relatively constant in the period 1974–94.

13. There is a cost ceiling on prescribed drugs. The patient pays maximum U.S.$134 per year on drugs that are listed by the National Insurance Board. Should a patient choose some brand that costs more than the reference price listed for the active substance, he/she has to pay for the difference.

14. These is also an ongoing discussion of whether to add one more objective, the "value for money" aspect (Johannesson and Jönsson 1993).

15. The primary assessment time for a new chemical entity is 210 days.

16. The thoracic surgery clinic in Uppsala introduced a monetary bonus system in 1992 to enhance productivity at the clinic. For every extra operation performed, the staff received 0.05 percent of the annual salary as a bonus. The productivity grew, but it was more due to loyalty to the new organization structure that was introduced (Svensson and Nordling 1995).

17. In acute cases the patient is of course admitted to the nearest hospital regardless of which county council he/she belongs to.

18. The private alternatives are extremely few in Sweden when it comes to hospital care. In some areas (notably the largest cities), there are a significant number of private practitioners. During a brief period between January 1, 1994, and December 31, 1995, a reform was introduced by the government that allowed every patient the right to choose his/her family doctor (GP). Private doctors could also be chosen. This meant that the county councils could no longer regulate the establishment of private practices. After a change in the political majority the law was withdrawn. The county councils could, if they wished, continue using the family doctor system, but it was no longer compulsory (Lindgren 1995).

19. This is the case with five county councils in the western Swedish health care region. They have a collaboration that entitles the patients to choose a primary health center in a nearby county council. This possibility to choose exists also in the southern Swedish health care region with its six county councils. In these two regions, two of the largest cities in Sweden are included (Anell and Svarvar 1995). The result of this has been some movements across the council "borders," mainly for the reason to seek treatment closer to home or work (Svensson and Nordling 1995, 60).

20. Limitations existed for treatments for highly specialized care in the regional hospitals.

21. In 1991 a phone survey was conducted in the west of Sweden. Only 15 percent of the respondents in the county council of Bohuslän claimed that they had received information about their freedom to choose from a physician. Most of the respondents had received the information from the media.

22. The survey was done by the Swedish medical journal *Dagens Medicin.*

23. Clinical experiments are an exception from the obligation that the treatment should be conducted in accordance with scientific knowledge and professional experience.

24. That is, the patient no longer needed to prove that negligence had occurred. It was enough that the probable cause of injury was the treatment received or some other action taken by health care staff.

25. In 1997 a new law for patient damages came into effect, containing some changes. It became possible to claim compensation for psychic injuries, and the compensation limit was increased to SKr 7 million (U.S.$915,600 at current exchange rates) per individual.

26. In addition, even if one obtained data from individual hospitals, there are large differences in the use of technology between hospitals that would make the overall picture difficult to establish.

27. In a study in the area of Gothenburg between 1968 and 1977, including 1,222 patients under the age of 65 who faced myocardial infarction for the first time, a drop in posthospitalization mortality rate of 50 percent was found (from 12 to 6 percent) two years after discharge from the hospital. The two most likely reasons behind the drop were that more patients had quit smoking (47 vs. 65 percent) and more patients where treated with beta-blockers for a longer time span (4 vs. 70 percent). These studies were all conducted before patients routinely were given intravenous treatments with beta-blockers, nitroglycerin, thrombolytics, and prophylactic aspirin.

28. Direct PTCA means to give PTCA immediately after an AMI as an alternative to thrombolytic drug treatment. Like direct PTCA, rescue PTCA is rare and also performed at regional hospitals when treatment with thrombolysis does not give satisfactory results. Subacute PTCA is when the treatment is given within 48 hours after the patient suffers from an unstable situation.

29. These figures are based on data from the National AMI Register, where there is underreporting of PTCA. Hence, the number of AMIs treated with PTCA is probably larger. However, the virtue of this register is in the possibility to compare different age groups, and different uses of PTCA, assuming that the underreporting is unbiased in these reports.

30. The annual consumption of prescribed drugs is not included in the indirect cost.

31. Direct costs mean purely the health care costs. Included in the indirect costs for society are costs for sick leave, pension, and the cost of death.

References

Anell, A. 1994. *Sjukhusets kontrakt.* Stockholm: SNS Förlag.

Anell, A., and P. Svarvar. 1995. "Reforms in the Swedish Health Care Sector: Survey and Analysis." In *The Nordic Lights: New Initiatives in Health Care Systems,* ed. A. Alban and T. Christiansen. Odense: Odense University Press.

Beerman, B. 1995. "Trombolysbehandling i Sverige—en nationell översikt." In *Hjärtattack—akut eller hotande hjärtinfarkt* (consensus report from conference in Stockholm, April 26–28, 1995), 220–27. Stockholm: SPRI (Swedish Institute for Health Services Development) i samarbete med Medicinska forsknirgsrådet.

Danzon, P. M. 1994. "The Swedish Patient Compensation System: Myths and Realities." *International Review of Law and Economics* 14:453–66.

Hjalmarsson, Å. 1995. "Historisk återblick med avseende på behandling och prognos nationellt och internationellt." In *Hjärtattack—akut eller hotande hjärtinfarkt* (consensus report from conference in Stockholm, April 26–26, 1995), 94–106. Stockholm: SPRI i samarbete med Medicinska forsknirgsrådet.

Högberg, M., and S. Håkansson. 1995. "Hur kan hjärtinfarktvården göras mera kostnadseffektiv?" In *Hjärtattack—akut eller hotande hjärtinfarkt* (consensus report from conference in Stockholm, April 26–26, 1995), 262–302. Stockholm: SPRI i samarbete med Medicinska forsknirgsrådet.

Johannesson, M., and B. Jönsson. 1993. *Ekonomisk utvärdering av läkemedel.* SNS Förlag: Stockholm.

Kranskärlssjukvårdens utbyggand i Sverige (KRUS). 1987. *Kranskärlssjukvårdens utbyggand i Sverige: Rapport från expertgruppen.* Stockholm: Landstingsförbundet and Socialstyrelsen.

Liedström, G. 1995. *Lagen om medicintekniska produkter.* Stockholm: Publica.

Lindgren, B. 1983. *De samhällsekonomiska kostnaderna för akut hjärtinfarkt,* Vård vid hjärtinfarkt, Konsensuskonferens 7–9 juni 1983. Stockholm: MFR.

———. 1995. "Health Care Organization and Finance in Sweden." In *The Nordic Lights: New Initiatives in Health Care Systems,* ed. A. Alban and T. Christiansen. Odense: Odense University Press.

Lindgren, B., and P. Roos. 1985. *Produktions-, kostnads- och produktivitetsutveckling inom offentligt bedriven hälso- och sjukvård 1960–1980.* Rapport till expertgruppen för studier i offentlig ekonomi, Ds Fi 3.

Lyttkens, C. H., and L. Borgquist. 1995a. "Organisational Change in the Swedish Health Care Sector." In *The Nordic Lights: New Initiatives in Health Care Systems,* ed. A. Alban and T. Christiansen. Odense: Odense University Press.

———. 1995b. "Swedish Health Care in the Late 1980s and Early 1990s—a Story of Institutional Changes." In *The Nordic Lights: New Initiatives in Health Care Systems,* ed. A. Alban and T. Christiansen. Odense: Odense University Press.

Murray, R., O. Lundvall, and N. Hallerby. 1994. *Kvalitets- och produktivitetsutvecklingen i sjukvården 1960–1992,* ESO DS: 22. Stockholm: Fritzes.

Paulsson, E. M. 1995. "Hospital Financing in Sweden." In *Hospital Financing in Seven Countries,* ed. M. Wiley, M. Laschober, and H. Gelband. Office of Technology Assessment, U.S. Congress. Washington, D.C.: U.S. Government Printing Office.

SBU-rapport. 1997. *Att förebygga sjukdom i hjärta och kärl.* No. 134.

SoS-rapport. 1995. *Sjukvården i Sverige.* No. 25. Stockholm: Fritzes.

SOU. 1993. *Hälso- och sjukvården i framtiden.* No. 38. Stockholm: Fritzes.

———. 1995. *Reform på recept.* No. 122. Stockholm: Fritzes.

———. 1996. *Behov och resurser i vården—en analys.* Del A och B 163. Fritzes: Stockholm.

———. 1997. *Patienten har Rätt.* No. 154. Stockholm: Fritzes.

Svensk Författningssamling. 1993. SFS 584.

Svensson, H., and S. Nordling. 1995. "Effekter av nya styrformer i sjukvården-en litteratur översikt." In *Den planerade marknaden.* Socialstyrelsen följer upp och utvärderar, vol. 7. Stockholm: Socialstyrelsen.

Sverne, E., and T. Sverne. 1993. *Patientens Rätt.* Stockholm: Norstedts Juridik.

Westerhäll, L. 1992. *An Introduction to Medical Malpractice Law in the United States and Sweden.* Stockholm: Norstedts Juridik.

———. 1994. *Medical Law.* Stockholm: Fritzes.

Yearbook of Health and Medical Care. 1995–97. National Board of Health and Welfare, Official Statistics of Sweden.

CHAPTER 12

Determinants and Consequences of Technological Change in the Care of Acute Myocardial Infarction Patients in Finland

Unto Häkkinen, Ilmo Keskimäki, and Kimmo Asikainen

Until the 1980s, mortality from cardiovascular diseases and especially from coronary heart disease (CHD) in Finland was one of the highest in the world. In 1976, CHD mortality for men was 550 per 100,000 and 235 per 100,000 for women. In addition, surveys on morbidity and mortality due to coronary heart disease showed large regional and socioeconomic variations. Lowering the health burden of coronary heart disease has consequently been a main issue in Finnish health policy. Public health efforts have focused on preventive measures, such as nutrition and tobacco control policies (Puska et al. 1995), but analysis of the treatment of heart diseases has also been an important topic in health services research.

As figure 12.1 shows, between 1975 and 1995 CHD mortality decreased dramatically for both men (by 33 percent) and women (by 22 percent). A considerable part of the decline in CHD mortality has been attributable to decreased numbers of deaths from acute myocardial infarction (AMI), which have fallen over this period from 415 to 232 per 100,000 (44 percent) among men and from 172 to 112 per 100,000 (35 percent) among women. Since the late 1980s the decline in both CHD and AMI mortality has accelerated. About one-third of the AMI mortality decrease of 1976–95 occurred in the 1990s.

At the same time, figure 12.1 shows that real health care expenditure in Finland has risen substantially. To what extent do these aggregate trends in resource use and mortality from CHD and AMI reflect a causal relationship between the use of high technology in medical care

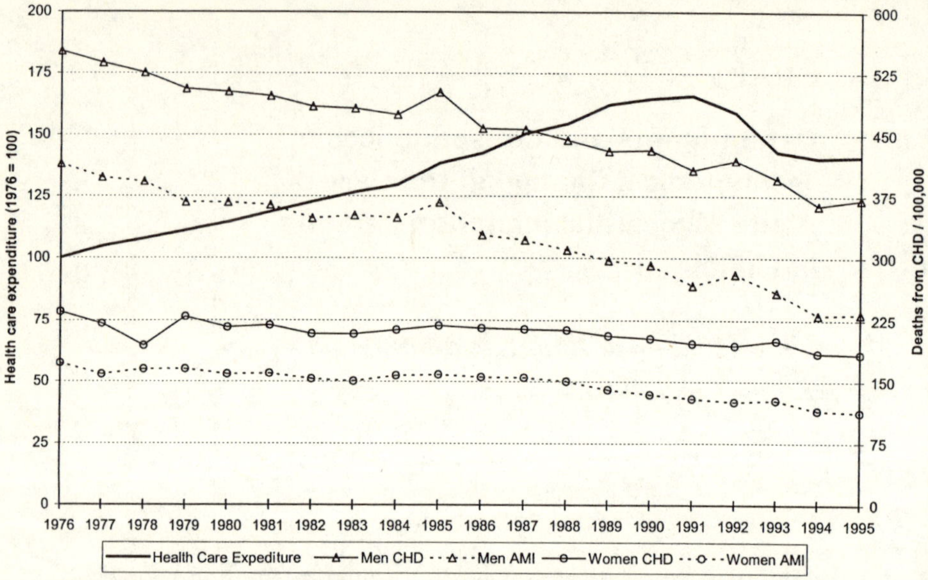

Fig. 12.1. Health care expenditure at constant prices (1976 = 100) and age-standardized mortality from coronary heart disease in Finland, 1976–95

and patient health outcomes? The purpose of this chapter is to explore the relationship between technological change, the use of intensive treatments for AMI, and patient health. We first describe the Finnish health care system and the economic and regulatory incentives that it provides for technological change in the treatment of AMI. The second section of the chapter documents how technological change has affected medical treatment for AMI in Finland over the 1987–96 period, primarily using data on inpatient records from the Finnish Hospital Discharge Register. The third section presents information on in-hospital mortality of these patients; unfortunately, neither information on out-of-hospital mortality nor information on resource use is available in Finland at the individual patient level. The fourth section of the chapter discusses our findings and offers some tentative conclusions about the causes and consequences of technological change in Finland over the 1980s and 1990s.

Incentives for Technological Change in Finland

The Finnish health care system covers the whole population. Health services are mainly produced by the public sector and financed through general taxation. In Finland, the local administrative units, that is, municipalities, are responsible for providing health services for their residents (fig. 12.2). The municipalities are governed by elected councils that levy taxes that provide the primary source of financing for health care services (central government subsidies and user charges supplement municipal tax revenue). The median size of the 452 municipalities is about 5,000 inhabitants, but municipalities range in size from about 200 people to over 500,000 in the capital.

Hospital care is primarily provided by the public sector, through 22 hospital districts that are administrative federations of municipalities. The hospital districts own and run over 50 acute care general hospitals, which are divided into three categories: regional, central, and university hospitals. Regional hospitals provide services only in most common specialties. University hospitals are central hospitals for their own districts and provide tertiary level services for other districts in their responsibility area.

Although the private sector has a significant role in production of elective, nonurgent health services (in ambulatory care, private practitioners provide about 20 percent of doctor visits), its role in inpatient care is much more minor (about 5 percent of all hospital admissions). However, in some services the share of private hospitals is more substantial. In 1996, private hospitals produced about 12 percent of all coronary angiograms and bypass operations. Patients' expenses for the use of private services are partly reimbursed by the National Health Insurance (NHI), which is mandatory and managed by the Social Insurance Institution (SII). Besides the expenses for private sector examinations and treatments, the NHI reimburses part of the expenses for prescription drugs, dental care for young adults, transportation services, and rehabilitation.

Financing of Care for Heart Disease

In the 1990s, two factors markedly affected the Finnish health care system: the revision of the central government subsidy system in 1993, and an extraordinarily severe economic recession in 1991–93. The main content of the central government subsidy reform was a revision of the

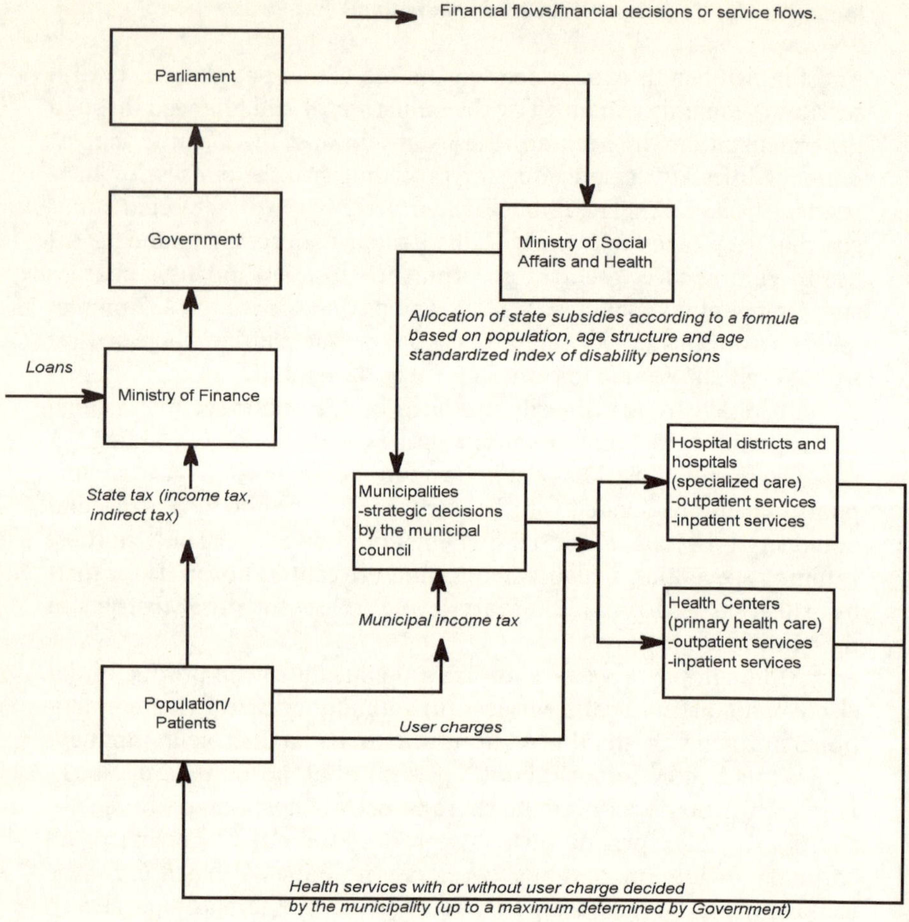

Fig. 12.2. The finance and production of municipal health services in Finland

principles for determining operating-budget subsidies to hospitals. While the central government subsidies for operations under the former system were related to actual expenditures and split between municipalities and direct payments to hospital districts, they are now lump sum grants paid to municipalities that are calculated prospectively. Thus, municipalities—which control the hospital districts—now are faced with either a global budget constraint or the prospect of imposing a tax increase on their residents.

This reform has dramatically changed the way that hospital operations in Finland are financed. The aim of the reform was to reduce central government control and to increase local freedom in the provision of services. The reform was intended to allow the municipalities to adopt a more active role as a purchaser of services instead of the previous role of a provider-producer.

Before 1993, hospitals received about half of their revenues from the central government via the provincial boards. The other half of revenues came from municipalities. Charges were usually assigned to municipalities according to bed-days used by their residents without taking severity of cases or actual costs of treatments into account. Since 1993, hospital charging has depended more directly on the quantity and quality of services purchased by municipalities. In 1997, two hospital districts introduced pricing systems based on DRGs. For elective surgical services, such as coronary revascularization, the prices for municipalities or other hospital districts are now based mainly on two methods: (1) a service package including all services required by a "standard" treatment of a "normal" inpatient defined by causes or types of treatment or (2) a combination of an average price per bed-day and an additional fee for the procedure. However, the hospital districts managing hospitals determine prices for hospital services without national guidelines. Consequently, methods and procedures of defining services and setting prices vary across districts.

Financing of capital expenditures by hospitals was less affected by the 1993 reforms. The central government still subsidizes capital investments directly. Central government subsidies for investments in municipal health services vary between municipalities from 25 percent to 50 percent of the value of a capital investment according to the per capita income of the municipality.

Evaluation of the effects of the subsidy reform are complicated by radical changes in the Finnish economy that occurred contemporaneously. Due to a severe recession, the unemployment rate increased from 3 percent to 18 percent from 1990 to 1993; since then it has only slowly fallen, to 16 percent in 1996. GDP in Finland at constant prices fell 15 percent from 1991 to 1993. Although some economic growth occurred during the two following years, the GDP in 1995 was below the figures of the late 1980s. The recession was also reflected in health care spending. In 1991–94 the health care expenditure decreased by 15 percent (fig. 12.1).

Technology Regulation

At the macro level, the adoption of medical technology in Finland is mainly regulated by the above discussed budgeting system. The final decision-maker is the district council consisting of members appointed by the member municipalities. However, professional opinion has a strong influence. Budgets and operative plans are prepared by leading physicians from districts and hospitals (Saltman 1987). There are few formal restrictions to investing in any specific technology.

Nevertheless, the spread of high medical technology, such as invasive cardiac procedures, has remained restricted and regionalized in Finland. In public health care, coronary bypass operations and angioplasties are performed in six hospitals and angiograms in eight hospitals in different parts of the country. In addition, these procedures are performed in three private clinics. Since the 1980s coronary revascularizations have been the subject of intense public discussion, with the main focus on scarcity and regional disparities in the supply of procedures. Several central government working groups have considered the need for, and development of, additional capacity to provide invasive treatments of CHD. In the late 1980s Parliament even voted for an appropriation to increase the supply of revascularization procedures.

Compared to these rather strict overall constraints, the role of "microregulation" is minor in Finland. For example, doctors' prescription patterns are not controlled, and there are no formal mechanisms to regulate individual practitioners' medical decisions.

Competition

Since the 1993 reform, hospital financing has been based on utilization of services more directly than in the past. This change has the potential to increase price competition among providers. Yet price competition in specialized hospital care is still rather limited: the hospital districts are local monopolies in their areas, and membership in the regional hospital district is mandatory for the municipalities. In fact, a municipality has a disincentive to buy services outside its own hospital district, because such behavior could lead to the deterioration of the hospitals for which it is legally responsible. Most municipalities are also economically weak in relation to hospital districts and are unlikely to have sufficient power to make hospitals compete. Moreover, because the supply of intensive services for AMI patients is regionalized and concentrated in the six major hospitals located in different parts of the country, hospitals have the opportunity to use revenues from intensive cardiac procedures to cross-subsidize less intensive services, in which they may face greater competition.

On the patients' side, choices are generally restricted. In general, a patient cannot choose his or her hospital of treatment; the primary-care health center in the patient's municipality of residence makes decisions on referrals. There is also minimal competition for postacute treatment of patients with AMI: these treatments are mainly centralized in university hospitals with catchment areas decided administratively. A patient can choose to go to a private hospital. However, private hospitals do not provide emergency services, and in the private sector a patient must pay for a substantial amount of treatment costs out of pocket.

Other Incentives for Technology Adoption and Use

Public hospital doctors do not have clear incentives for adopting new technology, since they draw monthly (uniform) salaries with limited allowance for variation in performance. On the other hand, the emphasis on equity in Finnish health policy implies a pressure on health care providers to make new technologies available to all patients regardless of age, income, or geographical residence. Other factors that may affect incentives for technology adoption and use include those discussed in the ensuing subsections.

Malpractice Liability

Malpractice liability pressure is not significant in Finland. All patients are covered by mandatory first-party, no-fault medical accident insurance. Compensation does not require a mistake or negligence on the part of providers; any unexpected injury or complication is sufficient. However, the level of compensation is relatively low. Employers pay insurance premiums for their employees; private practitioners are covered by a collective insurance as a membership benefit of the medical association. In cases of negligence, patients can also file a civil lawsuit against the doctor. Yet lawsuits are very infrequent.

Regulation of Physician Supply

The central government (Ministry of Education) controls the numbers of enrollees in health care education and training. Until 1992, hospital personnel decisions were regulated jointly by the central government and provincial boards. If a hospital district employed any new personnel that were not approved in its officially accepted plan, it did not get state subsidies for the post and had to acquire financing for all incurred costs from its "client" municipalities. Since the 1993 reform, personnel decisions are no longer regulated by the central government; they are solely the responsibility of the hospital districts.

In the private sector, permission of the relevant provincial board is required in order to found a private hospital or other private service. An individual doctor starting a private practice does not need such permission, but does have to notify the provincial board about the practice.

Technological Change in Heart Attack Care in Finland

Sources of Data

Our analysis of the changes in the treatment of AMI patients in Finland are principally based on two data sources: hospital discharge data, for information on high-technology treatments and health outcomes, and data collected for the FINMONICA study, for information on low-technology drug treatments. We validate these results with aggregate data collected by the Finnish Heart Association (1998).

Hospital Discharge Data

For this study, the annual cohorts of AMI patients were constructed from longitudinal data files of inpatient records in the 1987–96 Finnish Hospital Discharge Register. The register has been operating since the 1960s, and it covers all hospitals in Finland. The register contains personal, administrative, and clinical data on hospital stays, such as the patient's identity code, hospital number, admission and discharge dates, principal and two subsidiary diagnoses, and discharge status. Data on surgical procedures were gathered starting in 1986.

Patients were identified for inclusion on the basis of a principal diagnosis of AMI (ICD9: 410). The patients with an admission due to MI within one year prior to their hospitalization were excluded from the sample of that year. Patients were also excluded if they were admitted as transfers from other hospitals, unless the principal diagnosis for the preceding admission was AMI. Moreover, patients were excluded if their stays in hospital were over 365 days or too short to constitute a true AMI (patients admitted for less than three days were included only if the admission concluded with an in-hospital death). We present results on procedure use during the first admission, and within one year of the initial admission.

After exclusions, the annual study cohorts covered about 80 percent of all AMI admissions in each year; the share remained stable during the study period. The proportion of outliers excluded due to stays longer than one year was about 1 percent of annual admissions. Moreover, in about 10 percent of the outlier cases, the patient had already been included in the study cohorts of the previous years. The total number of new AMI patients (study cohorts) decreased from 12,747 in 1988 to 10,672 patients in 1996. There was considerable decrease in the rates of new cases in all four age and gender groups, although the decline was relatively (per population) steepest (about 40 percent) among those ages 40–64 in both sexes.

Due to the current Finnish classification of surgical procedures, coronary artery bypass grafting (CABG) was the only relevant cardiac procedure on which the discharge register collected data for the total study period. Since 1994, the register has also recorded angioplasties (PTCA), and since 1995, angiographies. However, these procedures appear to have been underreported by all hospital districts except one, the Varsinais-Suomi district. For this reason, our analysis of PTCA and angiography is limited to this single university-hospital-based district.

FINMONICA MI Register

The description of changes in low-tech treatments (drugs) is based on the FINMONICA study (Miettinen et al. 1996). Since the mid-1980s, treatment practices for myocardial infarction in Finland have been monitored by the acute coronary care surveys of the registers accumulating data from three regions in Finland. However, the study regions are not necessarily representative of Finland; thus, the results from the FINMONICA study may give a biased picture of the treatment of AMI in Finland.

Changes in the Use of High-Tech Procedures

Data collected by the Finnish Heart Association (1998), presented in table 12.1, shows the total number of CABG, PTCA, and angiography procedures performed in Finland over the 1988 to 1996 period. Over this period, the total number of coronary bypass operations increased from 2,114 to 4,577. The annual rate of increase was fastest (15–25 per-

TABLE 12.1. Total Number of Bypass Surgery, Angioplasty, and Angiography Procedures in Finland, 1988–96

	1988	1989	1990	1991	1992	1993	1994	1995	1996
Bypass surgery	2,114	2,231	2,294	2,486	3,105	3,693	4,279	4,403	4,577
Annual increase (%)		5.5	2.8	8.4	24.9	18.9	15.9	2.9	4.0
Angioplasty	272	430	652	876	1,068	1,390	1,604	1,803	2,102
Annual increase (%)		58.1	51.6	34.4	21.9	30.1	15.4	12.4	16.6
Angiography						8,371	8,927	9,312	11,733
Annual increase (%)							6.6	4.3	26.0

Source: Finnish Heart Association 1998.

cent) in 1991–94. The number of angioplasties has increased even more in percentage terms but from a lower base level; the number of angioplasties in 1996 was only about half as great as the number of bypass operations.

The upward trend in the total number of coronary bypass operations is reflected in figure 12.3. Figure 12.3 presents trends in CABG rates for AMI patients in the year after their MI, by age group and gender, based on data from the Finnish Hospital Discharge Register. Figure 12.3 shows that CABG rates have risen dramatically for all age groups and for both men and women over the 1988 to 1995 period, with the fastest increases occurring between 1992 and 1994. Nonelderly males (ages 40–64) experienced the greatest absolute increase in CABG rates, from approximately 8.5 percent in 1998 to 22.1 percent in 1995. However, elderly females (65 and older) showed the greatest relative increase in CABG, from 3.8 percent to 11 percent, an almost threefold increase. Information not presented in the figure suggests that few of these additional procedures occurred during the patient's first admission; a constant small fraction (about 1–2 percent) of AMI patients received CABG during their initial hospital stay.

Table 12.2 shows the fraction of AMI patients receiving intensive cardiac procedures within one year of their MI in 1995 in the hospital district of Varsinais-Suomi (as discussed above, national trend data on procedures other than CABG are not yet available in Finland). The distribution of coronary procedures in this hospital district is exceptional: in 1995 hospitals this district produced more angioplasties than bypass operations, while in the whole country the total number of bypass operations was about 2.4 times higher than the number of angioplasties. In addition, a comparison between table 12.2 and figure 12.3 suggests that the rates of procedure use in the elderly were abnormally low in this hospital. According to table 12.2, nonelderly males were more than three times as likely to be treated with CABG within one year in 1995, relative to elderly males; but according to figure 12.3, nonelderly males were only 1.36 times more likely to be treated with CABG within one year in 1995.

Changes in the Use of Low-Tech Treatments

Although the Finnish Hospital Discharge Register does not contain information about the use drug treatments for AMI, a recent study revealed marked changes in the role of pharmaceuticals (Miettinen et

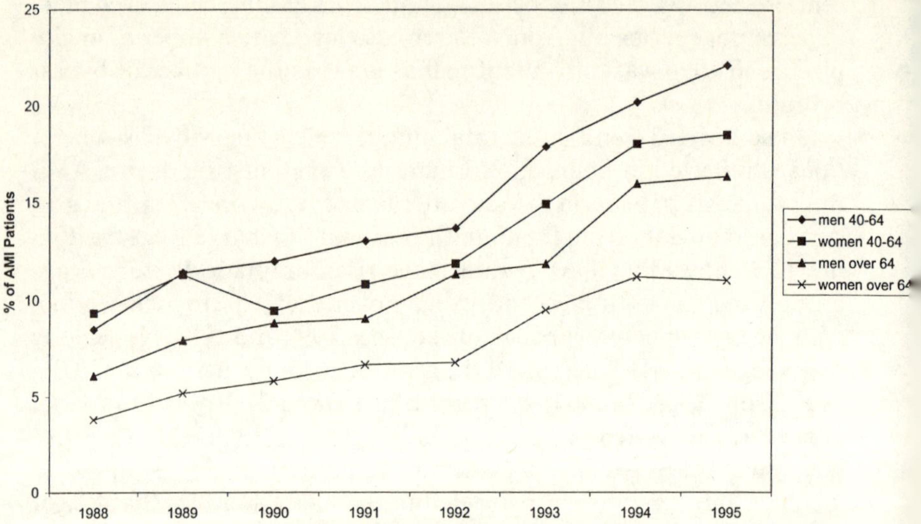

Fig. 12.3. One-year CABG rates, AMI Patients in Finland, 1988–95

TABLE 12.2. Bypass Surgery, Angioplasty, and Angiography Rate for AMI Patients Hospitalized in the District of Varsinais-Suomi in 1995 after One Year

Procedure	%
Bypass surgery	
Men 40–64	11.8
Men over 64	3.5
Women 40–64	10.5
Women over 64	0.6
Angioplasty	
Men 40–64	25.7
Men over 64	3.5
Women 40–64	18.4
Women over 64	1.2
Angiography	
Men 40–64	46.7
Men over 64	9.7
Women 40–64	34.2
Women over 64	3.9

al. 1996). Table 12.3 documents the use of drugs in the hospital treatment of AMI patients in the three FINMONICA study areas—North Karelia, Kuopio, and Turku/Loimaa—for the years 1986, 1989, and 1992. Most notably, the use of acetylsalicylic acid (aspirin) during hospitalizations for definite or probable AMIs increased from about 30 percent (28–42 percent depending on the study area) to over 80 percent (80–90 percent) during the study period. The use of thrombolytic therapy in AMI hospitalizations increased from 3–5 percent to 19–29 percent. Moreover, the use of beta-blocking agents and nitrates increased, whereas the use of calcium channels blockers decreased. Results not presented in the table show that similar trends occurred in the drugs prescribed for AMI patients at hospital discharge.

Recent evidence suggests that the use of thrombolytic drugs to treat AMI is still increasing in Finland, at least in part due to the fact that advocates have emphasized the importance of the availability of thrombolytics in all municipal heath centers having emergency services. According to a recent study (Turunen 1998), the availability of thrombolytic therapy increased from 16 percent to 32 percent of health centers between 1990 and 1995. But even in 1995, there was still considerable variation in the supply of the therapy across health centers.

TABLE 12.3. Use of Drugs in Hospital Treatment of AMI Patients in Three FINMONICA Study Areas, 1986–92 (%)

	North Karelia			Kuopio			Turku/Loimaa		
	1986	1989	1992	1986	1989	1992	1986	1989	1992
Beta-blocking agents	68	79	82	68	75	78	66	65	74
Nitrates (long acting)	70	93	95	75	72	76	78	84	83
Calcium channel blockers	42	50	33	45	40	32	51	49	35
Acetylsalicylic acid	42	81	80	28	71	80	33	74	90
Anticoagulants	23	19	39	49	23	19	51	13	28
Antiarrhythmics	25	23	22	32	31	14	18	20	16
Diuretics	40	36	34	40	43	45	43	51	33
Inotropic agents	27	30	20	36	32	23	33	40	24
ACE inhibitors		11	23		19	24		9	15
Cholesterol-reducing agents		10	6		8	9		4	8
Nitrate infusion		52	77		40	56		32	53
Thrombolytic drugs	3	14	26	5	16	19	3	15	29
Number of patients	117	98	79	151	137	139	101	75	76

Source: Miettinen et al. 1996.

The Consequences of Changes in Heart Attack Care in Finland

Information on the consequences of changes in AMI treatment is also based on the cohorts of AMI patients constructed from the Finnish Hospital Discharge Data. We evaluate outcomes with data on 1-, 7-, and 30-day in-hospital mortality; unfortunately, we cannot link hospital discharge data with death records to provide information on out-of-hospital mortality. In addition, in Finland it is not possible to get reliable information on the trends of costs or expenditure attributable to the treatment of AMI patients. As a resource indicator, we consider trends in the length of stay of the first admission, and in the total days in hospital for all admissions during the year after the AMI.

Changes in Health Outcomes

Figure 12.1 suggests that, at least in part, the decline of CHD mortality has been attributable to decreased population mortality from AMI. However, this may be due to declining incidence, or to declining case fatality. Earlier studies suggest that case fatality from AMI may not have contributed substantially to the decreased population mortality observed in the aggregate Finnish data. Salomaa, Miettinen, et al. (1996) analyzed data on CHD mortality in the three FINMONICA study areas. Over the 1983 to 1992 period, they found that in Turku/Loimaa—the study area with the smallest change in population mortality—declining case fatality contributed substantially to declines in mortality from AMI, but that declining case fatality was less important in the other two areas (Salomaa, Miettinen, et al. 1996). Moreover, according to statistics on the occurrence of coronary heart disease in the whole country over the 1991 to 1994 period, there were no changes in case fatality of AMI patients (Salomaa, Tamminen, et al. 1996).

Our analysis of hospital discharge data, presented in figures 12.4 and 12.5, is consistent with these results. Over the 1988 to 1991 period, 1-, 7-, and 30-day in-hospital mortality from AMI declined, with substantial declines for some demographic groups. For example, in the nonelderly (fig. 12.4), 30-day in-hospital mortality declined from 12.7 percent to 8.2 percent (for women), and from 9.5 percent to 7.2 percent (for men); in the elderly (fig. 12.5), 30-day in-hospital mortality declined from 27.0 percent to 24.4 percent (for men), and from 28.5 percent to 27.5 percent (for women). However, over the 1991 to 1995

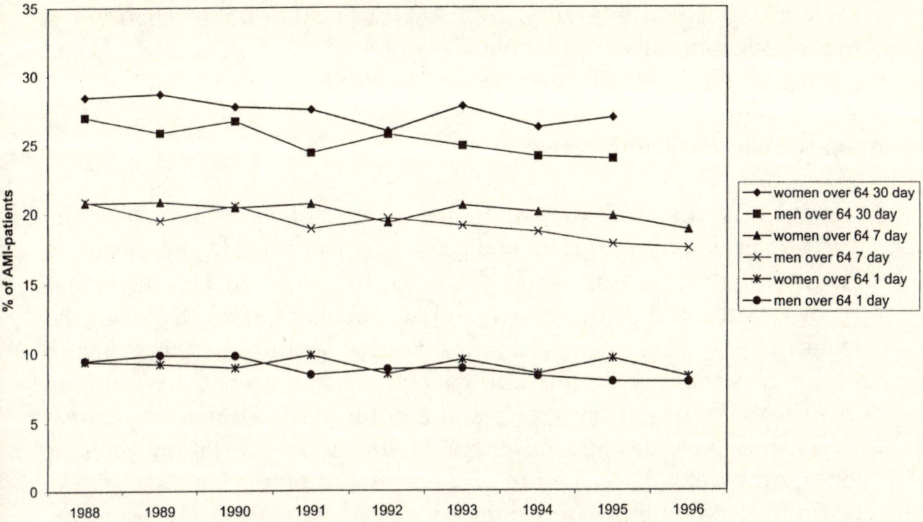

Fig. 12.4. In-hospital mortality rates, elderly AMI patients in Finland, 1988–96

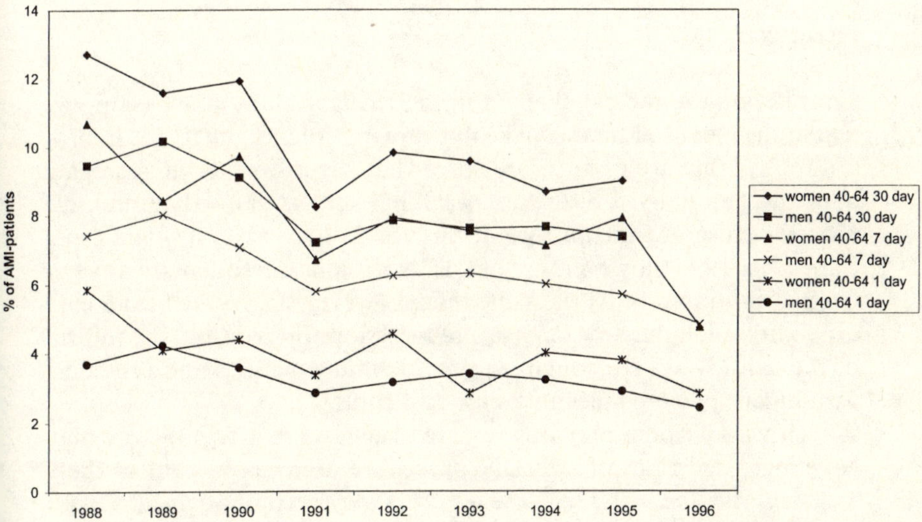

Fig. 12.5. In-hospital mortality rates, nonelderly AMI patients in Finland, 1988–96

period, in-hospital mortality from AMI was either flat or slightly rising. In addition, figures 12.4 and 12.5 present the potentially unusual finding that in-hospital mortality was greater for women than for men.

Changes in Hospital Utilization

Figures 12.6 and 12.7 present trends in hospital utilization over the 1988–95 period by age group and gender. The average length of stay of AMI patients' first admissions decreased from 12.7 to 11.5 days, that is, by 9 percent. The decrease mainly occurred in 1992–95, when the length of stay shortened by about one day. In absolute terms, figure 12.6 shows that the decline in the length of stay was greatest among men in the younger age group and among older women; in relative terms, however, declines in length of stay were substantially larger among the nonelderly. Figure 12.7 shows the gender and age breakdown for total number of bed-days for AMI patients in the year after their initial admission. Overall, there was a slight decrease of about one day over the 1988 to 1995 period.[1] Information not presented in the figures shows that this was due to a gradual upward trend in the number of admissions per patient in the year after an AMI.

Discussion

Considering the radical changes in the 1990s in the Finnish economy and in the means of financing health care in Finland, the trends in procedure use that we observe are somewhat surprising. Both aggregate data and our analysis of the use of CABG surgery show that intensive procedure use in Finland rose during the 1980s and 1990s, and especially after 1990 (however, use of PTCA remains infrequent, relative to CABG, in Finland). At the same time, however, aggregate health care expenditure fell due to a very severe recession. In addition, the reform of the subsidy system sought to provide municipalities and providers with higher-powered incentives for cost control.

However, some previous research suggests that two factors may have increased rates of intensive procedure use even in light of these factors. First, the increase in the numbers of procedures coincided with a general increase in hospital productivity (Häkkinen 1999). Indeed, according to a recent study, hospital productivity was already improving before the 1992 financing reforms, which indicates that the recession may have had a marked additional impact on hospital productivity (Linna 1998). However, for the expansion of intensive cardiac

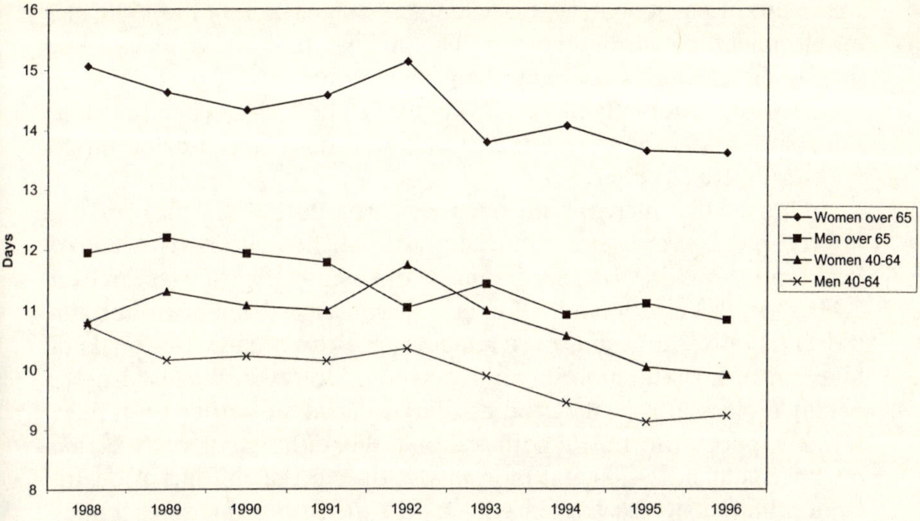

Fig. 12.6. Average length of stay of initial admission, AMI patients in Finland, 1988–96

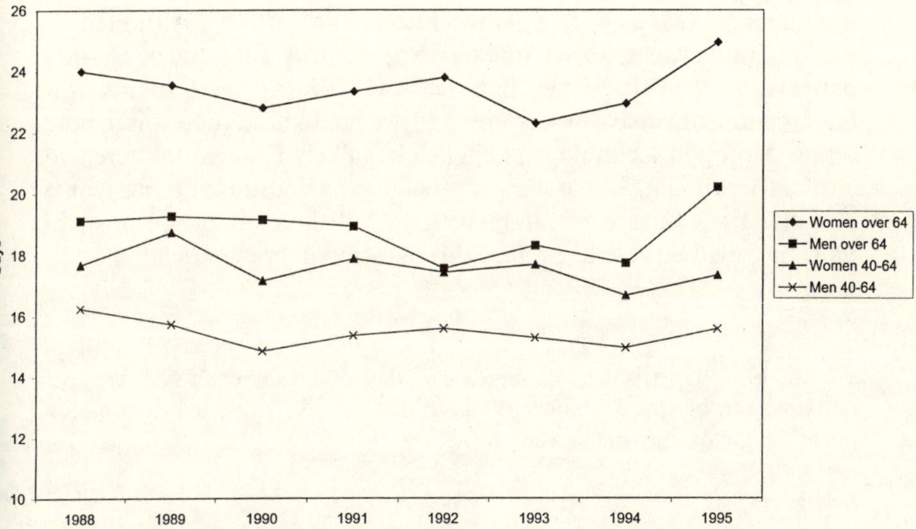

Fig. 12.7. One-year average hospital utilization, AMI patients in Finland, 1988–96

treatment in particular there is a simpler explanation: in the 1980s the development of cardiac surgery had a high political priority. The investment decisions enabling the growing numbers of procedures in the 1990s were actually made already in the late 1980s, when the planning of new operating theaters and catheterization laboratories started and staff were recruited.

Unlike the increase in intensive procedure use, the greatest improvement in in-hospital mortality for patients with AMI occurred between 1988 and 1991. This finding is consistent with other research on AMI mortality in Finland. Of course, because we examine in-hospital mortality only, our results must remain suggestive because we could not take out-of-hospital mortality into account. However, because lengths of stay (at least for the index admission) declined most after 1991, there is no support for the hypothesis that the differential early-period improvement in in-hospital mortality is due to the shifting of deaths from admitted to discharged patients. In the future this shortcoming can be improved by linking hospital data to the cause-of-death register, which will provide data on both sudden, out-of hospital AMI deaths and follow-up data on mortality after the patient's discharge.

The treatment of AMI patients has developed markedly in Finland during the last 15 years. New methods have been adopted in acute treatment of AMI as well as in prevention of new attacks. Although we could not investigate the changes in expenditure on treatment of AMI patients, our results show that the AMI patients in Finland now undergo more invasive procedures and are readmitted to hospital more often. Although technological change has likely resulted in increased costs of treatment, it is not clear whether the additional treatment is cost-effective. Future research, with linked data on out-of-hospital mortality, will be able to explore this question in greater detail.

Note

1. In 1994–95 there was an increase in the total number of bed-days per AMI patient, of approximately 1.8 days; this was likely due to a two-month nurses' strike during that period.

References

Airaksinen, J., E. Pokela, M. Niemelä, A. Ylitalo, and M. Ikäheimo. 1996. "Välitön pallonlaajennus—uhkaavan infarktin paras hoito" (Immediate angioplasty—the best treatment for imminent myocardial infarction). *Duodecim* 112:1345–49.

Finnish Heart Association. 1998. *Sydänleikkausrekisteri 1996* (Cardiac operation register, 1996). Helsinki: Sydäntautiliitto.

Häkkinen, U. 1999. "Cost-Containment in Finnish Health Care." In *Health Care and Cost Containment in the European Union,* ed. E. J. Mossialos and J. Legrand, 661–99. Ashgate: Aldershot.

Linna, M. 1998. "Measuring Hospital Cost Efficiency with Panel Data Models." *Health Economics* 7:415–27.

Miettinen, H., M. Mähönen, V. Salomaa, M. Ketonen, M. Arstila, P. Immonen-Räihä, E. Kaarsalo, S. Lehto, H. Mustanimemi, M. Niemelä, P. Palomäki, P. Puska, K. Pyörälä, J. Torppa, J. Tuomilehto, and T. Vuorenmaa. 1996. "Sydäninfarktiin sairastuneiden lääkehoitokäytäntö Suomessa vuosina 1986–1992" (Drug treatment practices for AMI patients in Finland, 1986–1992). *Suomen Lääkärilehti* (Journal of the Finnish Medical Association) 51:543–52.

Pohjola-Sintonen, S., P. Siltanen, J. Haapakoski, and J. Romo. 1987. "The Declining Trend in the Incidence of Acute Myocardial Infraction in Finland: The Results of Helsinki Coronary Registers during 1970–1977." *European Heart Journal* 8:354–59.

Puska, P., J. Tuomilehto, A. Nissinen, and E. Vartiainen, eds. 1995. *The North Karelia Project: Twenty Years Results and Experiences.* Helsinki: National Public Health Institute.

Salomaa, V., H. Miettinen, K. Kuulasmaa, M. Niemelä, M. Ketonen, T. Vuorenmaa, S. Lehto, P. Palomäki, M. Mähönen, P. Immonen-Räihä, M. Arstila, E. Kaarsalo, H. Mustaniemi, J. Torppa, J. Tuomilehto, P. Puska, and K. Pyörälä. 1996. "Decline of Coronary Heart Disease Mortality in Finland during 1983 to 1992: Roles of Incidence, Recurrence and Case-Fatality. The FINMONICA MI Register Study." *Circulation* 94:3130–37.

Salomaa, V., M. Tamminen, R. Salmela, I. Keskimäki, H. Hämäläinen, and A. Reunanen. 1996. *The Occurrence of Coronary Heart Disease in Finland, 1991–1994.* Helsinki: National Public Health Institute.

Saltman, R. B. 1987. "Management Control in a Publicly Planned Health Care: A Case Study from Finland." *Health Policy* 8:283–98.

Turunen, A. 1998. *Terveyskeskuksessa vai erikoissairaanhoidossa? Muutokset sairaanhoidon porrastuksessa 1990-luvulla* (In health center or in specialist care? Changes in division of tasks between primary and secondary health care in 1990s). Kuopio: Kuopio University Publications D, Medical Sciences 152.

Vartiainen, E., P. Puska, J. Pekkanen, J. Tuomilehto, and P. Jousilahti. 1994. "Changes in Risk Factors Explain Changes Mortality from Ischaemic Heart Disease in Finland." *British Medical Journal* 309:23–27.

CHAPTER 13

Determinants and Consequences of Technological Change in Health Care: Acute Myocardial Infarction in Denmark

Ivar Sønbø Kristiansen, Jørgen Clausen, Terkel Christiansen, and Jes Søgaard

Denmark shares many health and health care characteristics with other industrialized countries: a public health care system with free access to care, a substantial increase in health care expenditure since World War II, an aging population, and morbidity and mortality dominated by chronic diseases. However, Denmark is different from other industrialized countries—even the Nordic ones—in important aspects. First, life expectancy has been remarkably stable over the last 15 years, while most other industrialized countries have seen substantial increases. The lack of a substantial increase is attributable to lung cancer, intestinal cancer, chronic obstructive lung diseases, and suicide, due to smoking, alcohol consumption, and unhealthy diet (Danish Ministry of Health 1994). Even though there has been a substantial decline in mortality from coronary heart disease, only Finland and Scotland have higher mortality rates than Denmark. Second, despite a high per capita GDP, the proportion devoted to health care has been consistently below 7 percent. Even if the national statistics may be somewhat misleading because in Denmark some health services for the elderly are categorized as social services, there is little doubt that fewer resources are devoted to health care in Denmark than in most other industrialized countries. With respect to cardiovascular diseases, the lack of real growth in hospital expenditure and tight budget controls create a gap between supply and demand in a system where demand is not constrained by patient payments. Therefore, waiting lists are prevalent in many parts of the health care system. Clearly, acute cases as AMI are handled immediately, but elective interventions may have considerable waiting lists. By the end of 1997, about 2,050 patients (corresponding to more than 10 percent of new AMIs) were on waiting lists for CABG with a mean waiting time of about 10 weeks (Danish Ministry of Health 1998b).

The aim of this chapter is twofold. First, we describe changes in the occurrence of acute heart disease, changes in the medical management of this disease, and changes in the cost to society for caring for those having diseases related to acute heart disease. Second, we try to explain why technology use and the costs of cardiac care have changed; financing and organization of health care are likely to have had a substantial influence. Unfortunately, Denmark's health care statistics currently provide only a small fraction of the information needed for a thorough analysis. The chapter therefore can only suggest some causal mechanisms through which changes in incentives for care have affected technology use, and in turn affected medical treatment decisions and patient health outcomes. Better data collection and further research is needed to gain a better understanding of this important aspect of health policy. We conclude with a discussion these avenues for further research.

Incentives for Technological Change in Denmark

Financing of Care for Heart Disease Care

In Denmark, the organization and financing of health care have been relatively stable over the last 20 years with no major reforms. The health care system is decentralized to the 14 county councils and to the public hospital authority of the capital area (Copenhagen Hospital Corporation). These 15 units are responsible for primary as well as hospital care. About 83 percent of the total health care expenditure comes from public funds, while the remaining 17 percent is paid out of pocket through various cost-sharing arrangements (Danish Ministry of Health 1998a). The National Health Insurance (in Danish: Sygeforsikringen) reimburses general practitioners, medical specialists, dentists, and physiotherapists. It also finances prescriptions with some patient copayments (see below). The National Health Insurance is financed by general taxation.

The 87 public general medical hospitals and the 13 psychiatric hospitals have global budgets, and there are no user charges for inpatient or outpatient care (Danish Ministry of Health 1998a). The physicians and other staff are salaried. In sum, the county councils play a crucial role in the planning, provision, and financing of health care in

Denmark. While several countries have tried to split purchaser and providers, Denmark has an integrated system with small incentives for competition. To offset the cost-containing incentives of global budgeting, some county councils have introduced contracts with their hospitals on an experimental basis that reimburse hospitals for some specified services in addition to the global budget.

In 1997, there were three private general medical hospitals with a total of 130 beds representing about 0.5 percent of national hospital bed capacity. Private hospitals are financed through out-of-pocket payments and private insurance. They mainly offer elective surgery, but none of them offer cardiac catheterization, CABG, or PTCA. Additionally, there are some private clinics offering various specialized services including cardiologic examinations. The number of private hospitals and clinics is increasing. Although they play a very limited role in caring for patients with AMI, they do provide services for patients with other types of coronary heart disease (angina, heart failure, etc.).

The general practitioner (GP) plays a pivotal role in Danish health care, acting as a gatekeeper to hospital and other specialized services. Most often working in private group practices, the GPs own their premises and equipment and hire their own staff. They are financed by the National Health Insurance through a combination of capitation payments (representing approximately one-third of total physician revenue) and fee-for-service reimbursement (Kristiansen 1993). There are no direct patient payments except for some special services (immunizations, issuing of health certificates, etc.).

There are about 900 medical specialists who run private practices in agreement with the county councils. They are reimbursed entirely on a fee-for-service basis. The fee schedule for all types of physicians and the size of the capitation payments for GPs are decided in negotiations between the Danish County Council Association and the Danish Medical Association. The salary for hospital physicians is settled in similar negotiations. It should be noted that in a country with a strong egalitarian culture, it is very difficult to pay a much higher salary to physicians than other academicians such as engineers or high school teachers. As a result, a hospital lacking medical manpower has a limited ability to raise the salary of physicians. Also, the worker protection regulations and the global budgeting make it difficult to increase hospital capacity for needed services (e.g., CABG or catheterization) through overtime or evening operations. Even if the staff is willing to work longer hours than they currently do, worker protection regulations and budget constraints limit expansion of capacity.

Prescription drugs are paid in part by the patients (except in the hospitals), while the rest is paid by the county councils. The patient payment is generally 25 percent or 50 percent of the cost. A few drugs (e.g. tranquilizers, sleeping pills, painkillers) are paid in full by the patients, while a few others (e.g. insulin) are fully reimbursed. In total, about 50 percent of the national drug expenditure is publicly financed. For drugs used in relation to coronary heart disease, about 75 percent of the drug costs are publicly financed. Lipid-lowering agents are paid in full by the patients, who may apply for public reimbursement according to quite liberal rules. Retired and disabled patients have higher reimbursement rates than others because the local governments (the municipalities) supplement the ordinary reimbursements. About 25 percent of Danish citizens have supplementary private insurance to cover patient copayments for pharmaceuticals.

Technology Regulation

The regulation of technology adoption and use is relatively limited in Denmark (Poulsen et al. 1998). The Ministry of Health in principle decides what types of services (e.g. heart transplantation) are to be provided by one national center and what types to be provided only by the four university hospitals. In practice, however, the hospitals are relatively free to introduce new technologies. In fact, by 1966, coronary units or intensive care departments had been established in all Danish general medical hospitals. This means that almost all patients admitted to hospital for AMI are cared for in coronary units.

In effect, then, there is very little formal regulation of technologies such as cardiac catheterization, CABG, PTCA, and coronary intra-arterial stents. For example, according to ministry guidelines, there should be one national center for heart transplantation, but in practice there are two. Usually, new technologies are introduced by clinicians who learn about them abroad and propose their adoption to the hospital managers.

Rather, the binding regulation lies in hospitals' budget constraints. Since the early 1980s the total health care budget has been very tight with a very low growth rate. Taking into account the aging population, which places an increasing burden upon the hospitals, they have a limited scope for adopting new and costly services. Adopting new services means that older ones have to be used less or be abolished. Therefore, hospitals see a constant conflict between clinicians (and patients) who wish to introduce new technologies or expand the use of existing ones, and managers and politicians who cannot finance them.

One of the major and explicitly formulated goals within the Danish health care system is free and equal access to health care services. However, it would be more realistic to reformulate this slightly by appending the provision: "if the capacity is available." In a publicly owned, controlled, and financed health care system, it is not easy to make immediate adjustments to capacity, so the only way to restrict entry is by establishing waiting lists. Nor does free access to health care ensure that the newest—and often quite expensive—technologies are available.

The adoption and the use of pharmaceuticals are regulated according to European Market rules that are much like the FDA regulations in the United States. In practice, the introduction of new drugs is strictly regulated, while the use is not, once a drug is approved. Medical devices are regulated by the gradual implementation of the European Commission Directives focusing on safety and not efficacy or cost-effectiveness (EEC 1993).

The pharmaceutical market in Denmark used to have no strict rules or control regarding the setting of prices. Because of a high growth rate of pharmaceutical expenditure, a reference price system was introduced in 1993 together with generic substitution (i.e., pharmacists are required to deliver the cheapest generic drug if the physician prescribes a more expensive one). Because this provision had little impact on the growth rate, industry and the government in 1997 reached an agreement about total drug expenditure. According to the agreement, expenditure growth beyond an agreed limit will be met by reductions in the price of certain drugs. It is yet too early to draw conclusions about the effect of this new agreement. The concern about drug costs probably explains the fact that lipid-lowering agents are not reimbursed by the National Health Insurance despite their effectiveness.

Competition

In a system with queuing and waiting lists for public hospitals, and very limited private hospital supply, there is no need for hospitals to compete for patients. There is a slight shortage of medical manpower, which means that physicians in most cases can get the kind of job they want. Hospitals may compete for medical and other manpower, but such competition is rarely based on salary or other payments, but on working environment, research facilities, and other factors.

Other Incentives for Technology Adoption and Use

In a health care system with limited use of competition and financial incentives, other mechanisms will tend to influence the adoption and use of medical technologies. Here, special interest groups, both professional and lay, have been important. The Danish Medical Association, subcommittees of this organization, informal medical networks, patient organizations, and individual patients and relatives have all to a greater or lesser extent influenced health policy in the area of heart disease. Through mass media, frequently in the form of media headlines with a "sad heart story," lay and professional people put pressure on the politicians to allocate more resources to care for heart patients. Such initiatives may result in extra funds or the establishments of committees to plan expansion of services. The gap between supply and demand for services frequently makes headlines in the mass media.

The Heart Plan 1993

The Heart Plan 1993 is an example of how private professional and lay interest groups may create initiatives within the public health care system. Despite various recommendations, queues were a constant problem for patients with heart disease. The National Board of Health met the criticism with a new initiative called the Heart Plan 1993. The background for this plan was a committee under the National Board of Health, which in 1987 recommended that over a period of four years, an annual capacity of 2,300–2,550 for cardiac catheterizations, 380 for PTCAs, and 1,800 for CABGs should be reached.

The Heart Plan 1993 sought to double 1993 revascularization capacity by 1996, to a planned capacity for cardiac catheterizations of 6,800–8,200 per year, and approximately 5,000 revascularizations per year (approximately 1,500 angioplasties and 3,500 bypass operations) (National Board of Health 1993). However, even with the accompanying increased funding, existing heart centers were not able to meet these targets due to lack of resources, including qualified manpower. In 1997, the central government earmarked an additional DKK 250 million (U.S.$40 million, at current exchange rates) for a so-called change-and-incentive pool to finance increased activity in the health care sector. A share of this sum was assigned to increase capacity at the heart centers. Each center would receive funds for expanding its activity beyond specified levels. Each center would receive DKK 9,000 for each cardiac catheterization (U.S.$1,435) and DKK 36,000 for each CABG or PTCA (U.S.$5,742). The incentive to perform PTCAs was much stronger than the incentive to perform CABGs since the cost of the former is about one-third of the latter.

Regulation of Physician Supply

Denmark has three medical schools for a population of 5 million. The supply of physicians is currently somewhat less than the demand. There is little immigration of physicians, which means that some geographic areas and medical specialties have a manpower "shortage." However, cardiology and cardiac surgery are popular specialties among physicians. To the extent manpower shortage is the problem in the care for AMI patients, the reason is funding rather than personnel per se.

Technological Change in Heart Attack Care in Denmark

In the following, we will present some aspects of change in the management of patients with coronary heart disease. Even in a public, homogeneous health care system like that of Denmark, readily available health care statistics currently provide only a small fraction of the information needed for a thorough analysis. However, in one respect the public system has a great advantage: all citizens are assigned a 10-digit unique personal number (so-called CPR number). This creates an important potential for follow-up of individuals in electronic databases and linkage of various data sources.

Much of the following presentation is based on the National Patient Register (NPR). Since 1977, all discharges from Danish hospitals have been recorded in this register. Administrated by the National Board of Health, the registration of discharges from hospital is mandatory. For each discharge, personal number, sex, address, dates of admission and discharge, diagnoses, and procedure codes (surgical operations and some major diagnostic procedures) are recorded. The classifications of diseases was based on ICD8 until 1993 and on ICD10 from 1994. Because all hospitals are encompassed by the register and individuals are identifiable by their personal number, the medical history of each individual can be traced. Also, the register can be linked with other registers, such as the birth register or causes-of-death register. Although the current chapter reports neither links of discharges across individuals nor links of NPR data with data from the causes-of-death register, we will seek to undertake this analysis in future work.

Changes in High-Tech Care: Intensive Cardiac Procedures and Hospital Use

Here, we define high-tech procedures as those that require costly equipment (i.e., high fixed costs), or specialized personnel (i.e., high variable costs), or both. This section will therefore focus on revascularization technologies and in-hospital care. However, ambulance services can also represent high-tech medicine. Provided by one national, private company, ground ambulances are all equipped with defibrillators and ECG according to national guidelines (National Board of Health 1985). There is no air ambulance service due to the short distances to hospital in all parts of Denmark. A major problem in the prehospital care for AMI patients is the delay in admission. In a study of 26 Danish hospitals, the mean delay was 9.1 hours (median 3.5) in 1990–92 (Ottesen et al. 1996). Only 34 percent of the AMI patients were admitted within 2 hours of symptom onset, 68 percent within 6 hours, and 81 percent within 12 hours.

There exist several different technologies for revascularization. Catheterization, followed by CABG and PTCA in combination with stents, constitutes the most common high-tech treatment. Newer high-tech procedures such as coronary angioscopy, intracoronary ultrasound, and rotational artherectomy have been employed on a more experimental basis in Denmark. Laser intervention has also been tried, but the results are not promising.

Figure 13.1 presents the total number of intensive cardiac procedures per million population for the years 1988–96. Cardiac catheterization is the basic diagnostic procedure needed for all routine revascularization procedures. The rate of catheterizations per million population has almost tripled during the period. Since there is no indication that the incidence of AMI has increased substantially during this period, this suggests that the utilization rate may have increased.

Performed primarily on patients below the age of 40, the first CABGs in Denmark were carried out in 1967. At this time, the procedure was reserved for patients with severe, stable angina. In recent years the outcome has been relatively good with an operative mortality on the order of 2 percent among patients without symptoms or sign of cardiac failure (National Board of Health 1993). When patients with

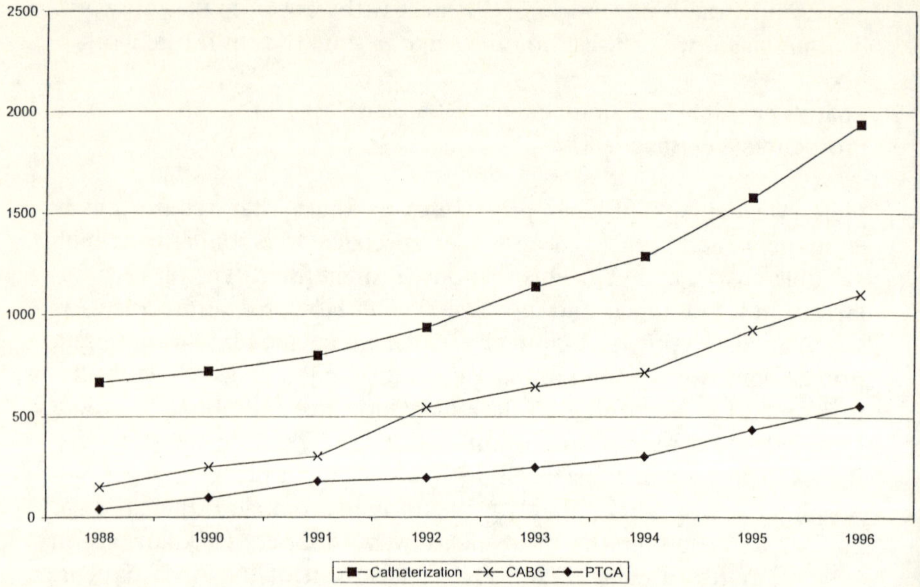

Fig. 13.1. Intensive cardiac procedure rates per 1,000,000 population

unstable angina or heart failure are included, the figure is about 5 percent. Five years after a bypass operation about 95 percent of the patients show no sign of new or recurrent AMIs. Expanding the time horizon to 10 and 15 years, the corresponding percentages are 85 percent and 65 percent, respectively (National Board of Health 1993).

Figure 13.1 suggests that the various "heart programs" have been effective in increasing the utilization of revascularization. The capacity for cardiac catheterizations indeed increased, except for 1996, when the capacity lagged behind the plan, and the magnitude of waiting lists per unit population remained roughly constant. Clearly, the increased capacity appears to have induced the demand for services in a "free" health care system. Most likely, this does not represent real demand inducement as defined by health economists (Reinhardt 1985), but rather demand revelation. When the capacity is very limited, patients needing or wanting catheterization may not be referred. The more capacity is expanded, the more patients are referred.

Not surprisingly, waiting list data indicate that a substantial number of patients are still queuing for intensive cardiac procedures. For example, in 1997, about 65 percent of patients having PTCA had less than one month waiting time, while the corresponding percentages for catheterization and CABG was about 40 percent.

Hospital Use

In 1979, the total number of admissions for AMI (ICD8: 410) was 16,579 (227,690 bed-days); in 1993, the total number of admissions was 16,468 (for a total of 124,048 bed-days), according to the National Patient Register. As figure 13.2 shows, the number of discharges per unit population rose by about 10 percent from 1980 to 1987 but has since declined to the 1980 level. The changes were for the most part attributable to changes in the admission rates for the elderly (65 years or older). We note here that the admission rates should not be interpreted as incidence rates for AMI. First, nonhospitalized AMIs (fatal as well as nonfatal) are not included. Second, one AMI may be registered as two because the register is based on admissions. When a patient is transferred from one unit (department or hospital) to another, two admissions are recorded. Third, some admissions categorized as AMI may in fact be angina or other types of coronary heart disease. Nor is it possible to identify first AMIs in the individual patients, because this is not registered.

While the number of admissions for AMI has been relatively stable over the last 15 years, the number of bed-days declined by 45 percent during the 1979–92 period. As figure 13.3 shows, this decrease was due to a decline in the average length of stay for AMI patients from about 14 days in 1979 to 7.5 days in 1992. Currently, the national guidelines recommend 5–7 days in hospital for an uncomplicated AMI (National Board of Health 1992).

This decline in average length of stay masks substantial variation across hospitals and individuals. A survey of 79 Danish hospitals revealed a substantial variation in AMI care (Madsen et al. 1987). The median time of cardiac monitoring was 5 (with a range of 1–14) days, the median time of immobilization (in bed) was 6 (with a range of 1–14) days.

The decline in bed-days and length of stay is in line with the decline in the number of hospital beds. During the last 15 years, the total number of admissions (i.e. any diagnosis) has increased, while the average length of stay and the number of bed-days has declined substantially. For AMI, the decline may be attributable to improved technology (e.g., thrombolytic therapy, faster postoperative recuperation, more effective analgesics). Other explanatory factors include tighter

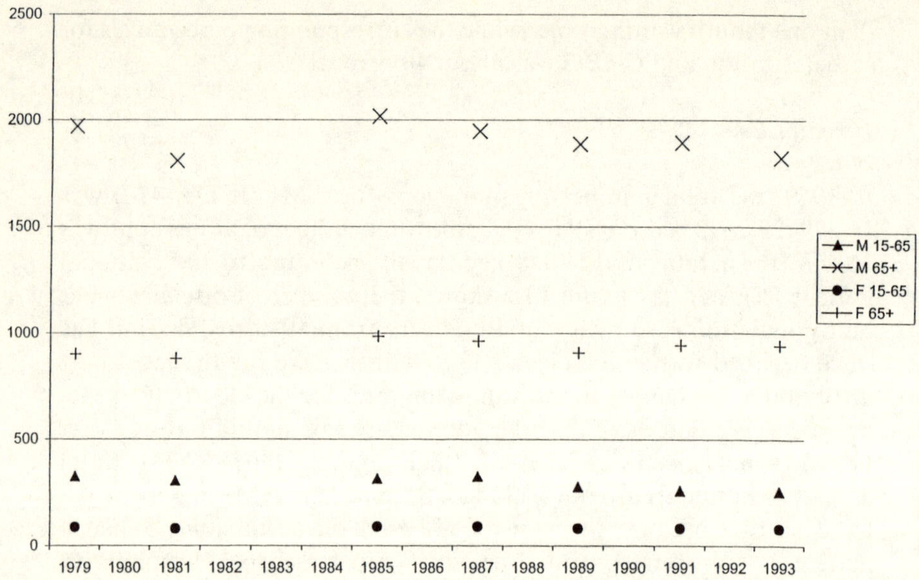

Fig. 13.2. Discharges from hospital for AMI per 1,000,000 population by age and sex, 1979–93

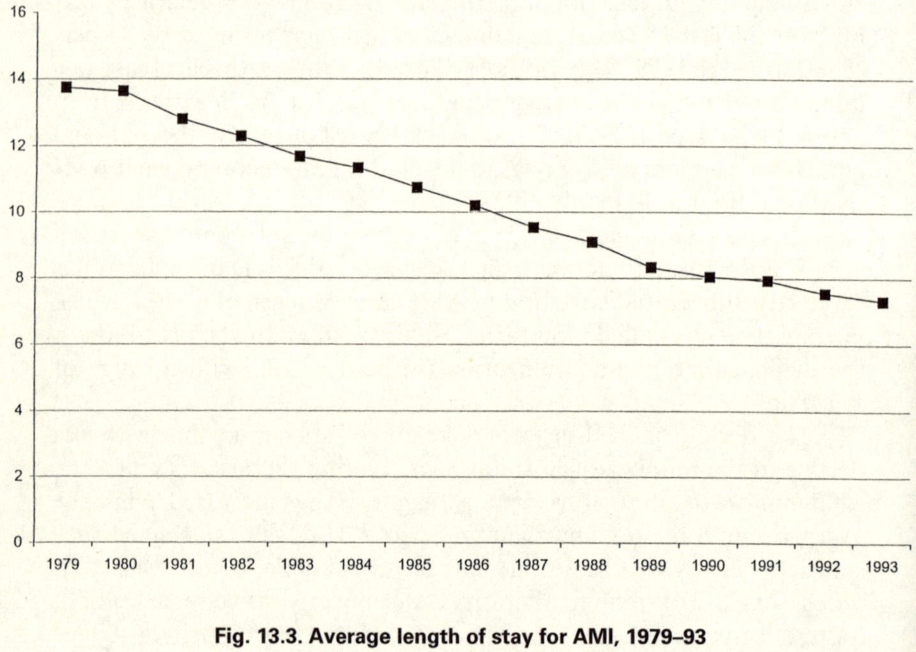

Fig. 13.3. Average length of stay for AMI, 1979–93

budgets combined with increasing demand and thereby extended waiting lists; and a general recognition that long-term placement of patients in beds does not imply better treatment.

Changes in Low-Tech Care

In Denmark, total drug sales are well known from public statistics, and prescriptions to individual patients can be monitored in some databases. A major problem, however, is the lack of information on prescription indication or diagnosis. Several drugs (ASA, warfarin, beta-blocking agents, etc.) can be used for AMI, but also for several other conditions. The number of published Danish studies are few in this area, and the following presentation is therefore based on a more qualitative description.

Based on sales of thrombolytics, about 5,500 of AMI patients had thrombolytic therapy. This would represent about 30 percent of all patients admitted for AMI (Haastrup, Gill, and Haagfelt 1994). Streptokinase has been used as the drug of choice, while tissue-plasminogen activator is normally offered to patients who have had streptokinase before (i.e., second-time AMI).

Beta-blocking agents are used to alleviate angina and to prevent recurrent AMI. In 1995, the consumption of such agents was DKK 157 million (U.S.$18.7 million at a 1995 PPP exchange rate), equivalent to 16 DDD per 1,000 population per day. A survey of 79 hospitals showed that in 1986, 16 percent of the hospitals prescribed beta-blocking agents routinely at discharge, while anticoagulant treatment was used in 44 percent of the hospitals (Madsen et al. 1987). Statins are increasingly used even though the public funding is limited. In 1991, the sales were DKK 23 million, while in 1996 they were DKK 116 million.

At Odense University Hospital in 1992 for example, 25 percent of patients with AMI were treated with ASA during their hospital stay, 7 percent with beta-blockers, 20 percent with calcium antagonists, 26 percent with nitrates, 9 percent with ACE inhibitors, 35 percent with diuretics, and finally 16 percent received other heart drugs (Haastrup, Gill, and Haagfelt 1994). About 40 percent of the admitted patients did not receive any specific pharmaceutical treatment.

Changes in Expertise or Appropriateness of Care

While studies of appropriateness have been frequently undertaken in the United States, such studies are rare in Denmark, with none performed in the area of AMI management. Taking into account the excess demand and waiting lists, it is unlikely that patients have CABG or PTCA inappropriately. Rather, it is likely that patients who would benefit from such interventions are not offered them because of insufficient capacity. Pharmaceuticals may be used inappropriately, but the extent of such use is largely unknown.

The Consequences of Changes in Heart Attack Care in Denmark

Because the current chapter does not provide any new analysis of the impact of heart attack care on patient health outcomes in Denmark, we summarize some recent studies here.

While most industrialized countries have had an almost continuous decline in mortality and a consequent increase in life expectancy since World War II, life expectancy improvements leveled off around 1978 in Denmark. However, with respect to coronary heart disease, mortality has declined. The best study on mortality from AMI covers the years 1982–92 (Osler et al. 1996). This study was based on merged NPR/causes-of-death register data. The study period began with 1982; patients who had not been admitted to hospital for AMI the previous five years were classified as incident cases of AMI if they either were admitted for a first AMI or were registered as dead from AMI without previous hospitalization. During the period 1982–92, the age-adjusted incidence of AMI fell from about 450 to 375 per 100,000 per year for men, and from 230 to 200 in women. The corresponding changes in population mortality figures were a decline from 260 to 180 in men and from 150 to 110 in women.

There are no data available on post-1992 AMI incidence, but declining mortality indicates that the decline in incidence is continuing. In 1992 the number of AMI fatalities was 8,723 (Osler et al. 1996), while it was 6,117 in 1995 according to the causes-of-death statistics. It should be noted that Denmark switched from ICD8 to ICD10 in 1994. Due to somewhat different classification of patients with coronary heart disease, the real decline in AMI mortality is likely to be less than the figures may indicate. However, a real increase is most unlikely, and the rapid rise in utilization of PTCA and CABG means that medical needs have been met to a greater extent since 1990.

The Danish part of WHO's MONICA project also provides recent information on the magnitude of mortality from AMI in Denmark (Salomaa et al. 1997). The one-year case-fatality for nonelderly males (ages 35–64) was 52 percent for men with a new AMI, and 60 percent for men with recurrent AMI. For women, the figures were 61 percent and 54 percent, respectively. This study also indicates a higher AMI prehospital fatality rate in Denmark than other industrialized countries. In particular, for women ages 35–64, prehospital AMI mortality was 37 percent, considerably higher than for men in the same age group (28 percent). These were the highest rates reported in the MONICA study.

The National Board of Health in Denmark also published a study on AMI mortality in 1993 (National Board of Health 1993). This study found that 13.7 percent of nonelderly males with AMI, and 12.4 percent of nonelderly females, died before admission to the hospital. Although the fatality rate is increasing with age, this study reported substantially different findings than did the MONICA study discussed above.

Changes in Medical Expenditure and Resource Use

Because Danish hospitals are on global budgets, they have few incentives to account for use of procedures or costs. Accounting systems are quite primitive, and costs are measured at an aggregate level. The medical record contains a lot of information on procedures, but they are for the most part manual and cannot be searched electronically. In other words, there is no tradition (or any particular need) for detailed cost accounting in the Danish health care system. Information on costs is therefore based on ad hoc studies.

However, it is surely true that Denmark (and several other industrialized countries) has lower unit health care costs than the United States. An important factor here is the income level of physicians. A Danish cardiologist or heart surgeon may have an income of approximately U.S.$100,000, well below the level in the United States. Such income differences also apply for nurses and other personnel groups, but to a lesser extent. One study estimated the cost in 1992 of a cardiac catheterization to be DKK 15,000 (1995 PPP U.S.$1,875), a PTCA DKK 33,000 (U.S.$4,125), and a CABG DKK 100,000 (U.S.$12,500) (National Board of Health 1993). Relatively low unit costs combined with low utilization rates make the total costs of AMI care quite modest.

Discussion

The relatively early adoption of new cardiac technology in Denmark cannot be explained by financial incentives. In fact, in a health care system with hospitals on global budgets and physicians on salary, there are hardly any incentives to adopt new costly procedures. Instead, through various professional networks, physicians learn about new technological possibilities for their patients and persuade the hospital managements and boards to adopt them.

The diffusion of heart technologies has been slower in Denmark than the other Nordic and most other industrialized countries. Here, the lack of financial incentives is likely to be important. Being on tight global budgets, the hospitals have difficulties expanding the services even though all patients and most clinicians would wish to see greater capacity for treatment of patients with heart disease. Admittedly, a few physicians have publicly advocated primary prevention instead of high-tech treatment of AMI, but this has had only minimal impact on policy.

When financial incentives favoring the diffusion of heart technologies are lacking, other mechanisms seem to play an important role. First, clinicians, in particular cardiologists and heart surgeons, are active in persuading politicians to fund increases in the capacity for heart patients. Such initiatives may take the form of letters to politicians or public outcry in the mass media. However, much of the professional activity is channeled through the various "heart plans." Heavily influenced by physicians, the National Board of Health set up a commission of specialists to issue reports or "heart plans" that later was used in the political decision-making process. Second, patient interest groups play an important role. Physicians frequently collaborate with patient groups and mass media in the struggle to fund increased capacity for heart patients.

In conclusion, the high incidence of coronary heart disease has not been met by a high utilization of cardiac technologies. Relatively small national health budgets and lack of financial incentives (hospitals on global budgets and physicians on salary) are likely to explain the low utilization of cardiac technologies. When financial incentives for technology adoption are lacking, they seem to be replaced by other mechanisms such as patient and professional pressure.

References

Danish Ministry of Health. 1994. *Heart Disease in Denmark* (in Danish). Copenhagen: Life Expectancy Commission.

———. 1998a. "Health Care in Denmark. Internet Presentation 1998." <http://www.sum.dk/health/sider/print.htm>.

———. 1998b. *Waiting List Information* (informational pamphlet for the public, in Danish). Copenhagen.

European Economic Community (EEC). 1993. *Council Directive 93/42/EEC of June 1993: Medical Devices.* Brussels: European Commission.

Haastrup, B., S. Gill, and T. Haghfelt. 1994. "Thrombolysis in Acute Myocardial Infarction: The Implementation of Thrombolytic Therapy in a Coronary Care Unit in 1992." *Cardiology* 85: 397–406.

Kristiansen, I. S. 1996. "Factors Affecting Doctors' Decision Making." Ph.D. diss., Institute of Community Medicine, University of Tromsø.

Madsen. E. B., and P. E. Nielsen. 1987. "The Treatment of Acute Myocardial Infarct in Denmark" (in Danish). *Ugeskr Laeger* 149:2585–89.

National Board of Health. 1985. *Ambulanceservice til patienter med akutte hjertelidelser. Underudvalget vedrørende hjerteambulancers behandlingsmæssige værdi* (Ambulance service for patients with acute heart diseases: Subcommittee for the Effectiveness of Intensive Care Ambulances). Copenhagen.

———. 1992. *Referenceprogram. Blodprop i hjertet* (Model for treatment program: Acute myocardial infarction). Copenhagen.

———. 1993. *Hjertekirurgi i Danmark—Behov, kapacitet og organisation* (Cardiac surgery in Denmark—needs, capacity, and organization). Copenhagen.

Osler, M., T. I. Sorensen, S. Sorensen, K. Rostgaard, G. Jensen, L. Iversen, T. S. Kristensen, and M. Madsen. 1996. "Trends in Mortality, Incidence, and Case Fatality of Ischaemic Heart Disease in Denmark, 1982–1992." *International Journal of Epidemiology* 25:1154–61.

Ottesen, M. M., L. Kober, S. Jorgensen, and C. Torp Pedersen. 1996. "Determinants of Delay between Symptoms and Hospital Admission in 5,978 Patients with Acute Myocardial Infarction: The TRACE Study Group. Trandolapril Cardiac Evaluation." *European Heart Journal* 17:429–37.

Poulsen, P. B., S. Adamsen, H. Vondeling, and T. Jørgensen. 1998. "Diffusion of Laparoscopic Technologies in Denmark." *Health Policy* 45, no. 2: 149–67.

Reinhardt, U. E. 1985. "The Theory of Physician-Induced Demand: Reflections after a Decade." *Journal of Health Economics* 4:187–93.

Salomaa, V. V., V. Lundbergh, U. Agnarsson, R. Radisauskas, M. Kirchoff, and L. Wilhelmsen. 1997. "Fatalities from Myocardial Infarction in Nordic Countries and Lithuania." *European Heart Journal* 18:91–98.

CHAPTER 14

Technological Change in Heart Attack Care in England

Michael B. Robinson, Rob Manning, Mark Petticrew, Nigel Rice, Mark Sculpher, and Trevor Sheldon

The United Kingdom National Health Service (NHS)[1] reached its 50th anniversary in July 1998. Surveys of public opinion show it remains a popular national institution, despite its less attractive features such as waiting lists for elective surgery and many old hospital buildings. Almost all NHS care remains free at the point of delivery, and the whole resident population is covered. Although the health proportion of gross domestic product (GDP) devoted to health care rose by 1.3 percent between 1986 and 1995 in England (see figure 14.1), the absolute level is lower than many other OECD countries, and no further increase is estimated to have occurred since (Office of Health Economics 1997).

The time period upon which this book is focused was well chosen from an English point of view. In 1991, about half way through the period concerned, the NHS underwent its most radical reform since its inception. Before that date, management was similar to that of a command economy, with highly centralized planning, national pay agreements, and very limited incentives for financial efficiency at local level. At the same time however, there were hardly any external constraints on individual clinicians. After 1991, selected hospitals were allowed more independence, including the power to retain surpluses, sell assets, and set their own terms and conditions for staff, while remaining in public ownership in the form of hospital trusts. Along these lines, the role of the district health authorities changed, from the organization responsible for both the planning and delivery of care, to that of purchaser, responsible for selecting a set of services and then contracting with hospitals and providers for their supply. In addition, selected general practitioners (GPs) were allocated funds for the purchase of a lim-

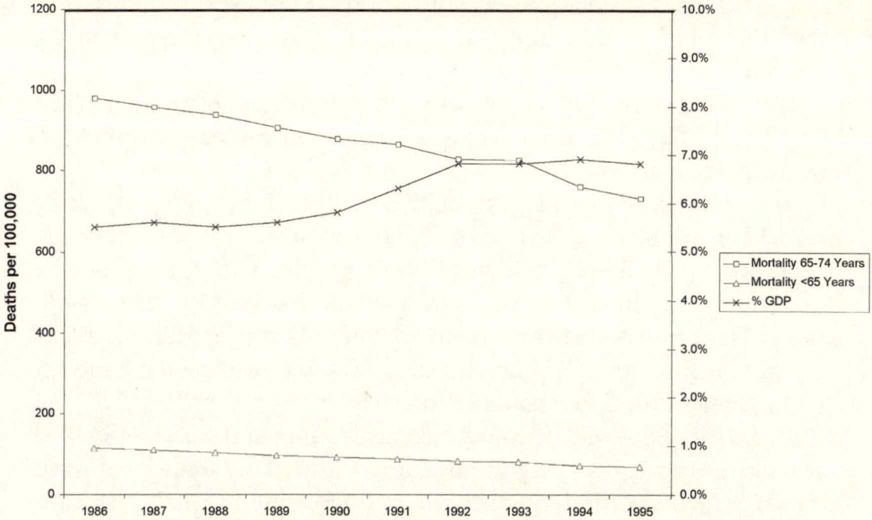

Fig. 14.1. Age-standardized mortality from CHD, elderly and nonelderly population of England, versus share of GDP spent on health care. (Data from Department of Health 1996.)

ited range of hospital services, again with the power to retain surpluses for reinvestment in primary or secondary care.

Although these reforms sound quite radical and have indeed transformed the organizational structure of the NHS, at a more fundamental level, arguably, little has changed. Hospital and community health services remain subject to a global annual budget. Contracts between Health authorities and providers are not legally enforceable, but are subject to arbitration by the secretary of state. Borrowing for capital investment is regulated by "external financing limits" set for each hospital trust by the Treasury. Competition between hospitals has been managed to avoid politically embarrassing downsizing or closures. Clinicians have retained considerable clinical freedom, with very little external oversight and management of clinical activity. In summary, the NHS reforms have had less effect on the incentives for technological change described below than might have been expected.

England has one of the highest rates of CHD in general, and acute myocardial infarction (AMI) in particular, among the OECD countries, and has shown a slower rate of decline than elsewhere. CHD is the most common cause of death among both men and women, responsible for over one-quarter of all deaths in both sexes. Figure 14.1 shows the trend in mortality for both the nonelderly (less than 65 years) and the elderly (65–74 years) populations. The 1986–95 average annual rates of decline of 4.0 percent and 2.5 percent, respectively, are little different from those for the preceding 10 years. Deaths from AMI show a similar pattern.

It is uncertain to what extent the decline in mortality (or lack thereof) has been due to changes in incidence, or to changes in mortality conditional on illness; neither has been routinely monitored across the country as a whole. An expert group commissioned by the Department of Health has drawn up plans for more comprehensive surveillance of MI outcomes (Birkhead et al. 1997), but to date there are no firm implementation proposals. For these reasons, analysis of the causes and consequences of change in cardiac care and care for AMI in particular in the United Kingdom is important. To what extent have the 1991 reforms of the organization and financing of the health care sector affected trends in the use of high technology in the treatment of AMI? How have these changes in medical treatment decisions affected resource use and patient health outcomes? The purpose of this chapter is to provide a new analysis of data on individual AMI patients, primarily but not exclusively based on data from the Oxford Record Linkage Study (ORLS), details of which are given at the start of section 2.

Mortality data is included in the ORLS, but no details of cost or medication usage. In addition, the ORLS covers only one part of the country in the relatively prosperous southeast, and cardiothoracic surgery was not well established in the main tertiary hospital in Oxford until the early 1990s. Although the generalizability of our results may be limited by these facts, our analysis suggests how the financing and regulation of health care in the United Kingdom, and changes in those policies, may have affected treatment decision-making and health outcomes for AMI.

This chapter proceeds as follows. Section 1 reviews the economic and regulatory incentives that the NHS has provided for technological change in the treatment of AMI, focusing on how these incentives have changed in response to the 1991 reforms. The second section of the chapter documents how technological change has affected medical treatment for AMI in England over the 1989–93 period, using data from the ORLS, compared with information from the national Hospital Episode Statistics; the Clinical Standards Advisory Group study; and the Nottingham Heart Attack Register. The third section presents information on the mortality of these patients, and a review of some previous studies regarding trends in resource use for treatment of heart attack. The fourth section of the chapter discusses our findings and offers some tentative conclusions about the causes and consequences of technological change in the United Kingdom, and some suggestions for future research.

1. Incentives for Technological Change in England

Financing of Care for Heart Disease

Hospital inpatient care accounts for the largest proportion of health care spending in the United Kingdom overall, and for heart attacks in particular. Virtually all initial admissions are to NHS hospitals, whereas a small minority, perhaps 20 percent, of subsequent revascularization procedures are insurance-funded within the private sector. The true private sector share of such work is unknown; the quoted figure was suggested by a cardiothoracic surgeon from the Yorkshire Heart Centre.

Incentives for technological change are likely to be quite different in the public and private sectors. In the NHS, until 1991 hospitals had fixed annual budgets. This provided a disincentive for changes that required an initial capital outlay (e.g., for equipment or training), but encouraged change that was immediately cost saving, such as day case surgery. In general there was a strong incentive to deliver less costly care, at least from a management perspective. (On the other hand, medical staff, unlike managers, were not at risk of losing their jobs if the hospitals overspent, thereby weakening incentives for cost control in certain cases.) After 1991, and the introduction of the purchaser-provider split, some hospital trusts negotiated "cost and volume" or "cost per case" contracts with health authorities for particular procedures, such as coronary artery bypass grafts (CABG) or angioplasties (PTCA). In these specific instances, hospital income was related to volume of activity, and an incentive was thereby created to deliver more and more intensive treatments. However most acute care for heart attacks continued to be provided under fixed-cost "block" contracts, essentially equivalent to the prereform situation. Even for CABG and PTCA, in practice there was a fixed cap on expenditure at health authority level. Hence the impact of the new financial incentives was blunted. Overall each health authority purchaser was still cash limited with a local global budget, and so the ability of a hospital trust to generate more income depended on the degree of competition allowed between neighboring hospitals, which was limited in most cases. Increased spending on technology for heart disease therefore largely depended on the ability to shift resources from other clinical activity.

In the small private sector, there were no incentives to limit volume or intensity of activity. Most insurance schemes did not require copayments. Physician and surgeon income was sensitive both to the volume and to the intensity of treatment, providing strong personal incentives for use of medical technologies. As part of the 1991 reforms, health care insurance premiums became tax-deductible for the elderly, further encouraging an expansion of private insurance and provision. However, the early 1990s featured a general economic recession in the United Kingdom that counteracted these forces, and the private sector did not undergo any substantial expansion.

The financial incentives for use of pharmaceuticals are quite different. Before 1991, GP prescribing was not cash-limited, and after 1991 only became so for those GPs who volunteered to take on fundholding. Patients had to make a copayment of approximately U.S.$6 per NHS prescription, but the elderly and those on low incomes, among others, were exempted. Moreover, drugs for hospital inpatients were excluded, being accounted for within inpatient costs.

Over the period 1986–95, the prescription copayment increased somewhat in real terms, and after 1991 some GPs had their prescription budget capped. Prices charged by the pharmaceutical companies to the NHS for their products were regulated by a voluntary agreement with the Government. In summary, there existed a mixture of financial incentives to introduce new drugs that taken together might favor higher-cost treatments. However, in the specific case of acute heart attacks, most prescribing costs fell into the inpatient sector with its clear fixed budgets and overall cap, both before and after 1991.

Technology Regulation

Within the overall context of a cash-limited pubic health service, technology regulation per se has not been a prominent feature of the NHS, and commercial interests have been free to market new drugs and devices. For many years hospital specialists were given free rein to introduce these as best they could within the financial constraints imposed by fixed budgets. Before 1991, decisions on capital investment were made by regional committees of hospital specialists with minimal input from other interest groups, but with the total amount of new capital for each region being strictly fixed by central government. Also there was a loosely defined national strategy to concentrate specialist services such as CABG in a small number of regional centers. After 1991, hospital trusts were in theory free to make their own investments in new technology, but the imposition of external financing limits on each trust by the Treasury had much the same effect as before the reforms. More recently, formal technology regulation has been suggested, but so far only a voluntary register of unevaluated new interventional procedures and devices has been introduced (Sheldon and Faulkner 1996).

In 1987, the Government adopted a national target for CABGs of 300 per million total population per year for each NHS region, leading to planned expansion in certain areas. Higher targets have been suggested since by patient and professional associations, but none has been formally adopted by the Government. No formal target has ever been set for PTCA or coronary angiography.

At the "microregulatory" level, some changes were introduced in 1991. All doctors were required to participate in "medical audit," without defining clearly what this involved. In only a minority of cases has this resembled utilization review as undertaken in the United States. Some hospitals and GP practices have introduced drug formularies, mainly on a voluntary basis. GP fundholders have a financial incentive to limit referrals to secondary care, but few if any have introduced formal review mechanisms. As argued above for the macro level, microregulation per se is insignificant compared to the general constraints of the global budget cap.

Other Incentives for Technology Adoption and Use

Competition

The 1991 reforms introduced an internal market within the NHS and the possibility of competition between hospitals. This meant there was considerable potential for shifts in patient flows, especially for elective surgeries purchased by GP fundholders (defined by a cost threshold that included coronary angioplasty and PTCA but not CABG), particularly in areas such as Greater London with a choice of providers and some oversupply of facilities. In practice, this was limited by the need to avoid politically damaging financial crises in individual hospitals, and patients' reluctance to travel long distances for care. However, the threat of losing business may have provided a lever for hospital managers to introduce changes against the will of reluctant clinicians, although this may have been more significant for conditions whose management was dominated by outpatient care rather than for heart attacks.

Regulation of Physician Supply

Second only to budget caps, this is likely to be a major influence on technological change in England. The overall number of doctors in training is strictly controlled by the Government, with stiff penalties for universities that recruit more students than their annual quota. Once qualified, numbers entering higher specialist training are regulated by the medical royal colleges. Only fully accredited specialists are likely to have significant numbers of private patient referrals, so there is an incentive to established specialists in high-earning fields such as cardiothoracic surgery to limit their own numbers. In contrast, in less prestigious areas such as geriatric medicine (an area with a substantial minority of heart attacks) numbers are limited by the cost to the NHS of employing more doctors. After 1991, trust-owned hospitals were allowed to appoint new specialists without consent from health authorities, and anecdotal evidence suggests that shortages in certain fields including cardiology did develop. (Reversal of this freedom was one of the first changes made by the new Government in 1997.)

Physician Payment and Culture

Most cardiologists and surgeons are fully or nearly fully employed by the NHS on fixed salaries that are independent of the volume or complexity of their activity. A minority receive graded salary and pension supplements, awarded by their peers, for contributions to the NHS greater than normal expectations. This may encourage some technological innovation, but on the whole physicians are more conservative than in many other countries, for example in the prescription of new drugs.

National Expectations

The NHS originated at a time of postwar rationing, and a tolerance of waiting lists and limited facilities is a national characteristic that has continued since. A related factor is that those with money or connections can expedite care directly or indirectly, so many of the potentially most vociferous may be satisfied while the majority remain passive.

Although such aspects of the medical and popular culture are important, they are not considered further in this chapter.

2. Technological Change in Heart Attack Care in England

A basic data set is collected for every admission to an NHS hospital including patient date of birth and postcode; principal and subsidiary diagnoses; operative procedures and status on discharge. Although since 1948 every UK resident has been assigned his or her own NHS number, until recently this has been very poorly recorded in the basic data set and so routine linkage of individual episodes of care has not been possible.

Fortunately, in one part of the country, there has been a long-running special project to overcome this, known as the Oxford Record Linkage Study (ORLS). This includes details of all admissions to hospitals in the area covered, and all deaths, whether these occurred in hospital or elsewhere. Records are organized so that successive admissions can be linked together, and all hospital admissions and death certificates are also linked. Death outside hospital following hospital care can therefore be studied (Seagroatt and Goldacre 1994; Goldacre, Seagroatt, and Hawton 1993). Beginning in 1963 with a population base of 350,000, it now covers about 2.5 million people (Gill et al. 1993). The preliminary analysis for this chapter covers only 1989–93.

Table 14.1 summarizes the information contained in the ORLS data, and the three other data sets used in this chapter—the Hospital Episode Statistics data, the Nottingham Heart Attack Register, and the Clinical Standards Advisory Group study.

Our analysis of the ORLS has some limitations. No details of cost or medication usage are included, and only one part of the country in the relatively prosperous southeast is included, so results may not be representative of England as a whole. Cardiothoracic surgery was not well established in the main tertiary hospital in Oxford until the early 1990s, so the procedure rates in the ORLS may be particularly nonrepresentative.

Interpretation of trends from the Hospital Episode Statistics is limited by changes made to the system in 1987. Financial years replaced calendar years as the basic time unit, and episodes of care

TABLE 14.1. Main Data Sources Available for the Study of Technological Change in Heart Attack Care in England

Name	Population Covered	Major Variables Included	Time Period Covered	Linked Episodes	Comments
Oxford Record Linkage Study	4 counties: Buckinghamshire, Berkshire, Oxfordshire, Northamptonshire, approximately 2.5M	Discharge diagnoses, procedure codes, cause of death, GP practice, postcode	1963 to present	Yes; also to death registrations	Only 1989–93 analyzed to date; longer series may follow
Hospital Episode Statistics	England, approximately 48M	Discharge diagnoses, procedure codes, cause of death, GP practice, postcode	1988 to present	No	Only aggregate results routinely available. Future access to individual data uncertain
Nottingham Heart Attack Register	Catchment population of 2 general hospitals of 600,000	Prehospital care, procedures and medication during hospital stay and on discharge, mortality	1973 to present	No	Results abstracted from previous publications, possible access for further analysis
Clinical Standards Advisory Group study of use of revascularization	3 NHS regions, approximately 8–9M	Demographics, surgeons, procedure	1988–92	No	One-off study; results abstracted from previous publications, MI status unknown

under individual consultants rather than hospital admissions began to be counted. Implementation throughout the NHS took some time, so only data prior to 1986, and from 1989–90 onward are generally regarded as reliable.

Another weakness common to most English data is the absence of data from the private hospitals. The Clinical Standards Advisory Group study of 1987–95 is therefore a particularly valuable ad hoc data source, as its basic method (data from clinical databases run by the clinician) was equally applicable to the private as well as the public sectors. The aim of the study was to determine if overall trends in revascularization had been affected by the 1991 reforms, rather than to study any particular diseases, so patients' MI status was not recorded.

In line with the paucity of expenditure data at patient level, there is a lack of information about low-tech care such as medication and rehabilitation. Many individual audits of these treatments are reported in the peer-reviewed literature, but comparing separate studies is difficult, and hardly any single study covers a substantial period of time. The Nottingham Heart Attack Register is a notable exception, having run for selected intervals since 1973. Only results from a previous publication are presented now, but customized analysis of the entire database is a future possibility. Results are likely to be representative of the whole country, as the standardized mortality rate for CHD is close to the English average, as are the age and socioeconomic profiles. Its contributing hospitals are of typical size. It should be possible to confirm this by comparing Nottingham with other sites in routine data and cross-sectional ad hoc studies, but this has not been performed to date.

Table 14.2 compares ORLS trend data to those from the unlinked but nationally comprehensive Hospital Episode Statistics. As table 14.2 shows, the mean length of stay for heart attack from the ORLS is lower than the national average, but the downward trend in length of stay is quite similar. The finding of shorter lengths of stay in the Oxford region than in England as a whole for AMI is not surprising; it has been observed for a wide range of medical conditions.

Changes in High-Tech Care

Figure 14.2 shows the trend in overall population rates for angiography, CABG, and PTCA, based on the Hospital Episode Statistics for 1989–93. As explained above, Hospital Episode Statistics are unavailable before 1988 and of doubtful reliability immediately thereafter. All procedures are included, not just those delivered to patients with AMI. Procedures performed during the index admission for AMI could be specifically identified and counted, but numbers would be very small, as NHS patients are usually discharged then readmitted for such care. This means the trends shown are not necessarily representative of invasive procedures overall post-MI. Angiography rates increased the most dramatically, almost tripling between 1989 and 1993. PTCA rates show the next-largest increase, with most of the change occurring 1992–93. Data covering the 1987–95 period from the Clinical Standards Advisory Group (not presented in the figure), however, suggest that there was a substantial increase in the aggregate number of revascularization procedures (both CABG and PTCA) prior to 1990, possibly due to the setting of a target for CABG and its identification as a priority by the Government in 1987. In addition, the Clinical Standards Advisory Group data show substantial variation across regions in the level and the rate of change of intensive procedure use, suggesting that local factors may be just as important as national ones in explaining changes in technology use.

Trends in the use of high-tech procedures for patients with AMI, based on analysis of the ORLS, are shown in figures 14.3 and 14.4. Figure 14.3 presents trends in the use of angiography, PTCA, and CABG during patients' initial admission; figure 14.4 presents trends in the use of these procedures at any time during the first 90 days after the patient's initial admission to the hospital, including procedures administered in the initial admission. Baseline rates of procedure use in 1989

TABLE 14.2. Characteristics of AMI Patients in the Oxford Record Linkage Study, and Corresponding National Characteristics, 1989–93

	1989	1990	1991	1992	1993	Average Annual Change (%)
Oxford Record Linkage Study						
Number	3,234	3,120	3,232	3,398	2,986	–2.1
Mean age	67.7	67.6	67.6	68.1	67.8	+0.4
Mean length of stay (unadjusted)	8.9	8.8	8.5	8.3	7.8	–3.1
England[a]						
Mean length of stay	10.2	9.8	10.6	9.3	9.2	–2.5

[a]Hospital Episode Statistics.

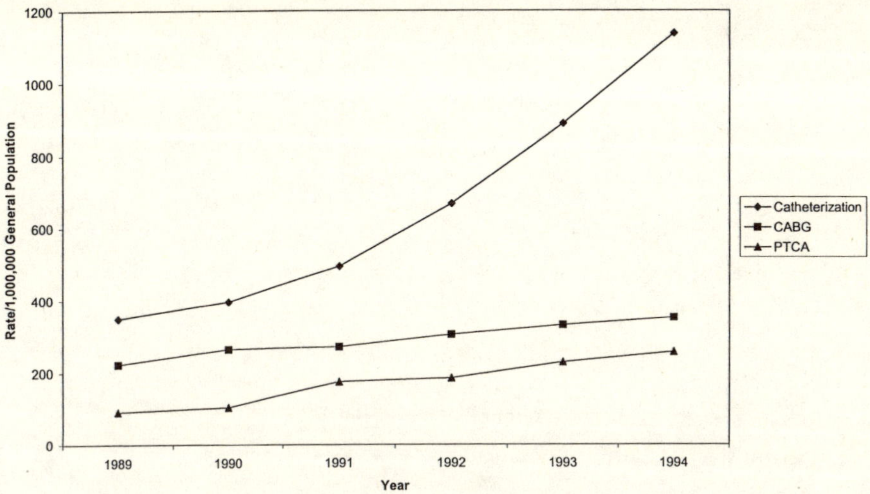

Fig. 14.2. Trends in rates of use of intensive procedures per 1,000,000 population. (Data from Hospital Episode Statistics.)

were very low by international standards: less than 0.5 percent of AMI patients received either CABG or PTCA within the initial admission, and less than 2 percent received CABG or PTCA within the first 90 days. Procedure use increased rapidly over the period. Average annual increases in the 90-day rates between 1989 and 1993 were 11 percent for CABG, 39 percent for PTCA, and 15 percent for angiography. These rates of increase are broadly similar to the national trends shown in figure 14.2.

Day 1 angioplasty is rarely performed in the United Kingdom; precise numbers could be obtained form the Hospital Episode Statistics. None of the four NHS cardiologists interviewed in preparation for this project mentioned day 1 angioplasty or stenting when asked to list the most important recent changes in heart attack management. A database on stent use is maintained by the specialist association, the British Cardiac Intervention Society, and analysis of their data is a possibility in future.

Changes in Low-Tech Care

In our interviews the respondents reported that changes in low-tech care were the most important; in particular, use of intravenous throm-

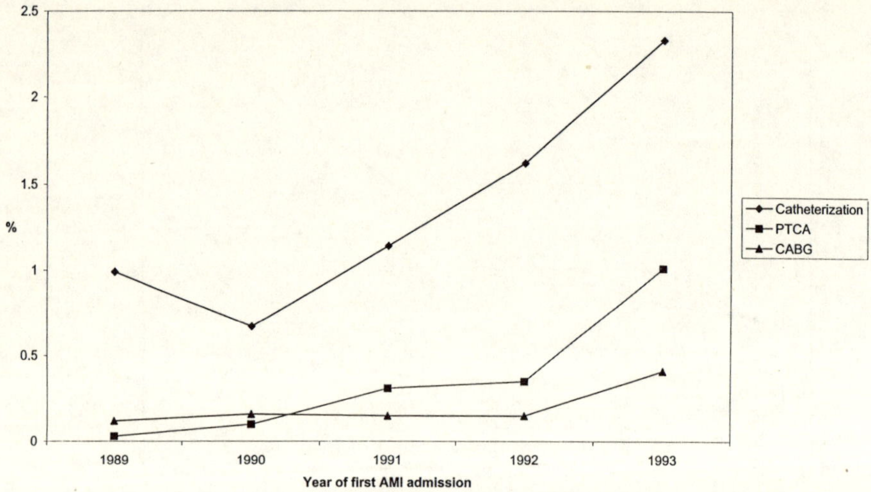

Fig. 14.3. Rates of use of intensive procedures during initial admission for AMI in England. (Data from Oxford Record Linkage Study.)

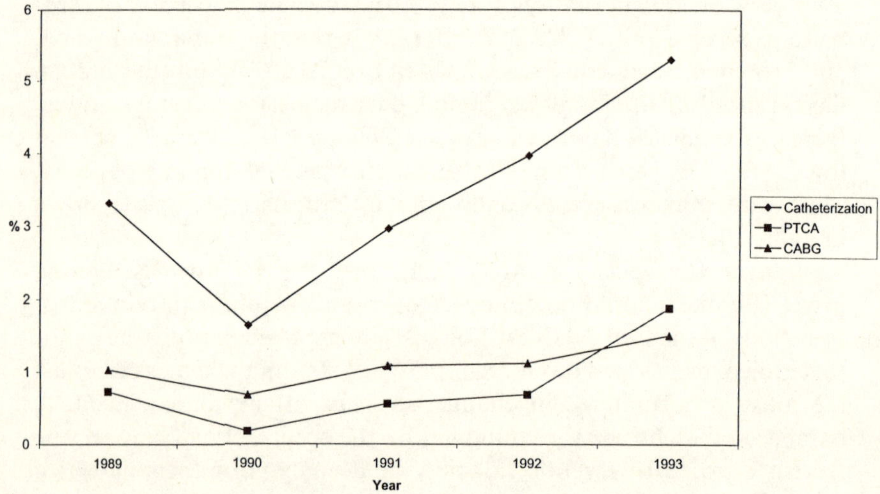

Fig. 14.4. Rates of use of intensive procedures within 90 days of AMI. (Data from Oxford Record Linkage Study.)

bosis, use of aspirin, and organizational changes aimed at getting thrombolysis administered more promptly.

Trends in the use of low-tech care, based on analysis of the Nottingham Heart Attack Register, are shown in figure 14.5. Figure 14.5 presents the rate of use of selected medications during initial admission for AMI during selected years from 1982 to 1992. Aspirin and thrombolysis were not used in 1982–84; between 1989 and 1992 their annual average rates of increase were 3.9 percent and 11 percent, respectively. Between 1984 and 1992, anticoagulant use (mainly heparin) increased by 19 percent per year, beta-blockers by 29 percent. In contrast, data not shown in the figure indicate that use of antiarrhythmics decreased by 4 percent per year.

More detailed information for certain drugs is available from ad hoc studies, particularly for thrombolytics. In one NHS region, thrombolytics treatments were found to have increased from virtually zero in 1987 to about 1,200 treatments per million population per year in 1991 (Ketley and Woods 1993). A similar change is likely to have taken place throughout the country.

Changes in Expertise or Appropriateness of Care

As in most countries, there are considerable local variations throughout the health care system in the use of both high- and low-tech care. Performance indicators based on Hospital Episode Statistics and other routinely collected NHS data were published annually from 1989–90 to 1994–95 and could be used to explore changes in interdistrict variations for a number of factors related to heart attacks, such as length of stay and the overall CABG or PTCA rates. Existing results from published studies show a mixed picture. Results from the Clinical Standards Advisory Group show substantial regional variation through 1995. For thrombolysis, Ketley and Woods (1993) showed a sixfold variation between health authorities in one region in 1989–90, falling to a 2.2-fold variation in 1991–92. Introduction of compulsory medical audit as part of the 1991 reforms might have been expected to have further reduced interdistrict variations, but no studies specifically addressing this question are known to have been published to date.

3. The Consequences of Changes in Heart Attack Care in England

Trend data concerning the outcomes of heart attack in England are scarce, and even when available cannot easily be used to assess the

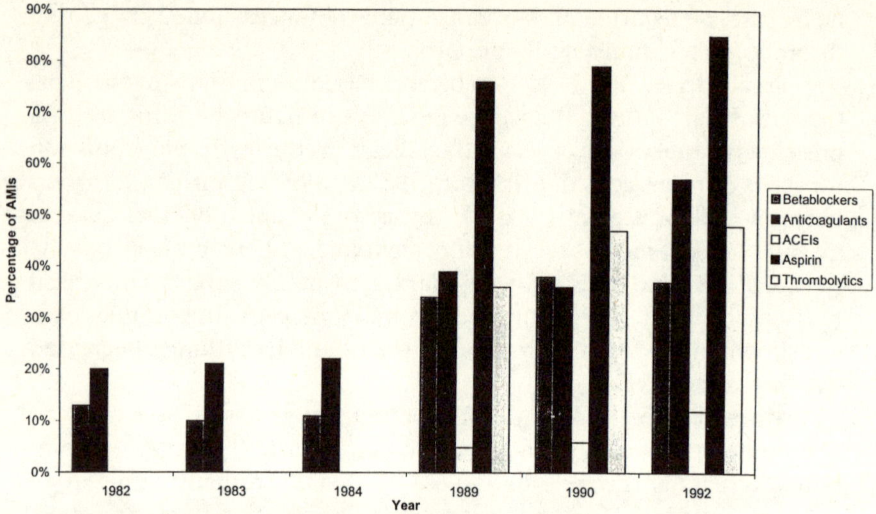

Fig. 14.5. Medication use during initial AMI admission, 1982–92. (Data from Nottingham Heart Attack Register. Adapted from Brown et al. 1997.)

causal link with changes in care. Hospital Episode Statistics provide information on aggregate in-hospital mortality but little else. The Oxford Record Linkage Study is the source of the main results below, with which we calculate total post-AMI mortality at 1, 7, 30, and 365 days after the index AMI admission. Apart from the ORLS, there are a number of localized registries or cohort studies that have reported outcome trends, mainly mortality. Brown et al. (1997) showed little change in in-hospital mortality (about 20 percent) in the Nottingham Heart Attack Register between 1982 and 1992, whereas Greenbaum et al. (1995) reported a decrease from 25.4 percent to 20 percent over a similar period in the North West Thames region.

Changes in Health Outcomes for AMI Patients

Figure 14.6 shows unadjusted mortality (in- and out-of-hospital deaths) among patients with AMI, based on our analysis of the ORLS database. Between 1989 and 1993 there was a slight decrease in mortality rates. 1-, 7-, and 30-day rates fell by a mean of 0.1 percent, 0.6 percent, and 0.2 percent, respectively, per year. The trend in one-year mortality was also quite flat over this period. The overall impression from these limited data and the published studies mentioned above is

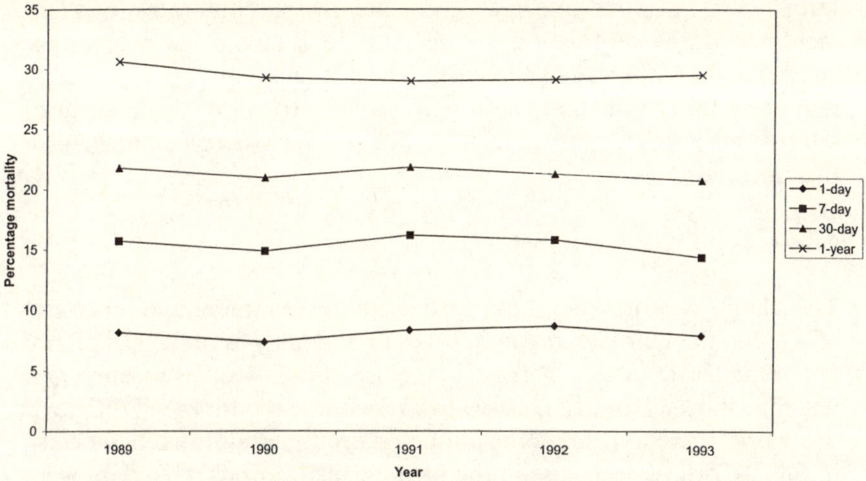

Fig. 14.6. Post-AMI mortality rates (including deaths outside hospital). (Data from Oxford Record Linkage Study Database.)

that post-AMI survival has changed little, in contrast to overall IHD mortality in general, which has constantly fallen, as shown in figure 14.1. This implies that most of the reduction in IHD mortality is due to reduced incidence, not reduced case fatality. This is an interesting finding that needs to be confirmed or refuted by further investigation.

Changes in Medical Expenditures and Resource Use

As explained earlier in the chapter, this is the weakest area of English data. Reports from the Office of Health Economics (1997) show a substantial increase in the medical workforce in both cardiology and cardiothoracic surgery, which has accelerated since 1991, findings that have been confirmed by the Clinical Standards Advisory Group over a shorter time period. Heart attack bed-days have fallen, due to a combination of reduced incidence and shorter length of stay. Detailed analysis of Hospital Episode Statistics might be able to decompose this trend into intensive and nonintensive components.

The estimated cost per bed-day for AMI is the most uncertain figure, as it is derived from average specialty cost reports collected by the Chartered Institute of Public Finance and Accounting. The quoted figure of a real increase of 3.2 percent per year in constant U.S. dollar terms seems intuitively correct, given the low baseline rates for high-tech procedures, and their absolute increase of only a few percent per year. Total resources consumed by heart attack care have probably remained fairly constant, although a rising trend in acute medical admissions and greater use of intensive coronary care facilities make this uncertain.

4. Discussion

This chapter reports on four key trends in the treatment and outcomes of AMI in the United Kingdom. First, in our analysis of the ORLS, we find a moderate rate of increase in the use of high-tech procedures but one that started from a relatively low baseline. Second, based on previous work, there appears to be a much more rapid and timely increase in the use of low-tech care in the form of medications. (No data were available on other low-tech aspects such as rehabilitation). Third, based on our analysis of the ORLS, post-AMI survival has changed little, in contrast to overall CHD mortality. Fourth, also based primarily on previous research, total resources consumed by heart attack care are unlikely to have increased significantly.

There is some evidence that these overall national trends obscure considerable regional and local variations. Between 1987–88 and 1991–92, the rate of increase in PTCA varied 10-fold across the three regions studied (Clinical Standards Advisory Group 1993). At health authority level, the variations were even greater. There was conflicting evidence regarding whether these geographical variations were widening or narrowing during the study period.

How might incentives operating in the NHS have caused this pattern of change? The most appealing explanation is that the system of global budgets is a highly effective restraint on the relatively expensive high-tech procedures, but has much less effect on low-cost, low-tech ones. The latter are also relatively easy to adopt in terms of their limited need for additional infrastructure and training. Supporting evidence is that when there was an explicit intention to increase high-tech procedures, and budgets were adjusted accordingly, this appears to have come about. The interviews with cardiologists offer further support, in that pressure to control costs was perceived as the main reason why new technology was not introduced more quickly.

However, two factors specific to England may have produced an exaggerated impression of the power of global budgets to restrain change. First, the incidence of heart attacks appears to have been falling by about 3 percent per year, effectively freeing up a margin of resources every year. Second, the small private sector may have acted as a buffer, absorbing some of the pressure for change that a fixed budget produces. Without these two relieving factors, the pressure to introduce more high-tech care might have been greater, and the costs of care might have increased despite the global budget caps.

There is an alternative explanation for the relatively slow growth of high-tech care compared to low-tech care that concerns the quality of scientific evidence for its effectiveness. Medical culture in England may place greater value on the scientific basis of clinical practice, and on the principle that treatment should be based on need or ability to benefit rather than ability to pay. During the period of study, several large randomized controlled trials were published in leading journals demonstrating the effectiveness of low-tech care such as thrombolysis and antiplatelet agents, whereas few large trials were completed demonstrating the benefits of high-tech care such as stenting or bypass surgery. It is possible that had the converse occurred and the effectiveness of high-tech care had been demonstrated in a similar fashion, its use would have been rapidly increased despite the financial disincentives. As explained at the beginning of the chapter, doctors do not lose their jobs if financial control is lost, and such events have occurred several times in the history of the NHS.

Circumstantial evidence in support of this second hypothesis is provided by Ketley and Woods (1993). Hospitals that participated in thrombolysis trials took up this new technology more rapidly than those that did not, and practice was changed more rapidly in the subgroups of patients well represented in the trials. Comparison of English trends with other countries with and without the same characteristics may throw light on which, if either, of these two hypotheses is correct.

Relatively little can be said at this preliminary stage about trends in resource use and outcomes specific to heart attack care in England. The only outcome for which data have been obtained is mortality, and this suggests only a marginal improvement between 1989 and 1993. More extensive information on this and other outcomes should be available after more work.

With regard to resource use for patients with AMI, there appears to have been a modest increase in costs per bed-day in hospital, but the average length of stay has fallen, so the overall effect is roughly neutral. In the meantime, there has been an increase in the number of medical staff working in cardiology and cardiothoracic surgery. There are three possible explanations for this apparent paradox. First, heart attacks may not have been a priority for service development permitted by extra staff. Second, and more likely, the apparent increase in medical staff time devoted to cardiology may be an artifact caused by less input from other physicians as cardiology numbers have increased. Third, new costs attributable to AMI treatment (for example those associated with the follow-up and retreatment of survivors) may have been underestimated, because these would not have been ascribed to heart attacks in the relatively simple costing models currently used.

The apparent lack of improvement in survival after heart attack is surprising in light of the increase in the use of low-tech treatments of proven effectiveness during the same time period. Possible explanations are, first, an increase in the number of heart attack victims reaching hospital alive as awareness of a new treatment that should be given promptly has spread; and second, an increase in the proportion of elderly people whose unexpected death is ascribed to a heart attack. In support of this, the average age has increased slightly. Survival rates are highly age-dependent.

Priorities for further work on the costs and consequences of technological change in England are as follows:

1. Extension of the analyses undertaken for this chapter to a longer time period and with other data sets, to allow for a more robust comparison of trends before and after the 1991 reforms.
2. Checks on the stability over time of the coding process, both for mortality and hospital activity data. Almost all the conclusions derived from trend data assume a high degree of stability in coding practice, and this may be incorrect. The 1991 reforms stimulated efforts to improve the completeness of routine discharge coding; they may also have induced some diagnostic "creep" similar to that produced by introduction of payment by DRGs in the United States in the 1980s. Furthermore, small changes in the coding of deaths in the emergency room could have major effects on apparent survival rates.
3. Exploitation of "natural experiments" within the NHS regarding the timing of changes to budgets and staffing levels. Although developments in the NHS are nationally driven, the speed and intensity of any particular change has varied considerably from one region to another. For example, the provision of extra cardiothoracic surgeons and theaters is a discrete, not a continuous, process. Not all regional or health authority budgets caps have risen at a constant rate; preference has been

shown to those regions below their notional target based on a weighted capitation formula. Study of such intracountry differences may allow the impact of budget caps and/or restrictions on staffing levels to be better understood.

Notes

Thanks to Michael Goldacre and David Yeats of the Unit of Health Care Epidemiology, University of Oxford, for allowing us access to data from the Oxford Record Linkage Study and for their comments; Kent Woods and Diane Ketley from the University of Nottingham for their comments; and to the NHS consultant cardiologists who agreed to be interviewed in preparation for this study.

1. Although the basic system is constant throughout the United Kingdom, with separate budgets and management systems for the NHS in England, Wales, Scotland, and Northern Ireland, this chapter focuses exclusively on England. Parallel studies of technology change in the other parts of the United Kingdom could be undertaken and might show interesting differences.

References

Audit Commission. 1995. *Dear to Our Hearts? Commissioning Services for the Treatment and Prevention of Coronary Heart Disease.* London: HMSO.

Birkhead, J., M. Goldacre, A. Mason, E. Wilkinson, M. Amess, and R. Cleary, eds. 1997. *Working Group on Outcome Indicators for Myocardial Infarction: Report to the Department of Health.* London: Royal College of Physicians Research Unit; Oxford: Oxford University Unit of Health-Care Epidemiology.

Black, N., S. Langham, C. Coshall, and J. Parker. 1996. "Impact of the 1991 NHS Reforms on the Availability and Use of Coronary Revascularisation in the UK." *Heart* 76 (suppl. 4), no. 4: 1–31.

Black, N., S. Langham, and M. Petticrew. 1995. "Coronary Revascularisation: Why Do Rates Vary Geographically in the UK?" *Journal of Epidemiology and Community Health* 49, no. 4: 408–12.

Brown, N., T. Young, D. Gray, A. M. Skene, and J. R. Hampton. 1997. "Inpatient Deaths from Acute Myocardial Infarction, 1982–92: Analysis of Data in the Nottingham Heart Attack Register." *British Medical Journal* 315:159–64.

Central Health Monitoring Unit. 1994. *Coronary Heart Disease: An Epidemiological Overview.* London: HMSO.

Clinical Standards Advisory Group. 1993. *Access to and Availability of Coronary Artery Bypass Grafting and Coronary Angioplasty.* London: HMSO.

Department of Health. 1996. *Public Health Common Data Set, 1995.* Vol. 3. London: Department of Health.

Gill, L., M. J. Goldacre, H. Simmons, and G. Bettley. 1993. "Computerised Linking of Medical Records: Methodological Guidelines." *Journal of Epidemiology and Community Health* 47:316–19.

Goldacre, M., V. Seagroatt, and K. Hawton. 1993. "Suicide after Discharge from Psychiatric Inpatient Care." *Lancet* 342:283–86.

Greenbaum, R. A., R. Morris, P. Sritara, D. Shanit, and K. L. Chan. 1995. "Reduced In-Hospital Mortality from Acute Myocardial Infarction with General Adoption of Thrombolytic Therapy in North West Thames Health Region, 1979–1991." *British Heart Journal* 74:493–96.

Hospital Episode Statistics. 1988–. London: Department of Health.

Ketley, D., and K. L. Woods. 1993. "Impact of Clinical Trials on Clinical Practice: Example of Thrombolysis for Acute Myocardial Infarction." *Lancet* 342:892–94.

Office of Health Economics. 1997. *Compendium of Health Statistics.* 10th ed. London: Office of Health Economics.

NHS Executive. 1997. *Clinical Indicators for the NHS (1994–95): A Consultation Document.* London: Department of Health.

Seagroatt, V., and M. J. Goldacre. 1994. "Measures of Early Post-operative Mortality: Beyond Hospital Fatality Rates." *British Medical Journal* 309:361–65.

Sheldon, T. A., and A. L. Faulkner. 1996. "Vetting New Technologies." *British Medical Journal* 313:508.

CHAPTER 15

Technological Change in Heart Attack Care in France: Causes and Consequences

S. Jacobzone, Brigitte Dormont, and Isabelle Durand Zaleski

Among the French population of 60 million, cardiovascular diseases are the primary cause of mortality, accounting for 32 percent of deaths (Haut Comité de la Santé Publique 1996). For example, ischemic heart disease represented 46,400 deaths in 1994, of which 6,400 occurred in those younger than 65 years of age (9.4 percent of all deaths). However, there has been a rapid decline in mortality from ischemic heart disease, a reduction of 14 percent for men and 9 percent for females between 1980 and 1987, and a steeper reduction of 27 percent for men and 32 percent for females between 1987 and 1994. Heart attack (AMI) patients experienced similar declines in mortality over this period (Haut Comité de la Santé publique 1994, 1996).

In terms of GDP share, health care costs in France have been steadily rising since the beginning of the 1970s. Until 1982–83, health care spending was increasing at a yearly nominal rate of 10 to 15 percent per year (with around 10 percent inflation). The very strict Beregovoy public finance stabilization package in 1984 included a global budget for public hospitals and a freeze on medical fees. This action made it possible to stabilize the GDP share until 1987–88. From that point forward, however, the share of GDP devoted to health care began to rise again. Favorable macroeconomic conditions led to less stringent cost control: hospital staff salaries were raised, and global budgets were not always enforced. The incentive power of the global budget decreased over time, partly due to the strategic abilities of the players (Jacobzone 1995). In spite of a freeze in doctor's fees, large increases in volume led to strong growth of ambulatory spending.

Various policy reforms were implemented in order to slow the growth in health care costs in the 1990s. In 1993, for example, global budgets with a joint adjustment of volume and prices were implemented for private hospitals (Brocas 1993), supplemented by additional copayments for patients. In addition, collection of "DRG-like" case-type information was made mandatory for public hospital budget approval, in order to adjust reimbursement based on hospital activity levels (Ministère des Affaires Sociales 1994, 1995). In 1996, the Juppé Plan led to a revision of the constitution, the vote of a "social budget" by Parliament each year, and a global budget both for ambulatory care (one global budget for GPs, and one for specialists) and for hospital care. Yearly increase targets for expenditure were set at low levels, including an increase for inflation, set at 2.1 percent in 1995 and 1.6 percent in 1996–97.

What has been the role of technological change in the treatment of AMI patients in France, and how have budgetary and policy reforms interacted with the presence of new cardiac technologies to affect medical treatment decisions and medical costs? In the context of changes in health care spending, the rest of this chapter provides a more detailed review of incentives for the causes and consequences of technological change in heart attack care. Although our ability to examine trends in the causes and consequences of technological change is limited by the fact that detailed individual-level claims data is only available for the years 1994–95, supplemented by other data, our analysis suggests how health care finance in France may affect treatment decision-making for heart attack. Section 1 outlines the incentives for technological change for heart attack care, including those due to health care financing and other regulatory policies. Section 2 describes the data that we use and explores the extent and the implications of technological change for treatment of heart attack, and section 3 concludes.

1. Incentives for Technological Change in France

Financing of Care for Heart Disease

French health care is financed through a two-pillar system. Public and mandatory health care coverage is organized through public sickness funds, and supplementary individual insurance is delivered both by not-for-profit *mutuelles* and private insurance companies. Altogether there are about 15 public sickness funds covering about 99.6 percent of the population. A law ensuring universal coverage for the remaining 0.4 percent of the population was passed in 1998. Although financing of the sickness funds varied in the past, recent financing reforms have caused a shift toward general public financing based on a fixed 6.7 percent tax on all income. In addition, for less than 1 percent of the population, copayments can be waived due to major chronic disease (e.g., diabetes), under the "100 percent clause."

Supplementary insurance covers the copayments required under the public insurance scheme. Although supplemental coverage is not mandatory, most employed people choose it. There is a mandatory community uniform rating by the not-for-profit *mutuelles,* with no coverage exclusions allowed for preexisting conditions if affiliation is chosen at time of hiring. There are also "private for profit" insurance companies, where prices are set according to the market.

Hospitals are either public or private-not-for-profit. Public hospitals, with approximately 75 percent of the acute care beds, are financed by a global budget, which is shared by sickness funds in proportion to their affiliated population (but not depending on relative hospital use). Global budgeting was introduced in 1984 to replace a system with a reimbursement per diem. Until recently, budgets were capped and did not vary with increased activity, case mix, or utilization of new technologies. (One small exception to this financing scheme was a daily inpatient copayment of around $10–$15.) Doctors are salaried in public hospitals, although in a few cases, private practice may exist within public hospitals.

Until 1993, private hospitals and clinics were financed by per diem charges, split between the sickness funds, supplemental insurance, and out-of-pocket payments by patients. In 1993, modified global budgets financed by the sickness funds were imposed on private hospitals. However, doctors in private hospitals are paid by the patients directly; physician charges are not included in the per diem or more recently, the global budget.

Another special feature of the French health care system, particularly worth being noted in the case of heart attacks, is its general emergency service, the SAMU (Service d'Aide Médicale d'Urgence), financed through a separate global budget process and available at no cost to all patients on a nationwide basis. The SAMU team includes doctors who are able to deliver thrombolytic drugs immediately.

The public insurance system covers a substantially greater portion of hospital expenses than ambulatory care expenses. The public system covers 89 percent of hospital expenses (total net copayments by households represent 6.4 percent of hospital expenditure, and supplementary insurance 4.5 percent); in contrast, the public insurance system covers 59 percent of ambulatory care expenses (total copayments by households represent 22 percent of ambulatory care expenses, supplementary insurance 19 percent).

Ambulatory care is mostly financed through a fee-for-service system in which patients pay for care up front and are partly reimbursed by the public sickness funds. However, the rapid rise of supplementary insurance covering ambulatory care expenses, to 80 percent of the population in 1980, has favored a general homogenization in terms of access to care and patterns of consumption (Mormiche 1997). Hence, for middle-class patients, there is virtually free access to GP care and prescription drugs, as well as simple tests. This may explain the relatively high level of consumption of pharmaceuticals in volume in France, which is close to double those observed in other European countries for certain types of drugs that may have preventive effects for coronary disease. The only constraint is that the patient must in most situations pay cash up front and then obtain reimbursement, which is a restriction for some less wealthy individuals. Poorer patients, typically unemployed and thus without supplemental coverage, may either get less ambulatory care or go to outpatient consultations in public hospitals, although in practice this constraint applies to less than 5 percent of the population. Due to rising unemployment, constraints of access may have worsened, however, for the more deprived groups over recent decades (Mormiche 1997).

Technology Regulation

CABG versus PTCA Incentives and Regulations

In addition to general financing considerations that may affect practice patterns, the most expensive and sophisticated technologies are highly regulated and mostly limited to the public sector. For example, there is extensive regulation and planning by the Department of Health of cardiac surgery facilities where coronary bypass surgery (CABG) procedures are performed using a key technology for open heart surgery, extracorporeal circulatory surgery device (ECSD). In the public sector, regional hospital centers had to be able to perform cardiac surgery, and ECSD buying decisions had to be made at the Ministry of Health. In the planning process, there has been a legitimate concern on the one hand to favor diffusion of useful procedures. On the other hand, such decisions are subject to an intense bargaining process, with an intense joint lobbying of local authorities to obtain the desired equipment. After 1989, a national target was set at 850,000 inhabitants per cardiac surgery unit, to regulate further placements (there are in fact about 70 units in France today, which is close to the target) (Bourgueil 1994). The evidence from surveys reveals still significant regional inequalities (Baubeau et al. 1996). In practice, the degree of control of central national authorities over general hospital investment is quite weak.

Under the current situation, the private sector has disproportionally adopted cardiovascular technologies requiring neither a surgical facility nor difficult regulatory hurdles (PTCA and stents). With favorable economic incentives (lower start-up cost, in particular), the private sector has gained 50 percent of the PTCA market even though on an acute bed basis this sector only makes up 25 percent of the health care market. A deterrent to public-sector entry into the PTCA market is the financing of supplies from the global budget, which creates difficulty for expensive devices. For example, quality regulations favor single use for catheters and angioplasty balloons, while hospital budget managers prefer resterilization and multiple uses.

Drug and Device Regulation

In the private sector, device prices have to be approved through the Interministry Price Setting TIPS (Tarification Interministérielle des Prestations Sanitaires) process. The price is set generally according to a survey study by the National Health Care Evaluation Agency (ANDEM), on a de facto cost-based approach. Once the TIPS price is set, devices can be freely reimbursed by sickness funds. Difficulties may exist for very innovative devices such as stents or new coronary care procedures. Sometimes, "informal" agreements may exist between local sickness fund offices and clinics, which allow for some reimbursement. When these arrangements do not exist, availability is still possible on the basis of private payment. Usually, the TIPS procedure is used to clarify and unify rules on a national level. Cardiac catheters and angioplasty have been subject to TIPS for a long time. In addition, the Health Care Evaluation Agency (ANDEM) undertakes formal technology assessment to investigate the relevance of new technologies, such as new coronary procedures (laser, rotablator), with a report early in 1992, and updated in 1994 (ANDEM 1992, 1994). This assessment may influence the diffusion of drugs and devices, as it is sometimes the first step before the investigation of official approval for reimbursement.

Thrombolytic drugs are mainly used for emergency services, either in SAMU or in public hospitals out of a global budget. This budget allows for a significant use of tPA (greater than 50 percent). Private clinics are faced with a $20 cap per day on drug expenditure. This allows only for streptokinase but not tPA. In any event, emergency care is mainly public. Prices of drugs used in hospitals, such as thrombolytics, are not regulated: they are bought after a bidding process between hospitals and drug companies. On the other hand, prices for drugs available both in hospitals and pharmacies are centrally regulated by the government once the drugs have been officially approved and made eligible for public reimbursement.[1] This creates some strategic incentives for the release of new drugs on the market (Jacobzone 1997).[2]

Microregulation of Provider Decisions

There is very little regulation of provider decisions in France. There are no precertification programs for performing procedures. The only regulation to date refers to ambulatory care with negative reference guidelines, Regulatory Medical References (RMO).[3] In theory, physicians who do not comply with these can be fined by sickness funds. In practice, there are seldom any penalties. Under the present global budget for specialists, physicians are collectively responsible at the national level for their activity, but this exerts a negligible influence on micro decisions.

Other Incentives for Technology Adoption and Use

Competition

Competition is important where there are dense resources in health care professionals and equipment. In France, patients have an absolutely free choice insofar as they have the time and the opportunity to look for doctors or hospitals. Patients are courted, and often more aggressive treatment or additional prescriptions help to keep them. There is no real competition among health plans even if this may formally exist. In areas with limited care resources, competition is not very intense and patients use the closest resource.

Regulation of Physician Supply

The total number of physicians is regulated through a cap on the number of students admitted to the second year of medical school, introduced at the end of the 1970s. The total number of specialists is controlled, through the number of places offered in internship, after an intensive exam at the end of the first six years of medical study. The cap is not maintained by specialty, resulting in an oversupply of ophthalmologists and dermatologists, and an undersupply of surgeons and obstetricians. The relative number of cardiologists among specialists is steadily increasing (Letouzey, Genet, and Amoretti 1996).

2. Technological Change in AMI Care in France

Based on previous research (Jacobzone, Durand Zaleski, and Chaix 1997), figure 15.1 reports aggregate trends in use of catheterization (CATH), PTCA, and CABG for 1986 through 1994 (data were only available for 1990–94 for CATH). Figure 15.1 shows that there was significant technological change in heart attack care in France during the 1980s and 1990s. For example, the number of catheterizations performed in France increased by over 60 percent during the early 1990s. Trends in PTCA and CABG were fairly similar until 1989–90, at which point angioplasty became much more prevalent.

Unfortunately, analysis of long-term trends in the causes and consequences of technological change is not feasible in France if using only DRG-type data (see below). Discharge abstracts for patients have only become available after the government mandated "DRG-like" case-type reporting for hospitals after 1993. For this reason, we only have claims data on individual AMI patients for the years 1994 and 1995. In addition, our data do not enable us to follow the same patient from one hospital stay to the other. Therefore, it will not be possible to have detailed information on the long-term outcomes of AMI treatment, except for hospital mortality during the initial AMI stay. For each stay (observation), we know the principal diagnosis (AMI), secondary diagnoses (comorbidities), procedures used,[4] entry mode in the hospital, exit mode, length of stay, age, gender, and county of residence of the patient.

Our data come from three sources. First, we analyze data from the National Cost Base for Public Hospitals (Cost Base). This database provides additional detailed information about costs of each stay on a restricted sample of 25 hospitals[5] for the years 1994–95. This sample contains information about 5,623 stays due to AMI over these two years. This sample is assumed to be quite representative of the whole public system, as it has been used to construct the French resource scale to determine the relative value of procedures for different case-type groupings.

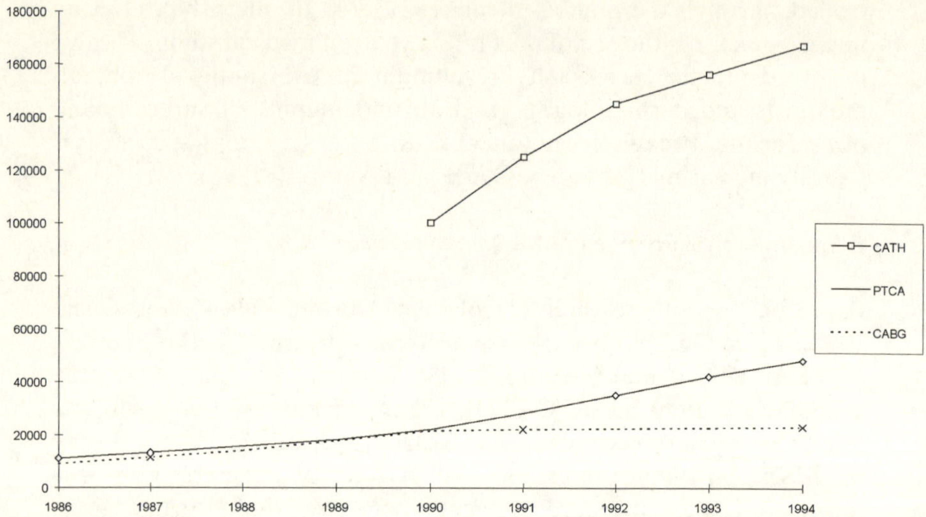

Fig. 15.1. Counts of invasive procedures in France, 1986–94. (Data from Bourgueil 1994; Letouzey, Genet, and Amoretti 1996; IGAS 1988.)

The second database is the National Base for Public Hospitals (National Base). At the time of the study, the data was available only from July through December of 1994. It includes the discharge abstract information describing the 8 million stays in 430 French public hospitals a year. Information about costs is not provided by the National Base. Furthermore, it covers public hospitals only, as similar data for private clinics[6] were not readily available on a national basis. However, it is worthwhile to exploit it, as it provides information about most of the hospitals of the French public sector. When selecting stays due to AMI treatment, the National Base contains information about 17,931 stays for the second half of 1994.

The National Base contains more small hospitals proportionately than the Cost Base. In the National Base, 100 hospitals provide 66 percent of observations. The French public hospital system is in fact highly hierarchical, with most heart disease related interventions performed in approximately 160 centers, which are equipped for cardiac surgery with extracorporeal circulation devices, and with many other hospitals performing small numbers of invasive interventions.

The third source is the cost accounting system from a large

Parisian metropolitan hospital, which enabled us to perform more detailed cost analysis of the selected cardiac interventions.

Table 15.1 shows the characteristics of the individual patients in the first two databases. The demographic characteristics of patients in our two databases are quite similar. The majority of AMI patients are males (approximately 70 percent). Approximately 40 percent are ages 40–64; 57 percent are ages 65–89. One difference between patients from the two data sources is the higher number of transfer patients in the Cost Base compared with the National Base.. In the National Base sample of hospitals, only 4.9 percent of admissions are transfer patients; in the Cost Base, 7.2 percent are transfer patients.

Table 15.2 presents statistics on treatment decisions, lengths of stay, and mode of exit from the hospital for Cost Base and National Base patients. Based on the National Base, 20.6 percent of patients received treatment with catheterization during their initial admission to the hospital for AMI in 1994. Angioplasty and bypass surgery were administered to 6.9 and 4.3 percent of patients, respectively. Patients initially admitted to Cost Base hospitals, not surprisingly, generally receive slightly more intensive treatment for their AMI. Treatment decisions for transfer patients in the Cost Base and National Base differ more substantially. For example, fully 29.1 percent of Cost Base transfer patients receive catheterization, whereas only 19.2 percent of National Base transfer patients do; 28.1 percent of Cost Base transfer patients receive angioplasty, whereas 5.7 percent of National Base transfer patients do. CABG rates among initial admissions and trans-

TABLE 15.1. Characteristics of AMI Patients, Cost Base and National Base for Public Hospitals

	Cost Base 1994–95		National Base, Second Half of 1994	
	Frequency	Percentage	Frequency	Percentage
Entry mode to the hospital				
From home	5,217	92.8	17,050	95.1
From another hospital	406	7.2	881	4.9
Age				
40–64	2,235	39.7	7,092	39.6
65–89	3,178	56.5	10,325	57.5
90 and over	210	3.8	514	2.9
Gender				
Male	3,958	70.4	12,548	70.0
Female	1,665	29.6	5,383	30.0

fer patients are similar in the two databases, suggesting that hospital size has a greater effect on hospitals' propensity to perform PTCA than it does on hospitals' propensity to perform CABG. The proportions of patients receiving intensive procedures rises significantly when the sample is limited to patients initially admitted to hospitals operating CATH, PTCA and CABG labs. In the Cost Base, 56 percent of hospitals perform CATH, and 28 percent perform PTCA and/or CABG. In the National Base, these proportions fall to 34.7 percent for CATH, 9.8 percent for PTCA, and 11.6 percent for CABG.

Consistent with these differences, table 15.2 also shows that lengths of stay are longer in the Cost Base hospitals than in the National Base hospitals. Just as fewer patients are transferred into a National Base hospital, a greater share of patients are transferred to

TABLE 15.2. Treatment Decisions, Length of Stay, and Mode of Exit from the Hospital for AMI Patients, Cost Base and National Base for Public Hospitals

	Cost Base, 1994–95, Share of Patients (%)	National Base, Second Half of 1994, Share of Patients (%)
Procedure use during initial admission		
CATH	22.3	20.6
PTCA	8.3	6.9
CABG	3.2	4.3
Procedure use, transferred patients only		
CATH	29.1	19.2
PTCA	28.1	5.7
CABG	8.4	8.3
Procedure use, only those patients admitted to hospitals performing the relevant procedure[a]		
CATH	30.3	33.1
PTCA	11.4	11.2
CABG	4.3	6.9
Length of stay		
1 to 7 days	35.0	41.1
8 to 14 days	43.8	41.2
Over 14 days	21.2	17.7
Mode of exit from hospital		
Other service or hospital	30.2	35.2
Death	9.3	9.2
Death among those who had been transferred from another hospital	4.4	6.0
Home	60.5	55.6

[a]Nationwide, 56 percent of hospital perform CATH, and 28 percent perform both PTCA and CABG.

another hospital from a National Base hospital. Death rates are about the same (9.2 versus 9.3 percent)[7] in the two databases.

Table 15.3 presents selected characteristics of patients, treatment decisions, and initial-admission mortality, by age for patients admitted to Cost Base and National Base hospitals. The majority of young AMI patients are male (approximately 88 percent), whereas older patients tend to be female (approximately 73 percent of patients aged 90 and over are women). Intensive cardiac procedures are performed disproportionately on young (and therefore, all else constant, male) patients. Lengths of stay are longest for younger elderly (patients ages 65–89), and death rates are monotonic in age.

Tables 15.4 and 15.5 report descriptive statistics on the cost of treating AMI patients over the 1994–95 period, in francs and U.S. dollars, converted at 1995 PPP exchange rates. Because public hospitals are subject to a global budget, table entries do not represent actual reimbursements to hospitals; rather, they are accounting measures of differential resource use based on hospital cost reports. Table 15.4 shows the breakdown of cost of treatment by case type, and the mean and standard deviation of the cost of each patient's initial admission. Six case types are represented in our databases.[8] Case codes 178 and 179 represent the bulk of the observations. Hospitals from the Cost Base sample provide a higher proportion of complicated AMI (21.1 percent) than do hospitals of the National Base (only 15.8 percent).

TABLE 15.3. Selected Characteristics of Patients, Treatment Decisions, and Health Outcomes, by Age, Cost Base and National Base for Public Hospitals

	Cost Base, 1994–95, Share of Patients (%)			National Base, Second Half of 1994, Share of Patients (%)		
	40–64	65–89	90+	40–64	65–89	90+
Male	88.1	60.7	27.6	87.7	60.0	27.0
Procedure use during initial admission						
CATH	32.3	16.7	0	29.1	15.8	0.4
PTCA	13.5	5.2	0.5	10.5	4.8	0.0
CABG	4.7	2.3	0.5	6.6	2.3	0.0
Length of stay						
1 to 7 days	41.3	30.6	34.3	48.6	36.1	37.6
8 to 14 days	43.5	44.0	41.9	40.6	41.9	36.2
Over 14 days	15.2	25.3	23.8	10.8	22.0	26.2
Death	2.3	12.6	35.7	2.2	12.8	34.0

Patients who die from their AMI are the least costly to treat; patients who receive catheterization and CABG are the most costly. Table 15.5 provides information on changes in average costs per admission, and average costs per day. The table shows that the costs of treating AMI are rising dramatically in France. In francs, the average cost per stay rose 8.2 percent between 1994 and 1995. This is perhaps due to a rise in the procedure use. But even more striking is the rate of growth of the average daily cost during the same period. From 1994 to 1995, the average cost per day of an AMI admission rose by 18.1 percent. This result reveals the shortening of the average length of stays (see above), and underscores the two trends in AMI treatment in France: greater intensity delivered during shortened hospital stays. Another noteworthy feature of table 15.5 is the trend in the variability of costs across patients. Standard deviations are as large as or larger than means, and increasing even more rapidly.

Table 15.6 provides the costs of admission for AMI in 1996 at a large Parisian teaching hospital (Henri Mondor), converted to 1995 U.S. dollars at a PPP exchange rate. The cost of treatment for patients with an uncomplicated AMI is in line with the results from the Cost Base. The cost of treatment for patients who died is slightly lower. On the other hand, the cost of the complicated AMI is much higher than in the Cost Base, due primarily to a higher intensity of care (the 1996

TABLE 15.4. Frequency and Cost for AMI Patients, by Case Type, Cost Base for Public Hospitals, 1994–95

Case Code and Case Type	Frequency	Percentage	Mean Cost of Admission (standard deviation) Fr	$
154 CABG with cardiac cath	24	0.4	147,107 (88,705)	23,557 (14,205)
155 CABG elective	22	0.4	130,743 (39,157)	20,937 (6,271)
157 Other cardiac procedures without extracorporeal circulation	161	2.9	57,456 (55,829)	9,201 (8,940)
178 Complicated AMI	1,189	21.1	36,363 (23,051)	5,823 (3,691)
179 Uncomplicated AMI	3,718	66.1	26,197 (19,384)	4,195 (3,104)
180 AMI deceased	509	9.1	24,148 (32,321)	3,867 (5,176)

data reflect a high proportion of stents placed and intensity of care is generally higher in teaching hospitals), and to some cost differentials present in teaching hospitals.

Although our analysis is primarily cross-sectional, prior studies have analyzed longitudinal data from the French MONICA centers (e.g., Haas et al. 1996); for comparability with other chapters, we discuss these studies here. The French MONICA registers cover both public and private hospitals and characterize AMI care in three regions of France between 1985 and 1991. During this period, CATH rates increased 20–25 percent in two of the centers, reaching levels of 81 percent of all AMI patients in Strasbourg and 96 percent in Toulouse. Similarly, PTCA rates increased two- to fivefold from 1985 to 1991, with the 1991 levels at approximately 25 percent in two of the registers, and 50 percent in the third one. In fact, the intensity of care has increased more in highly competitive environments such as the

TABLE 15.5. Changes in Mean and Standard Deviation of Costs per Admission, Cost Base for Public Hospitals, 1994–95

	Total Cost of Admission (standard deviation)		Mean Daily Cost of Admission (standard deviation)	
	Fr	$	Fr	$
1994	28,795	4,693	3,434	560
	(25,498)	(4,156)	(3,429)	(559)
1995	31,152	4,989	4,057	650
	(28,142)	(4,507)	(4,710)	(754)
Percentage change	8.2%	6.3%	18.1%	16.1%

TABLE 15.6. AMI-Related Costs at Large Parisian Teaching Hospital, 1996

	Costs
Treatment for AMI	
Uncomplicated AMI	4,759
Complicated AMI, discharged alive	10,451
AMI, deceased	4,348
Invasive cardiology procedures	
Coronary angiography	898
PTCA	4,186
PTCA, 1 stent	5,869
PTCA, 2 stents	8,631

Note: Costs are 1995 U.S. dollars, converted at PPP rates.

Toulouse area. CABG rates were rather stable. The use of thrombolytics increased significantly and is higher in areas where less intensive use was made of invasive procedures in early years. The use of beta-blockers and antiplatelets increased, while the use of calcium channel blockers decreased over time.

3. Conclusion

The French data provide insights regarding the joint effects of economic incentives and medical progress on the type and intensity of treatments made available to AMI patients. The French system appears to be very mixed and cannot be easily generalized, as it results from a complex interaction of publicly regulated and market-based mechanisms. In this setting, there has been a significant, though sometimes unbalanced, diffusion of intensive technologies in the health care system, while unit costs have been kept in line with most other results in major Western countries, except the United States.

Although it is quite possible to draw a detailed cross sectional overview, it is more difficult to reflect trends in outcomes per se. In France, the absence of linkage between the episodes of care for the same patient presents a challenge for longitudinal economic studies that investigate the delayed benefit of an expensive initial therapeutic procedure. Under the past global budget, hospitals have had no incentive to spend more on an index admission in order to decrease the number or severity of readmissions. Incentives at the margin may be changed, however, as the implementation of the new (DRG) related payment system proceeds further. The adoption of new technologies that have a high purchase price for the hospital, but may decrease length of stay, has not been encouraged since the savings from bed-days does not offset the high cost of new technologies. On the other hand, one may explain the still significant rate of diffusion of new technologies through the general pressure resulting from the advance of medical knowledge together with the competitive pressure from private clinics (though this assumption would need to explored with data). In the future, the progressive generalization of DRG-related information will make it possible to produce a more detailed longitudinal assessment of trends in health care interventions and outcomes, as more years become available. Also, increased linkage possibilities, including those allowing follow-up of each patient, will allow for a more longitudinal assessment of outcomes after a health intervention.

Finally, the ongoing extension of the DRG data system to the private clinics will also allow for a more complete overview.

Notes

We thank the Mission PMSI/Direction des hôpitaux and the SESI from Ministère de l'Emploi et de la Solidarité for respectively allowing access to French DRG data and providing financial support for this research. We thank CITI-2 Center in Paris for the help with data as well as M. McClellan and M. C. Closon for useful discussions. This research has benefited from the research assistance of K. Milcent and L. Rappegno. The views expressed here are the authors' sole responsibility and do not represent those of their institutions. This research began while S. Jacobzone was at CREST-INSEE.

1. After the grant of a Market Entry Authorization for the Drug (Autorisation de Mise sur le Marché, AMM).
2. In this study, a specific insight on the evolution of prices for French antihypertensive drugs can be found.
3. Références Médicales Opposables. For details see Durand Zaleski, Colin, and Blum Boisgard 1997.
4. Up to 50 comorbidities or diagnoses are being coded for each stay.
5. Our cost base is slightly smaller than the original cost base because we eliminate hospitals not observed during the two years 1994 and 1995.
6. The available data were too scanty and too biased to be really exploited. Further generalization of the collection should make it possible to use them for such a study in a near future.
7. This does not include deaths before arrival at the hospital (about 2 percent).
8. Information relative to other types of cases was eliminated because it was too scarcely observed to be considered as representative.

References

Agence Nationale pour le Developpement de l'Evaluation Medicale (ANDEM). 1992. *New Techniques of Coronary Angioplasty: State of the Art.* Paris: Agence Nationale pour le Developpement de l'Evaluation Medicale.

———. 1994. *New Techniques of Coronary Angioplasty: State of the Art, Update.* Paris: Agence Nationale pour le Developpement de l'Evaluation Medicale.

Amouyel, P., D. Arveiler, J. P. Cambou, M. Montaye, J. B. Ruidavets, A. Bingham, P. Schaffer, and J. L. Richard. 1994. "Myocardial Infarction Case-Fatality, Gradient in Three French Regions: The Influence of Acute Coronary Care." *International Journal of Epidemiology* 23, no. 4: 700–709.

Baubeau, D., H. Q. Gong, M. P. Chaillet, M. N. Vibet, M. Marty, G. Hoffman, S. Ruelle, Y. Bourqueil, and J. C. Mino. 1996. *Activité des unités de chirurgie cardiaque française en 1994.* Direction des Hôpitaux, Caisse Nationale d'Assurance Maladie, Groupe Image Ministère de l'Emploi et de la Solidarité.

Bourgueil, Y. 1994. "L'organisation de la chirurgie cardiaque dans plusieurs pays de la CEE et le Québec." Groupe Image, National School of Public Health (ENSP), Rennes.

Brocas, A. M. 1993. "La maîtrise des dépenses dans le secteur de la santé, après la loi du 4 janvier 1993." *Droit Social,* March, no. 3: 235–43.

Durand Zaleski, I. 1992. "An Economic Model of Coronary Care." Ph.D. diss., University of Paris IX Dauphine.

Durand Zaleski, I., C. Colin, and C. Blum Boisgard. 1997. "Usefulness of Regulatory Medical References." *British Medical Journal* 315:943–46.

Fédération Française de Cardiologie. 1996. "L'infarctus du Myocarde en France: Données des trois cardiopathies ischémiques de Lille, Strasbourg et Toulouse. Période 1985–1992." In *Les Registres Français de Cardiopathies Ischémiques,* 32. Paris: Fédération Française de Cardiologie.

Haas B., D. Arveiler, J. P. Cambou, P. Amouyel, A. Bingham, J. L. Richard, and P. Schaffer. 1996. "Prise en charge thérapeutique de l'infarctus du myocarde: évolution dans le projet MONICA France entre 1985 et 1991." *Revue d'Epidémiologie et de Santé Publique* 44:S53–S61.

Haut Comité de la Santé Publique. 1994. *La santé en France, rapport général* (Health in France, General Report). Documentation Française. Paris.

———. 1996. *Health in France.* Documentation Française. Paris.

Inspection Général des Affaires Sociales (IGAS). 1988. National Survey on Cardiac Surgery. June. Inspection Général des Affaires Sociales.

Jacobzone, S. 1995. "Les apports de l'économie industrielle pour définir la stratégie économique de gestion du secteur hospitalier public" (The contribution of industrial economics in defining the management strategy of public hospitals). *Sciences Sociales et Santé* 13, no. 1: 5–46.

———. 1997. "A Perspective on the Pricing of French Prescription Drugs: Are Price Indices Biased Downward?" Centre de Recherche en Economie et Statistique—Institut National de la Statistique et des études Economiques (CREST-INSEE), presented to the Franco-American seminar, NBER Summer Institute.

Jacobzone, S., I. Durand Zaleski, and C. Chaix. 1997. "Impact de la diffusion de l'innovation: Le cas du traitement invasif de la pathologie coronarienne" (The impact of diffusion of innovation: The case of invasive treatment of coronary pathology). *Minutes of the Tenth Anniversary of French Health Economists.* John Libbey Eurotext.

Letouzey, J. P., A. Genet, and R. Amoretti. 1996. *Cardiologie 2000.* Syndicat National des Spécialistes des maladies du coeur et des vaisseaux, with J. De Kervasdoué, R. Cash, C. Meyer, J. N. Colling, and F. Bousquet. SANESCO.

Ministère des Affaires Sociales, de la Santé et de la Ville. 1994. "Manuel des Groupes Homogènes de Malades." *Bulletin Officiel de la République Française,* fascicule spécial no. 94/2 bis.

———. 1995. "L'échelle nationale de coûts relatifs par Groupe Homogène de Malades." *Bulletin Officiel de la République Française,* fascicule spécial no. 95/5 bis.

Mormiche, P. 1997. "Inégalités de santé et inéquité du système de soins." In *Economie de la Santé, Trajectoires du futur.* INSEE-ECONOMICA, ed. S. Jacobzone. Paris: Institut National de la Statistique et des études Economiques.

World Health Organization Multinational Monitoring of Trends and Determinants in Cardiovascular Disease (WHO MONICA). 1994. "Myocardial Infarction and Coronary Deaths in the WHO MONICA Project: Registration Procedures, Event Rates, and Case Fatality Rates in 38 Populations from 21 Countries in Four Continents." *Circulation* 90, no. 1: 583–611.

CHAPTER 16

Technological Change in Heart Attack Care in Belgium: Causes and Consequences

N. Maes, P. M. De Coster, M. C. Closon, and J. Perelman

Like most other developed countries, Belgium has in recent decades experienced both substantial growth in expenditures on health care and substantial improvements in health outcomes. From 1970 to 1992, aggregate expenditure on health care has risen dramatically, from 4.1 percent to 8.2 percent of GDP (OECD 1995). Correspondingly, the annual percentage change in mortality rates from cardiovascular disease between 1970 to 1992 has been –2.3 percent per year for men and –2.9 percent for women ($p < 0.0001$, age 45 to 74 years). The annual percentage change in mortality rates from ischemic heart disease between 1970 to 1992 is similar.

The purpose of this chapter is to identify the extent of technological change in heart attack care in Belgium, and to explore the extent to which it is responsible for observed trends in medical expenditures and health outcomes. To this end, we analyze hospital data from the Center for Interdisciplinary Study in Health Economics (Centre d'Etudes Interdisciplinaires en Economie de la Santé, or CIES) database for the years 1989 to 1995. The subsample of CIES data we use contains hospital-based information for 11 of the 33 hospitals in Belgium that have cardiac surgery centers. For this reason, the levels of procedure use we report are not representative of those in the nation as a whole and are not comparable to rates of procedure use in other countries. Nonetheless, the trends in procedure use over time are indicative of how technological change has affected cardiac care in Belgium, and its implications for health care costs and outcomes more generally.

We first describe the economic and regulatory incentives for technological change in Belgium. We then turn to our analysis of Belgian microdata. We begin with broad descriptive information from the public and nonprofit health insurers *(mutualités)* and conclude with our analysis of CIES data from patients admitted to hospitals that have cardiac surgery centers.

Incentives for Technological Change in Belgium

Financing of Care for Heart Disease

The Belgian health care system is financed through five private nonprofit insurance funds and a single public fund. Together, these funds cover more than 99 percent of the Belgian population for major health risks such as heart attack. (There is private voluntary insurance for minor health risks, sold by the *mutualités* and by for-profit insurers, but this is only a small part of health care spending in general, and an even smaller part for major illnesses such as heart attack.) Membership in one of the six funds is compulsory for most individuals, although there is free choice among funds, which are organized largely according to political and religious affiliation. The funds are financed almost entirely through social security taxes on wages (slightly more than half), and public subsidies, with the remainder of financing arising out of other taxes. Individuals' tax rates do not depend on their choice of fund. In addition, no fund is allowed to make a profit or loss; surpluses and deficits are pooled among funds by the government. There is free choice of doctors and hospitals; all funds reimburse for care supplied by any provider. Not surprisingly, the funds compete on the basis of customer service and provision of supplementary health care, since other avenues for competition are largely foreclosed.

Care for heart attack is reimbursed through three different payment mechanisms. First, hospitals are reimbursed on a per diem basis, with a per diem rate that is declining in the total number of days for which a given hospital seeks reimbursement. As part of efforts toward cost control, the Belgian government has implemented a policy in which it fixes a "global budget" of allowable days for each hospital. This budget is adjusted based on each hospital's case mix, in terms of illness severity and patient demographics. Hospitals seeking reimbursement for fewer than their budgeted number of days receive a higher marginal per diem reimbursement than do hospitals seeking reimbursement for more than their budgeted number of days. Second, physicians are reimbursed on a fee-for-service basis for the procedures that they perform, with the fee schedule subject to agreement by 60 percent of the relevant physicians. However, physicians remit a portion of this fee-for-service reimbursement back to the hospital in which they practice, which provides hospitals with somewhat weaker incentives for cost containment. Third, hospitals are reimbursed for drugs, diagnostic tests, and medical devices on a fee-for-service basis. Patients pay substantial copayments for certain prescription drugs for treatment of minor illnesses, but pay very minimal copayments for drugs used on an inpatient basis, and minimal copayments for other inpatient care as well (in total, patient copayments account for 2 to 5 percent of total hospital costs).

To the extent that this payment system has changed over time, it has sought to provide hospitals with higher-powered incentives to contain costs. For example, there is a trend to finance the hospitals on a "DRG-like" basis that is more related to the severity of pathologies and the functions of the hospitals (e.g., specialized cardiac care center), rather than on the basis of historical costs or levels of activity. However, there are still substantial incentives for hospitals to supply patients with high levels of intensive treatment and costly pharmaceutical therapy, for the reasons described above.

Technology Regulation

Apart from regulation for purposes of safety, Belgium has minimal regulation of technology use. The Belgian government has attempted to undertake some "macroregulation" of technology, by essentially freezing the supply of hospital beds in general, and the supply of intensive cardiac beds and cardiac care facilities in particular. However, there is substantial evidence that this constraint is not binding. Belgium has a high number of cardiologists and cardiac surgery centers given its small size—in 1993, for example, 33 cardiac surgical centers served a population of approximately 10 million. And, there are no waiting lists for intensive treatment for cardiac illness in Belgium.

There is virtually no "microregulation" of technology use in Belgium. Utilization review (the main mechanism for microregulation of technology use in the United States) is virtually unknown in Belgium, although some peer-review programs have been implemented recently. There are no "gatekeeper" requirements, such as those in use in the United States and Britain. And, inpatient pharmaceutical and medical device use is reimbursed on a fee-for-service basis, including reimbursement without restriction for expensive thrombolytic drugs such as tPA and streptokinase.

Technological Change in Heart Attack Care in Belgium

In order to study the technological changes in heart attack care, we used two data sources: the CIES database and the Health Insurance database. The CIES hospital database contains information from hospitals that account for approximately one-third of the hospital admissions in Belgium. Sixty out of a total of 200 hospitals in Belgium are included in the CIES database; for hospitals with cardiac surgical centers, 11 of 33 are included. We have the ability to follow the admissions of one patient inside the same hospital but not between hospitals. We know also if patients are transferred to or from an "unknown" hospital only if it is during the same hospitalization.

We know for each stay the admission and discharge dates, the age and sex of the patient, the patient's diagnosis, and the surgical procedures performed. We have also very detailed information about all hospital charges, including per diem charges, drug charges, and other hospital charges. We do not have information on physician fees paid in connection with inpatient care, or on the portion of physician fees rebated to the hospital in connection with the supply of such care. Patients were identified for inclusion on the base of a principal diagnosis of ICD9 code 410. Patients were excluded if they were transferred from another hospital or if their length of stay was too short to constitute a true AMI (three days or fewer). Data from 1989 to 1995 were analyzed by age and sex.

We have specifically analyzed data on patients admitted for AMI in hospitals in which a catheterization lab and interventional cardiology/cardiac surgery facilities were available. As explained in the introduction, this means that the levels of procedure use we report are not representative of those in the nation as a whole and are not comparable to rates of procedure use in other countries. Nonetheless, the trends in procedure use over time are indicative of how technological change has affected cardiac care in Belgium, and its implications for health care costs and outcomes more generally.

The Health Insurance database provides us with aggregate information concerning the number of procedures performed at the national scale. We can follow one patient in the time in this database, but it does not provide information on diagnosis. Data from this source were analyzed from 1988 to 1997.

Changes in High-Tech Care

Figure 16.1 shows the evolution of the frequency of coronary artery bypass graft (CABG) and percutaneous transluminal coronary angioplasty (PTCA) surgery from 1988 to 1997 (1997 data are from January to September). This table is based on Health Insurance data and does not take account of patients' diagnosis. These data confirm that the use of intensive, high-tech cardiac procedures in Belgium has grown dramatically in the early 1990s. The prevalence of intensive cardiac procedures in Belgium cannot be accounted for by increases in the population or in the prevalence of cardiac illness. Bypass surgeries nearly doubled, from fewer than 5,000 in 1988 to almost 10,000 in 1996; annualized 1997 numbers indicate further rapid increase. Even more striking, angioplasty rates tripled over the shorter 1991–96 period, growing from approximately 5,500 in 1991 to 14,000 in 1996, with the annualized 1997 count still greater.

Our analysis of the CIES hospital database begins with figure 16.2, which presents the rate of catheterization (coronary angiography) in the first or second hospital admission after myocardial infarction. Although trends in catheterization are relatively flat over the study period, there is a clear relationship between patient age and the catheterization rate. Throughout the study period, more than 80 percent of patients under 65 years old underwent catheterization. On the other hand, only approximately 30 percent of patients who were more than 75 years old received catheterization. As the high levels of the rates indicate, catheterization had diffused thoroughly to cardiac care facilities in Belgium before 1989, although catheterization rates increased significantly for the oldest old (elderly aged 75 or more years) over the 1989–95 period. In particular, among this group, catheterization rates rose approximately one-third for men, from approximately 30 percent to approximately 40 percent. Similarly, for women in the oldest old group, rates rose by a factor of five, from around 5 percent to more than 25 percent.

The trend in catheterization in the oldest old reflects a feature of intensive cardiac procedure use that appears both in younger populations (and in other procedures): the narrowing of gender differences in the prevalence of intensive procedure use. For example, among the oldest old, the male/female catheterization rate differential was almost 25 percentage points in 1989; this differential had shrunk by approximately half as of 1995. Similar changes, although proportionately smaller, are found in the young elderly and nonelderly AMI populations.

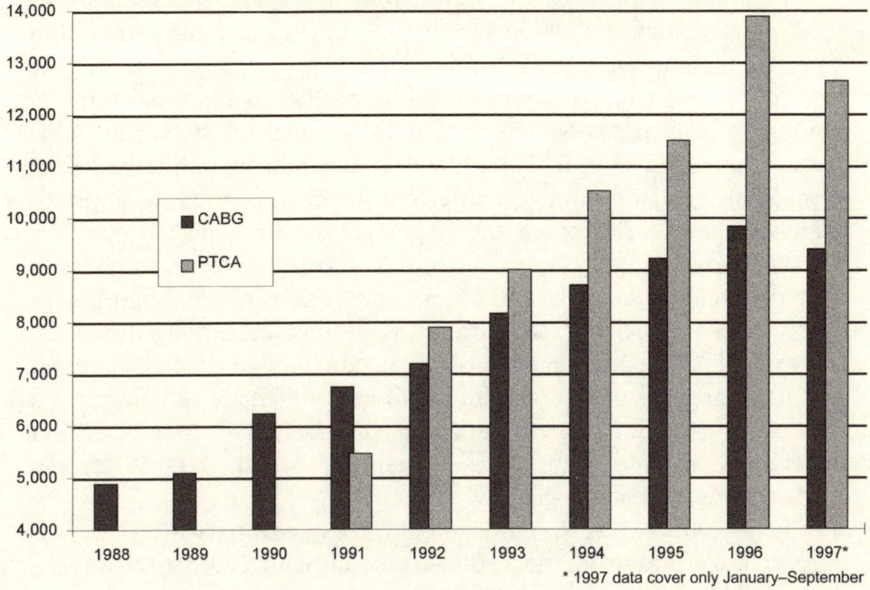

Fig. 16.1. CABG and PTCA volume in Belgium, 1988–97

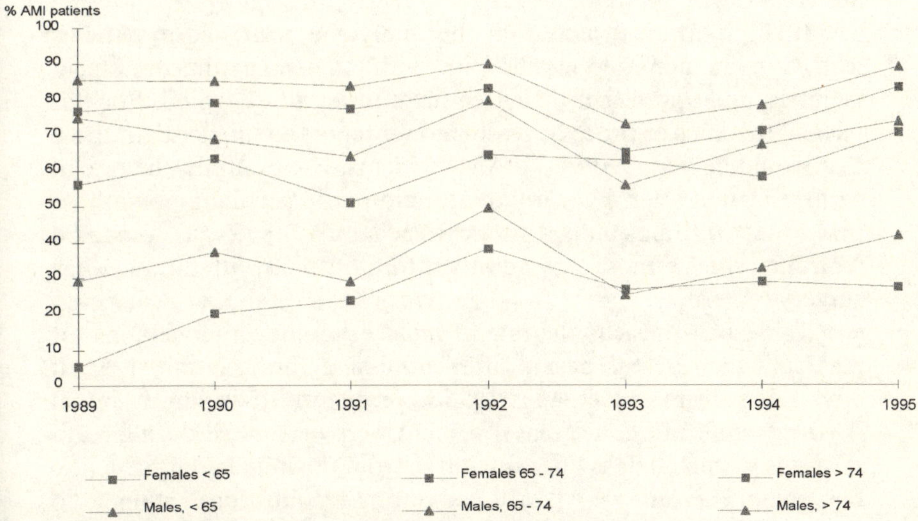

Fig. 16.2. Fraction of AMI patients who underwent catheterization during first or second hospital stay

Figures 16.3 and 16.4 analyze the rate of intensive therapeutic cardiac interventions (PTCA in figure 16.3, CABG in figure 16.4), and compare them to the rate of thrombolytic drug therapy (fig. 16.3). The rate of PTCA increased significantly from 1989 to 1995, particularly among younger patients. The probability of angioplasty for an AMI patient under 65 essentially doubled in Belgium in the early 1990s, from 20 percent for women (28 percent for men) in 1989, to approximately 45 percent of women and 50 percent of men with AMI in 1995. This increase is much greater in absolute terms than that experienced by patients aged 75 years and older, who even as of 1995 had angioplasty rates under 20 percent after AMI. However, among the oldest old women AMI patients, angioplasty rates exhibited relative increases almost as great as the increase in the oldest old female catheterization rate. And, as with catheterization, the shrinkage over time in gender differences within age groups is substantial, with the largest changes evident in the oldest age groups.

In percentage terms, trends in the rates of coronary artery bypass surgery are not as dramatic, as illustrated in figure 16.4. However, the rate of CABG for older patients (more than 75 years) increased from near zero in 1989–90 to about 5 percent in 1995. Excepting an outlying fall in the rate of bypass surgery for females ages 65–74 in 1995, the trend toward decreased gender differentials in procedure rates is manifested in CABG as well.

It is important to note that this analysis is restricted to patients who were first admitted in a hospital with intensive cardiac treatment facilities, and underwent their treatment inside this hospital. For this reason, the rates of procedure use that we report are higher than those that would be observed for all AMI patients. For example, the rate of catheterization after myocardial infarction is 58 percent among those first admitted to hospitals with a cardiac surgery center, as compared to 15 percent for those first admitted to a hospital without a cardiac surgery center.

Table 16.1 presents the rate of high-technology interventions for AMI patients, by the period after admission for their initial AMI. About 91 percent of PTCAs in 1995 were performed during the initial AMI hospitalization, whereas 4 percent were performed during readmissions within 30 days after discharge from the initial admission (the remaining 5 percent were performed during readmissions within 30 to 90 days after the initial admission). The percentage of PTCAs performed during the initial AMI hospitalization decreased slightly from 1989 (93 percent) to 1995. This trend over time is similar for catheteri-

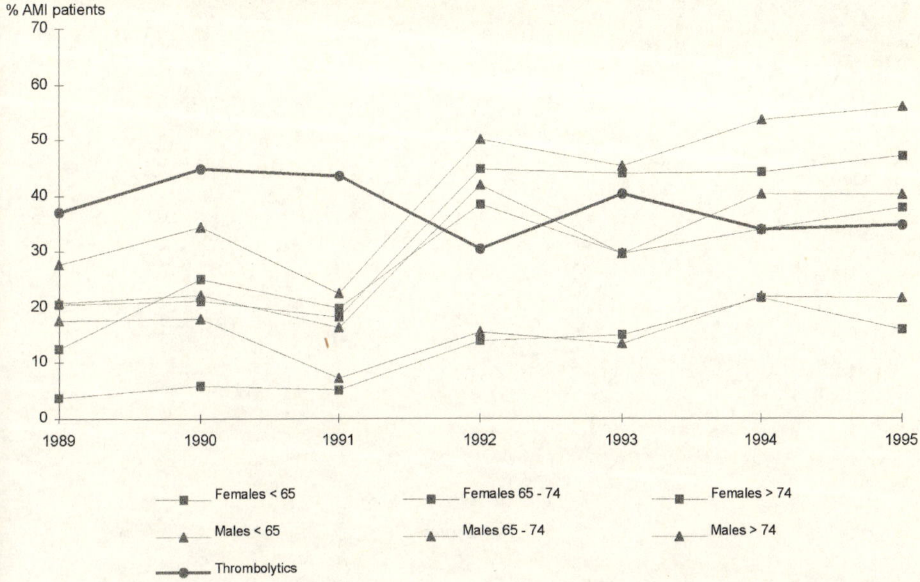

Fig. 16.3. Fraction of AMI patients who underwent PTCA or thrombolytic drug treatment during first or second hospital stay

zation. Thus, there is no evidence of increasing use of primary angioplasty, for example, PTCA immediately after initial admission for AMI. On the other hand, in 1995, about 57 percent of CABGs are performed during the first AMI admission, whereas 25 percent are performed during readmissions within 30 days after initial discharge, and 18 percent during readmissions within 30–90 days. The percentage of CABGs performed during the first AMI admission has increased from its 1989 base (45 percent) but has been quite stable since 1992.

Changes in Low-Tech Care

Table 16.2 shows the proportion of AMI patients receiving each of the different types of drug treatments during their initial hospitalization. Thrombolytic drug treatment rates vary with no particular trend, ranging from 37.1 percent in 1989, to 43.3 percent in 1991, to 34.5 percent in 1995. Beta-blocker use trended downward for most of the period, with calcium channel blocker use following a similar pattern. In con-

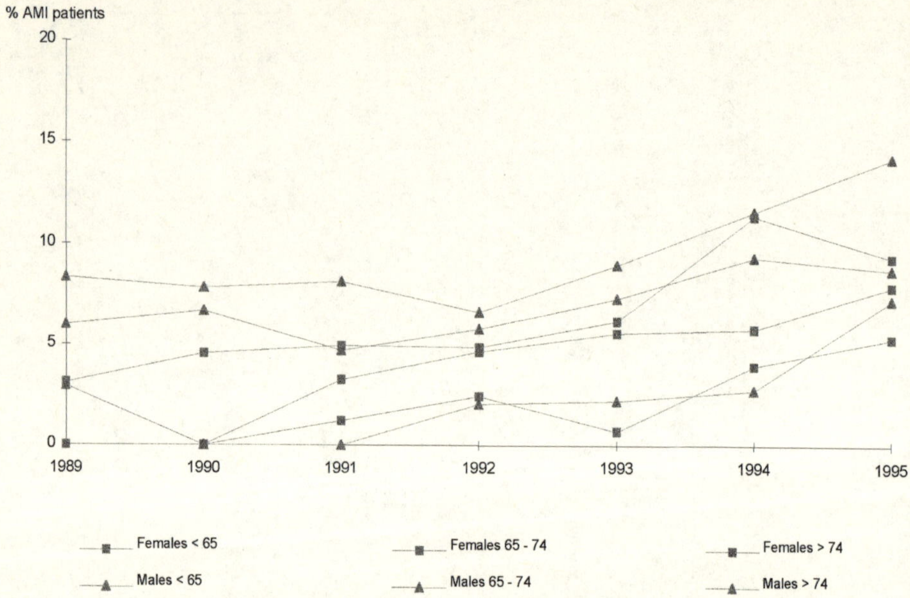

Fig. 16.4. Fraction of AMI patients who underwent CABG during first or second hospital stay

trast, antihypertensive drug use rose consistently and substantially, from under 20 percent to over 40 percent over the same period.

Data not presented in table 16.2 show that the rate of patients who received thrombolytic drug therapy is lower in hospitals with a cardiac surgery center than in hospitals without a cardiac surgery center. This may be due to the fact that thrombolytic therapy might serve as a substitute for high-tech intensive treatments, allowing a hospital without a cardiac surgery center to avoid transferring patients to another hospital to receive high-tech care such as PTCA or CABG.

The Consequences of Changes in Heart Attack Care in Belgium

Changes In Health Outcomes for AMI Patients

Figure 16.5 shows the percentage of in-hospital deaths among patients with AMI. It is clearly related to patient age and shows a slight trend

TABLE 16.1 Rate of High-Tech Interventions in AMI Patients, by Period after Discharge from Initial Admission (%)

	1989	1990	1991	1992	1993	1994	1995
Rate of catheterization	66.6	65.3	62.9	73.8	56.0	61.4	68.5
Share of catheterizations:							
Performed during initial admission	97	97	97	97	92	91	91
In 7 days after discharge from initial admission	0	0	0	0	0	0	0
7–30 days after discharge from initial admission	1	1	1	2	3	5	4
30–90 days after discharge from initial admission	2	2	2	1	5	4	5
Rate of PTCA	20.5	24.3	16.8	38.3	32.1	39.7	39.4
Share of PTCAs:							
Performed during initial AMI episode	93	95	95	94	95	92	91
In 7 days after discharge from initial admission	0	0	1	0	0	0	0
7–30 days after discharge from initial admission	3	2	2	2	2	6	5
30–90 days after discharge from initial admission	4	3	2	4	3	2	4
Rate of CABG	3.8	4.2	4.3	4.7	5.4	7.6	8.9
Share of CABGs:							
Performed during initial AMI episide	45	50	23	57	57	61	57
In 7 days after discharge from initial admission	0	0	0	0	2	0	0
7–30 days after discharge from initial admission	11	14	16	15	15	17	25
30–90 days after discharge from initial admission	44	36	61	28	26	22	18

TABLE 16.2. Medication Received by AMI Patients during Initial Hospitalization

	% of Patients						
	1989	1990	1991	1992	1993	1994	1995
Any blood or blood-forming compound	99.4	99	99.3	99.5	98.4	88.7	99.7
B01AA: Vitamin K antagonists	10.5	7.7	8.7	11.7	12.8	7.8	8.3
B01AB: Heparin group	89.3	74.9	83.0	88.7	90.2	84.5	95.8
B01AC: Platelet aggregation inhibitors excluding heparin	10.1	19.0	24.8	14.0	11.6	13.5	19.9
B01AD: Thrombolytics	37.1	44.7	43.3	30.3	40.1	33.7	34.5
Any cardiovascular system compound	97.5	98.1	98.2	98.0	98.4	87.1	99.7
C01A: Cardiac glycosides	12.4	12.3	9.4	12.0	11.6	8.8	8.5
C01B: Antiarrhythmics, class I and II	11.4	12.3	13.4	14.9	14.3	11.6	14.4
C01C: Cardiac stimulants excluding cardiac glycosides	19.4	18.8	21.8	30.0	24.4	26.1	28.4
C01D: Vasodilators used in cardiac diseases	69.3	79.1	82.2	84.3	87.8	80.9	89.2
C02: Antihypertensives	19.2	20.9	23.0	26.1	30.6	33.2	41.2
C03: Diuretics	33.1	28.0	31.2	32.7	31.3	29.4	34.1
C04: Peripheral vasodilators	2.1	2.7	2.8	2.4	2.6	2.4	1.5
C07: Beta-blocking agents	58.9	58.7	51.6	54.3	46.0	42.1	56.4
C08: Calcium channel blockers	34.9	29.9	23.2	24.3	23.0	22.0	28.5
All other therapeutic products[a]	73.7	72.9	70.9	75.4	60.9	60.3	64.5

[a]Including contrast media.

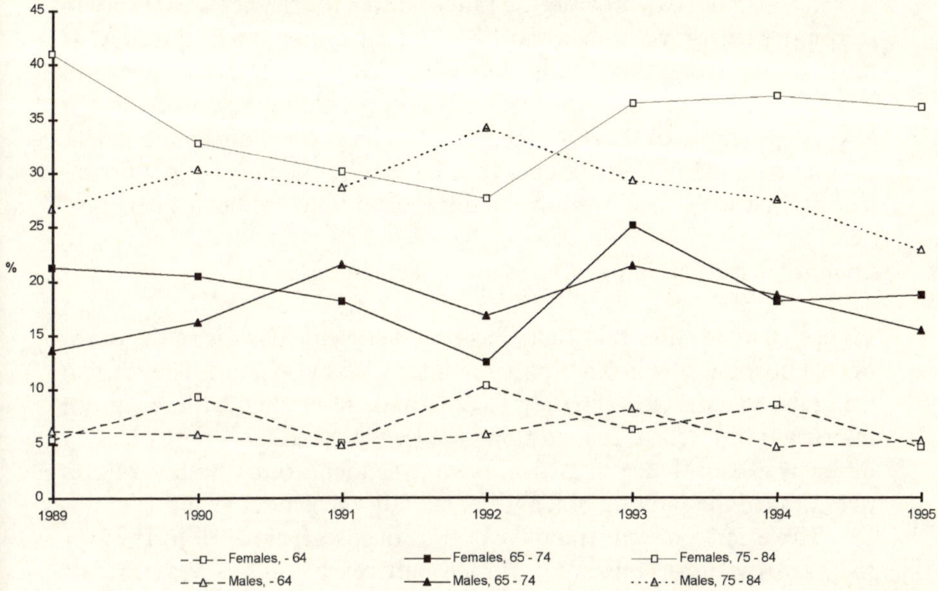

Fig. 16.5. AMI patient in-hospital mortality rate

decrease from 1989 to 1995. Of course, because the figure only presents improvements in in-hospital mortality, it may understate the total trend reduction in mortality (given that lengths of stay have remained roughly constant over this period, discussed below). Nonetheless, figure 16.5 presents important information about the possible effects of technology on mortality in Belgium in the 1990s. On one hand, in-hospital mortality of the age/gender group that experienced the greatest increase in intensity of medical treatment—the oldest elderly females—showed the greatest improvement in mortality. In addition, just as gender differences in intensive treatment rates shrank for all age groups, so did gender differences in in-hospital mortality. On the other hand, in-hospital mortality rates for nonelderly AMI patients did not improve much, despite the fact that they as a whole saw their angioplasty rates rise greatly. However, because this group is more healthy in general (in-hospital mortality rates of around 5 percent, in comparison to much higher rates for the elderly), the lack of evident progress in their in-hospital mortality rate may be due to the fact that it is a poorer measure of health outcome for them.

We also have compared the rate of death for the first AMI stay in hospital with or without a cardiac surgery center. In-hospital AMI mortality is 13 percent in hospitals with a cardiac surgery center, and 19 percent in hospitals without a cardiac surgery center. This finding is also consistent with the hypothesis that at least some of the incremental intensive cardiac treatments that have become increasingly prevalent at high-tech hospitals have had important patient health benefits.

Changes in Medical Expenditures and Resource Use

Figure 16.6 indicates that there has been very little change in the duration of hospital stay in AMI patients since 1989 in Belgium. The median length of stay is approximately 11 days and, surprisingly, there are not important differences related to age or gender. Median lengths of stay differ by at most a day or two across age/gender groups, with variation over time in the ranking of length of stay by age/gender group.

Table 16.3 presents trends over time in costs from 1989 to 1995 for the first AMI hospitalization of men between 65 and 74 years. Costs are inflated to a constant-currency 1995 basis using the CPI deflator and converted to U.S. dollars based on a 1995 PPP conversion. The median real total cost per AMI hospitalization has increased 13 percent from 1989 to 1995. There has been very little change in the total cost per patient, given the intensive treatment they received (plus 5 percent for CABG patients and minus 2 percent for PTCA patients). Rather, the increase in expenditures on AMI is mainly due to the increase of the drugs and implants costs (58 percent) and surgery and anesthesiology costs (39 percent), both of which are attributable to the increased rate of intensive procedure use. Drug, implant, and surgery costs for AMI patients who receive either CABG or PTCA are a more important component of total expenditures than they are for AMI patients who are not treated intensively.

Another source of the increase in expenditures for AMI patients is the use of the patented thrombolytic drug tPA. It is important to note that despite the fact that the rate of thrombolytic drug use was relatively stable from 1989 to 1995, information not presented in table 16.3 indicates that the median cost per patient of thrombolytic therapy (among those receiving thrombolytics) increased from U.S.$435 to U.S.$1,135 (costs are inflated to a constant-currency 1995 basis using the CPI deflator and converted to U.S. dollars based on 1995 PPP conversion). This is mainly due to the use of more expensive thrombolytic drugs like tPA.

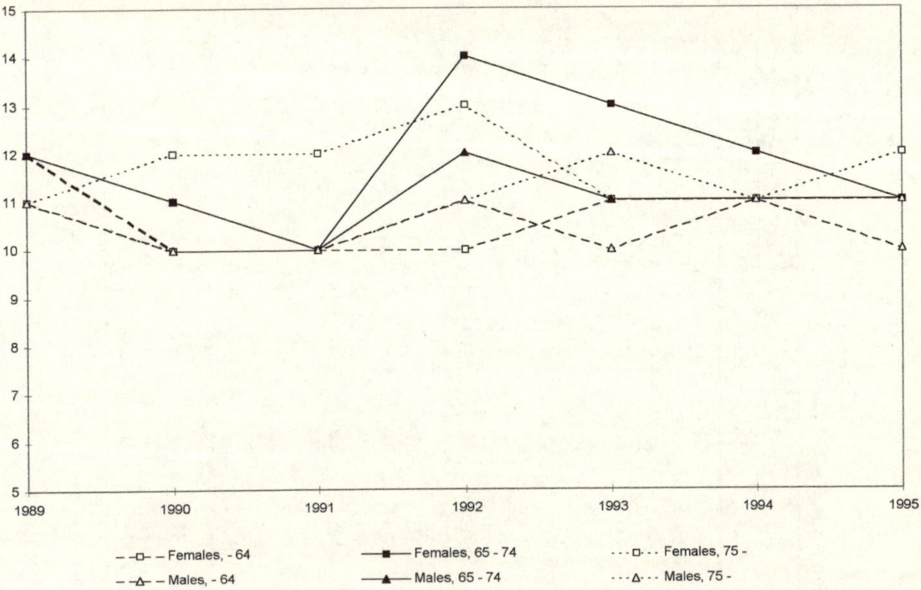

Fig. 16.6. Median duration of hospital stay for AMI patients (days)

Discussion

Effects of Incentives for Technological Change

In Belgium the rate of high-tech interventions like PTCA and CABG increased significantly from 1989 to 1995. The rate of growth for PTCA is much higher than for CABG, although the level of hospital reimbursement for CABG is more than twice as large, and reimbursement conditional on treatment has been relatively constant over time. These observations suggest that some factor other than the simple price levels in the hospital reimbursement system is responsible for the increased prevalence of intensive treatments.

Although this chapter does not directly explore this possibility, the increase in procedure use in general, and in PTCA use in particular, may be partly due to the fee-for-service reimbursement schedule offered to physicians. Particularly because physicians remit a portion of the fee-for-service reimbursement back to the hospital, this reimbursement mechanism encourages use of intensive cardiac procedures.

TABLE 16.3. Median Hospital Costs for the First AMI Hospitalization of Men Aged 65–74 Years

								% Change		
	1989	1990	1991	1992	1993	1994	1995	1989–92	1992–95	1989–95
First AMI hospitalization										
Total costs	5,715	6,742	5,712	6,018	4,448	5,732	6,533	0.05	0.08	0.13
Hospital bed-day costs	1,976	2,338	2,100	2,018	1,604	1,617	1,850	0.02	–0.09	–0.07
Drug and implants costs	612	1,471	1,047	1,131	987	1,325	1,470	0.46	0.23	0.58
Surgery and anesthesy costs	203	298	232	281	244	325	331	0.28	0.15	0.39
Medical (cardiology) costs	481	568	386	435	337	347	407	–0.11	–0.07	–0.18
Other costs	2,443	2,067	1,948	2,153	1,277	2,118	2,474	–0.13	0.13	0.01
First AMI hospitalization, CABG patients										
Total costs	14,489	17,484	14,895	15,303	14,602	13,405	15,210	0.05	–0.01	0.05
Hospital bed-day costs	2,792	3,815	2,746	1,892	2,337	2,396	3,347	–0.48	0.43	0.17
Drug and implants costs	3,824	3,756	3,208	4,617	3,772	3,374	3,631	0.17	–0.27	–0.05
Surgery and anesthesy costs	3,554	3,916	3,205	2,858	3,604	3,819	3,667	–0.24	0.22	0.03
Medical (cardiology) costs	767	557	394	555	481	390	597	–0.38	0.07	–0.28
Other costs	3,552	5,440	5,342	5,381	4,408	3,426	3,968	0.34	–0.36	0.10
First AMI hospitalization, PTCA patients										
Total costs	8,637	9,411	10,002	8,871	8,409	8,065	8,443	0.03	–0.05	–0.02
Hospital bed-day costs	1,396	1,831	2,100	2,182	1,948	1,896	2,090	0.36	–0.04	0.33
Drug and implants costs	2,433	2,686	2,578	2,154	2,275	2,254	2,212	–0.13	0.03	–0.10
Surgery and anesthesy costs	600	587	556	378	348	334	382	–0.59	0.01	–0.57
Medical (cardiology) costs	670	727	505	550	515	449	461	–0.22	–0.19	–0.45
Other costs	3,538	3,579	4,264	3,608	3,324	3,133	3,298	0.02	–0.09	–0.07

Note: Costs are 1995 U.S. dollars converted at PPP rates.

The lack of either macro- or microregulation of technology also contributes to this effect.

Implications for Changes in Expenditures and Outcomes

The median total cost per AMI hospitalization has increased only modestly from 1989 to 1995. This is mainly due to increases in the drugs and implants costs, and surgery and anesthesiology costs. The increase in surgery costs is the consequence of increases in the rate of intensive cardiac procedures, especially CABG (discussed above). The increase in drugs and implants costs is not due to increasing rates of treatment with thrombolytic and other drugs, but rather to the use of more sophisticated and costly drugs. This shift toward more costly cardiac drugs in Belgium is the consequence of virtually unrestricted fee-for-service drug reimbursement. In particular, the median cost per patient of pharmaceuticals has increased mainly due to the use of more sophisticated drugs like tPA.

Despite the increasing of the rate of high-tech intervention, we observe a very small decrease in the rate of hospital death in patients with acute myocardial infarction. However, this decrease in in-hospital mortality may understate the total benefits of intensive cardiac care, particularly for nonelderly individuals, who are much less likely to die in the hospital. Nevertheless, there is some evidence that at least some of the incremental intensive cardiac treatments that have become increasingly prevalent have had important patient health benefits. First, the dramatic decline in most measures of the differential rate of intensive cardiac treatment between men and women has been accompanied by an analogous decline in the differential male/female in-hospital mortality rate. Second, the rate of in-hospital mortality is slightly higher in hospitals without a cardiac surgery center.

References

Banta, H. David, ed. 1995. *Health Care Technology and Its Assessment in Eight Countries.* Washington, D.C.: U.S. Government Printing Office.

McGovern, P. G., J. S. Pankow, E. Shahar, K. M. Doliszny, A. R. Folsom, H. Blackburn, and R. V. Luepker. 1996. "Recent Trends in Acute Coronary Hearth Disease." *New England Journal of Medicine* 334, no. 14: 884–90.

Organisation for Economic Cooperation and Development (OECD). 1995. *New Directions in Health Care Policy.* Paris: Organisation for Economic Cooperation and Development.

Rogers, W. J., L. J. Bowlby, N. C. Chandra, W. J. Franch, J. M. Gore, C. T.

Lambrerr, R. M. Rubison, A. J. Tiefenbrunn, and W. D. Weaver. 1994. "Treatment of Myocardial Infarction in the United States (1990 to 1993)." *Circulation* 90, no. 4: 2103–14.

Sans, S., H. Kesteloot, and D. Kromhout. 1997. "The Burden of Cardiovascular Diseases Mortality in Europe." *European Heart Journal* 18, no. 12: 1231–48.

Tunstall-Pedoe, H., K. Kuulasmaa, P. Amouyel, D. Arveiler, A. M. Rajakangas, and A. Pajak. 1994. "Myocardial Infarction and Coronary Death in the World Health Organization MONICA Project." *Circulation* 90, no. 1: 583–612.

CHAPTER 17

The Determinants and Consequences of Technological Change in the Care of Acute Myocardial Infarction in Italy

Vincenzo Atella, Simona Giampaoli, Lorenza Pilotto, and Diego Vanuzzo

According to a recent report on the health status of the Italian population (Ministry of Health 1997), heart disease represents a significant problem with still high mortality rates, even though technological improvements in treatment and more timely and frequent hospitalizations have contributed to a dramatic secular decline in mortality for cardiac illness. Figure 17.1 shows the trends in death rates from ischemic heart disease for nonelderly Italians (ISTAT 1995); trends for elderly individuals are similar, though not quite as large. Similar to other countries such as the United States, mortality rates have declined considerably since 1980, by approximately one-third for elderly people and by more than one-third for nonelderly people.

In this chapter, we explore the causes and consequences of technological change over the 1984–93 period for cardiac illness in general, and for one of the most prevalent and costly forms of cardiac illness: heart attack (AMI). To what extent have the incentives provided by the system of health care finance in Italy affected technological change? And how has this technological change affected treatment decisions, resource use, and patient health outcomes? In order to understand the effects that technology has had on expenditures and outcomes, we have had to rely on fragmented and, sometimes, preliminary information. This limitation is particularly true for our investigation of the impact of technology on resource use, a relationship for which data are available only from 1995. For our investigation of the effects of technological change on treatment decisions and health outcomes, we analyze data from the MONICA project for the Friuli region. In this case, even though residents of Friuli may not be fully representative of the

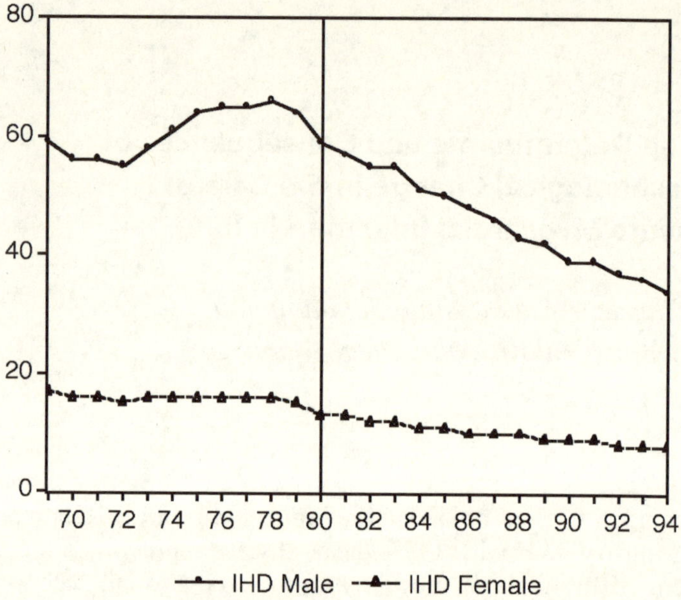

Fig. 17.1. Trends in ischemic heart disease mortality, nonelderly Italian population (ages 35–64), 1969–94

Italian population, the MONICA data are extremely useful for understanding how technology has affected the health of individuals with heart disease.

This chapter proceeds as follows. Section 1 outlines the regulatory and financial incentives for use of high- and low-technology care for heart disease, and how they have changed during our study period. Section 2 describes both the high-technology and the low-technology changes in AMI care that occurred in Italy during the 1980s and 1990s. Section 3 suggests how these changes in treatment decisions have affected resource use and health outcomes. Section 4 concludes with some hypotheses about the impact of incentives on technological change and its consequences, and some possibilities for future research.

1. Incentives for Technological Change in Italy

Financing of Heart Disease Care

The provision of health care in Italy comes almost entirely through the National Health System (NHS), which is financed through compulsory employer-paid health insurance of workers (with the share of covered individuals ranging from 47.5 percent in 1983 to 55 percent in 1996) and from other general tax revenues. Introduced in 1978, the NHS represented a radical transformation that, according to several experts (see, e.g., Piperno 1986 and Ferrera 1989) had few precedents in the Italian history of social reforms. At its beginning, this new scheme was based on the "universalism principle"; namely, every citizen could have free access to a homogeneous level of service. It replaced an old system based on more traditional compulsory social insurance with limitation and segmentation of coverage, organizational fragmentation, and normative and procedural disparities among the different insurance schemes. The NHS affected the provision of health care services as well as their financing. Most important, under the NHS, control of hospitals shifted from the hospitals to a political organization called the Local Health Unit, or USL.[1]

In this system, the role of private insurance has been negligible. For example, in 1994, out of total spending on health care of 130 trillion lira (U.S.$74.3 billion),[2] 73 percent has been financed by the NHS, 26 percent by the private sector through household out-of-pocket spending, and only 1 percent financed through private insurance funds.

Unfortunately, during the 1980s, full implementation of the universalism principle has encountered several problems. First, sharp increases in health expenditures undermined what had been a strong consensus. Over the years, copayments have been added to the NHS in order to limit the demand for services,[3] thus limiting the principle of "free" access to care. However, the use of these measures to limit the demand has proven to be inefficient and ineffective, due to the contemporaneous creation of exemptions from the copayment (by income, pathology, age, and employment status) and to the total lack of control on expenditures.[4] Due to alarming trends in public deficits during the 1980s, curbing health care expenditure growth became a major goal for policymakers. This goal became even more important when, at the beginning of the 1990s, the long awaited European Union became a reality.

In 1992, several major changes to the NHS—"a reform of the reform"—took place. Among the many changes, the following are the most significant:

1. USLs became "public enterprises" with organizational autonomy and responsibility (the acronym changed to ASL). Management shifted to general managers with private contracts appointed by the regions based on professional qualifications.

2. Large hospitals can request permission to act as independent public hospital agencies, thus regaining autonomy, if they accept responsibility for operating with balanced budgets.
3. While retaining overall planning functions and the responsibility to pay for a standard set of services that must be guaranteed to every Italian citizen, the central government imposed full financial responsibility on regional governments for expenditures above a fixed annual budget. Regional governments are allowed to set higher copayments or taxes, thus being encouraged to contain costs and promote efficient use of resources.[5]
4. Reimbursement for the standard set of services changed, from a system based on historical expenditure to one based on a prospective payment system (PPS) with tariffs determined by diagnosis-related groups (DRGs). Under this new system, the central government sets rules by which DRG payments are determined; regional governments determine the maximum DRG reimbursements, on the basis of regional costs of production; finally, the ASLs bargain with all producers (internal and external) for the most favorable conditions for the provision of goods and services. In this way the ASLs can choose to make or buy goods and services, depending on the relative efficiency of internal versus external production. (This system of financing applies only to certain acute hospital admissions: excluded are emergency and intensive care, teaching and research, rehabilitation, and long-term care. According to data provided by the Ministry of Budget, in 1995 the PPS covered 83 percent of expenditures related to hospital admissions.

There is no doubt that this reorganization has helped the Italian health sector to become more competitive and productive (although further information is needed to quantify precisely the effectiveness of the PPS). Based on 1995 data, hospital expenditures have decreased by 0.3 percent compared to the previous year, while total health spending has decreased by 1.6 percent, and lengths of stay have been sharply reduced, by 9 percent. On the other hand, the number of hospital admissions has increased by 7.4 percent (such that the total number of days in hospital has remained almost unchanged), with same-day hospital admissions up by 36 percent.

As these statistics suggest, it is also true that several problems still remain to be solved, most of which arise out of the methodology used to set the DRG payment rates. The definition of the first set of DRG prices in 1994 came directly from the United States, with some modifications. First, Italian DRG prices are determined at the regional level and may vary across providers, while in the United States they are fixed at national level. After only one year, this system caused large differences in regional prices. These differences were decreased in 1997 by limiting to 20 percent the maximum reduction possible on the national tariff. Second, in Italy, the DRG system covers physicians' costs but excludes depreciation; in the United States, the opposite is true. Third, in Italy, there is only one buyer of health care services (the state acts as a monopsonist) with mostly public producers, while in the United States there are several, mostly private, buyers and producers.

Even though significant adjustments had been introduced in the Italian system to take into account the differences existing between the Italian and the American model of care delivery, in June 1997 the Ministry of Health was forced to work out a larger revision of the DRG price system. As a result, 256 tariffs were increased, 133 left unchanged, and 98 reduced. In particular, the average reimbursement for DRGs in the cardiovascular diseases group has increased from 786,000 lira (U.S.$550) in 1994 to almost 3.5 million lira (U.S.$2,000) in 1997—a 345 percent increase. In the case of PTCA, for example, DRG reimbursement has increased from 6.4 million lira (U.S.$ 3,657) in 1994 to 12 million lira (U.S.$6,857) in 1997—an 86.5 percent increase. We discuss some of the implications of these changes for future growth in intensity of cardiac treatment below.

Technology Regulation

The introduction of new medical technologies, such as medical devices and drugs, has been regulated by the Ministry of Health for quite some time. Over the last few years, due to agreements with the European Union, the introduction of new technologies has been regulated by the European Commission. In 1993 the European Commission issued several directives to regulate the introduction and commercialization of new medical devices and new drugs (for both human and animal use). In Italy these directives were adopted only in February 1997.

Differently from medical devices, drugs receive a centralized registration through the EMEA (European Medical Agency). Each new drug that receives the approval from EMEA can be automatically marketed in all 15 European Union countries. This has represented a very important step toward market unification for this kind of product. In the past, manufacturers had to go through each country's regulatory system to obtain approval.

For both drugs and medical devices, the authorization to sell the product in Italy does not mean that the product is accepted for payment by the NHS. In the case of drugs, the introduction of a new product in the list for reimbursement depends on the judgment of the CUF (Commissione Unica del Farmaco), a special committee of the Ministry of Health introduced in 1993 to evaluate new medicines. Over the last five years the CUF has totally revised the list of approved drugs and eliminated several products that have been recognized as ineffective. In case of new devices, experimentation is implemented according to rigid protocols and under the supervision of the Ministry of Health. While there is strict regulation for the pricing of new and existing drugs,[6] no regulation exists for the pricing of new medical devices, nor for the adoption of new approved technologies by hospitals.

Though few other government regulatory barriers to technology use exist, very often bureaucracy remains the most difficult barrier to overcome. In fact, in many cases, the adoption of a new technology depends primarily on the issuance of permits by local government authorities, which often slows down the whole process of technology acquisition. On the other hand, no internal or external auditing is performed regarding the proper use of these new technologies, nor do special bodies or organizations exist that can supervise their use.

In addition, even if formal "macroregulation" of technology use is minimal, Italy does use "microregulation" to control technology use in health care. Before having free access to specialist care, a patient needs to obtain a referral from his primary care practitioner. However, the number of referrals to a specialist has dramatically increased over time, raising questions about the effectiveness of this approach as well.

Competition

The way in which the NHS was organized in 1978 left no room for competition among health care providers; with financing based on historical expenditures, neither producers nor purchasers worried about competition. Furthermore, there were rather stringent restrictions on patients who sought to choose hospitals or physicians outside the jurisdiction of their USL.[7] With the new PPS several things have changed. Even though the central government is still the monopsony purchaser of all health care, the introduction of more stringent rules on economic and financial performance has pushed the local health units (ASLs) to be more careful in selecting health care providers, and in deciding between internal provision or external purchase of goods and services.

Physician recruitment is based on public competitions. However, physicians are hired according to a public contract and their base salaries are fixed at the national level. From this point of view hospitals cannot provide monetary incentives to attract physicians. And, given that the supply of practicing physicians in Italy has steadily increased over time, from less than 100,000 in 1970 to 322,000 in 1996, there is no real competition among hospitals due to the existence of a virtually unlimited supply of labor.

Other Incentives for Technology Adoption and Use

Other factors in Italy also affect technology adoption and use. We touch on two of them here: the rapidly growing number of lawsuits and judgments against physicians for medical malpractice, and the increasing number of physicians who lack practical experience, but have substantial technical training.

Over the last 10 years, medical malpractice and defensive medicine have become very popular topics in the profession. According to Iatrona (1997) both the frequency and the severity of civil and penal actions for malpractice have increased pressure substantially on physicians and insurers. Indeed, the judicial system is becoming very tough with physicians so that several lawyers have stated that the traditional widespread principle of *in dubio pro reo* has changed to *in dubio contra medicum.* Based also on the experience of other countries, especially the United States, recently two new proposals have been presented in parliament in order to reregulate the liability law. According to ANIA (the association of insurance companies) in 1990 about 60,000 out 288,000 physicians were insured, with total Italian malpractice insurance premiums of 25.4 billion lira (U.S.$14.5 million). Compensation represented about 90 percent of premiums and was sharply increasing; malpractice liability insurance became unprofitable shortly thereafter. It is for this reason that malpractice liability concerns are widely cited by doctors as a justification for additional diagnostic tests and therapeutic interventions (see Benciolini 1996; Fiori 1996; and Iatrona 1996).[8]

It is widely recognized that classroom-based methods of training physicians in Italy provide new doctors with little practical experience. This has the potential to result in physicians who are easily influenced by external pressures, such as malpractice or pharmaceutical representatives.[9] In addition, although the number of medical school students trained to be specialists is fixed by the Ministry of Education and Universities and by the Ministry of Health, there are doubts as to whether cost containment is an important influence on this process.[10] Taken together, these factors mean that competition among physicians for patients, and a concern not to disappoint, may contribute to the use and diffusion of technology.

2. Technological Change in AMI Care in Italy

The introduction of both new "high-tech" and "low-tech" treatments[11] for heart disease in Italy in the 1980s and 1990s has, as figure 17.1 shows, been accompanied by dramatic reductions in mortality. In order to explore the role of these technologies in changes in medical treatment decisions and health outcomes, we rely only on data collected from two geographic regions, because of the lack of reliable national longitudinal data on large populations of elderly or nonelderly AMI patients.

Our main analysis uses data from the MONICA project from Area Friuli, where a community registry was set up in 1984. Friuli is an autonomous region in northeastern Italy, with approximately 1.5 million inhabitants, a mixed economy, including heavy and light industry, agriculture, trades, and services. Compared to the Italian average, Friuli has high living standards but above-average mortality, morbidity. and cardiovascular risk factors.

There are several advantages in choosing this region for our case study. Each resident has a unique personal identifier through the regional health system; there are computerized health rolls of all the residents, including a computerized hospital admission and discharge system (Sistema Informatico Sanitario Regionale, SISR), which includes, besides the admitting and discharge dates, from one to four diagnoses, codified according to ICD9, and from one to four procedures, codified according to ICD9-CM, and, since 1994, DRGs; and a computerized death registry. All of this allows for fairly easy data retrieval and record linkages. In our analysis of treatment decisions, we include all patients diagnosed with AMI according to the MONICA project standards (Chambless et al. 1997). We validate our analyses of the MONICA-Friuli registry with some information from previous studies of the MONICA project from Area Brianza.

Trends in hospital admission for nonelderly AMI patients (ages 35–64) in the MONICA-Friuli region during the period 1984–93 are illustrated in figure 17.2, showing a steady decrease in admissions for both males and females. This may be due a real decline in incidence of

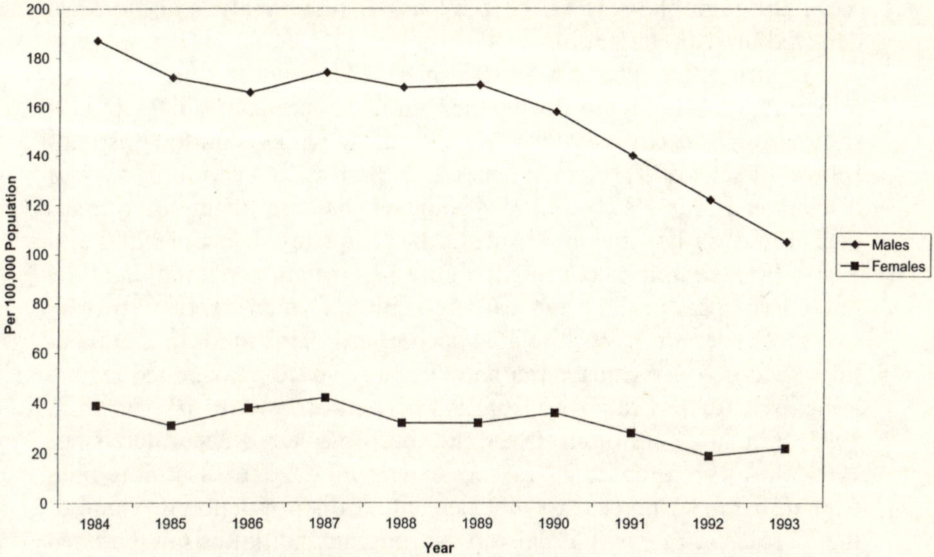

Fig. 17.2. Rate of hospital admission for AMI patients ages 35–64 in the MONICA-Friuli registry

AMI, due largely to the expansion in procedure use and drug treatment discussed below. However, two facts limit our ability to interpret figure 17.2 in this way. First, figure 17.2 includes only patients admitted to the hospital; it does not include those who died in the hospital emergency room, in the ambulance, or at home or work. Second, figure 17.2 includes all admissions, not just admissions for new AMIs; especially in the earlier years, some patients readmitted for intensive cardiac treatment after their initial infarct may have been misclassified, leading to an overstatement of incidence by admissions statistics in this period. This concern applies to the remainder of our analysis of treatment decisions below as well.

Changes in High-Tech Care: Intensive Cardiac Procedures and Hospital Use

The gold standard invasive procedure used to assess artery status is cardiac catheterization, which may be followed by either coronary artery bypass graft surgery (CABG) or percutaneous transluminal coronary angioplasty (PTCA) to bypass or remove areas of blockage detected on catheterization.

Figure 17.3 presents rates of intensive procedure use for nonelderly AMI patients during their initial hospitalization; figure 17.4 shows rates of intensive procedure use during patients' initial hospitalization or scheduled (but not necessarily performed) within 28 days of discharge. Figures 17.3 and 17.4 indicate that use of intensive treatment for AMI has increased substantially in Italy over the 1980s and 1990s. For example, according to figure 17.4, our approximation of the nonelderly patients' 28-day catheterization rate more than tripled, from 14.1 percent in 1984, to 46.4 percent in 1993. Trends in therapeutic procedures also charted impressive gains. The approximated 28-day nonelderly CABG rate rose from 3.3 percent in 1984, to 10 percent in 1993. Similarly, although it has only been measured accurately since 1989, the approximated 28-day nonelderly PTCA rate also more than tripled, from 3.3 percent to 11.1 percent. A disproportionate share of the increase in intensity is delivered in patients' initial hospital admission. According to figure 17.3, the rate of catheterizations on initial admission rose more than fivefold, with trends in the therapeutic procedures showing similar gains.

Data not presented in the figures show that trends in male/female relative rates of intensive therapeutic procedures are flat over the study period (although they do exhibit some variation around the mean). For example, the relative rate of PTCA per AMI admission was 1.37 in both 1986 and 1993; the relative rate of CABG was 1.32 in 1984, as compared to 1.33 in 1993. The catheterization rate for men was much closer to the catheterization rate for women throughout the study period. Surprisingly, the male/female relative catheterization rate was less than one in 1984 (0.73), increasing to almost 1 by 1993 (0.96). This finding could be consistent with male patients having a greater likelihood of catheterization than female patients, if the additional catheterizations administered to men were more likely to be administered in a subsequent readmission for AMI, particularly in earlier years. However, because figures 17.3 and 17.4 show roughly similar changes across procedures in their use in initial versus subsequent readmissions, the relative equality in male/female catheterization rates may reflect a true phenomenon.

The relative use of PTCA versus CABG for AMI in Italy is lower than in the United States and other European countries. This may be due to the fact that angioplasty was introduced in Italy in 1980, somewhat later than in other European countries. According to studies con-

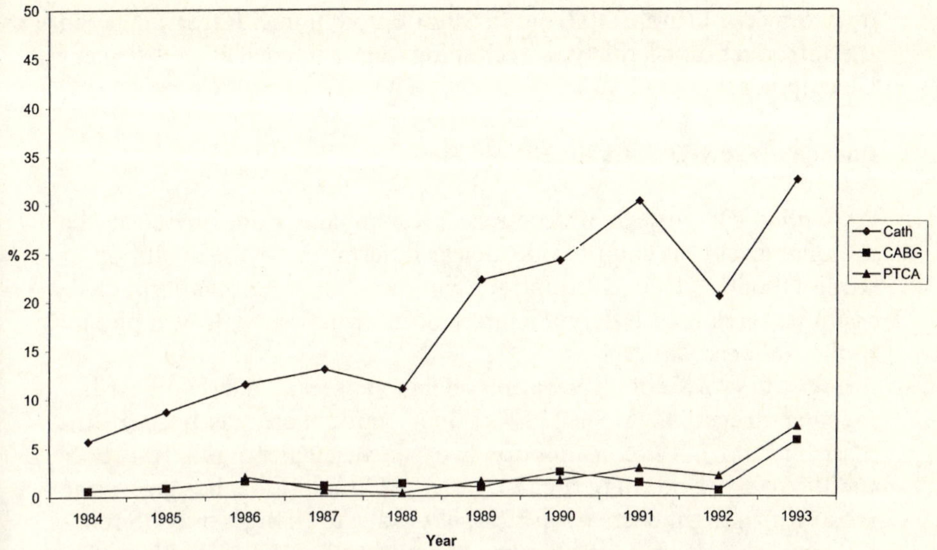

Fig. 17.3. Rates of intensive procedure use during initial hospitalization for AMI patients ages 35–64 in the MONICA-Friuli registry

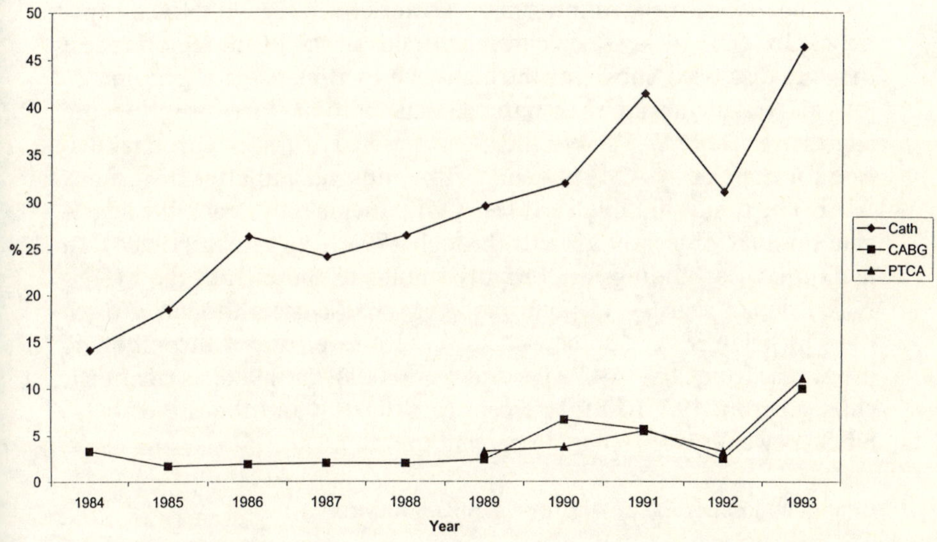

Fig. 17.4. Rates of intensive procedure use during initial hospitalization of scheduled (but not necessarily performed) within 28 days of discharge for AMI patients ages 35–64 in the MONICA-Friuli registry

ducted by the Gruppo Italiano di Studi Emodinamici (GISE) delay in the introduction of this new technology has impeded its subsequent development.

Changes in Low-Tech Care

As with the high-tech procedures, no complete study exists at the national level that can provide a clear description of the evolution of cardiovascular drug consumption in the Italian population. Once again we have used different sources of information to draw a picture of the Italian situation.

The first piece of information refers to aggregated data on cardiovascular drugs. As Atella (1998a) documents, there has been a dramatic increase in the consumption of cardiovascular drugs in Italy over the 1985–95 period. In particular, use of ACE inhibitors has grown the most, with a slight decrease in 1995, likely due to changes in NHS reimbursement policies. This parallels the more general finding that after 1993, the rate of growth for all classes, with the exception of ACE inhibitors, has became negative or very close to zero. Since 1993, use of diuretics and beta-blockers has decreased sharply, while all other classes have remained roughly constant.[12]

The second piece of information comes from the MONICA experience. In terms of low-tech care, the trends in the Friuli region reflect the ones discussed above for the high-tech treatments—the pharmacological treatment of AMI patients has become increasingly more aggressive. Table 17.1 shows the use of selected drugs for coronary disease for nonelderly AMI patients before, during, and after their index AMI. The trends in table 17.1, for AMI patients only, track the aggregate findings of steady growth through 1993 from Atella (1998a). In addition, these findings are broadly similar to those from the MONICA-Brianza registry in confirmed AMI patients, although growth rates in Brianza were somewhat lower. Rates of use of thrombolytic drugs rose from 29.3 to 43.2 percent ($p < 0.001$); antiplatelets treatment changed from 19.7 to 81.9 percent ($p < 0.001$); and the use of beta-blockers went from 16.6 to 44 percent ($p < 0.001$).

Changes in Expertise or Appropriateness of Care

Recently a study was conducted in the northern Italian region of Lombardy to assess the appropriateness of some medical practices (Valagussa et al. 1997). A multidisciplinary panel of experts convened by the

TABLE 17.1. Share of AMI Patients Aged 35–64 in the MONICA-Friuli Registry Receiving Specific Drug Treatments before, during, and after Hospitalization, 1984–93 (%)

	1984	1985	1986	1987	1988	1989	1990	1991	1992	1993
Antiplatelets										
Before	9.1	14.7	15.7	16.9	20.1	20.1	21.6	25.7	25.7	29.9
During	32.5	40.1	40.5	41.8	57.7	64.6	70.6	79.0	77.6	78.6
After	46.5	54.5	55.8	55.0	64.8	71.0	72.7	81.8	80.0	80.4
Beta-blockers										
Before	12.3	12.9	14.4	10.0	13.3	16.1	17.7	16.5	19.6	26.0
During	18.2	20.6	25.4	19.3	33.8	41.6	42.8	51.8	57.5	62.5
After	16.9	21.1	24.7	19.7	29.3	37.7	42.1	49.0	54.1	57.2
Thrombolytics										
Before		0.4	0.7	0.9	0.8	0.7	2.4	3.3	2.8	3.5
During	7.9	11.4	17.0	17.9	19.0	19.7	21.2	29.6	26.2	29.4
After										
ACE inhibitors										
During			6.7	4.2	4.5	9.7	15.6	22.6	25.4	25.9
After			4.8	3.4	4.3	8.8	14.5	21.4	22.7	23.8
Hypolipemics										
After		1.7	1.2	1.7	1.3	3.9	6.2	4.8	7.4	10.7

Italian Association of Hospital Cardiologists (ANMCO) rated the appropriateness of 898 "theoretical indications" for coronary artery bypass grafting (CABG) and percutaneous transluminal angioplasty (PTCA) using methods from the RAND Corporation. The most striking finding from this study is that the underuse of revascularization procedures constitutes a significant health care problem in the Lombardy region, and probably in the rest of Italy too, at least for the time period under consideration. This study in itself, though, does not make it possible to understand whether these results reflect a structural shortage of services (limited accessibility and/or "unprioritized" waiting lists) or a more general quality-of-care problem.

There is also evidence of substantial regional differences in care in Italy, due at least in part to differences in facilities across areas. Catheterization rates were significantly greater in northern and central Italy than in southern Italy. In 1995, in the northern part of Italy, hemodynamics centers performed more than 46,000 procedures (1,847 per million population), as compared to central Italy with 15,102 procedures (1,139 per million population) and the south, at 16,190 procedures (819 per million population). A similar situation had been noted for PTCA, with northern Italy performing 9,942 PTCA (330 per million population), central Italy 3,159 (252 per million population) and the south at 2,651 PTCA (131 per million population). These results are neither explained by differences in the incidence of ischemic cardiopathy, nor by differences in risk factors.

3. The Consequences of Changes in AMI Care in Italy

In this section, we describe some of the potential consequences of these changes in care. Unfortunately, data limitations preclude definitive conclusions about the consequences of changes in care for AMI patients. We begin with a discussion of the changes in case fatality within 28 days of discharge, for all heart disease patients. In addition, as discussed above, it is essentially impossible to obtain information on resource use until 1995, three years after the 1992 reforms imposing the PPS. For this reason, we do not present any new analysis of the cost of treatment for AMI and instead review two recent studies.

Changes in Health Outcomes for AMI Patients

As figure 17.5 shows, there has been a substantial decrease in case fatality from heart disease in the nonelderly in Italy over the 1984–93 period. Mortality from heart disease dropped by 18 percent between

1984 and 1993, from 50.2 percent to 41.3 percent. Both men and women showed similar declines. Male 28-day case fatality dropped slightly more, by 19 percent, as compared to the female decline of approximately 13 percent. There is some relationship between these indicators and technology use over time, even if the year-by-year relationship is somewhat noisy. The MONICA-Brianza data show similar trends in 28-day case fatality from heart disease, albeit at much lower levels. Between 1986 and 1989, figure 17.5 shows that 28-day fatality from heart disease in Friuli in the nonelderly declined from 52.7 percent to 42.0 percent, that is, by approximately 20 percent; heart disease fatality rates in Brianza fell from 29.4 percent to 23.6 percent, a 19 percent decrease, for the same population. Supplementary analysis of the Brianza data shows that the 28-day fatality rate for nonelderly AMI patients is much greater, suggesting that similar gains may have occurred for AMI patients in Friuli. In Brianza, 28-day fatality of confirmed AMI in the nonelderly fell from 16.4 percent to 8.3 percent, a 49.4 percent decrease.

Changes in Medical Expenditures

There are only two studies that, to our knowledge, have investigated the costs of treatment for AMI patients, both of which focus on understanding the extent to which DRG reimbursement rates approximate production costs. Bezante et al. (1997) estimate the total cost of treatment for 45 patients over a three-month period discharged with a diagnosis of AMI (ICD9-CM code 410). Payments under four DRGs were considered in this study: DRG 112, 121, 122, 123.[13] The study found that the mean cost for each patient with AMI was 5.86 million lira (U.S.$3,350), ranging from 17.1 million lira (U.S.$9,771) for those patients reimbursed under DRG 112 to a minimum of 3.3 million lira (U.S.$1,885) for patients reimbursed under DRG 123. The results from this study suggest that in patients with AMI, the current DRG reimbursements are substantially lower than costs. In particular, in case of DRG 112, costs are 166 percent of reimbursement.[14] The second study by Lucioni, Pedrini, and Romero (1998) is limited to pharmacological costs, and finds analogous results.

4. Conclusion

Although the importance of technological change in treatment for AMI and heart disease is well known, there has been little evidence in Italy about the causes and consequences of the use of high-tech versus

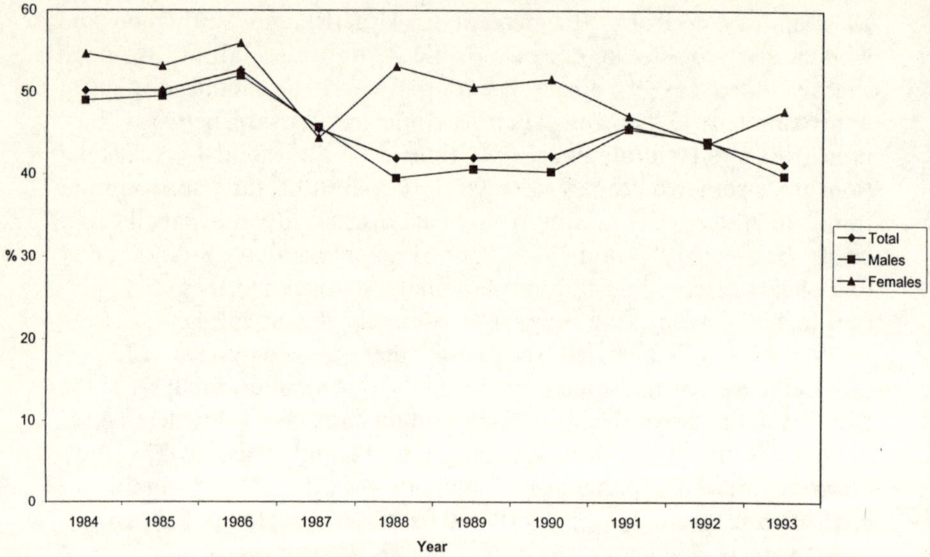

Fig. 17.5. Twenty-eight-day case fatality for heart disease patients ages 35–64 in the MONICA-Friuli registry

low-tech treatments for resource use and patient health outcomes. This chapter seeks to provide a framework in which further exploration of these issues can occur, by documenting trends in the use of three key intensive procedures for AMI, and how patient health outcomes have changed contemporaneously with these trends.

There is no strong evidence on the extent to which regulatory and financial incentives have affected the adoption of new technologies in this sector. Use of intensive procedures in the treatment of AMI has increased dramatically over the 1984–93 period, and case fatality from heart disease has decreased. Supplementary evidence suggests that declines in case fatality for AMI patients may be even greater than the overall decline for patients with heart disease. There is also some evidence that reforms undertaken in 1992, including the adoption of PPS, increased the use of intensive cardiac procedures. To the extent that this is the case, the dramatic 1997 increase in DRG reimbursement for patients given high-tech, intensive treatment should result in even greater increases in procedure use.

There is substantial evidence that other institutional factors play an important role in the adoption of new technologies. Italy exhibits substantial regional disparities in catheterization facilities, potentially due to lack of planning from the Ministry of Health. Indeed, other research suggests that treatment for cardiac illness remains inappropriate in a substantial number of cases.

The total absence of reliable cost data before 1995 prevents us from forming definitive conclusions about the effects that technological change will have on expenditures for AMI patients. However, several years after the DRG revolution, the debate is still on how closely DRG reimbursement approximates the true costs of treatment. To the extent that DRG reimbursements make intensive treatment more profitable, recent changes may result in substantially greater use of high technology in the treatment of AMI. Future research projects might make use of this newly collected information on treatment decisions and expenditures, matched with data on individuals' health outcomes, to assess the benefits and costs of technological change.

Notes

1. The health system is organized on three levels: State, region and local. The local health units are the operative branches of the system and are in charge of care delivery and management for the territory. For a long time they have been managed by politicians, who transformed these institutions in arenas of political parties' competition where career administrators were subordinated to "politicians and peripheral party cadres with little or no technical expertise or management skills, formally free of any hierarchical, administrative accountability, and only vaguely and indirectly responsible to the electorate at large" (Ferrera 1995).

2. Based on the current exchange rate of 1,750 lira per U.S. dollar.

3. As clearly demonstrated by several OECD analyses (1985), a prime cause of skyrocketing health care expenditures in most countries was the increasing use of services.

4. There was no responsibility at all for presenting balance sheets exhibiting losses, and the budget for each USL was based on the historical expenditures. These two conditions bear substantial responsibility for both the sharp increase in the public health expenditure and for the low levels of productivity.

5. Combined with the changes discussed below, this encouraged regions, and in turn ASLs and hospitals, to experiment with "contracting out" certain services. Hospitals are allowed to "sell" beds to patients willing to pay extra charges; hospital physicians are allowed to provide intramural professional services on a private basis if they grant a proportion of their extra income to the hospital. The regions are allowed to increase the rate of compulsory health care contributions from their residents by as much as 6 percentage points and local taxes by as much as 75 percent; they are also allowed to impose consumer copayments or to limits the care provided by ASLs and hospitals in their territory.

6. Over the last few years the mechanism for setting drug prices has changed several times. Presently, the European Average Price mechanism is

the one that fixes the price for existing drugs, while a new bargaining system between NHS and industries has been adopted for new drugs (see Atella 1998b for a detailed overview of the evolution of these mechanisms).

7. Patients had to request formal approval from the USL in order to use a different hospital or a specialist outside the jurisdiction of the USL. Approval was given only in those cases where a specific cure was not available locally (this was particularly true for certain surgeries).

8. The rising problem of "defensive medicine" is not only confined to a more intensive use of more sophisticated and expensive diagnostic tests. According to Benciolini (1996) the number of hospital admissions has increased as well as the length of stay in hospitals; there is a widespread tendency in the medical profession to redirect elsewhere patients with complicated pathologies or diagnosis, thus causing patients to travel often from one hospital to another.

9. One of the main concerns in the medical profession today is costly prescribing behavior that may actually be harmful to patients' health. Typical examples are the prescription of wide-spectrum, last-generation antibiotics and the prescription of triple therapy in the case of dyspepsia.

10. A typical example is represented by the powerful pediatrics lobby: in a country like Italy, where the birth rate is very low and the number of elderly is increasing sharply, the number of positions for specialization in pediatrics is still much higher than those available in geriatrics.

11. By *low-tech* treatment, we mean all those procedures, devices, and drugs with relatively modest costs of use that do not require large fixed investments. In contrast, by *high-tech* we mean the use of procedures and devices that require substantial fixed investments in equipment and specialized personnel, or that have high equipment and personnel costs with each use, or both.

12. Because drug manufactures have changed the "strength" or "dosage" and the "size" of the packages in order to overcome the strict regulation on price determination that prevented drug price adjustment, determining the true change in the use of cardiac drugs is difficult. For cardiac therapy drugs, the rate of growth of constant values has exceeded that of package quantities by an average of 58.2 percent per year during the later part of the study period. See Atella 1998a for further discussion.

13. DRG 112 is "percutaneal interventions on the cardiovascular system." DRG 121 is "cardiovascular diseases with AMI, with other problems and for patients alive." DRG 122 is "cardiovascular diseases with AMI, without other problems and for patients alive," and DRG 123 is "cardiovascular diseases with AMI, and for patients dead."

14. See Ramponi and Schweiger 1997 for criticism of the methods used to impute costs in this study.

References

Atella, V. 1998a. "Cardiovascular Drug Consumption: A Cross-Country Comparison." Photocopy.

———. 1998b. "Spesa farmaceutica pubblica e controllo dei prezzi: Venti anni di problemi e incomprensioni." *MECOSAN* 27:43–52.

Benciolini, P. 1996. ". . . a scopo medico legale." *Rivista Italiana di Medicina Legale* 2:71–181.

Bezante, G. P., C. Brunelli, A. Pasdera, P. Spallarossa, M. R. Merello, P. Rossettin, F. Zorzet, and S. Caponnetto. 1997. "Analisi dei costi per DRG e PRG del trattamento dell'infarto miocardico acuto in regime di ricovero ospedaliero." *Giornale Italiano di Cardiologia* 27:1290–98.

Bourassa, G. M, E. L. Alderman, M. Bertrand, L. de la Fuente, A. Gratsianski, M. Kaltenbach, S. B. King, M. Nobuyoshi, P. Romaniuk, T. J. Ryan, et al. 1988. "Report of the Joint ISFC/WHO Task Force on Coronary Angioplasty." *Circulation* 78:780–89.

Braunwald, E. 1990. "Coronary Artery Patency in Patients with Myocardial Infarction." *JACC* 16:1550–52.

Chambless L., U. Keil, A. Dobson, M. Mahonen, K. Kuulasmaa, A. M. Rajakangas, H. Lowel, and H. Tunstall-Pedoe. 1997. "Population versus Clinical View of Case Fatality from Acute Coronary Heart Disease: Results from the WHO MONICA Project, 1985–1990." *Circulation* 96, no. 11: 3849–59.

Ferrera, M. 1989. "The Politics of Health Reform: Origins and Performance of the Italian Health Service in Comparative Perspective." In *Controlling Medical Professionals: The Comparative Politics of Health Governance,* ed. G. Freddi and J. Bjorkman. London: Sage.

———. 1995. "The Rise and Fall of Democratic Universalism: Health Care Reform in Italy, 1978–1994." *Journal of Health Politics, Policy, and Law* 2:275–302.

Fiori, A. 1996. "La medicina legale difensiva." *Rivista Italiana di Medicina Legale* 4:899–910.

Fuster, V. 1993. "Coronary Thrombolysis: A Perspective for the Practicing Physician." *New England Journal of Medicine* 10:723–25.

Granger, C. B., R. M. Califf, and E. J. Topol. 1992. "Thrombolytic Therapy for Acute Myocardial Infarction: A Review." *Drugs* 44:293–325.

Grines, C. L., K. F. Browne, J. Marco, D. Rothbaum, G. W. Stone, J. O'Keefe, P. Overlie, B. Donohue, N. Chelliah, G. C. Timmis, et al. 1993. "A Comparison of Immediate Angioplasty with Thrombolytic Therapy for AMI." *New England Journal of Medicine* 328:673–79.

Iatrona, F. 1996. "L'epidemiologia del contenzioso in Italia." *Rivista Italiana di Medicina Legale* 1:71–181.

———. 1997. "Commento a: Proposta di legge n.3244 su Norme in materia di assicurazione obbligatoria della responsabilità civile derivante dall'esercizio dell'attività sanitaria." *Rivista Italiana di Medicina Legale* 4–5: 1120–38.

National Statistical Institute (ISTAT). 1995. Statistiche sulla Sanità.

Kessler, D. P., and M. B. McClellan. 1996. "Do Doctors Practice Defensive Medicine?" *Quarterly Journal of Economics* 111, no. 2: 353–90.

Klugmann, S. 1990. "L'angioplastica coronarica in Italia: Perché il ritardo?" *Giornale Italiano di Cardiologia* 20:272–76.

Linchoff, A. M., and E. J. Topol. 1993. "Illusion of Reperfusion: Does Anyone Achieve Optimal Reperfusion during Acute Myocardial Infarction?" *Circulation* 87:1792–1805.

Lucioni, C., M. Pedrini, and M. Romero. 1998. "Il sistema di finanziamento dell'attività di ricovero (DRG) edi costi delle terapie farmacologiche." *Giornale di Farmacoeconomia* 47, no. 2: 106–15.

Marzocchi, A. 1996. "Attività dei laboratori di emodinamica italiani 1995." *Emodinamica* 5:24–29.

McClellan, M. B., N. Every, A. Garber, P. Heidenreich, M. Hlatky, D. P. Kessler, J. Newhouse, and O. Saynina. 2002. "Technological Change in Heart Attack Care in the United States." In this volume.

Organisation for Economic Cooperation and Development (OECD). 1985. *Measuring Health Care.* Paris: OECD.

———. 1987. *Financing and Delivering Health Care.* Paris: OECD.

Piperno, A., ed. 1986. *La politica sanitaria in Italia.* Milan: Franco Angeli.

Ramponi, C., and C. Schweiger. 1997. Commento editoriale a: "Analisi dei costi per DRG e PRG del trattamento dell'infarto miocardico acuto in regime di ricovero ospedaliero." *Giornale Italiano di Cardiologia* 27:1299–1301.

Stritoni, P. 1988. "Attività negli anni 1985 e 1986 dei laboratori di emodinamica italiani aderenti al registro nazionale dei cateterismi cardiaci." *Notiziario di emodinamica GISE* 1:2–3.

———. 1989. "Attività nel 1987 dei laboratori di emodinamica italiani." *Notiziario di emodinamica GISE* 3:2–3.

Topol, E. J., R. M. Califf, M. Vandormael, L. L. Grines, B. S. George, M. L. Sanz, T. Wall, M. O'Brien, M. Schwaiger, F. V. Aguirre, et al. 1992. "A Randomized Trial of Late Reperfusion Therapy for Acute Myocardial infarction." *Circulation* 85:2090–99.

Valagussa, F., A. P. Maggioni, L. Valagussa, G. Filardo, G. Mura, and A. Liberati, for the Gruppo Interdisciplinare Valutazione Appropriatezza Rivascolarizzazione Coronarica. 1997. "L'appropriatezza della indicazione al by-pass aorto-coronarico e alla angioplastica coronarica: i risultati di uno studio osservazionale prospettico in regione Lombardia." *Giornale Italiano di Cardiologia* 27:1264–70.

Veen, G., A. Meyer, F. W. Verheught, C. J. Werter, H. de Swart, K. I. Lie, J. M. van der Pol, H. R. Michels, and M. J. van Eenige. 1993. "Culprit Lesion Morphology and Stenosis Severity in the Prediction of Reocclusion after Coronary Thrombolysis: Angiographic Results of the APRICOT Study." *Journal of the American College of Cardiology* 22:1755–62.

CHAPTER 18

Technological Change in Treatment of Acute Myocardial Infarction in Switzerland, 1986–1993

Fred Paccaud and Alberto Holly

Over the last decade, the age-adjusted rate of mortality from ischemic heart disease (IHD) in Switzerland has declined. As figure 18.1 shows, this decline has been most dramatic for nonelderly men (ages 35–64), who experienced a 34 percent reduction in IHD mortality from 136 per 100,000 population in 1980 to 89 in 1992. Despite a much lower level of mortality from IHD, the decline was similarly impressive for nonelderly women, from 27 per 100,000 population in 1980 to 18 in 1992. In contrast, mortality remained constant over the same period among the elderly, especially among elderly women.

Over the same period, costs of health care have increased substantially, from U.S.$12.3 billion in 1985 to U.S.$23.4 billion in 1995 (*Annuaire statistique de la Suisse* 1997, 407, 7) (converted at a rate of 1.5 Swiss francs/U.S.$). Expenditures as a share of GDP have increased substantially as well, from 7.3 percent in 1980 to 9.4 percent in 1992. To what extent has technological change in the care of heart disease generally, and heart attack (AMI) specifically, contributed to real growth in health expenditures in Switzerland? And how have the methods of financing and the regulation of provision of care for AMI in Switzerland affected technological change and resource use? Several sources of data are potentially relevant to these questions, but none are currently available that cover the whole Swiss population. Switzerland has recently established a uniform national Hospital Discharge Data System by federal law, but this system is not yet fully implemented. In fact, only a few cantons are currently able to provide even the number of heart attack cases seen in acute care hospitals. It is expected that all acute care hospitals will be reporting to the data system by 2002; however, it is clear that the information available from this system will be

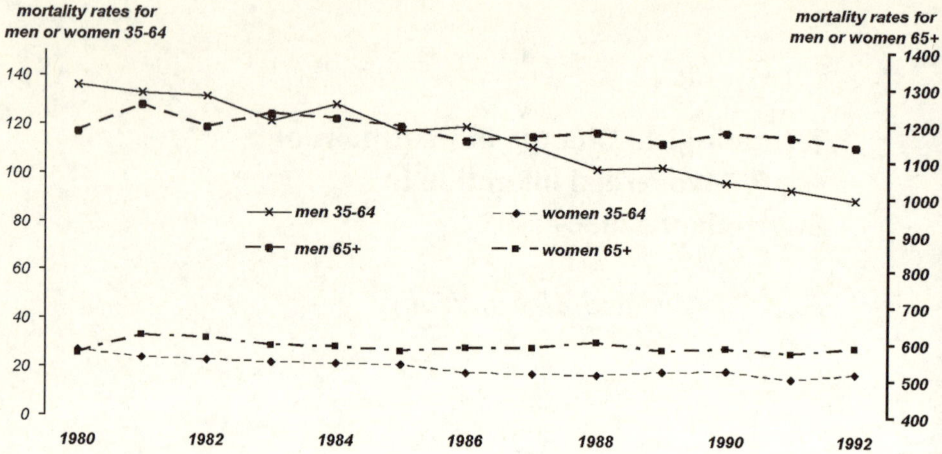

Fig. 18.1. Age-standardized trends in mortality rates per 100,000 from ischemic heart disease, by gender and age, Switzerland, 1980–92

for some time too limited to provide information on trends in technology related to AMI. There is an additional ongoing effort to collect detailed national data on care for AMI at the hospital level, but this data source is also not yet complete.[1]

For this reason, this chapter seeks to explore these two questions with an analysis of data from the international MONICA project (Monitoring of Trends and Determinants in Cardiovascular Disease). Unlike other existing data sources (Schilling et al. 1996), MONICA is not limited to only one hospital and provides population-based information. As part of MONICA, patient intake and the treatments dispensed during hospitalization for myocardial infarction were recorded in 1986, 1990, and 1993 in a single Swiss region (cantons of Vaud and Fribourg) for men aged between 25 and 64 years. This material contained in this section is largely based on this effort; a more complete account has been published elsewhere (Bourquin et al. 1998). The changes in therapeutic practices for the treatment of myocardial infarction during these three consecutive inquiries are reported. Some comparisons of these results with the timing of significant scientific publications in the field are also presented. Unfortunately, the MONICA data on all AMI patients cannot be linked over time, and data for multiple years on individual AMI patients are not available. In addition, we do not have AMI patient-level information on expenditures.

Although our ability to examine trends in the causes and consequences of technological change for heart attack care is limited by our data, our analysis suggests how health care finance in Switzerland may affect treatment decision making for heart attack. This chapter proceeds as follows. Section 1 outlines the incentives for technological change in treatment of heart attack care under the Swiss system of financing of care. Section 2 presents our analysis of technological change in AMI care, based on the MONICA data. Section 3 concludes with some hypotheses about technological change in Switzerland and suggestions for future research.

1. Incentives for Technological Change in Switzerland

Financing of Care for Heart Disease

In this section we review some of the relevant aspects of the Swiss health system over the 1986–93 period covered by the MONICA project. We begin with a discussion of the Federal Law on Sickness and Accident Insurance (KUVG) in effect at this time. We outline some important changes to the KUVG that were implemented in 1992, with a set of emergency measures designed to address sharply escalating premiums and health care costs. We conclude the section with a brief summary of the provisions of the new Federal Law on Sickness Insurance (KVG), effective January 1, 1996, which may provide important incentives for technological change in the future. This review makes use of the expositions of the Swiss health system contained in OECD (OECD 1994) and Swiss Federal Social Insurance Office (*Sickness Insurance in Switzerland* 1997).

Until 1996, health insurance was not compulsory (although certain cantons and municipalities did make insurance compulsory for all residents). However, the federal government encouraged the private purchase of insurance by granting subsidies to nonprofit sickness funds. As a result, approximately 99 percent of the population was insured during the 1980s.

The KUVG specified various requirements that nonprofit funds had to satisfy. The KUVG specified a minimum benefits package, often described as "basic" or "social insurance" benefits. In addition, the KUVG required that all applicants for insurance had to be accepted; prohibited preexisting conditions exclusions of more than five years, and any preexisting conditions exclusions for individuals who changed insurers involuntarily; and in the event of disability, required that unlimited hospitalization be offered. Insurers were allowed to establish rules regarding age limits for coverage, an initial waiting period during which the insured did not receive benefits, and preexisting conditions exclusions that did not violate the KUVG. Both nonprofit and for-profit sickness funds were also allowed to offer more extensive supplementary benefits, which respond to specific wishes of the insured persons, such as hospitalization in a private or semiprivate ward, or supplementary inpatient and outpatient services.

The KUVG also regulated premiums. First, the KUVG prohibited insurers from increasing existing customers' premiums based on their age or gender; as long as an individual was affiliated with the same sickness fund, he was entitled to pay the same premium he was charged when he first purchased insurance from the fund, with adjustments allowed only for aggregate growth in health care costs. In addition, women's premiums were not allowed to be more than 10 percent higher than men's premiums, controlling for age. Not surprisingly, these premium regulations resulted in large adverse selection problems in markets for individual insurance. If a person was covered by group insurance, for example through his or her employer, the premium could be much lower than it would be in the individual insurance market. In some extreme cases, premiums could differ by a factor of 12.

Under the KUVG, care delivered under basic insurance coverage is financed primarily through premiums (approximately 75 percent), with patient copayments and public subsidies accounting for most of the remainder. Copayments include a fixed annual deductible and a coinsurance rate of 10 percent on outpatient expenses that exceed the amount of deductible. Under the KUGV, the deductible was FR 150 (U.S.$100) with a maximum annual patient contribution of FR 750 (U.S.$500). There were no copayments or deductibles for inpatient care.

Payments from insurers to hospitals was based on historical costs, so the financial incentives for hospitals to provide cost-effective treatment were at best weak. However, hospitals and cantonal health insurance associations did bargain over reimbursement rates, providing some check on costs. In addition, for patients with supplementary insurance, hospitals could levy an additional daily surcharge, to which fees for medical and technical care are added. (Unfortunately, due to lack of data, it is presently impossible to work out the effect of the incentives for technological change for heart attack care provided by the supplemental health insurance system in Switzerland.)

In 1992, when the KUVG was still in force, a number of federal emergency measures were adopted, aimed at limiting increases in expenditures and prices of benefits and reinforcing equity in health insurance. Patient copayments were extended to inpatient hospital care: inpatients became responsible for a copayment of FR 10 (U.S.$7) per hospital day, plus 10 percent of costs, up to FR 500 (U.S.$333). This cost-sharing measure was intended to encourage patients to choose outpatient treatment whenever possible, as it is less expensive than inpatient treatment. However, it had almost no effect in the case of AMI treatment because such treatment was, and still is, only available in public hospitals. Since no alternative outpatient treatment was available, patients paid very little directly out of pocket for care for this illness, and nothing at the margin. Another more radical change was the introduction of an insurance system with an expanded choice of deductibles. In exchange for a choice of a higher deductible by the insured person, the insurer reduces its premiums by a given percentage. The choice of deductibles and the associated premium reductions are set annually by the Federal Council. Even so, given the fact that the total amount of the initial deductible, the coinsurance, and the ceiling on out-of-pocket expenditures is low compared to AMI hospital inpatient costs, the financial incentives for patients to seek less costly treatment is very small.

The 1992 measures also took other steps to control costs and address adverse selection problems in the market for insurance. For example, the measures included some caps on premiums and reimbursement rates for providers. In addition, the measures prohibited new insurers being created, restricted the activities of existing insurers, and required that insurers with low-risk populations make equalization payments to insurers with high-risk populations. The restrictions on women's premiums relative to men's was also lifted.

The new Federal Law on Sickness Insurance (KVG), effective January 1, 1996, may provide important incentives for technological change in the future. The most important reform imposed in 1996 by the KVG for treatment for heart attack was a shift to funding hospitals with global budgets (although some hospitals were funded with global budgets before the KVG, the number of hospitals funded in this way increased dramatically). The amount of this global budget is determined through annual negotiations between the hospital and the canton government. Although the KVG allows for the introduction of DRG-like payment schemes, expensive therapies are largely funded from the global budget. Another important change contained in the KVG is the fact that hospital inpatient cost sharing has been put on an equal footing with outpatient cost sharing.

Other reforms introduced in 1996 by the KVG include the following. Insurance was made compulsory for medical and pharmaceutical care. In addition, nonprofit sickness funds must accept applicants without any reservations. Finally, the public subsidization of health insurance was changed from a system in which subsidies were granted to nonprofit sickness funds for all members, to a system aimed at reducing premiums of persons whose financial circumstances are modest.

Other Incentives for Technology Adoption and Use

Competition

The insured has in principle the freedom to choose a doctor and hospital. However, free choice of the physician does not necessarily exist for hospitalized patients who only purchased basic insurance. And if an individual uses a hospital other than the one nearest his or her home, the insurer generally only reimburses what it would have paid to the nearest hospital.

Under both the KUVG and the KVG, there is a free choice as to the sickness fund with which the basic insurance is taken out. Under the KUVG, if the insured was constrained to change funds, he could change freely, that is to say that his new nonprofit insurer could not impose either a waiting period or new exceptions to insurance, although premiums could be increased.

Microregulation

The lack of microregulation of Swiss physicians is apparent on several dimensions. They can practice where they wish and have complete autonomy in choice of treatment, the limits being due to the availability of these treatments. Cost containment mechanisms and utilization review were not used during the study period for individual providers, except possibly in 1993, in reaction to the federal emergency measures adopted in 1992. However, even before the emergency measures, sickness funds could demand an efficiency examination when a physician was suspected of overtreatment, although this provision was rarely used.

2. Technological Change in Heart Attack Care in Switzerland

Several sources of data are potentially relevant to monitor technological change, but none of them covers the entire Swiss population. The only study that provides some population-based figures is the MONICA project. As part of the international project, patient intake and the treatments dispensed during hospitalization for myocardial infarction were recorded in 1986, 1990, and 1993 in a Swiss region (cantons of Vaud and Fribourg) for men aged between 25 and 64 years. Unfortunately, the MONICA data on all AMI patients cannot be linked over time, and data for multiple years on individual AMI patients are not available.

Changes in High-Tech Care

Table 18.1 shows changes in the use of coronary angiography, percutaneous transluminal coronary angioplasty (PTCA), and coronary artery bypass surgery (CABG)—the three main high-tech procedures used in AMI care—among nonelderly males with a diagnosis of definite AMI. Coronary angiography has increased in use constantly since 1986 and was carried out in 53 percent of patients in 1993. Information not in the table indicates that the mean time to carrying out this procedure rose from 8.2 days in 1990 to 11 days in 1993. The use of PTCA remained stable during the last two inquiries, and, like coronary angiography, it was performed longer after admission, the delay increasing from an average of 7.1 days in 1990 to 11.4 days in 1993. In 1993, 2 percent of patients underwent implantation of a coronary stent (data missing for 1986 and 1990). Finally, the frequency of CABG, carried out within 27 days following the onset of symptoms, fell during the three inquiries. Corresponding figures in Zurich in 1993 are 31 percent for angiography, 15 percent for PTCA, and 11 percent for CABG (Schilling et al. 1996).

TABLE 18.1. Use of Intensive Procedures during Hospitalization: Frequency of Coronary Angiography, Percutaneous Transluminal Coronary Angioplasty, and Coronary Artery Bypass Surgery

	Levels			Statistical Significance of Trends		
	1986	1990	1993	1986–90	1990–93	1986–93
Coronary angiography	35%	41%	53%	Ns	$p < .05$	$p < .05$
PTCA	11%	17%	18%	$p < .05$	Ns	$p < .05$
CABG	9%	5%	3%	Ns	Ns	$p < .05$
Number of cases	218	224	167			

Notes: Cantons of Vaud and Fribourg, men aged 25 to 64 years hospitalized with a diagnosis of "definite myocardial infarction" and survived more than 27 days. *Ns:* not statistically significant at the 5 percent level.

Changes in Low-Tech Care

Two low-tech approaches to improving treatment of AMI include increased rapidity of response of emergency care (for example, through mobile coronary care units) and administration of in-hospital treatment, especially thrombolytic drugs, immediately upon admission to the hospital. Table 18.2 explores the first of these alternatives and presents the distribution of patients according to their first medical contact, which may have been carried out by the general practitioner, in the mobile coronary care unit, or directly at the hospital. There was no statistically significant variation between the three inquiries for this distribution. More than half the patients consulted a general practitioner prior to their arrival at the hospital. The time to initial medical treatment and to arrival at the hospital, given in the same table, remained relatively stable in terms of the median value (two and three hours, respectively) over the period studied.

Table 18.3 shows the trends in use of drugs during hospitalization. Almost all the patients were treated in an intensive care unit. In the

TABLE 18.2. Distribution of AMI Patients According to Type of, and Time to, First Medical Contact

	1986	1990	1993	Statistical Significance of Trend, 1986–93
Type of first medical contact				
General practitioner	51%	60%	53%	Ns[a]
Hospital	48%	40%	44%	Ns[a]
Mobile coronary care unit	0%	0%	2%	Ns[a]
Unknown	1%	0%	1%	Ns[a]
Number of cases with nonmissing data	218	224	167	
Time to first intervention				
Median delay (in hours)	2.0	2.3	1.9	Ns[b]
Number of cases with nonmissing data	109	136	82	
Time to arrival at hospital				
Median delay (in hours)	3.3	3.0	3.0	Ns[b]
Number of cases with nonmissing data	164	182	130	

Note: Cantons of Vaud and Fribourg, men aged 25 to 64 years hospitalized with a diagnosis of "definite myocardial infarction" and survived more than 27 days.

[a]Not statistically significant at the 5 percent level. Chi-squared test.

[b]Not statistically significant at the 5 percent level. Test of difference between medians.

three studies, the most frequently used medications were anticoagulants and nitrates. An increase in frequency of use was observed for antiplatelets between 1986 and 1990 and for beta-blockers and ACE inhibitors between 1990 and 1993. In contrast, the use of calcium antagonists fell significantly and regularly over the three inquiries, while the use of antiarrhythmics dropped dramatically from 1990 onward. Use of diuretics and intropic agents declined as well. Information not presented in table 18.3 shows that these trends in in-hospital drug use were largely paralleled by the prescription of different treatments on release from hospital.

Perhaps the most striking finding from table 18.3, however, is the dramatic increase in the use of thrombolytic drugs over the 1986–90 period. Thrombolytic use rose from only 9 percent of patients in 1986 to more than 40 percent in 1990. The introduction corresponds to the increase of experimental evidence regarding the efficacy of thrombolysis during this period (Herman, Stüdemann, and Greiser 1993; Doggen, Van der Palen, and Beaglehole 1993). Table 18.4 provides additional information on the use thrombolysis for the years 1990 and 1993. Thrombolytics were administered in 98 of 224 patients (44 percent) in 1990 and in 70 of 167 patients (42 percent) in 1993. By far the most frequently used route of administration was intravenous, while the intra-

TABLE 18.3. Medication Use during Hospitalization

	% of Patients Treated			Statistical Significance of Trends		
	1986	1990	1993	1986–90	1990–93	1986–93
Nitrates	97	95	99	Ns	$p < .05$	Ns
Anticoagulants	98	99	98	Ns	Ns	Ns
Antiplatelets	51	96	95	$p < .005$	Ns	$p < .005$
Beta-blockers	57	57	78	Ns	$p < .005$	$p < .005$
ACE inhibitors		26	43		$p < .005$	
Antiarrhythmics	69	75	43	Ns	$p < .005$	$p < .005$
Calcium antagonists	72	55	43	$p < .005$	$p < .05$	$p < .005$
Thrombolytics		44	42	$p < .005$	Ns	$p < .005$
Diuretics	47	38	32	$p < .05$	Ns	$p < .05$
Inotropic agents	33	24	17	$p < .05$	Ns	$p < .005$
Digitalin, oral		8	7	$p < .05$	Ns	
Digitalin, IV		9	4		$p < .05$	
Hypolipidemic agents		8	12		Ns	
Number of cases	218	224	167			

Notes: Cantons of Vaud and Fribourg, men aged 25 to 64 years hospitalized with a diagnosis of "definite myocardial infarction" and survived more than 27 days. *Ns:* not statistically significant at the 5 percent level.

coronary route was only rarely used. Streptokinase was generally used rather than other drugs (APSAC, tPA, and urokinase). According to information not in the table, the time from arrival at the hospital to beginning of the thrombolytic treatment remained stable at 48 minutes between 1990 and 1993, and when no thrombolytic treatment was used, the reasons given were as follows: lack of indication according to the clinician's judgment (40 percent of cases), delay from the onset of symptoms that exceeded the limits adopted by the clinician (43 percent of cases), or contraindication to the treatment (9 percent of cases).

In Switzerland, the proportion of patients receiving thrombolytic agents did not continue its rise between 1990 and 1993. Table 18.4 suggests that this proportion could still be increased since excessive delay was the reason for not receiving thrombolytic treatment in 43 percent of patients for these two years. The median times to hospitalization (three hours) and to implementation of treatment (47 minutes) have not fallen in the Vaud-Fribourg region. Although several means of reducing time-to-hospitalization in Vaud-Fribourg have been suggested, it seems more difficult to reduce the intrahospital "door-to-needle time" (Rogers et al. 1994).

Another Swiss region conducted a similar MONICA study during the same period and using the same methods for data collection (Bordoni et al. 1998). The 1993 inquiry into care in Ticino found 118 hospitalizations diagnosed as "definite myocardial infarction." The Ticino patients were, on average, older than those from the Vaud-Fribourg

TABLE 18.4. Medications Used for Thrombolysis, Route of Administration, and "Door-to-Needle Time"

	1990 ($N = 98$)		1993 ($N = 70$)	
	%	*n*	%	*n*
Route of administration and substance				
IV: streptokinase	56	55	87	59
IV: urokinase	3	3	2	1
IV: APSAC	21	20	0	0
IV: tPA	11	11	4	3
IV: unknown medication	2	2	4	3
Intracoronary	7	7	3	2
"Door-to-needle time"				
1-30 minutes	30	27	29	17
31–60 minutes	33	29	31	18
61+ minutes	37	33	41	24

Notes: Cantons of Vaud and Fribourg, men aged 25 to 64 years hospitalized with a diagnosis of "definite myocardial infarction" and survived more than 27 days.

region (53.4 years compared with 51.5 years in 1993, a nonsignificant difference), with a comparable frequency of ischemic cardiopathy history. Over the course of the three studies, Ticino patients received their first medical treatment directly at the hospital with increasing frequency (50 percent in 1986 and 60 percent in 1993), which contrasted with the trend observed in the Vaud-Fribourg region (49 percent in 1986 and 44 percent in 1993). In Ticino, the mobile coronary care unit is now used frequently: in 1993, 10 percent of Ticino patients (in contrast to only 2 percent of Vaud-Fribourg patients) received their first care from a specialized mobile team. The median time to arrival at hospital declined in Ticino, from 4.5 hours in 1986 to 2 hours in 1993, while it remained stable at 3 hours in the Vaud-Fribourg region. Furthermore, for thrombolized patients, door-to-needle time fell in Ticino, from a median value of 70 minutes in 1990 to 50 minutes in 1993, while the median delay remained at 48 minutes in the Vaud-Fribourg region.

In the two Swiss regions, there was a parallel development in the use of antiplatelet treatment and thrombolytics, which increased significantly in use between 1986 and 1990, and then stabilized. The use of beta-blockers increased steadily in Ticino, while an increase in the Vaud-Fribourg region was only noted from 1990. Calcium antagonists were used less and less frequently in both regions, with a more rapid decrease in Ticino, followed by a stabilization in use. Insofar as medical procedures are concerned, the use of coronary angiography increased greatly between 1990 and 1993 in Ticino (from 15 percent to 46 percent), while in the Vaud-Fribourg region the use of coronary arteriography was already at 35 percent in 1986. PTCA increased in use in both regions (from 5 percent to 16 percent in Ticino, in contrast to 17 percent to 18 percent in the Vaud-Fribourg region). Finally, the proportion of patients who underwent CABG increased in Ticino, while it fell in the Vaud-Fribourg region (from 2 percent to 9 percent in Ticino versus 5 percent to 3 percent in the Vaud-Fribourg region).

In the two regions, trends in prescriptions at discharge from hospital are comparable to those observed during hospital stay for all medications. The percentage of patients referred for rehabilitation on discharge from hospital increased between 1986 and 1990, then fell in both regions.

3. Discussion

How have the methods of financing and the regulation of provision of care for AMI in Switzerland affected technological change and resource use? Several important features regarding both the adoption of technological change and economic incentives emerge from the material contained in sections 1 and 2. From 1986 to 1993, financing of hospitals was largely based on retrospective reimbursement of costs. In addition, as a result of the cost-sharing structure of the KUVG, patients paid very little directly out of pocket for AMI hospital treatment. Furthermore, the federal emergency measures adopted in 1992 are unlikely to have produced much effect on treatment for AMI. In summary, there were weak financial incentives at best either for hospitals or for patients to seek cost-effective treatment paths for AMI in Switzerland over this period. This conclusion applies to both patients covered by basic insurance and those covered by private insurance, and perhaps even more so for the latter.

The above statement implies that medical knowledge was the principal constraint on the speed and the nature of technical change in AMI care in the 1980s. For example, the reduction in the diameter of catheters allowed broader use of coronary angiography with a lower risk of complications. Similarly, the speed of introduction of innovation of agents and drugs seems to be mainly due to the increase of experimental evidence regarding their efficacy, although both streptokinase and aspirin were relatively cheap, which certainly facilitated their rapid adoption.

This situation is likely to have changed for hospitals (although not for patients) with the new KVG, which became effective on January 1, 1996. As noted before, the newly introduced hospital inpatient cost-sharing measure is intended to reduce costs by encouraging patients to choose outpatient treatment whenever possible. However, AMI treatment is largely done on an inpatient basis. In addition, the amounts paid by the insurance beneficiary, as a result of deductibles, coinsurance, and the ceiling on out-of-pocket expenditures, are small compared to AMI hospital inpatient costs. Thus, the financial incentives for patients to seek less costly treatment is very small even under the KVG.

In contrast, the KVG created economic incentives for hospitals to use less expensive treatments: to substitute low-tech for high-tech treatment, and cheaper for more costly drugs. This new incentive comes about because most hospitals are now funded with an annual global budget that includes cardiac care. Note, however, that the supplemental health insurance system still provides an incentive to introduce innovations for heart attack care, which may result in the use of high-tech treatments and more costly drugs or agents. The introduction of the new KVG offers a unique opportunity to examine how financial incentives affect the adoption of new technologies, by comparing treatment decisions of patients with supplemental insurance to those with only basic insurance. Projects aimed at capturing data routinely on AMI patients will allow for the study of the effects of this change.

Note

1. Registry of Acute Myocardial Infarction events in Switzerland (AMIS). See <www.epidemiology.ch/amis>.

References

Annuaire statistique de la Suisse, 1998. 1997. Zurich: Verlag Neue Zürcher Zeitung.

Bordoni, A., V. Wietlisbach, F. Barazzoni, M. Rickenbach, and F. Paccaud. 1998. "L'évolution récente du traitement de l'infarctus du myocarde en Suisse reflète-t-elle les résultats des essais cliniques?" Manuscript.

Bourquin, M. G., V. Wietlisbach, M. Rickenbach, F. Perret, and F. Paccaud. 1998. "Time Trends in the Treatment of Myocardial Infarction in Switzerland from 1986 to 1993: Do They Reflect the Advances in Scientific Evidence from Clinical Trials?" *Journal of Clinical Epidemiology* 51, no. 9: 723–32.

Doggen, C., J. Van der Palen, and R. Beaglehole. 1993. "Trends in Medical Management of Acute Myocardial Infarction, Auckland 1983–90." *New Zealand Medical Journal* 106:278–81.

Herman, B., G. Stüdemann, and E. Greiser. 1993. "Trends in Acute Myocardial Infarction Mortality, Morbidity, and Medical Care in the City of Bremen: Results of the MONICA-Bremen Acute Coronary Event Register, 1985 to 1988." *Annuals of Epidemiology* 3 (suppl.): S62–S68.

Organisation for Economic Cooperation and Development (OECD). 1994. "Switzerland." In *The Reform of Health Care Systems: A Review of Seventeen OECD Countries.* Paris: OECD.

Rogers, W. J., L. J. Bowlby, N. C. Chandra, W. J. French, J. M. Gore, C. T. Lambrew, R. M. Robinson, A. J. Tiefenbrunn, and W. D. Weaver. 1994. "Treatment of Myocardial Infarction in the United States (1990 to 1993): Observations from the National Registry of Myocardial Infarction." *Circulation* 90:2103–14.

Schilling, J., M. Schwendinger, N. Vranjes, and F. Gutzwiller. 1996. "Thrombolyse nach Herzinfarkt." European Secondary Prevention Study Group. *Schweizerische Rundschau fur Medizin Praxis* 85:1311–15.

Sickness Insurance in Switzerland. 1997. Bern: Swiss Federal Social Insurance Office.

CHAPTER 19

Determinants and Consequences of Technological Change in Heart Attack Care in Israel

Jeremy D. Kark, Amir Shmueli, Sylvie Goldman, and Ziona Haklai

Israel has experienced growth in the cost of medical care over the last decade similar to that seen in most developed countries. In 1986, 6.8 percent of the Israeli GDP was spent on health. By 1995, this share reached 8.1 percent (*National Expenditure on Health* 1997) (fig. 19.1). Although some of this increase has been accounted for by population growth, much has not. Total expenditures in constant prices have increased, on average, by 5 percent yearly, whereas per capita expenditure in constant prices has increased, on average, by 2 percent. In 1994, per capita expenditure reached U.S.$1,221 (measured in 1995 U.S. dollars, converted at PPP exchange rates).

Trends in coronary heart disease (CHD) mortality (as coded by the Israel Central Bureau of Statistics, ICD codes 410–414) have changed. After a steady decline since the early 1970s there was an overall age-adjusted increase in the 1990s. When examined in more detail, mortality from acute myocardial infarction (AMI, ICD 410) has continued to decline steadily, whereas the rate of other CHD mortality (ICD 411–414) was stable in the 1980s and increased in the 1990s (Israel Center for Disease Control 1997). Our age-sex specific analysis of Israeli CHD mortality (ICD 410–414) between 1984 and 1994 revealed that the steepest decline occurred in the younger age groups, whereas the increase in the 1990s was restricted largely to ages 75 and over in both sexes. Increase at this age is evident in 9 of 10 sex-ethnic origin groups (and is not attributable to immigration from the former USSR, as has been suggested [Israel Center for Disease Control 1997]), and is seen in all regions of the country. The main competing explanations for this increase include possible misclassification of underlying cause of death, which is supported by the uniformity of the change in

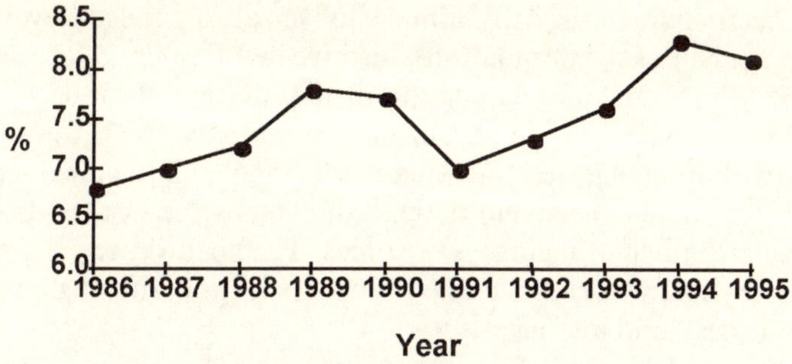

Fig. 19.1. National health expenditure as share of GDP, Israel, 1986–95

this age group, and the possibility of delayed increased mortality following earlier successful treatment of CHD, and in particular of AMI.

To what extent has technological change in treatment for coronary heart disease been responsible for these trends in resource use and population health? What roles have government regulation and, more generally, the mechanisms for financing care for CHD in Israel played in influencing technology use, medical treatment decisions, and ultimately, health outcomes? In order to gain some insight into these questions, this chapter presents analyses of five data sources: the Ministry of Health's (MOH) centrally collected data on invasive cardiac procedures; a regional study of trends in care of AMI in Jerusalem; a nationwide biennial survey of patients in coronary care units (CCUs); the nationwide MOH Hospitalization Database; and the General Sick Fund database. We first describe some of the economic and regulatory incentives for technological change in Israel, and how these incentives have changed over time. Then, we discuss our five sources in some detail and present data on how trends in care for and health outcomes of CHD have changed in the 1980s and 1990s. We conclude with a discussion of the potential implications of our findings for the determinants and consequences of care for heart disease.

Incentives for Technological Change in Israel

Financing of Care for Coronary Heart Disease

Recently, Israel has experienced important changes in its system of health care finance. Since the establishment of Israel in 1948, the system has been characterized by almost universal insurance coverage (about 95 percent of the population), massive involvement of the Ministry of Health (MOH) in the regulation and provision of services, and monopolistic competition in the insurance industry, with four sick funds providing integrated insurance coverage and medical care. Members' fees were collected in the past directly by the sick funds as a regulated percentage of members' incomes. The health care provision system as a whole was characterized by politicization, dissatisfaction, industrial unrest, and inefficiency.

Per Diem Reimbursement

Until 1989, hospitals were reimbursed for all care on a fee-for-service, per diem basis. Hospitals were reimbursed equally for days spent in internal medicine wards and in intensive coronary care units (CCUs), serving as a disincentive for development of CCU capacity for management of AMI. With the exception of admissions in which invasive procedures are performed, this mode of reimbursement remains up to the present. This may have contributed to the current situation in Israel whereby about half of all acute MI patients are admitted to internal medicine rather than CCUs, where appropriate care can be provided.

Shortening-of-Queues Campaign

In 1989, in response to long queues for invasive cardiac procedures, the MOH launched a "shortening of queues" campaign that introduced special additional payments for intensive cardiac treatment directly to the operating medical staff to increase the number of procedures performed.

Prospective Payment

And in 1990, the MOH went a step further by introducing a "prospective" (DRG-like) payment system for hospitals for about 15 procedures (now extended to 40 procedures), including CABG, catheterization, and PTCA. However, because these "prospective" payments are made on a per procedure basis, they do not provide incentives for providers to limit costs. Indeed, the generous marginal reimbursement that the prospective system offered (in 1995 U.S. dollars, converted at

PPP exchange rates, the prices were about $1,900, $4,500, and $10,000 for catheterization, PTCA, and CABG, respectively) provided incentives for hospitals to perform invasive procedures rather than manage patients with noninvasive care. Based on data from the four largest medical centers in Israel (Shmueli and Israeli 1998), it was found that during 1990, the volume of CABG performed increased by nearly 80 percent, and hospital income per CABG hospitalization by 126 percent, and per inpatient day by 180 percent. Furthermore, the cost containment features of the mixed prospective payment and per diem system (e.g., the absence of specific reimbursement for certain expensive procedures such as thallium scanning) may be undone by practice patterns; such procedures may be postponed until after release, at which point they would be reimbursable on an outpatient basis.

Also in 1990, the Netanyahu Commission of Inquiry recommended the introduction of national health insurance and privatization of government-owned hospitals. The national health insurance law was enacted January 1, 1995, guaranteeing medical care to all citizens, although the privatization of hospitals had not yet started as of mid-1998. The law separates centralized income-related tax collection by the National Insurance Institute from decentralized provision of care in a market designed along the lines of "managed competition."

Capping

In conjunction with the implementation of national health insurance in 1995, the MOH introduced certain cost-containment measures, including a partial cap on reimbursement to hospitals. According to the capping, each hospital was reimbursed by each of the sick funds in any given year up to its previous year's total reimbursement from that sick fund plus a small adjustment. Care given beyond that point was not reimbursed. In 1996, the system was modified and hospitals were reimbursed 50 percent of costs above the capping cutoff point. This system of capping does not relate specifically to invasive coronary procedures, but rather is imposed on total inpatient costs.

With respect to diagnostic catheterization and PTCA, a decreasing marginal reimbursement policy became effective in 1995 as well. At present, for example, a hospital is to be fully reimbursed (according to the prospective price) from each sick fund for the first 1,250 procedures. For the next 125 procedures the payment is 97 percent of the full price, for the next 125 procedures 94 percent, and so on. For 1,876 procedures or more, the payment is 64 percent of the full price. This scale is not effective in controlling costs since only one hospital reached this volume with any single sick fund. It should be noted that there is no overt indication of existing queues for cardiac procedures after the introduction of capping. However, this question of waiting time has not been formally examined.

Two further attempts at limitation of reimbursement for cardiac procedures are of particular interest. First, percutaneous coronary revascularization is reimbursed the same amount with and without stenting. This should have served as a disincentive for rapid diffusion of stent technology. However, anecdotal evidence suggests that there has been wide-scale adoption of stenting by invasive cardiologists in Israel (A. Battler, president, Israel Cardiology Society, personal communication, 1998). Second, ReoPro (a costly new platelet glycoprotein IIb/IIIa receptor inhibitor) initially indicated in high-risk PTCA and stenting, was introduced in 1997. Originally, there was no additional reimbursement for ReoPro. Nevertheless, there was a rapid diffusion of this drug, with about 1,000 patients treated the first year, representing 10–15 percent of all PTCAs done. In 1998, the MOH decided to reimburse this drug (following lobbying by the Israel Cardiology Association) to a capped level of 25 percent of all PTCAs performed.

Technology Regulation

In general, the establishment of a new department or medical unit (including catheterization clinics) or purchase of major capital equipment such as MRI must be authorized by the MOH. Authorization is granted based on actual geographical availability and demand (documented in a "Certificate of Need"). In departments that perform cardiac procedures, authorization of medical staffing (specialists) is required as well. Drugs must be approved by the MOH. Regulation of high-tech procedures, medical devices, and drugs by licensing or other direct administrative restrictions do not appear to have had a marked effect on technology diffusion in this country. Furthermore, there is little "microregulation" of technology by means such as utilization review. On the other hand, all providers (the sick funds, hospitals) have drug committees that attempt to regulate the use of expensive drugs. For example, streptokinase remains the predominant thrombolytic agent, whereas expensive alternatives such as r-tPA are reserved for patients in whom streptokinase is contraindicated.

Competition

Competition between providers exists but is based largely on reputation rather than on pricing, with no data available to consumers to substantiate differences in outcomes between hospitals. However, competition, fostered by the sick funds, has developed between hospitals in the price of services such as stress testing and outpatient specialist visits; secondary referrals for invasive procedures are probably being influenced by this policy. There is currently no price or package-of-basic-benefits competition among the sick funds, which operate under open enrollment. The National Insurance Institute allocates revenues to the sick funds on a per capita basis, with risk adjustment based on nine age groups. However, the sick funds differ slightly in the copayment that they require for outpatient services (there are no copayments for inpatient services), although all copayments are low. There is emerging competition on supplemental insurance. And sick funds compete on the facilities they offer and on issues such as ease of access to specialists.

Other Incentives for Technology Adoption and Use

Physicians are either employed by a sick fund on a salary or they contract with one or more on a capitated basis. During the last year, a capping of expenditures was introduced at the district level by the General Sick Fund. This new constraint is intended to limit the services purchased outside the GSF, for instance from hospital outpatient clinics. Most invasive cardiologists work exclusively in hospitals. Referral within the sick fund to less invasive cardiologists outside the hospitals thereby introduces a gatekeeping process in the GSF that may decrease the number of referrals for catheterization.

Israel has one of the highest ratios of physicians per population, particularly considering its young age structure. In 1993, there were 4.6 physicians per 1,000 population, 38 percent of whom were specialists. Of the specialists, 14 percent were internists; 3 percent were cardiologists and 0.6 percent were cardiothoracic surgeons (*Medical Professions in Israel* 1993). At the beginning of 1998, Israel had 402 registered board certified cardiologists (6.8 per 100,000 population) (A. Battler, personal communication, 1998) and in 1997, 77 registered cardiothoracic surgeons (1.3 per 100,000) (*Health in Israel* 1996). The actual number of active specialists in these fields is smaller, however, as retirees and those abroad are also counted. For example, the rates for cardiologists and surgeons below age 65 were about 5.8 and 1.1 per 100,000, respectively (*Health in Israel* 1996). We are unaware of planned regulation of the supply of physicians by the MOH in accord with predicted need or demand. For example the number of cardiac surgeons is predicted to increase by about 50 percent by the year 2005 (Lauffer 1997), despite a reduction in the absolute number of CABG procedures in Israel from 1994 to 1997, reflecting a change in practice patterns. The influential Israel Medical Association (IMA) controls the training and licensing of specialists and has strong bargaining power with the government and the sick funds. For example, the IMA succeeded in raising physicians' real wages by 65 percent between 1990 and 1995, in spite of the dramatic increase in the supply of physicians due to massive immigration from the former USSR.

In terms of medical culture, the Israeli public is increasingly critical of medical care, providers, and the medical establishment, as evidenced by enhanced media interest and increased litigation and costs of provider insurance. These factors may also have contributed to the recent passage of a law that defines patient rights and seeks to increase patient access to information concerning his or her own care; its effects have yet to be assessed. The IMA blocked attempts by the MOH to set and monitor practice guidelines and is currently publishing its own guidelines for various conditions including invasive cardiology. The IMA strongly opposes any comparison of outcomes between hospitals, a position to which the MOH has acquiesced. Therefore, Israelis do not have information available to make informed decisions in this regard.

Technological Change in Heart Attack Care in Israel

Data Sources

For the assessment of trends in treatment of heart attack in Israel, we use five data sources. These data sources are of three types: aggregate-level data on procedure use (type 1), individual-level data that are not linked across hospitalizations, that is, events or attacks (type 2), and fully linked longitudinal individual-level data, that is, persons (type 3).

Data from two sources both relate to invasive treatment of CHD overall, rather than AMI specifically. First, we use the Ministry of Health's centrally collected data on invasive cardiology procedures in the last decade, whereby each catheterization facility and cardiac surgery department reports on the overall number of procedures performed during a time period (I. Berlovitch, Medical Administration Division, MOH, unpublished data, revised 1998). A limitation of these data is the absence of stratification by age, sex, or place of residence of patients. In addition, we analyze the General Sick Fund database on procedures, which covered over 60 percent of the population of Israel (but 78 percent of the 65-plus age group) in 1996. This data source is valuable because it permits small-area analysis in provision of care (to assess inequality and appropriateness). However, it cannot as yet supply data on time trends. An additional limitation of this source is the possibility of selection bias, in that it may not be representative of the population of Israel. This source is also accessible as an individual-level longitudinally linked administrative file that links hospitalizations (currently without discharge diagnoses), procedures, day hospital, and hospital outpatient visits.

We also use two sources of data for our assessment of trends in care of AMI. First, we examine the results of two regional studies, conducted in 1987–89 and 1995. The Jerusalem AMI registry, since 1995, covers all hospitalized AMIs and in- and out-of-hospital CHD death for ages 25–74 in the population of the Jerusalem district served by the four general hospitals in west Jerusalem. The Arab population of east Jerusalem is not included since it is only partly served by these hospitals, and hence is underrepresented. Comparisons of the first six months of 1995 data can be made with a similar Jerusalem survey done in 1987–89 for first-MI patients ages 25–64, using WHO MONICA criteria. Although only first-AMI patients are included in the comparison, the 1995 data suggest that treatment was similar for first- and recurrent-AMI patients in this age group. The Jerusalem registry permits analysis of events (attacks, i.e., type 2 data) as well as longitudinal linkage across hospitalizations (type 3 data). Second, we present findings of a nationwide biennial two-month survey of admissions for AMI in all CCUs, initiated in 1990 by the Israel Society for the Prevention of Heart Attacks. The main limitation of this survey is the fact that about half of all AMI patients are admitted to internal medicine wards, thus limiting inference to a selected group of patients. However, this source is useful for assessing trends in CCU care and case fatality of AMI patients admitted to the CCU, by linkage with the National Population Register.

The national MOH Central Hospitalization Database is accessible as both a type 2 and a type 3 data source. It includes information on admission ward, in-hospital transfers, length of stay, procedures performed during the episode (and permits calculation of cumulative rates across repeated admissions), comorbidity assessed from the list of diagnoses, the incidence over time of selected diagnoses such as congestive heart failure (from the diagnosis list), in-hospital mortality, and, by linkage with the National Population Registry, cumulative mortality (the latter is currently being developed). Information on drug use, dates of procedures, and linkage with outpatient data are not available. This data set, established in 1993, is currently incomplete with an estimated 70 percent coverage of all admissions in 1994 and 80 percent in 1995. Reporting to this database has now become obligatory, which should increase completeness. The usefulness of this resource is dependent on the validity and correct order of diagnostic recording, the completeness of recording of procedures, and their stability over time. We make comparisons with previous hospitalization surveys done by the Central Bureau of Statistics (CBS) and the MOH in 1987 and 1990 for length of stay and in-hospital case fatality (type 2 data). Informativeness of these earlier surveys is compromised by the intentional absence of any patient identification that prevents data linkage. Longitudinal analysis of defined cohorts (type 3 data) was performed for invasive cardiological procedures and for assessing the prevalence and incidence of congestive heart failure.

Changes in High-Tech Care

We now consider invasive procedures in CHD patients: aggregate trends in overall CABG, catheterization, and PTCA use for coronary heart disease patients for which no age and sex breakdown is available (type 1 data).

CABG

At present, there are 15 facilities performing CABG in Israel. In 1987 there were 7 such facilities. Since 1988, the rate of CABG procedures performed increased three- or fourfold. In 1997, the rates were 94 per 100,000 for the entire population and 350 per 100,000 when the population aged 45 and over is used as the denominator and the total number of procedures as the numerator (this latter figure is a slight overestimate due to the small proportion of procedures performed in those under age 45) (fig. 19.2). There were four distinctive subperiods: 1985–88, 1989–91, 1992–94, and 1995 on. From 1985 to 1988 the rate of CABG was approximately constant at 29–34 per 100,000. Due to

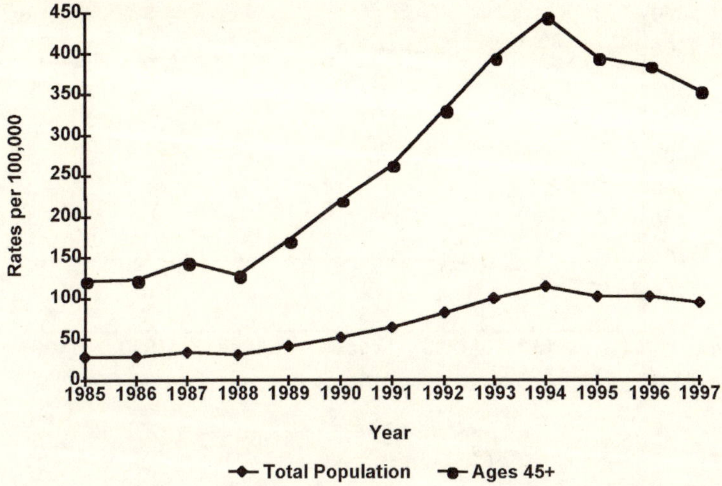

Fig. 19.2. CABG procedures per 1,000, Israel, 1985–97

public pressure to reduce waiting times, in 1989 the MOH started to reimburse hospitals and the relevant staff at higher rates for afternoon sessions, with striking results. In mid-1990, a prospective payment system was introduced, with the price set at an attractive level. The rate of CABG continued to increase until 1994. During the period 1989–94, the rate of CABG per 100,000 Israelis increased on average by 25 percent annually. From a peak of 113 per 100,000 in 1994, the rate of CABG per population decreased by 6 percent annually. Possible additional explanations for these substantial changes over time will be addressed below.

Diagnostic Catheterization

This category includes only angiographic procedures in which no revascularization was performed. At present there are 21 cardiac clinics in Israel licensed to perform catheterization. The rate of diagnostic catheterization per capita doubled between 1991 and 1997 and stood at 409 procedures per 100,000 population or 1530 procedures per 100,000 individuals aged 45 and over in 1997 (fig. 19.3). Although there are no comparable national data available on the number of procedures performed prior to 1991, we speculate that the pattern resembles that

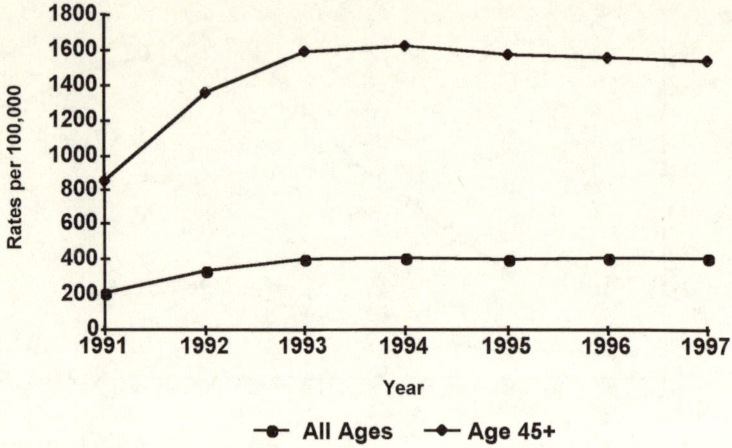

Fig. 19.3. Diagnostic catheterization per 100,000, Israel, 1991–97

found for CABG. After a sharp increase of 63 percent in 1992 following introduction of the attractive prospective payment, and a continued increase to 1994, the rates per population remained steady since 1994 and even declined slightly when computed for ages 45 and over. Part of this stability and decline may be attributed to the increased proportion of catheterizations that end up as a PTCA procedure and are tallied there.

PTCA

The rate of PTCA increased on average by 23 percent annually between 1991 and 1997 (fig. 19.4). Between 1991 and 1994 the rate almost tripled, increasing from 46 to 121 per 100,000. The rate of increase declined after 1994, with a sharper increase evident in 1997 versus the previous year (possibly related to the wide-scale adoption of stenting), for an average annual rate of growth of 7 percent. The 1997 rates were 148 per 100,000 population or 550 per 100,000 individuals aged 45 and over. Here again, no comparable data are readily available for the period prior to 1991.

The ratio of PTCA to CABG has been changing. While in early years CABG was a more popular procedure than PTCA, by 1993 the rates were equal, and subsequently the use of PTCA increasingly

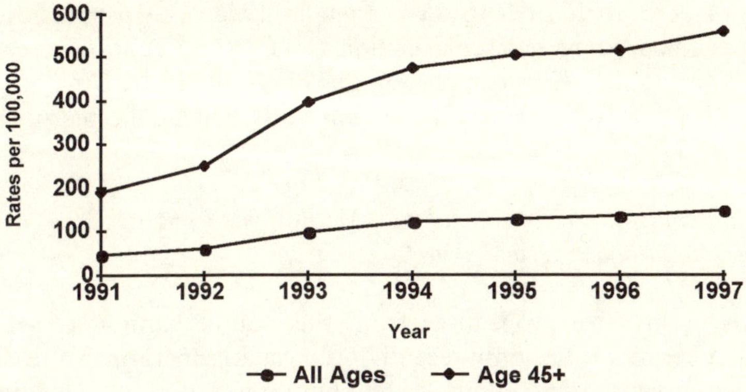

Fig. 19.4. PTCA per 100,000, Israel, 1991–97

exceeded that of CABG. All coronary angiographies in Israel are performed solely by cardiologists, who also make the decision as to revascularization using PTCA or referral to CABG. Clearly these specialists play a crucial role in determining the relative frequency of these often competing procedures. Therefore, while the rate of CABG declined from 1994 onward, the overall rate of revascularization remained more or less constant, with PTCA claiming an increasingly dominant role. The ratio of PTCA to CABG changed from 0.73 in 1991 to 1.58 in 1997.

We now analyze the use of invasive procedures for AMI admissions (during their hospital stay) with the data in the Jerusalem registry and the periodic national CCU survey (type 2 data). Among first-AMI patients ages 25–64 hospitalized in Jerusalem, the proportion undergoing diagnostic catheterization (coronary angiography) alone was similar in 1987–89 and the first half of 1995 (21 percent and 23 percent) (table 19.1b). However, the in-hospital proportion of revascularization doubled, increasing from 22 percent to 41 percent. Information not in the table shows that only 2 percent of first-MI patients received a stent during their hospitalization during the first semester of 1995, and only 4 percent of patients underwent primary PTCA. (Subsequently, stenting has become very frequent in Jerusalem.) Part b of the table presents results from the periodic national CCU survey, which showed a high rate of growth in procedure use in CCUs. Among AMI patients in CCUs nationwide, the rate of diagnostic catheterization increased from 14 percent in 1990 to 35 percent in 1996. The proportion of patients undergoing revascularization (PTCA or CABG) increased from 3 percent in 1990 to 26 percent in 1996 (table 19.1). Data on primary PTCA, as yet unavailable, are currently being collected nationally in CCUs.

Longitudinal Analysis of Individual AMI Patients from the MOH Database (type 3 data)

Trends in invasive procedures from this source cannot as yet be assessed because it has only recently been established; for this reason, we relate briefly to the follow-up data but do not display the findings. We constructed a cohort of AMI patients. An index admission of AMI was defined as the first admission of a patient in 1994 (n = 7,592) and 1995 (n = 7,919) and excluded patients with length of stay of less than 3 days if released home. There was a strong inverse association with age in the frequency of invasive procedures during the index hospitalization, and at 90 days and 365 days postdischarge (data not shown). The proportion of patients who underwent an invasive procedure during the index admission in 1995 and during a one year follow-up was substantially larger in those admitted to a CCU than in those admitted to an internal medicine ward, taking account of age differences. This

TABLE 19.1. Use of Intensive Procedures during Hospitalization for AMI, 1987–96

Year	A. CCU Admissions Receiving Intensive Procedures		
	N	Catheterization (%)	PTCA or CABG (%)
1990	413	14	3
1992	941	22	10
1994	999	29	18
1996	923	35	26
	B. Share of Nonelderly in Jerusalem Receiving Intensive Procedures (%)		
	Catheterization	PTCA	CABG
1987–89	21	22	0.3
1995	23	37	4

Sources: Part A: Israel Society for the Prevention of Heart Attacks; part B: Jerusalem MI registry, Israel Center for Disease Control.

held also for the proportion of revascularization procedures. Use of stents was extremely unusual in 1994 and 1995, confirming the finding in the Jerusalem registry. Stenting has subsequently proliferated rapidly and at present is estimated at about half of all PTCA (A. Battler, personal communication, 1998). This rapid diffusion is consistent with an international change in practice whereby coronary stenting has been adopted as the main approach for percutaneous coronary revascularization (Topol 1995). Stenting has been demonstrated to be superior to balloon angioplasty in terms of reduced need for coronary revascularization, but has not proved preferable with respect to the main outcomes: myocardial infarction and death.

Assessing the share of AMI patients admitted to CCUs versus internal medicine wards is important, largely because nonadmission to a CCU may result in suboptimal care of a subset of patients. Between 1977 and 1996, CCU beds per capita increased by 27 percent (*Hospitals and Day Care Units* 1997). Israel has 25 functioning CCUs. CCU days per capita increased by 41 percent (to 12.8 days per 1000), and admissions per capita nearly doubled to 4.3 per 1000. Length of stay in the CCUs decreased from 3.9 days in 1977 to 2.9 days in 1996. In 1997, there were 255 licensed CCU beds, or 0.18 beds per 1,000 population aged 45 and over. In comparison internal medicine beds per capita decreased by 20 percent between 1975 and 1995. Inpatient days per capita decreased by 5 percent, admissions per capita increased by 84 percent, and average length of stay decreased by almost 50 percent. In 1997, there were 2.5 internal medicine beds per 1,000 population aged 45 and over. There was, however, significant geographical variation in these rates.

Based on the MOH Central Hospitalization Database for 1995, less than half of all the AMI admissions (total n = 8,360) were initially to the CCU. There is a very strong inverse association of admission rates with age and a consistently lower proportion of women with AMI admitted to the CCU than men in every age group (fig. 19.5). Since this policy may influence patient outcomes, it becomes necessary to study the characteristics and determinants of CCU versus internal medicine admissions in Israel. Furthermore the overall use of CCU beds needs to be evaluated. The MOH is considering a prospective ("DRG") price for AMI that stipulates admission to the CCU with increased reimbursement. One result of such a change could be an effect on the current balance between ICD codes 410 (AMI) and 411 (other acute ischemic events, unstable angina), with a shift to preferential 410 labeling.

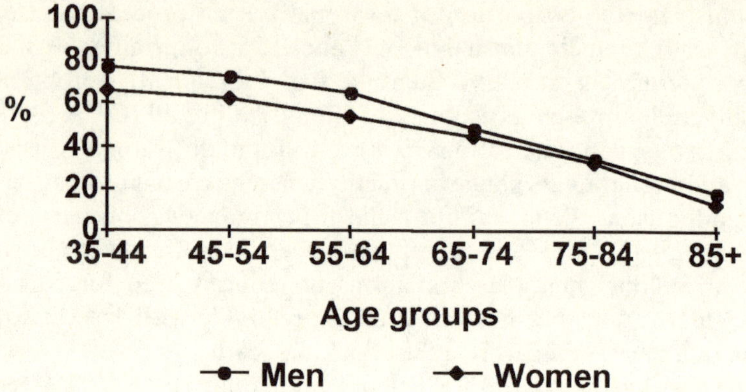

Fig. 19.5. Share of AMI patients admitted to intensive coronary care, 1995

Changes in Low-Tech Care

We assessed use of drugs and other low-tech services for individual AMI admissions in the periodic national CCU survey and the Jerusalem studies.

Drugs

The national CCU survey of AMI patients (table 19.2a) shows that the use of aspirin, beta-blockers, ACE inhibitors, and nitrates increased dramatically between 1992 and 1996. The use of calcium channel blockers remained low and fairly constant. The use of thrombolysis has increased from 35 percent in 1990 to 52 percent in 1996. The Jerusalem studies suggest that similar changes have occurred among first-AMI nonelderly patients hospitalized in Jerusalem (table 19.2b). A marked and rapid change in medical management occurred between 1987 to 1989 following reports of major clinical trials at meetings and in widely circulated journals. There was a rapid diffusion of thrombolysis into clinical practice; 37 percent of all patients received this therapy in 1987. This proportion increased to 57 percent in 1989 and remained constant (54 percent) in 1995. The predominant agent used was streptokinase. Aspirin was adopted rapidly; at discharge, 53 percent of the patients received aspirin in 1987, 81 percent in 1989, and 94 percent in 1995. In 1987–89, upon discharge, 4 percent received ACE inhibitors, and in 1987 24 percent received beta-blockers. By 1995, the respective rates were 30 percent and 65 percent. The use of calcium channel blockers decreased from 67 percent in 1987 to 25 percent in 1995.

Cardiac Rehabilitation

Cardiac rehabilitation provides another example of low-tech care that may have important implications for patients' quality of life. Between 1985 and 1987 there were no formal facilities for cardiac rehabilitation in Jerusalem; 7 percent of patients reported participation in a program. A unit attached to one of the city hospitals opened a broad program in 1994, whereas another developed a small external program in 1993. Patients are required by the sick funds to participate with out-of-pocket copayments. In the first half of 1995 only 16 percent of patients were referred at discharge for rehabilitation.

Small-Area Geographic Variation: Inequalities and Appropriateness of Care

Small-area variation indicating differences in care provided to basically similar patients is well recognized in all medical services. This reflects different practice styles, expertise and skills, population needs, and availability of services. Such differences are found even in a small country like Israel. Table 19.3 shows the rates of cardiac procedures in

TABLE 19.2. Use of Thrombolysis and Cardiac Drugs in AMI Patients, 1987–96

Year	*N*	Thrombolysis (%)	Aspirin (%)	Beta-Blockers (%)	ACE Inhibitors (%)	Ca-Blockers (%)	Nitrates (%)
	A. CCU Admissions Receiving Thrombolysis or Drug Treatment						
1992	941	44	72	31	19	17	55
1994	999	44	83	43	31	22	80
1996	923	52	89	57	48	16	78
	B. Share of Nonelderly in Jerusalem Receiving Thrombolysis or Drug Treatment (%)						
1987		37	53	24		67	
1989		57	81	39	4	38	
1995		54	94	65	30	25	

Sources: Part A: Israel Society for the Prevention of Heart Attacks; Part B: Jerusalem MI registry, ICDDC.

Note: Cardiac drugs used at discharge.

1994 in eight geographical districts of the General Sick Fund, the largest Israeli sick fund, covering over 60 percent of the population. For PTCA, for example, the estimated annual rates vary from 155 procedures per 100,000 insurees above age 45 per month in the southern district to about 615 per 100,000 in the Jerusalem district.

Consequences of Changes in Heart Attack Care in Israel

To examine the consequences of these changes in heart attack care, we use information from three sources. First, we examine overall trends in CHD mortality based on Central Bureau of Statistics death records. Second, we investigate trends in case fatality based on the national CCU survey, the Jerusalem AMI registry, and the MOH and CBS hospitalization surveys. Third, we present an analysis of congestive heart failure (CHF), a complication of AMI, based on the MOH Hospitalization Database.

Changes in Health Outcomes for AMI Patients

CHD Mortality Trends: Central Bureau of Statistics Death Records

Mortality attributed to acute MI (ICD8, in use in Israel up to 1978, code 410, and ICD9, in use from 1979, code 410] declined steeply between 1969 and 1994, evident in both sexes and in Jews and Arabs (*Medical Professions in Israel* 1993). On the face of it this appears

TABLE 19.3. Intensive Procedure Rates per 100,000 Insurees Aged 45 or Over by Geographic District, the General Sick Fund, January–August 1994

District	Catheterization	PTCA	Total	Ratio Catheterization/PTCA
Jerusalem	90.9	51.3	142.2	1.77
Dan	98.0	44.9	142.9	2.18
Tel Aviv	79.1	27.2	106.3	2.91
Haifa	88.2	27.9	116.1	3.16
Sharon	90.6	39.7	130.3	2.28
North	98.2	15.4	113.6	6.38
Center	85.2	22.7	107.9	3.75
South	69.0	13.0	82.0	5.31

Source: Dr. Gad Rennert, unpublished data.

entirely consistent with trends in case fatality of acute MI patients (see below). On the other hand, mortality attributed to other coronary heart disease categories (ICD 411–414) has shown a different pattern with a precipitous decline between 1978 and 1979–80 when the ICD9 was adopted, and a trend toward increase thereafter, particularly in the 1990s. The drop between 1978 and 1979 is likely to reflect coding artifacts, in particular the transfer of ASHD (atherosclerotic heart disease) from ICD8 412 to ICD9 429. To overcome possible bias due to coding inconsistency over time an analysis of all heart disease mortality (ICD 398–390, 402, 404–429) showed a decline up to 1990 with a flattening and increase thereafter (*Medical Professions in Israel* 1993). We performed an age-specific analysis of CHD mortality (ICD 410–414) between 1984 and 1994; this revealed an increase in the 1990s that was limited largely to the 75-and-over age group and was consistent in the various ethnic groupings and regions of the country. Age-specific analysis of ICD 410 and ICD 411–414 shows a decline in 410-mortality in both sexes in all age groups between 1984 and 1994, whereas the pattern for 411–414 is quite different, with an increase evident among patients aged 55–74 and particularly among those aged 75 and over.

Whether these discrepant findings between ICD 410 and 411–414 reflect coding practices or real changes in patterns of CHD mortality remains to be answered. The increase in overall CHD mortality (ICD 410–414) in the 1990s is reflected also in overall heart disease mortality. The findings for ICD 410 (AMI) are consistent with improved acute coronary care, but may also relate to reduced incidence of AMI (which cannot be assessed due to absence of systematic data over time), and to the possibility of a reduced lethality of acute MI due to a postulated change in the natural history of the disease (a reduced tendency to lethal arrhythmias would be a potential explanation). The decline in case fatality (see below) attributed to use of efficacious therapies such as thrombolysis may have led to an increase in the prevalence of CHD and of congestive heart failure among patients in whom mortality early after MI was averted. This suggestion would be consistent with the divergent patterns of ICD 410 and 411–414 mortality, more evident in the 1990s, and with the age association described. On the other hand, the increase in CHD mortality consistent across regions (in which effective acute and chronic coronary care was unlikely to have been equally delivered) and across ethnic groups in the 1990s supports an interpretation of a consistent bias in death notification recording or coding.

Case Fatality: The Jerusalem AMI Registry, the National CCU Survey, and the MOH and CBS Hospitalization Surveys

According to results from the Jerusalem AMI registry for AMI cases between the ages of 25 and 74, prehospital case fatality appears to be exceptionally low in Jerusalem, about 15 percent in 1995 versus a median of 32 percent (range 18–49 percent in women and 23–42 percent in men) recorded in 29 MONICA centers between 1985 and 1990 (Chambless et al. 1997). Explanation of this finding remains elusive, but may relate to a postulated reduced susceptibility in the Jerusalem population to lethal arrhythmias, rather than greater success in prehospital treatment. The determinants of these differences in early mortality, both environmental and genetic, remain to be unraveled.

Similar improvements in mortality are present in the CBS-MOH surveys of 1987 and 1990 and the MOH Central Hospitalization Database (1994–95). For this comparison patients were included if an AMI code appeared first in the list of diagnoses. In both sexes there has been a consistent reduction in age-adjusted in-hospital case fatality of AMI patients from 14.2 percent to 9.9 percent in men and from 18.0 percent to 12.2 percent in women. The reduction was evident in both the 25–64 and 65-and-over age groups, with a steeper rate of decline in the younger age group (table 19.4a). Similar results from the national CCU survey show that case fatality in patients admitted to the CCU has declined consistently between 1990 and 1996 (table 19.4b). Seven-day mortality was reduced from 10.2 percent to 6.3 percent and one-year mortality from 22.5 percent to 13.8 percent.

At all ages, women experienced higher case fatality than men. This was evident in those admitted to internal medicine and even more so in those admitted to the CCU. Women admitted to the CCU had a higher mortality than those admitted to internal medicine. This difference was relatively greater than for men, suggesting a stronger selection on severity in decisions as to where to admit women, who are less likely to be admitted to the CCU than men (see above).

It is of interest that no sex differences were evident for in-hospital mortality due to unstable angina (ICD 411) in 1994. In our population, as in many others, the ratio of discharge diagnoses of AMI to unstable angina is higher among men than women below age 75. This could well reflect differences in the presentation of acute CHD between the sexes and may play a role in decisions as to admission to the CCU or internal medicine divisions.

Sequelae of AMI: Assessment of Quality of Life by Measures of Cardiac Complications after an AMI Using the MOH Hospitalization Database (type 3 data)

Here we assess the potential usefulness of a measure derived from an administrative data set—the incidence of a subsequent discharge diagnosis of congestive heart failure in a defined cohort of AMI patients derived from the MOH database. This is of interest in light of the altered trend in CHD mortality in the 1990s, evident particularly in the elderly (aged 75 and over), which may relate to increasing proportions of patients with CHF among AMI survivors.

We used discharge diagnoses of CHF as a measure of complications due to AMI in the 1994 cohort of AMI patients who survived the index admission. We analyzed the prevalence of CHF recorded anywhere in the list of discharge diagnoses, and its incidence among AMI patients free of a CHF diagnosis upon discharge. Time trends in this measure cannot currently be assessed. Expectedly, the prevalence and incidence of CHF was strongly age dependent. The prevalence of CHF at index discharge was higher in women than men in all age groups, consistent with their increased case fatality. The incidence of CHF among women

TABLE 19.4. Case Fatality of AMI Patients in Israel (%)

	A. In hospital		
Year	Men	Women	Total
1987	14.2	18.0	15.5
1990	11.3	15.6	12.8
1994	9.8	13.3	11.2
1995	9.9	12.2	10.7
	B. All-Cause Mortality[a]		
	7 Day	30 Day	365 Day
1990	10.2	16.5	22.5
1992	8.8	13.5	19.1
1994	7.7	12.1	19.0
1996	6.3	9.5	13.8

Sources: Part A: CBS-MOH and MOH hospitalization databases, primary diagnosis of AMI, age adjusted; Part B: Israel Society for the Prevention of Heart Attacks.

[a]AMI patients admitted to CCU only.

initially admitted to the CCU was higher than in men, suggesting the selection of more severe cases in women relative to men (or alternatively, a gender difference in the natural history of the disease).

The prevalence of CHF was greater among AMI patients admitted to internal medicine than the CCU in both sexes and at all ages. The incidence of CHF after index discharge tended to be higher in those admitted initially to internal medicine, except for the youngest (25–44), and the oldest (85 and over) age groups. One wonders whether this may reflect differences in management or differences in the characteristics of patients admitted to the CCU versus internal medicine (i.e., patient selection).

Changes in Medical Expenditures and Resource Use

Changes in the financing of the Israeli health care system—from an historically regulated per diem reimbursement system, to a partially prospectively budgeted one—limit one's ability to obtain diagnosis- or procedure-specific expenditure data. For the analysis in this section we used two rough indicators of the trends in resource use. The first is the length of stay in-hospital (LOS). This is clearly a crude indicator, since hospitalization days are not homogenous with respect to resource use, and furthermore, LOS is sensitive to how hospitals are reimbursed: per diem reimbursement encourages longer stays, while prospective payment (introduced in July 1990) should induce shorter stays. Change in medical practice of course also plays a major role, with a trend toward earlier discharge of patients (as evident in non-AMI internal medicine patients) ostensibly being offset by extension of stay due to an increase in invasive procedures toward the end of the episode. The second indicator is the level of reimbursement. Although the per diem and the per-case prospective reimbursement rates regulated by the MOH are based on some cost calculation (and are updated regularly), they cannot reflect actual expenditures.

Trends in LOS are assessed for the period between 1987 and 1995 for acute MI patients, defined as those in whom the diagnosis appeared at the top of the list of discharge diagnoses. Both survivors and in-hospital deaths are included in the calculations. The sources are the CBS-MOS 1987 and 1990 surveys and the MOS Hospitalization Database for 1994 and 1995.

The age-adjusted mean LOS of AMI patients was 8.2 days in 1987, 8.5 days in 1990, 8.7 days in 1994, and 8.7 days in 1995, for a 6 percent increase in LOS over the nine years. This analysis probably slightly underestimates the increase in LOS because case fatality has declined and fatal MI is associated with shorter LOS.

Second, for the years after the "prospective" per-procedure reimbursement was implemented, table 19.5 presents the trends in expenditures on CABG, PTCA, diagnostic catheterization, and in total for these procedures. The average real reimbursement (the regulated rates) in 1995 U.S. dollars in PPP terms for all three procedures has increased on average by 5 percent annually. As was discussed above, the volume of procedures increased considerably during 1991–94. The number of CABGs increased on average by 25 percent annually, PTCAs by 43 percent, and diagnostic catheterization by 32 percent. The combined effect resulted in an average annual growth in real expenditures of 31 percent on CABG, 50 percent on PTCA, and 41 percent on diagnostic catheterization. Overall real expenditures on these cardiac procedures increased by 40 percent annually during this period. During 1995–97 the rate of change in the volume of these procedures declined markedly. The number of PTCAs continued to increase at an annual rate of 11 percent, and real average reimbursement increased by 3 percent annually (which was the rate of increase in the prospective rates of CABG and catheterizations as well). The result was a 14 percent average annual increase in real total expenditures on PTCA. The volume of CABG declined on average by 3 percent annually, and that of diagnostic catheterization increased by 3 percent annually. Real expenditures on CABG remained constant on average, and on catheterization increased by 6 percent annually. Total expenditures on these three procedures increased by 5 percent annually during 1995–97.

Another measure of the resources used by cardiac technology is the share of total expenditures accounted for by coronary procedures undertaken in internal medicine divisions (including, among others, internal medicine and cardiology wards). The total reimbursement for stays in the internal medicine divisions was calculated by multiplying total hospitalization days by the per diem rate. The results indicate a steep increase in this share from 22 percent in 1991 to 35 percent in 1994. Subsequently, the share leveled off and decreased slightly to 33 percent in 1996 (fig. 19.6).

Discussion: The Effects of Financial and Regulatory Incentives on Technological Change in Heart Attack Care

Effects on Technological Change

Technological change, indicated in this chapter by the trend in the volume of high- and low-tech cardiac procedures, appears to have been

TABLE 19.5. Trends in Resource Use for Cardiac Procedures

	CABG			PTCA			Catheterization			Total Payment for Cardiac Procedures
	N	Payment Per Case	Total	*N*	Payment Per Case	Total	*N*	Payment Per Case	Total	
1991	3,164	9,486	30,014,177	2,295	4,176	9,582,904	10,200	1,694	17,313,579	56,910,660
1992	4,208	10,150	42,711,200	3,190	4,343	13,854,170	17,272	1,813	31,314,136	87,879,506
1993	5,218	10,049	52,435,682	5,264	4,560	24,003,840	21,072	1,939	40,858,608	117,298,130
1994	6,105	11,355	69,322,275	6,527	5,153	33,633,631	22,336	2,192	48,960,512	151,916,418
1995	5,678	12,263	69,629,314	7,245	5,565	40,318,425	22,559	2,367	53,397,153	163,344,892
1996	5,735	12,386	71,033,710	7,752	5,621	43,573,992	23,236	2,391	55,557,276	170,164,978
1997	5,552	12,396	68,822,325	8,753	5,618	49,175,502	24,120	2,398	57,829,837	175,827,664

Note: Payment figures are 1995 U.S. dollars converted at PPP rates.

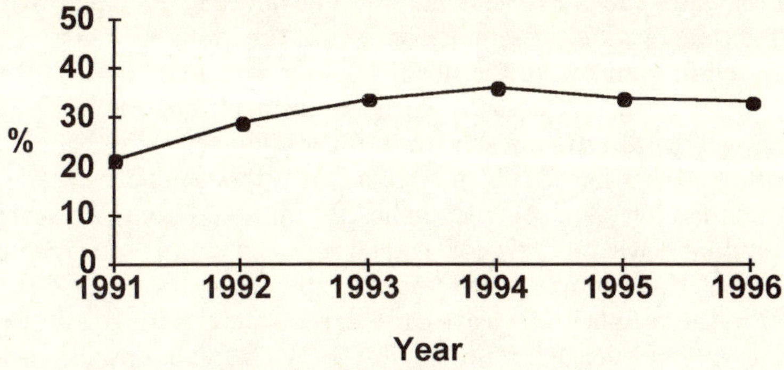

Fig. 19.6. Expenditures on invasive cardiology as share of total expenditures on internal medicine

strongly affected by administrative regulations. Two such regulatory actions appear to have shaped the trend in volume of cardiac procedures: the campaign to shorten waiting lists in 1989, followed by the introduction of "prospective" payment for these procedures in 1990. Possible effects of the third major action, the capping regulation enacted in 1995, are less obvious.

The 1989 campaign introduced financial incentives directly to the operating medical staff to increase the number of procedures performed. The 1990 prospective payments were instituted in order to enhance efficient use of hospital production capacity for specified procedures. By replacing per diem payment by prospective reimbursement, the MOS hoped to shorten length of stay. The levels of the prospective rates for cardiac procedures were very attractive, creating financial incentives for hospital management to increase the number of procedures performed. A reasonable interpretation and partial explanation is that the dramatic increase in volume that resulted from the campaign to shorten queues in 1989 was thus intensified, satisfying both the medical staff and the hospital administrators.

The main reason for the introduction of capping on hospitals' activities in 1995 was to limit national (hospitalization) expenditures and to help the sick funds to achieve financial stability. The general capping coincided with a sharp decline in the rate of increase in the volume of cardiac procedures performed during 1995–96. Capping may have played a role, but alternative or complementary explanations are equally tenable. For example, PTCA thrived again in 1997 under the same regulatory regimen. This may well have been stimulated by the wider acceptance and dissemination of stenting, notwithstanding the lack of reimbursement for the stents.

Several questions deserve further consideration. First, a more elaborated identification of the effect of the administrative changes on technology use is needed. In particular, attempts should be made to separate this effect from changes in health status and needs; however it is questionable whether this goal can be achieved in time-series ecological studies. For example, an alternative explanation for the 1995 leveling off in the volume of invasive cardiac procedures performed is simply that the prevalence pool of eligible patients created by the earlier lower volume of performance had been exhausted, and that a steady state had more or less been achieved between incidence and intervention. Second, little is known about how technology adoption is actually decided upon at the hospital level. It would be interesting to clarify this decision-making process and to relate it to hospital ownership, size, geographical location, academic status, relative bargaining power of the management versus the professional staff, and the level of market competition. Third, clearly, some of the regulatory acts come in response to the actual under- (or over-) use of technology. The shortening waiting lists for cardiac procedures in 1989 is an example. Further research should explore the implications of the possible endogeneity of the regulation on its effect on use.

Implications for Changes in Resource Use and Health Outcomes

Over the last decade, national expenditure on cardiac procedures has increased dramatically. Virtually all of that growth can be attributed to the technology diffusion and increasing quantities rather than to price inflation. The fundamental tension between satisfying individual needs and demand and limited national resources is fully reflected here. A central issue is the question of equity in the distribution of technological changes and its implications for population subgroups. The dramatic variation in availability and use of technology over geographical districts, age groups, and between men and women reported above underlines the need to further explore these differences, their causes and implications.

Two major and ostensibly conflicting trends in outcome are (1) the reduced AMI case fatality, supported by the MOH-CBS comparison, the national CCU survey, and additional sources (Behar et al. 1995;

Gottlieb et al. 1997), as well as the long-term reduction in mortality attributed to AMI (ICD code 410) and (2) increased overall CHD mortality, attributed to ICD 411–414, on the other. Whether the latter is a real finding or an artifact is a high-priority question in Israel. The phenomenon may result from an increasing prevalence of chronic ischemic heart disease, with an increase in chronic sequelae of AMI (namely congestive heart failure) relating to a postponement of acute phase mortality, or it may result from the misclassification bias of death notifications and coding. This currently unresolved issue has substantial consequences for health services and technology evaluation. Assessment of prevalence and incidence of congestive heart failure (apparently frequent in AMI patients in Israel), prevalence of angina, and other quality of life measures are relevant in this regard and will require further research.

The limitations of ecologic time-series studies in deriving cause-effect inferences are well recognized. To what extent technological change (both "low" and "high" tech) has actually affected health outcomes is difficult to determine. Such associations should be inferred largely from clinical trials that have demonstrated efficacy (e.g., thrombolytic therapy, aspirin, beta-blockers, ACE inhibitors) during the acute phase and subsequently in the community. The role that increased stenting and use of platelet glycoprotein IIb/IIIa blockade may play and how their diffusion is and will be affected by regulatory measures are topics worth pursuing. In light of recent evidence of the efficacy of these agents in reducing subsequent AMI and deaths, particularly when used in conjunction with stenting but also with balloon angioplasty (EPISTENT Investigators 1998), a major practice shift is likely whereby blockade will become standard treatment (Stables 1998). Wide-scale adoption of this treatment (likely to occur before further confirmation of the finding) will again lead to pressure to alter regulatory policy and to lift the newly imposed cap on these agents in Israel; immediate costs will again rise, although the long-term benefit may be substantial.

Concerning an important recent development in "low tech" care, we expect a substantial increase in the use of statins in CHD patients in general and in AMI patients after discharge. Here initiation of treatment and its persistence is more likely to be in the hands of primary care practitioners with whom the patients are registered than with the cardiologists. AMI patients do however return to the cardiology outpatient clinics of the hospitals from which they were discharged, at least for an initial clinic visit. Use of statins in CHD patients could have a substantial impact on patient outcomes. Diffusion of these drugs should be an informative topic for further collaborative evaluation.

Finally, the admission of a substantial proportion of AMI patients in Israel to internal medicine wards rather than CCUs, the apparent discrimination against women and the elderly in this regard, and the use of existing CCU beds will require attention. International comparisons of the latter, including the proportion of CCU beds per population, would be informative. It is a seeming anomaly that in a country that so rapidly and extensively embraces technological innovation, adoption of one of the first high-tech innovations in acute coronary care remains underused. Although Israel has experienced a steep reduction in in-hospital case fatality, treatment for a large proportion of AMI patients remains, on the face of it, suboptimal. More cost-effective solutions, in particular intermediate care facilities with expert monitoring and rapid access to trained personnel, might permit the achievement of health outcome improvements with more limited capital and operating expenditures.

Note

We thank Dr. I. Berlowitch for the Ministry of Health aggregate data on use of invasive coronary procedures, Professor S. Behar, representing the Society for the Prevention of Heart Attacks, for making the national CCU survey data available, and Dr. G. Rennert for access to the GSF (Kupat Holim Klalit) data on invasive cardiology.

References

Behar, S., U. Goldbourt, G. Barbash, and B. Modan. 1995. "Twenty-Five-Year Mortality Rate Decrease in Patients in Israel with a First Episode of Acute Myocardial Infarction." *American Heart Journal* 130:435–38.

Chambless, L., U. Keil, A. Dobson, M. Mahonen, K. Kuulasmaa, A. M. Rajakangas, H. Lowel, and H. Tunstall-Pedoe. 1997. "Population versus Clinical View of Case Fatality from Acute Coronary Heart Disease: Results from the WHO MONICA Project, 1985–1990." *Circulation* 96, no. 11: 3849–59.

EPISTENT Investigators. 1998. "Randomized Placebo-Controlled and Balloon-Angioplasty-Controlled Trial to Assess Safety of Coronary Stenting with Use of Platelet Glycoprotein-IIb/IIIa Blockade." *Lancet* 352, no. 9122: 87–92.

Gottlieb, S., U. Goldbourt, V. Boyko, G. Barbash, L. Mandelzweig, H. Reicher-Reiss, S. Stern, and S. Behar. 1997. "Improved Outcome of Elderly Patients (75 Years of Age) with Acute Myocardial Infarction from 1981–1983 to 1992–1994 in Israel." *Circulation* 95, no. 2: 342–50.

Health in Israel: Selected Data. 1996. Jerusalem: Israel Ministry of Health.

Hospitals and Day Care Units in Israel, 1996. 1997. Jerusalem: Israel Ministry of Health.

Israel Center for Disease Control. 1997. *The State of Health in Israel, 1997.* ICDC publication no. 202. Jerusalem: Israel Ministry of Health.

Lauffer, R. 1997. "Medical Manpower Planning in Israel: A Supply vs Demand Analysis of Cardiothoracic Surgeons." M.P.H. thesis, Hebrew University.

Medical Professions in Israel. 1993. Jerusalem: Israel Ministry of Health.

National Expenditure on Health, 1995. 1997. Jerusalem: Israel Central Bureau of Statistics.

Stables, R. H. 1998. "Routine Use of Abciximab in Coronary Stenting?" *Lancet* 352, no. 9122: 81–82.

Topol, E. J. 1995. "The Stentor and the Sea Change." *American Journal of Cardiology* 76, no. 4: 307–8.

CHAPTER 20

Conclusion

Mark B. McClellan and Daniel P. Kessler

In this book, 18 research teams from 15 countries have reviewed incentives for technological change in their health care system, and have presented representative, quantitative evidence on the trends in treatments and outcomes for heart attack patients that are associated with these health system characteristics. Here, we review some of the major findings across all of the chapters, and the implications for further comparative studies of the productivity of health care systems.

Major Findings

1. *Financial and regulatory incentives for technological change differ enormously across countries.* Table 20.1 summarizes differences in incentives for technological change in the six most important dimensions: the extent to which patients bear the cost of more intensive treatments, the generosity of payments to hospitals, the generosity of payments to physicians, the extent of "microregulation" of particular treatment decisions (e.g., through utilization review or gatekeeping), the extent of "macroregulation" of major investments in technology by health care organizations, and the extent of patient choice of health insurance plans (competition). As the table shows, many countries have correlated features across these dimensions. For example, countries with relatively stringent global budgets for hospital services often have global budgets (i.e., salaries) for physicians, strict macroregulation of the adoption of major technologies, and relatively little choice of providers and health plans. However, there are some exceptions. For example, Canadian provinces have global budgets for hospitals but some service-based payments for physicians, and some countries with relatively strict macroregulation of technologies also have microregulation. These large differences provide a potentially useful

foundation for careful cross-national comparisons of technological change and its consequences.

2. *Utilization of both high-tech and low-tech treatments for heart attack is increasing in virtually all countries.* Table 20.2 summarizes how the use of the three principal technologies studied in this book—cardiac catheterization, angioplasty, and bypass surgery—changed globally over the 1991–95 period. Table 20.2 divides countries into three categories, based on their rates of increase of technology use—no change/slow growth, intermediate growth, and rapid growth. Table 20.2 should be interpreted with caution. Even though the research teams made groundbreaking efforts to analyze large patient populations and utilization rates as consistently as possible, the quantitative results across countries are not likely to be fully comparable. First, some countries were not able to obtain data on the use of all of the three studied procedures for AMI patients only; these countries reported on procedure use per million population (these countries are noted in italics in the table). Second, among those countries reporting procedure use for AMI patients, the time base over which the procedure rate was measured differed in some cases. For example, some countries were not able to track patients after an initial hospitalization, and other countries were only able to report more limited follow-up periods (e.g., 30 days or 90 days, rather than one year, after the initial onset of illness). Third, the demographic base of patient populations was not always identical. For example, countries using MONICA data (such as Italy) focused on procedure use in the nonelderly, whereas other countries focused on procedure use in the elderly or in the population overall.

Although previous "macro" comparisons of technological capacity and some previous "micro" studies have provided complementary evidence (e.g., Tunstall-Pedoe et al. 2000), our results provide striking evidence of worldwide increases in the intensity of treatment for heart attack care. Even countries with quite low absolute rates of growth in high-tech procedure use in the mid-1990s increased the quantity of medical care for heart attack patients dramatically. For example, the number of heart attack patients in some regions in England receiving a revascularization procedure more than tripled in the 1990s, despite England's slow growth in percentage point terms relative to more technology-intensive countries (i.e., England started with a very low base rate). The Canadian provinces, which started from much higher base rates of high-tech procedure use, also expanded the use of intensive treatment despite relatively slow percentage growth rates. At the other

TABLE 20.1. National Differences in Economic and Regulatory Incentives for Technological Change in 1995

Type of Incentive	Strong Limit	Intermediate Limit	Weak Limit
Costs borne by patient	Substantial out-of-pocket payments: Japan Korea	Some out-of-pocket payments or significant optional private insurance sector with premiums borne directly by patients: Australia France Switzerland United States	Zero/very low patient payments for services: Belgium Canada Denmark Finland Israel Italy (for AMI patients) Sweden Taiwan United Kingdom
Generosity of payments to hospitals[a]	Fixed global budgets, more or less stringent: Canada[b] Denmark Finland[c] Sweden[c] United Kingdom	Some additional payments for the provision of more costly treatments: Australia[d] Belgium France[d] Israel Italy United States	Fee-for-service payments: Japan Korea Switzerland Taiwan Australia (private hospitals) France (private hospitals)
Generosity of payments to physicians[a]	Physicians are mainly salaried: Denmark (cardiovascular doctors) Finland France (public hospitals) Israel Italy Sweden United Kingdom	Some additional payments for the provision of more costly treatments: Australia United States Canada	Fee-for-service: Japan Korea Taiwan Belgium Australia (private hospitals) France (private hospitals) Switzerland

"Micro" technology regulation (mainly involves costly "high-tech" procedures, and potentially expensive patients)	Extensive reviews of individual treatment decisions: United States	Limited case-level review or "gatekeeping": Ontario, Canada (placement in bypass surgery queues) Denmark Israel United Kingdom	Little or no case-level review: Other countries
"Macro" technology regulation (includes regulation of physician supply)	Strict regulation: Canada United Kingdom	Intermediate regulation: Australia Belgium Denmark Finland France Sweden	Little regulation: Israel Italy Japan Korea Switzerland Taiwan United States
Choice and competition among insurance plans	No choice (universal insurance): Canada Denmark Finland Italy Sweden Taiwan United Kingdom	Limited choice (e.g., in supplemental coverage): Australia Belgium France Israel Japan Switzerland	Substantial choice: Korea United States

Note: Summary classification based on predominant incentives in each health care system in 1995.

[a]Both *level* of payments and *responsiveness* of payments to intensity of treatment may differ; this table focuses on responsiveness.

[b]Canadian provinces have varied in the extent to which their governments have expanded capacity for intensive treatments.

[c]Some districts have implemented DRG-like payments that provide additional revenues for supplying additional treatment.

[d]Has well-developed private hospital system, with relatively generous incentives for technological change, operating alongside public hospital system, with relatively strict incentives.

TABLE 20.2. Technological Change in Heart Attack Care: Trends in Intensive Cardiac Procedures, 1991–95

Type of Procedure	No Change/Slow Growth[a]	Intermediate Growth[b]	Rapid Growth[c]
Catheterization/ angiography	England; *Finland;* Quebec, Canada	*Denmark; France;* Manitoba, Canada;[d] Ontario, Canada; *Sweden*	Alberta, Canada;[d] Australia; *Israel;* Italy; Japan;[e] USA
PTCA	*Denmark;* England; *Finland;* Manitoba, Canada[d]	*Belgium; France* Quebec, Canada	Alberta, Canada;[d] Australia; *Israel;* Italy; Japan;[e] Korea,[e] USA
CABG	Alberta, Canada;[d] *France;* Japan[e] Korea;[e] England; Ontario, Canada; Quebec, Canada	Australia; *Belgium;* Manitoba, Canada;[d] USA	*Denmark;* Finland; *Israel;* Italy; Sweden

Note: Countries were divided into categories based on procedure growth rates for heart attack (AMI) patients if available. If procedure growth rates for AMI patients were not available, countries were divided into categories based on the total growth in procedures per million residents (italic font). An individual country may report differently across the three types of procedures (e.g., procedure growth rates for AMI patients for one procedure, total growth in procedures per million residents for another procedure, and no information for the third procedure). Time period used varies across countries but is always in the 1991–95 window.

[a]For catheterization and PTCA (CABG), no change/slow growth category includes countries with average annual procedure growth rates of less than 1.25 (0.5) percentage points per year for AMI patients; if linked data on AMI patients are not available, then category includes countries with rates less than 100 (50) procedures per million population per year.

[b]For catheterization and PTCA (CABG), intermediate growth category includes countries with average annual procedure growth rates of 1.25–1.75 (0.5–1) percentage points per year for AMI patients; if linked data on AMI patients are not available, then category includes countries with rates of 100–250 (50–100) procedures per million population per year.

[c]For catheterization and PTCA (CABG), rapid growth category includes countries with average annual procedure growth rates of greater than 1.75 (1) percentage points per year for AMI patients; if linked data on AMI patients are not available, then category includes countries with rates greater than 250 (100) procedures per million population per year.

[d]Growth rate may be nonrepresentative of technological change in province over a broader time period due to substantial nonrecurring changes in the health system during the study period.

[e]Classification should be interpreted with caution because the sample of hospitals on which the procedure rate is based may not be representative of hospitals in the country as a whole.

end of the spectrum, countries like Japan, Italy, Israel, and to a lesser extent the United States showed explosive growth in the use of both diagnostic and therapeutic procedures.

3. *There are enormous differences in patterns of technological change across countries, particularly for high-tech treatments.* Although the quantity of medical treatment expanded significantly virtually everywhere, we document substantial differences across countries. That is, although all countries have experienced substantial technological change, the nature and rate of technological change have differed greatly. As table 20.2 shows, the absolute differences in high-tech procedure use growth rates between rapid- and slow-growth countries amount to a factor of two or more, over at most a five-year period. For example, Australia reported annual average growth in one-year angioplasty for elderly AMI patients of approximately 2.6 percentage points per year over the 1991–94 period; the growth in the Australian nonelderly was even higher. By comparison, Ontario reported annual average 1992–94 growth in 180-day angioplasty rates for both elderly and nonelderly AMI patients of approximately 0.4 percentage points per year. In Finland, catheterization rates per capita were virtually flat, whereas in Israel, the per capita rate of catheterizations doubled over the 1991–94 period.

We also find substantial differences across countries in the type of revascularization procedures employed. Countries with the highest rates of high-tech procedure use at the start of the study period, such as Australia, the United States, Israel, and France, exhibited relatively more rapid growth in the use of angioplasty than in bypass surgery. This was in part due to the increasing use of primary angioplasty. Primary angioplasty involves performing a catheterization to identify the location of a coronary artery blockage, and then performing angioplasty to remove it, all within the 6- to 12-hour window after the heart attack. It requires the quick availability of a catheterization laboratory. Primary angioplasty has become quite widely used in the United States; to a lesser extent, it has also become widely used in countries like France that do not regulate the diffusion of angioplasty facilities extensively and that provide additional reimbursement for performing this treatment. Regionally, Asian countries exhibited much more growth in the use of angioplasty as opposed to bypass surgery, and Nordic countries exhibited much more growth in the use of bypass surgery as opposed to angioplasty. We return to the issue of the causes of these differences below.

As we explained in the introduction, the chapters did not detect systematic differences in the use of low-tech treatments. In part, this was due to less availability of relatively comparable information on trends in drug use for a large part of each country's population; this is an important area for further empirical investigation, and our findings here should be viewed as very preliminary. However, there were some important exceptions to the general lack of clear evidence of substantial differences in trends in drug therapies. In particular, use of drugs such as ACE inhibitors seems to have grown more rapidly in use in countries that had relatively larger increases in high-tech care. This may be because more use of relatively high-tech treatments like echocardiography are important for identifying milder cases of heart failure in which ACE inhibitor treatment is appropriate. We also find divergent trends in the use of thrombolytic drugs across countries. The goal of using thrombolytic drugs is to break down the blood clot responsible for the heart attack, restoring blood flow to the affected heart muscle before it dies. The higher-tech alternative to thrombolytics—primary angioplasty—has become an important substitute in countries like the United States that use primary angioplasty most heavily.

Finally, changes in the specific type of thrombolytic used have also differed across countries. In the United States, use of tissue plasminogen activator (tPA) has become widespread. This is a patented thrombolytic, which in some trials out of many has been shown to lead to slightly lower mortality than the much less expensive "generic" thrombolytics, streptokinase and urokinase. In contrast, streptokinase is used in Canada (except in severe blockages) and most other European countries, probably as a result of the price incentives for hospitals and medical regulation. For reasons that are not clear but may relate to institutional and regulatory factors, most of the growth in thrombolytic use in Japan has involved urokinase.

4. *Supply-side incentives appear to be important determinants of trends in high-tech treatments but are less influential in determining trends in low-tech treatments.* The responsiveness of payment systems to physicians' and especially hospitals' behavior, and the stringency of technology regulation, are important determinants of differences in the rate of growth of technology use across countries. Incentives have important *dynamic* consequences for a country's health care utilization, and so are an important determinant of international growth in the cost of health care—as well as being an important determinant of differences in levels of health care expenditures.

Countries with traditional fee-for-service reimbursement systems—such as Japan and Korea, and at least in the private hospital sector, Australia and France—report much higher growth in high-tech procedure use. Other countries (such as Belgium) have fee-for-service reimbursement for physicians and more limited reimbursement for hospitals; reimbursement systems found commonly in the United States, such as the Medicare Prospective Payment System, offer a blend of fee-for-service and reimbursement that is truly invariant to providers' medical treatment decisions (McClellan 1997). These countries report intermediate-to-rapid growth in utilization. At the other extreme of the reimbursement spectrum are the Nordic countries, the United Kingdom, and to a lesser extent the Canadian provinces. These countries finance hospitals with global budgets (although, as we point out below, global budgets can exhibit varying degrees of stringency) and employ mainly salaried physicians. In turn, these countries reported the lowest growth rates of intensive procedure use.

Macro technology regulation is also a key determinant of technological change in health care. Such regulation takes very different forms in different countries. In Denmark, for example, there is very little formal regulation of hospital technology adoption; the binding regulation lies in targeted expansions in hospitals' global budgets. The Danish "heart plans," as they are popularly known, have been used to expand revascularizations in that country several times over the past 15 years. The provincial government of Quebec added in 1991 three additional catheterization laboratories, plus two additional bypass surgery and one additional angioplasty facility, which led to a shift up in high-tech procedure use in subsequent years. Other Canadian provinces, such as Alberta, also experienced reorganizations in their health care systems that affected the supply of technologically intensive treatments. France regulates strictly the use of a key piece of capital equipment necessary for bypass surgery—the heart-lung bypass pump—and private hospitals have, in turn, expanded disproportionately their angioplasty capacity.

Regional differences in revascularization methods—the Asian/Nordic angioplasty/bypass puzzle—are more difficult to link clearly to differences in financial and regulatory incentives. In Japan, reimbursement for angioplasty has grown more rapidly over the study period than has reimbursement for bypass; and the Danish heart plans have focused on bypass capacity more than on capacity for angioplasty (although the most recent heart plan has sought to increase the marginal relative rewards to performing angioplasty). However, and perhaps more important, the Asian and Nordic countries also exhibit important differences in the industrial organization of the production of revascularization services, with the slower-growing type of revascularization being performed by a specialist with less access to patients. In Japan, angioplasty is the domain of internal medicine cardiologists, whereas bypass surgery is the domain of cardiovascular surgeons, and the two specialties in that country have very separate career paths. In Sweden, angioplasty is traditionally performed by radiologists, who work at clinics that do not have the primary responsibilities for managing AMI patients. The extent to which these organizational differences are the product of differences in reimbursement incentives, or an independent cause of differences in medical treatment patterns, is an important topic for further research.

Finally, although many previous studies including MONICA have documented some cross-country variations in trends in the use of drug therapies that are likely to reduce mortality (Tunstall-Pedoe et al. 2000), our preliminary results (albeit somewhat limited) suggest that differences in incentives across countries are not that important in explaining trends in low-tech treatments. For example, aspirin use has increased substantially in almost all of our countries over the past decade, and beta-blocker use has increased more variably but not in a way that is clearly related to incentives. The use of drugs found in clinical trials to be potentially harmful in heart attack care, including calcium channel blockers and lidocaine, also declined in use in the early to middle 1990s in most countries studied.

5. *The predominant cause of medical expenditure growth, among those countries with detailed information on resource use for AMI patients, was technological change.* As we observed in the introduction, it is difficult or impossible for countries that finance care with global budgets to identify the cost of care for a particular patient or subset of patients. Those countries with longitudinal data and per-case payment systems were able, to varying degrees, to decompose trends in total resources use to treat AMI patients into changes in population demographics, changes in AMI incidence, technological change (changes in use of specific treatments), and changes in the prices or costs associated with the major heart attack treatments. This represents a major advance over the traditional approach to identifying the expenditure consequences of technological change as a residual. As Cutler, McClellan, and Newhouse (1999) show using U.S. data, changes in medical treatments over time are difficult to measure without detailed information on treatment changes, so that traditional methods of measuring productivity changes in health care substantially overstate price

growth and understate the impact of technological change on medical expenditure growth.

In the countries for which the research teams were able to perform this decomposition analysis, the predominant cause of medical expenditure or cost growth was technological change. These results provide the first explicit international evidence on the importance of technological change for expenditure growth. It appears to be a universal phenomenon across many different types of health care systems. However, the way in which technological change affects expenditures differs. As we noted above, the nature and magnitude of technological change appear to be systematically related to the economic and regulatory incentives in a country's health care system. Moreover, price *levels* for medical technologies differ substantially across countries, with prices in the United States considerably higher than in most other countries for comparable treatments, despite the recent reductions in U.S. prices. As a result, a given rate of treatment change in the United States will tend to result in greater absolute expenditure growth in the United States.

6. *There is some evidence of significant differences in outcome trends across countries, but the trend differences are much more modest than the differences in treatment trends, and further analysis is needed to reach definitive conclusions.* Table 20.3 presents trends in all-cause one-year case fatality for the five participating research teams that were able to obtain and analyze longitudinal data on individual patients that were linked to national death records. Although any conclusions about the consequences of technological change are limited both by the coarseness of our single-outcome measure and by the limited number of countries for which comparable AMI mortality statistics are available, our preliminary analyses suggest that most countries have experienced significant improvements in the health of heart attack patients. The connection between high-tech procedure use and health outcomes across countries, however, is not as strong as the connection between economic incentives and high-tech procedure use. There are important differences in mortality trends between countries at opposite extremes of the utilization distribution, with AMI patients from very low utilization countries such as England experiencing more modest improvements in mortality than patients from very high utilization countries such as Australia and the United States. But the relationship between technological change and health outcomes toward the center of the utilization distribution is less clear cut. The Canadian province of Quebec, for example, showed intermediate to slow growth in technology

use, but had a relatively rapid decline in average case fatality. The province of Manitoba showed slow to intermediate growth in technology use as well, but relatively modest declines in mortality.

The apparently modest consequences of increasing use of high-tech procedures at the middle and upper end of the utilization distribution may be evidence of a declining marginal benefit of technological change in health care. However, even if the additional procedures had substantial mortality effects, precise quantitative comparisons of highly standardized data would be needed to identify trend differences reliably. For example, suppose the additional cardiac procedures have a one-year case fatality reduction of 3 percentage points, a substantial effect. Then even a difference in growth rates of revascularization procedures of 2 percentage points per year for five years would only lead to a difference in case fatality changes of 0.3 percentage points. Thus, our findings of differences in trends must be viewed as preliminary. Moreover, countries with greater high-tech changes usually reported somewhat slower growth in the occurrence of complications from heart disease in the additional AMI survivors, suggesting that the more rapid growth in intensive treatments did have some consequences for patients' quality of life. Some countries also identified important differences in the health effects of technological change in younger versus older elderly populations, health effects that might be masked in comparisons of overall population averages. In particular, because high-tech cardiac procedures are used early in the diffusion process to treat younger, healthier patients, and then later expanded to the older and more severely ill, it is possible that differences in technology diffusion may be particularly large for the elderly. Future analysis of the outcome effects of technological change at the middle and top of the utilization distribution might focus on the impacts in this subgroup.

TABLE 20.3. Trends in All-Cause One-Year Mortality for Heart Attack Patients, 1991–95

Increase or Slower Decline[a]	More Rapid Decline[b]
England; Manitoba, Canada	Australia; Quebec, Canada; USA

Note: Time period used varies across countries but is always in the 1991–95 window.

[a]Category includes countries with average annual increases in mortality and declines of less (in absolute value terms) than 0.5 percentage points per year.

[b]Category includes countries with average annual declines in mortality of greater (in absolute value terms) than 0.5 percentage points per year.

Future Work

We view the efforts reported by this volume as the foundation for a wide range of future work by the TECH research network and other international research collaborations. We focus on three possible extensions here.

1. *More precise assessment of the consequences of technological change for treatment decisions and health outcomes.* More precise assessment of the causes and consequences of differences across countries in technological change for patients with an illness like AMI would seem to require estimation of regression models of the determinants of specific high-tech procedure use and patient health outcomes with pooled individual-level data. However, confidentiality concerns and security restrictions are a frequent obstacle to this sort of analysis. In recent work, some TECH investigators have developed new methods that allows researchers to undertake formal cross-country regression analyses, while only sharing data in an aggregated form that has all individual-level information destroyed.

For simplicity, consider the problem of pooling data on two countries for a single year, country A and country B. The objective of the pooled regression model is to estimate the difference in technology use Y (where $Y = 1$ for each patient in either country receiving a specific high-tech treatment, and zero otherwise), and the standard error of the difference, adjusted for observable differences in patient populations and other factors X, where X is defined identically across countries as well. A linear regression model always provides an unbiased estimate of this difference (Greene 1999).

With a linear model, it is possible to estimate matrix components for each country separately, based on X variables (a matrix with dimension of N observations by K covariates) and Y variables (a matrix with dimension of N observations on each outcome of interest) for that country's observations. The key insight of this method is that the matrix manipulations necessary to obtain coefficients and standard errors from a linear regression can be performed after estimating the matrix components for each country's data separately—which destroys all individual-level information.

More specifically, $X'X$ covariate matrices can be estimated from patient-level data as two submatrices, $X_A'X_A$ for country A (where X_A had dimension $N_A x K$, where N_A was the number of country A observations and K was the number of model covariates) and $X_B'X_B$ for country B (where X_B had dimension $N_B xK$). To obtain the relevant matrix $X'X$ for the full-sample regression, add the country-specific components:

$$X'_A X_A + X'_B X_B = X'X.$$

The $X'Y$ matrix can be obtained similarly, providing least-squares coefficient estimates β using the standard multivariate regression formula:

$$\beta = (X'X)^{-1} X'Y.$$

Covariance matrices for calculating standard errors were estimated analogously.[1]

2. *Extension of this work to other illnesses.* As we have noted, heart attack care is an excellent first case study of the causes and consequences of technological change in health care. Heart attack is a common and costly health problem throughout the world. Heart attack patients are generally hospitalized; important treatments are delivered in an inpatient setting, for which reliable data is more commonly available, soon after hospitalization; and important health outcomes usually occur soon after the initial onset of illness.

However, the implications of technological change may be quite different for other illnesses. Stroke, for example, has had fewer major innovations in treatment to compare. Breast cancer and other common cancers are more dependent on effective screening technologies, which may be influenced by economic factors in different ways than are therapeutic procedures. For this reason, technological change may affect not only treatment conditional on diagnosis but also the measured incidence of illness. For example, the incidence of localized and regionalized prostate cancer in the United States increased through 1992 and then dropped, with the rate of distant-stage disease stable through 1992 and then dropping (Dennis and Resnick 2000). If this pattern of incidence by stage is due to increasingly early detection, then simple comparisons of fixed-term survival rates over time may not provide an accurate assessment of the health benefits of technological change. And, to the extent that the effect of technological change on early detection differs across countries, this "lead time" bias would make international comparisons of the productivity of cancer treatment particularly difficult to interpret. Furthermore, because important treatment for cancer occurs in outpatient settings, the data requirements for analyses of patients with cancer are much greater, requiring linkage of inpatient and outpatient data from particular hospitals longitudinally to describe course of treatment.

3. *The impact of socioeconomic factors on differences in population health.* There is an extensive literature on the effects of socioeconomic status on health (e.g., Fuchs 1993), but international comparisons of the effects of socioeconomic status face particular challenges. The most difficult of these involves the construction of measures of socioeconomic hardship that are comparable across countries. Stratifying patients by their income, converted at market exchange rates, is clearly incorrect, since it fails to account for differences across countries in the cost of living. Conversely, stratifying patients on the basis of relative income is also undesirable, insofar as differences in inequality make the definition of relative hardship noncomparable across countries. Similar problems exist, although perhaps in a less pronounced fashion, with measures such as educational or occupational attainment, since these factors also have very different meanings in different countries. Estimation of the effects of individuals' socioeconomic *environment*—which may be as important to health as *individual* socioeconomic status—is also plagued by comparability problems. The relevant socioeconomic "neighborhood" for a patient in the United States may differ substantially from the relevant neighborhood of her counterpart in France, Italy, or Japan.

Notes

1. To obtain consistent estimates of coefficients and covariance matrices with binary dependent variables (which violate the linear regression assumption of identically distributed observations), the methods uses two-step estimation techniques to account for heteroskedasticity, i.e., the fact that the random variables in our models were not identically distributed. The two-step method required a second iteration using optimal weights, based on the estimated coefficients of the first iteration.

References

Cutler, D., M. B. McClellan, and J. Newhouse. 1999. "The Costs and Benefits of Intensive Treatment for Cardiovascular Disease." In *Measuring the Price of Medical Treatments,* ed. J. Triplett. Washington, D.C.: Brookings Institution Press.

Dennis, L. K., and M. I. Resnick. 2000. "Analysis of Recent Trends in Prostate Cancer Incidence and Mortality." *Prostate* 42, no. 4: 247–52.

Fuchs, Victor R. 1993. *The Future of Health Policy.* Cambridge: Harvard University Press.

Greene, William H. 1999. *Econometric Analysis.* 4th ed. Saddle River, N.J.: Prentice-Hall.

McClellan, Mark B. 1997. "Hospital Reimbursement Incentives: An Empirical Analysis." *Journal of Economics and Management Strategy* 6:91–128.

Tunstall-Pedoe, Hugh, Diego Vanuzzo, Michael Hobbs, M. Mahonen, Z. Cepaitis, K. Kuulasmaa, and U. Keil. 2000. "Estimation of Contribution of Changes in Coronary Care to Improving Survival, Event Rates, and Coronary Heart Disease Mortality across the WHO MONICA Project Populations." *Lancet* 355, no. 9205: 688–700.

Glossary

ACE inhibitor. Angiotensin-converting enzyme. Used to treat hypertension (high blood pressure) and congestive heart failure (CHF).

acute myocardial infarction (AMI). Necrosis (death) of the cells of an area of the heart muscle (myocardium) occurring as a result of oxygen deprivation, which is caused by obstruction of the blood supply; commonly referred to as a "heart attack."

angina. Acute pain in the chest resulting from decreased blood supply to the heart muscle (myocardial ischemia), usually brought on during emotional or physically strenuous periods. This usually is a symptom of coronary atherosclerosis (clogging of the vessels supplying blood to the heart).

angiography. *See* **cardiac catheterization.**

angioplasty. *See* **percutaneous transluminal coronary angioplasty.**

antagonist. A drug that prevents stimulation of receptors in the cells by binding to them and blocking the normal cellular response to a particular compound.

aspirin. Acetylsalicylic acid, a drug commonly used to relieve pain and reduce fever. This drug also has anticlotting properties and is used prophylactically (as a preventive measure) for patients at risk of myocardial infarction or stroke.

atrial fibrillation. Extremely rapid, incomplete contractions of the upper chambers of the heart resulting in irregular and uncoordinated action of this part of the heart.

beta-blocker. A drug that blocks the action of epinephrine at beta-adrenergic receptors in heart and blood vessel tissue. These are used to treat hypertension (high blood pressure), angina, certain cardiac arrhythmias, and post–myocardial infarction. Through their actions, they decrease the workload of the heart, resulting in a reduced long-term risk of mortality and heart attack.

bypass surgery. Installation of an alternate route for blood flow around an obstruction in a blood vessel.

CABG. Coronary artery bypass graft. Surgical insertion of a new pathway in order to carry blood around an obstruction in a blood vessel. A surgical treatment for coronary artery disease.

calcium channel blocker. A drug that blocks the entrance of calcium ions into muscle cells of the heart and blood vessels. This action leads to a decreased need for oxygen in the muscle cells. Used to treat angina and cardiac arrhythmias.

cardiac catheterization (cath). A technique for imaging the interior of the arteries that provide blood to the heart muscle. A tiny plastic tube is put into the heart through a blood vessel. Indicated whenever it is necessary to establish a precise and definite diagnosis in order to determine whether heart surgery is necessary.

cardiac catheterization laboratory. Unit where the patient is prepared for a cardiac catheterization procedure and monitored once the catheter is in place.

coronary care unit (CCU). A specialized area of a hospital with advanced heart monitoring capabilities.

comorbidity. State where one disease coexists with another.

conduction disorders. Diseases in which cardiac electrical impulses are not transmitted properly throughout the heart.

congestive heart failure. Impaired pumping capability of the heart due to retention of water and sodium. Decreased cardiac output and increased congestion lead to symptoms such as weakness, shortness of breath, and edema (swelling) in the lower extremities.

coronary artery disease. Narrowing of the coronary arteries sufficiently to prevent adequate blood supply to the myocardium (heart muscle tissue).

coronary heart disease. Decreased flow of blood to the heart such that the minimal oxygen levels are not met. Usually due to atherosclerosis (clogging of the vessels supplying blood to the heart).

defibrillator. Electronic device, either external or implanted, that produces defibrillation of the heart. Defibrillation stops the quivering, spontaneous contraction of the muscle that leads to cardiac arrest.

electrocardiogram (ECG). A tracing of the electrical activity of the heart. An ECG provides information useful in assessing cardiac arrhythmias and myocardial damage.

heart attack. Common term for myocardial infarction (MI).

heparin. Anticoagulant, usually administered via intravenous (IV) or subcutaneous injection. Useful in prevention and treatment of clotting disorders, pulmonary embolism, myocardial infarction, and cerebrovascular accident (stroke).

intensive care unit (ICU). Hospital unit for the care of seriously ill individuals needing continuous attention. Equipped with specialized equipment and specially trained staff.

intra-aortic balloon pump. Mechanical aid to circulation consisting of a balloon inserted into the thoracic aorta via the femoral artery and a pump to inflate the balloon with helium or carbon dioxide. Rhythmic inflation and deflation serves to decrease the workload on the heart and increase blood flow to the coronary arteries.

intubation. Insertion of a tube, generally for drainage purposes or for maintenance of the air passages.

ischemic heart disease. Local and temporary lack of blood-oxygen supply to the heart due to a circulatory obstruction.

left anterior descending artery. One of four major arteries supplying blood-oxygen to the heart muscle.

nitrates. Medication used in the treatment of angina pectoris.

open heart surgery. Surgery involving the heart, coronary arteries, or cardiac valves that requires an incision to the chest cavity.

purchasing power parity (PPP) exchange rates. A PPP exchange rate between countries is the rate that leads a fixed set of goods and/or services to have the same cost in both countries.

primary angioplasty. Procedural intervention during a heart attack (within one day) to open blocked blood vessels so that delivery of oxygen to the heart muscle is restored.

percutaneous transluminal coronary angioplasty (PTCA). A common type of angioplasty used to open blocked arteries by compressing blockage against the artery wall with a balloon. An alternative to bypass surgery for some patients.

Q-wave infarction. A type of myocardial infarction.

secondary angioplasty. Different from primary angioplasty in that the procedural intervention is performed after, rather than during, a heart attack to reduce blockages of the blood vessels supplying oxygen to the heart muscle.

stent. A wire mesh tube or rim inserted in a blood vessel to help keep it open after angioplasty.

streptokinase. A medication that reduces the ability of the blood to clot (coagulate). As with other anticoagulants, it is used to reduce blood vessel blockage during a heart attack.

thoracic surgery department. Surgical department concerned with procedures that involve entrance into the chest cavity. Operations on the heart, lungs, and major blood vessels are types of surgery carried out in such a department.

thrombolytic therapy. Use of medications called anticoagulants to dissolve blood clots.

tPA. Tissue plasminogen activator. A genetically engineered drug used in thrombolytic therapy to dissolve blood clots. Administered during or shortly after a heart attack to reduce the chances of death.

urokinase. A medication that reduces the ability of the blood to clot (anticoagulant). Used during heart attacks to open blocked blood vessels.

ventricular arrhythmia. An irregular and rapid contraction of the lower chambers of the heart. This situation can lead to cardiac arrest and death.

Contributors

Kimmo Asikainen, M.Sc., National Research and Development Center for Welfare and Health (STAKES), Helsinki

Vincenzo Atella, M.Sc., Centro Interdipartimentale di Studi Internazionali Suill'economia e lo Sviluppo–Studi Economico-Finanziari e Metodi Quantitativi (CEIS-SEFEMEQ) Department of Economics, University of Rome, Tor Vergata

Peter C. Austin, Ph.D., Institute for Clinical Evaluative Sciences and University of Toronto

Brenden Bertuola, Melbourne, Australia

Terkel Christiansen, M.Sc., Health Economics, Institute of Public Health, University of Southern Denmark B Odense Campus, Odense

Jørgen Clausen, M.Sc., Center for Health and Social Policy, Odense University, Odense, Denmark

M. C. Closon, Ph.D., Centre d'Etudes Interdisciplinaires en Economie de la Santé (CIES), Université Catholique de Louvain, Louvain-la-Neuve, Belgium

P. M. De Coster, Centre d'Etudes Interdisciplinaires en Economie de la Santé (CIES), Université Catholique de Louvain, Louvain-la-Neuve, Belgium

Brigitte Dormont, Ph.D., Théma, Université Paris X–Nanterre

Alexander Dozet, Ph.D. candidate, Department of Community Medicine, Department of Economics, and Lund University Center for Health Economics, Lund University, Lund, Sweden

Isabelle Durand Zaleski, M.D., M.P.H., Ph.D., Public Health, Henri Mondor Hospital, AP-HP, Paris

Diana Edwards, Research Fellow, Health Economics Unit, Centre for Health Program Evaluation, Monash University, Melbourne

Mark J. Eisenberg, M.D., M.P.H., Jewish General Hospital, McGill University, Montreal

Nathan Every, M.D., M.P.H., Veterans Affairs, Puget Sound Healthcare System, School of Medicine, University of Washington, Seattle

Konrad Fassbender, Ph.D., Research Associate, Department of Public Health Sciences, University of Alberta, and Institute of Pharmaco-Economics

Alan M. Garber, M.D., Ph.D., Department of Veterans Affairs and Center for Primary Care and Outcomes Research/Center for Health Policy, Stanford University, Stanford, California

Elizabeth Geelhoed, MPH, Bec, Dip Nuc Med, Asthma and Allergy Research Institute, Sir Charles Gairdner Hospital, Perth, Western Australia, Australia.

Simona Giampaoli, Laboratorio di Epidemiologia e Biostatistica, Istituto Superiore di Sanità, Rome

Sylvie Goldman, M.D., Hadassah Medical Organization and Israel Center for Disease Control

David Hailey, Ph.D., Department of Public Health Sciences, University of Alberta, and Technology Assessment, Alberta Heritage Foundation for Medical Research, Edmonton

Unto Häkkinen, Ph.D., Research Professor, National Research and Development Center for Welfare and Health (STAKES), Helsinki

Ziona Haklai, M.A., Department of Health Information, Ministry of Health, Jerusalem

Paul Heidenreich, M.D., M.S., Department of Medicine, Stanford University, Stanford, California

Mark Hlatky, M.D., Department of Health Research and Policy and School of Medicine, Stanford University, Stanford, California

Vivian Ho, Ph.D., Department of Health Care Organization and Policy, University of Alabama, Birmingham

Michael Hobbs, D.Phil., M.B., B.S., F.R.A.C.P., Associate Professor, Department of Public Health, University of Western Australia, Nedlands

Richard Hockey, Data Analyst, Mater Children's Hospital, South Brisbane, Australia

Sören Höjgård, Ph.D., Department of Community Medicine (Malmö) and Lund University Center for Health Economics, Lund University, Lund, Sweden

Alberto Holly, Ph.D., Institut d'économie et de management de la santé, University of Lausanne, Lausanne, Switzerland

Saburo Ide, M.Med.Sc., St. Mary's Junior College

S. Jacobzone, Economist, OECD

Jeremy D. Kark, M.D., Ph.D., Department of Social Medicine, Hadassah Medical Organization and Hebrew University–Hadassah School of Public Health, Jerusalem, and Israel Center for Disease Control

Ilmo Keskimäki, M.D., Ph.D., Research Fellow (Academy of Finland), National Research and Development Center for Welfare and Health (STAKES), Helsinki

Daniel P. Kessler, M.D., J.D., Associate Professor of Economics, Law, and Policy, Graduate School of Business, Stanford University, Stanford, California

Akihiro Koike, M.D., Kyushu University, Japan

Ivar Sønbø Kristiansen, M.D., Ph.D., M.P.H., Health Economics, Institute of Public Health, University of Southern Denmark B Odense Campus, Odense, Denmark

Mei-shu Lai, M.D., M.P.H., Ph.D., General Manager, Bureau of National Health Insurance, Taipei, Taiwan

Frédéric Lavoie, M.Sc., Research Institute of the McGill University Health Centre, McGill University, Montreal

Anna Lindgren, Ph.D., Center for Mathematical Sciences and Department of Community Medicine (Malmö), Lund University, Lund, Sweden

Joan C. Lo, Ph.D., Research Fellow, Institute of Economics, Academica Sinica, Nankang, Taipei, Taiwan

Carl Hampus Lyttkens, Ph.D., Department of Economics, Department of Community Medicine (Malmö), and Lund University Center for Health Economics, Lund University, Lund, Sweden

N. Maes, Centre d'Etudes Interdisciplinaires en Economie de la Santé (CIES), Université Catholique de Louvain, Louvain-la-Neuve, Belgium

Rob Manning, M.Sc., Department of Economics and Related Studies, University of York, York, United Kingdom

Toru Maruyama, M.D., Kyushu University, Japan

Mark B. McClellan, M.D., Ph.D., Associate Professor of Economics and Medicine, Department of Economics, Stanford University, Stanford, California

Tsuruhiko Nambu, Ph.D., Gakushuin University, Japan

C. David Naylor, M.D., D.Phil., F.R.C.P.C., Office of the Dean, Faculty of Medicine, University of Toronto

Joseph Newhouse, Ph.D., Kennedy School of Government; Department of Health Care Policy, Harvard Medical School; Department of Health Policy and Management, Harvard School of Public Health; and Faculty of Arts and Sciences, Harvard University, Cambridge, Massachusetts

Haruko Noguchi, Ph.D., Faculty of Social Science, Toyo Eiwa University, Kanagawa, Japan; National Bureau of Economic Research, United States

Hans Öhlin, M.D., Ph.D., Department of Cardiology, Lund University Hospital, Lund, Sweden

Fred Paccaud, M.D., Institute of Social and Preventative Medicine, University of Lausanne, Lausanne, Switzerland

Mark Pettigrew, Ph.D., NHS Centre for Reviews and Dissemination, University of York, York, United Kingdom

J. Perelman, Centre d'Etudes Interdisicplinaires en Economie de la Santé (CIES), Université Catholique de Louvain, Louvain-la-Neuve, Belgium.

Louise Pilote, M.D., M.P.H, Ph.D, Research Institute of the McGill University Health Centre, McGill University, Montreal

Lorenza Pilotto, Centro per le Malattie Cardiovascolari, Az. Osped. S. Maria Misericordia, WHO Collaborating Centre, Udine, Italy

Nigel Rice, Ph.D., Centre for Health Economics, University of York, York, United Kingdom

Jeff Richardson, Ph.D., Professor and Director, Health Economics Unit, Centre for Health Program Evaluation, Monash University, Melbourne

Iain K. Robertson, M.Med.Sci., M.P.H., Research Fellow, Health Economics Unit, Centre for Health Program Evaluation, Monash University, Melbourne

Michael B. Robinson, M.D., M.P.H., Nuffield Institute for Health, University of Leeds, Leeds, United Kingdom

Leslie L. Roos, Ph.D., Manitoba Centre for Health Policy and Evaluation, Winnipeg, Manitoba, Canada

Noralee P. Roos, Ph.D., Manitoba Centre for Health Policy and Evaluation, Winnipeg, Manitoba, Canada

L. Duncan Saunders, M.B.B.C.H, Ph.D., Department of Public Health Sciences, University of Alberta

Olga Saynina, M.A., M.B.A., National Bureau of Economic Research, Stanford, California

Mark Sculpher, M.Sc., Ph.D., Centre for Health Economics, University of York, York, United Kingdom

Trevor Sheldon, M.Sc., Ph.D., York Health Policy Group, University of York, York, United Kingdom

Amir Shmueli, Ph.D., School of Public Health, Hebrew University, and Gertner Institute for Health Policy Research, Jerusalem

Jes Søgaard, M.Sc., Center for Health and Social Policy, Odense University, Odense, Denmark

Ruth-Ann Soodeen, B.A., Manitoba Center for Health Policy and Evaluation, Department of Community Health Sciences, Faculty of Medicine, University of Manitoba, Manitoba, Canada

Koon K. Teo, M.B.B.C.H., Ph.D., Division of Cardiology, University of Alberta

Jack V. Tu, M.D., Ph.D., F.R.C.P.C., Institute for Clinical Evaluative Sciences, and Sunnybrook and Women's College Health Sciences Centre, and University of Toronto

Naoto Uemura, M.D., Oita Medical University, Japan

Akinori Urae, M.D., Medical Company, LTA, Fukuoka, Japan

Diego Vanuzzo, M.D., Centro per la Lotta contro le Malattie Cardiovascolari, Friuli-Venezia Giulia, Azienda Ospedaliera S. Maria Della Misericordia, Udine, Italy

Randy Walld, B.Comm., B.Sc., Manitoba Center for Health Policy and Evaluation, Department of Community Health Sciences, Faculty of Medicine, University of Manitoba, Manitoba, Canada

Bong-min Yang, Ph.D., Professor, School of Public Health, Seoul National University, Seoul, Korea

Aki Yoshikawa, Ph.D., National Bureau of Economic Research, United States

Index

ACE inhibitors, 16, 97, 334, 351, 390; in Australia, 136, 139, 149; in Denmark, 263; in Israel, 370–71; in Japan, 169–70; in the U.S., 38, 49

ÄDEL-reform (Sweden), 208, 225

Advanced cardiac life support, 38, 98

Adverse selection problems, 346, 347

Age difference, 3, 21, 385, 394 (*see also* Elderly patients); in Israel, 382; in Italy, 332, 343; in Korea, 191; in the U.S., 31, 35

Alberta, AMI care in, 88–103; consequences of changes in, 99–102; expertise in, 98–99; financing of, 89–92, 100–102; health outcomes, 99–100; low-tech, 97–98; mortality and, 88, 99–100, 102–3; regulation and, 92–93; technological change in, 94–98

Alberta Acute Care Funding System, 91

Alberta Health Insurance System, 89

Alteplase. *See* Tissue plasminogen activator (tPA)

AMI (acute myocardial infarction), 16–17 (*see also* AMI care *in specific country, Canadian province*); recurrent, 42–45, 127, 136, 139, 145–46, 151, 222

Angina, 113, 130–32, 151, 220, 254, 261, 263; in Israel, 374, 381

Angiography, 48, 80, 98 (*see also* Cardiac catheterization); in Australia, 127–28, 130–32, 136, 146, 151; in England, 273, 277–79; in Finland, 238, 241; in Japan, 175; in Quebec, 76, 78; in Sweden, 210, 217

Angioplasty, 389, 390, 391–92 (*see also* PTCA); balloon, 293, 369, 381; in Canada, 76, 84– 86, 102; in Finland, 238, 241–43; in France, 297; in the U.S., 14–15, 24, 38, 41, 48, 49, 50

Anticoagulants, 263, 281, 351. *See also* Streptokinase

Antiplatelet agents, 284, 302, 334, 351, 353; in Australia, 128, 136–39, 149, 151

Arrhythmias, 216, 374

Aspirin, 15, 16, 151, 170, 392; in Canada, 97–98, 113; in Europe, 220, 245, 281, 354; in Israel, 370; in Taiwan, 200; in the U.S., 36–38, 41, 48, 50

Australia, AMI care in, 11, 12, 121–53, 389; cardiac complications and, 139–43; consequences of changes in, 139–42; effects of incentives on, 146–52; high-tech, 126–36; hospitals in, 13, 121, 122–23; incentives for technological change in, 122–25; insurance in, 123; low-tech, 136–39; medical expenditures and, 142–46; MONICA Project in, 122–25, 139; mortality and, 127, 136, 139–42, 393; payment in, 18, 124; in Perth,

Australia (*continued*)
125–32; specialists in, 122, 123, 150; technological change in, 125–39; treatment rates in, 150; in Victoria, 132–36
Balloon angioplasty, 293, 369, 381
Belgium, AMI care in, 306–21; consequences of changes in, 314–18; effects of incentives on, 319–21; financing of, 307–8; high-tech, 310–13; incentives for technological change in, 307–9; low-tech, 313–14; medical expenditures and, 318, 321; mortality and, 316–17, 321; payment system for, 18; physician supply in, 13; technological change in, 309–14; technology regulation and, 308–9
Beta-blockers, 15, 392; in Alberta, 97–98; in Australia, 136–39, 149; in Belgium, 313; in England, 281; in Finland, 245; in France, 302; in Israel, 370, 371; in Italy, 334; in Japan, 170; in Ontario, 70; in Sweden, 220; in Switzerland, 351, 353; in the U.S., 26, 36–37, 38, 48
Blue Cross, 90, 97
Brianza, Italy, 334, 337
British Cardiac Intervention Society, 279
Budget caps, 121
Budget systems, global, 18 (*see also* Financing of care); in Belgium, 108, 307; in Denmark, 253–54, 265–66; in England, 271, 284; in France, 289–90, 291, 293, 299; in Italy, 347; in Sweden, 211, 213, 223, 225; in Switzerland, 354
Bureau of National Health Insurance (Taiwan), 196, 205
Bypass surgery (CABG), 15, 24, 385, 389, 391–92 (*see also* CABG); in Australia, 133; in England, 284; in Finland, 238; in Japan, 175; in Quebec, 76–77, 78; in the U.S., 24, 29, 31, 48, 49

CABG (coronary artery bypass graft), 29, 133, 241, 253, 297–98 (*see also* Bypass surgery); in Australia, 127–28, 130, 151; in Belgium, 310–14, 318, 319, 321; in Canada, 55, 61, 63, 65–66, 68, 93, 95–97, 102, 109–11; in Denmark, 254, 255, 257–58, 259–60, 264, 265; in England, 271, 273, 277–79, 281; in Finland, 248; in France, 292, 295, 300, 302; in Israel, 358–59, 364–65, 366–67; in Italy, 331–32, 336; in Japan, 160, 164–65, 167, 171, 173; in Korea, 185, 186, 188–91; in Sweden, 210, 215, 217, 227; in Switzerland, 349; in Taiwan, 196–97, 198, 199–200, 204–5, 206
Calcium antagonists, 263, 351, 353
Calcium channel blockers, 392; in Alberta (Can.), 97, 98; in Belgium, 313; in Finland, 245; in France, 302; in Israel, 370, 371; in Japan, 169; in the U.S., 37, 38, 48
California, 28, 29, 42, 49
Canada, 12, 14, 18, 115–16 (*see also* Alberta; Manitoba; Ontario; Quebec); fee-for-service in, 55, 60, 75, 90; IHD in, 156; insurance in, 13, 116; medical expenditures in, 58, 100–102, 106
Canadian Health Act, 55, 73
Canadian Institute for Health Information (CIHI), 59, 63
Cancer, 4, 6, 7, 41, 116, 396–97
Cardiac catheterization (angiography), 14–15, 16, 338, 385, 389; in Belgium, 310–13; in Canada, 60, 65–66, 93, 95–97, 102; in Denmark, 254, 255, 257–58, 259–60, 265; in France, 295, 297, 298, 299,

300, 301; in Israel, 358–59, 365–66, 377; in Italy, 331–32; in Japan, 171, 175; laboratories for, 6, 12, 55, 309; in Sweden, 217; in Taiwan, 198, 199, 206; in the U.S., 29, 34, 48, 49, 50
Cardiac complications, 139–42
Cardiac surgery centers: in Belgium, 308, 309, 314, 318, 321; in Finland, 250
Cardiologists, 50, 176, 214, 258, 279, 367; in Belgium, 308; in England, 284; in Japan, 171; in Korea, 190
Cardiology, 283, 285, 309
Cardiothoracic surgery, 275, 283, 285
Cardiovascular disease, 184, 252, 330
CATH. *See* Angiography; Cardiac catheterization
Catheters, 293, 354
Cause of Death Data File (Taiwan), 194
Center for Interdisciplinary Study in Health Economics (CIES), 306–7, 309
Central Bureau of Statistics (Israel), 364
Charlson comorbidity index, 63, 65
Clinical Quality Improvement Network, 99
Clinical Standards Advisory Group (England), 270, 275–77, 278, 281, 283
Commissione Unica del Farmaco (Italy), 328
Commonwealth Department of Health (Australia), 123
Comorbidity, 63, 65, 94, 111, 143, 146, 364
Competition, 3, 13, 358; among managed-care plans, 27; in Belgium, 307; in Denmark, 256; in Finland, 238–39; in France, 294; in Italy, 328–29; in Korea, 187, 191; in Sweden, 225; in Switzerland, 348; in Taiwan, 197; in the U.S., 26–27
Congestive heart failure, 43–45, 373
Consumer information, 187, 191
Copayments, 11; in Australia, 133; in Belgium, 308; in England, 272; in France, 290, 291; in Italy, 325, 326; in Japan, 159; in Korea, 186; in Manitoba, 116; in Sweden, 211; in Switzerland, 346–47; in the U.S., 24
Coronary angiography. *See* Cardiac catheterization
Coronary arteriography, 353
Coronary artery procedures (CARPs), 113, 127, 130–32, 143, 151. *See also* Stenting
Costs (*see also* Financing of care; Medical expenditures): in Australia, 124; containment of, 102, 174, 308, 348, 359, 392; resource, 1

Danish Medical Association, 254, 257
Data limitations, 2, 177, 336
Death registry, 330. *See also* Mortality
Defibrillators, 36, 216, 259
Demographic data, 63–65
Denmark, AMI care in, 252–66; appropriateness of, 263–64; competition and, 13, 256; consequences of changes in, 264–65; financing of, 253–55, 265; high-tech, 259–61; incentives for technological change in, 253–58; low-tech, 263; medical expenditures and, 265; mortality and, 252, 264; physician supply in, 13, 258; regulation in, 12, 255–56; special interest groups in, 257; technological change in, 258–64; waiting lists and, 252, 256, 257, 259

Diabetes, 4, 6
Diagnosis-related group (DRG) systems, 211, 225, 237, 308, 338; of Australia and Taiwan, 11; in Canada, 91; codes, 143–46, 286, 330; data, 295; in France, 302–3; in Italy, 326–27, 330, 337, 347; payments for, 49; in the U.S., 24, 36, 47
Diagnostic catheterization. *See* Cardiac catheterization
Diagnostic testing, 113
Diuretics, 263, 334, 351
Drugs, 151, 159 (*see also* Low-tech treatments; Thrombolytic drugs; *and specific drugs*); antiarrythmics, 281, 351; in Australia, 124; in Belgium, 308, 318, 321; cardiac, 36, 70, 75, 79, 80, 83, 139; cholesterol-lowering, 7, 38, 49, 97, 136; costs in Taiwan, 201; in Denmark, 255, 263; and device regulation, 3–4, 293–94; expenditures, 92; in Finland, 245; in Italy, 327, 334; in Japan, 116, 159, 176; pharmaceuticals, 116, 214, 243; prescription, 24, 26, 272, 292; in Sweden, 211, 214
Drug therapies, 16, 28, 59–60, 75, 92–93, 97

Elderly patients, 34–36, 65–69, 375 (*see also* Age difference); in the U.S., 21, 29–30, 42, 47, 49
Electrocardiogram (ECG), 137, 259
England, AMI care in, 4, 6, 11, 16, 268–87, 393; appropriateness of, 281; consequences of changes in, 281; economy and, 272; expenditures for, 283–84; financing of, 18, 271–72; gatekeeper requirements in, 308; health outcomes in, 282–83; high-tech, 277–79; hospitals and, 13, 273–74; incentives for technological change in, 271–75; low-tech, 279–81; medical expenditures and, 283–84; mortality in, 270, 283, 284, 286; national expectations for, 274–75; reimbursement in, 391; technology regulation and, 12, 272–73
Equity, 380; of Canadian health care system, 106; in Finland, 239
European Commission, 256, 327
European Medical Agency (EMEA), 327
European Union, 325, 327
Expenditures. *See* Medical expenditures

Federal Law on Sickness and Accident Insurance (Switzerland), 345–46, 348
Federal Law on Sickness Insurance (Switzerland), 345, 347–48, 354
Fee-for-service system, 12, 390–91; in Belgium, 319; in Canada, 55, 60, 75, 90; in Denmark, 254; in France, 292; in Israel, 358; in Japan, 159; in Korea, 186; in Taiwan, 193, 196
Financing of care (*see also* Costs; Insurance; Medical expenditures; Reimbursement): in Canada, 59–60, 73, 75, 76, 89–92, 100–102; in Israel, 357–58; in the U.S., 22–25
Finland, AMI care in, 233–50, 252, 389; competition and, 238–39; consequences of changes in, 246–48; economy of, 237, 248; financing of, 18, 235–38; high-tech, 241–43; incentives for technological change in, 235–40; low-tech, 243–45; malpractice liability and, 239; MONICA study in, 240, 241, 245; mortality and, 133, 234, 246; municipalities of,

235–37; regulation and, 12, 238; regulation of physician supply and, 239–40; technological change in, 240–45
Food and Drug Administration (FDA), (U.S.), 25–26, 49, 256
France, AMI care in, 13, 289–303, 389; competition and, 294; drug and device regulation and, 293–94; financing of, 290–92; incentives for technological change in, 290–95; medical expenditures and, 289; MONICA Project in, 301; regional inequalities in, 293; regulation and, 12, 292–94; technological change and, 295–302
Fribourg, Switzerland, 344, 349, 352
Friuli region (Italy), 323, 330, 334, 337
Fukuoka Prefecture (Japan), 158, 164

Gallbladder disease, 4, 6
General practitioners, 253, 254, 268, 272, 292, 350
Geriatric medicine, 274. *See also* Elderly patients
Germany, 4, 156
Gruppo Italiano di Studi Emodinamici, 334

Health Care Insurance Plan, 89–92
Health Departments: England, 270; France, 292; Taiwan, 194; Western Australia, 126, 143
Health Insurance database (Belgium), 309
Health maintenance organizations (HMOs), 212
Health Ministry (Canada), 92
Health outcomes, 1, 5–8, 17, 72, 393 (*see also* Mortality); in Belgium, 306, 314–18; in England, 282–83; in Finland, 246–48; in Israel, 372–76, 380–82; in Italy, 336–37; in Japan, 171–74; in Manitoba, 113; regional differences in, 102, 336, 338; in Sweden, 220–22; in Taiwan, 200; in the U.S., 40–47
Heart disease, ischemic. *See* Ischemic heart disease
Heart failure, 16, 50, 145–46, 151, 220–22, 254; chronic, 163
Heart Plan 1993 (Denmark), 257–58
Heparin, 36–37, 170
High-tech treatments, 12, 14–15, 385, 389, 393 (*see also* Angioplasty; Bypass surgery; Cardiac catheterization); in Australia, 126–36; in Belgium, 310–13, 319; in Canada, 95–97, 108, 109–12; in Denmark, 259–61; in Finland, 241–43; in Israel, 364–69; in Italy, 330, 331–34, 337; in Japan, 166–69, 173; in Manitoba, 109–12; in Sweden, 216–20; in Switzerland, 349; in Taiwan, 199–200; in the U.S., 24, 29–36, 48, 49, 50
Hospital Claim File (Taiwan), 194–95, 198
Hospital Discharge Register (Finland), 234, 240–41, 243, 246
Hospital Episode Statistics (England), 270, 275–77, 281–82
Hospitalization Benefits Plan (Canada), 89
Hospitalization data, 94–95
Hospitals (*see also* Length of stay): in Belgium, 308; CCUs, 350, 358, 363; corporate, 191; in Denmark, 261–63; in Finland, 248; ownership of, 10, 13, 173, 197; private, 122–23, 173, 191, 229n. 18, 256, 291, 359; public, 121, 122, 256, 291, 293, 296, 347; reimbursement of, 24, 359; in Switzerland, 343–44, 347; teaching, 13, 106, 111; university, 235

Hypertension, 139, 314

ICD9 codes, 163, 198, 240, 258; in Belgium, 309; in Canada, 95, 108; in Israel, 356–57, 369, 381; in Italy, 330, 337
IHD. *See* Ischemic heart disease
Income, 3, 115, 116
Inpatient care, 2, 45–47, 211, 235, 259
Institute for Clinical Evaluative Sciences, 61
Institute for Pharmaco-Economics, 93
Insurance, 3, 13, 116, 291 (*see also* Financing of care; Payment systems; Reimbursement); in Australia, 123; in Belgium, 307–8; employer-provided, 24, 239; in England, 272; in Israel, 358; in Italy, 325, 347; in Japan, 158, 159; in Korea, 184; private, 11, 24, 75, 97, 150, 290; in Switzerland, 345–48, 353
Ischemic heart disease (IHD), 6–7, 84, 85, 163, 381; in Australia, 125, 131, 136, 139, 145–46, 150, 152; in Japan, 156; in Korea, 184; in Taiwan, 193, 205; in the U.S., 21, 25, 29, 42–45
Israel, AMI care in, 356–82, 389; data sources for, 357, 362–63; effects of technological change in, 377–80; health outcomes, 372–76, 380–82; high-tech, 364–69; incentives for technological change and, 357–62; low-tech, 370–71; medical expenditures and resources, 356, 376–77; mortality, 356–57, 364, 372–74, 375, 381; regional differences in, 371–72
Israel Central Bureau of Statistics, 356
Israel Medical Association, 362
Israel Society for the Prevention of Heart Attacks, 363
Italian Association of Hospital Cardiologists, 336
Italy, AMI care in, 323–39; appropriateness of, 334–36; competition and, 328–29; financing of, 324–25; health outcomes and, 336–37; high-tech, 331–34; incentives for technological change in, 324–30; low-tech, 334; medical expenditures and, 337; MONICA Project and, 339; mortality and, 330, 339; payment system and, 326–28, 336, 338; physician recruitment and, 329; regional differences in, 326, 336, 338; regulation and, 327–28; technological change in, 330–36

Japan, AMI care in, 12, 18, 156–80, 390; appropriateness of, 171; fee-for-service in, 173–74; health outcomes and, 171–74; high-tech, 166–69, 173; hospital ownership and, 13, 173; IHD in, 156; incentives for technological change in, 159–63; insurance for, 13, 158, 159; length of stay and, 173–74; low-tech, 169–71; medical expenditures and, 2, 173; mortality and, 163, 171–73, 176, 177; physician supply in, 13; reimbursement in, 159–60; technological change in, 163–71; thrombolytic drugs for, 164–65, 169–71

Korea, AMI care in, 12, 13, 184–91; financing of, 186–87; high-tech, 185, 188–91; hospitals in, 188, 191; incentives for technological change in, 186–88; incentives for technology use, 187–88; patient payments in, 11

Koseisho (Japanese Ministry of Health and Welfare), 159, 163

Length of stay (LOS), 376; in Canada, 99–100, 113; in European countries, 225, 248, 300, 318; in Japan, 173–74; in Taiwan, 203, 204–5; in the U.S., 34–36
Lidocaine, 37–38, 48, 97, 392
Life expectancy, 5, 115, 116, 252, 264
Lipid-lowering agents, 136, 149, 255, 256
Local Health Units (Italy), 325–26, 328
Lombardy, Italy, 334–36
Long-term care, 24, 208
Low-tech treatments (*see also* ACE inhibitors; Aspirin; Beta-blockers; Drugs; Thrombolytic drugs): in Australia, 136–39; in Belgium, 313–14; in Canada, 97–98, 112–13; changes in, 15–16, 390; in Denmark, 263; in England, 277–81, 286; in Finland, 243–45; in Israel, 370–71; in Italy, 330, 334, 338; in Japan, 169–71; in Sweden, 220; in Switzerland, 350–53; in Taiwan, 200; in the U.S., 49

Macroregulation, 12, 26, 384
Malpractice, 14, 27, 62, 214, 239, 329
Managed-care plans, 25, 26, 49, 50
Manitoba, AMI care in, 106–7, 112–13, 394; changes in resource use, 113–15; consequences of changes in, 113–15; high-tech, 109–12; low-tech, 108, 112–13; patient demographics, 109–10; queue management and, 109; technological change in, 108–13
McKinsey Global Research Institute, 4, 5–6
Med-Echo, 79, 80
Medicaid (Korea), 186
Medicaid (U.S.), 24, 26
Medical Benefits Regulations (Canada), 90
Medical expenditures, 2–5, 8, 18–19 (*see also* Costs; Financing of care; Insurance; Reimbursement); in Australia, 142–46; in Belgium, 318, 321; in Canada, 58, 100–102, 106; in Denmark, 265; in England, 283–84; in France, 289; in Israel, 356, 376–77; in Italy, 325, 337; in Japan, 2, 173; in Sweden, 223–25; in Switzerland, 343; in the U.S., 2, 22, 45–47, 124, 174
Medical Products Agency (Sweden), 212, 220
Medicare (Australia), 123
Medicare (U.S.), 12, 22–25, 26, 28, 47–48, 49, 116; reimbursement of, 50, 391
Medications. *See* Drugs; *and specific medications*
Medisave (Singapore), 11
Microregulation, 12–13, 348, 360, 384
Ministry of Budget (Italy), 326
Ministry of Education and Universities (Italy), 329–30
Ministry of Health (MOH): Denmark, 255; Israel, 357, 358–59, 362, 363, 364, 369, 372, 374, 380; Italy, 327, 328, 330, 338; Ontario (Can.), 60, 61
Ministry of Health and Welfare (Japan), 159, 163
Ministry of Health and Welfare (Korea), 185
MONICA Project, 6–8, 17, 136, 264–65, 385; in Australia, 122–25, 139; in Finland, 240, 241, 245; in France, 301; in Israel, 363, 373; in Italy, 330, 334; in Sweden, 216; in Switzerland, 344–45, 349

Mortality, 7, 17, 21, 393–94; in Alberta (Can.), 88, 99–100, 102–3; in Australia, 127, 136, 139; in Belgium, 316–17, 321; in Denmark, 252, 264; in England, 270, 283, 284, 286; in Finland, 133, 234, 246; in France, 289; in Israel, 356–57, 364, 372–74, 375, 381; in Italy, 336–37; in Japan, 163, 171–73, 176, 177; in Manitoba (Can.), 113; in Ontario (Can.), 55, 59, 66, 68–69; in Quebec (Can.), 80, 83–84, 86; in Sweden, 209, 216, 220; in Switzerland, 343; in Taiwan, 198, 200; in the U.S., 40, 41, 42, 49, 115
Mutuelles (France), 290–91

National Base for Public Hospitals (France), 296–99
National Board of Health (Denmark), 257, 258, 265, 266
National Board of Health and Welfare (Sweden), 208, 212, 215, 220, 227
National Corporation of Pharmacies (Sweden), 212, 220, 227
National Cost Base for Public Hospitals (France), 295–300
National Facility Survey (Japan), 160
National Health Care Evaluation Agency (France), 293
National Health Insurance, 359; Denmark, 253, 254, 256; Finland, 235; Korea, 186, 191; Taiwan, 193, 196–98, 198, 200, 205
National Health Service (England), 268, 270, 273, 274, 277, 284; data from, 281; hospitals of, 271, 275; incentives in, 284; patients of, 278
National Health System (Italy), 324–25, 328, 334
National Insurance Institute (Israel), 359
National Patient Register (Denmark), 258, 261
National Population Registry (Israel), 363–64
National Registry of Myocardial Infarction (U.S.), 28, 37
Netanyahu Commission of Inquiry (Israel), 359
Nitrates, 36–37, 97–98, 113, 136, 245, 351
Nitroglycerin, 170, 220
Nottingham Heart Attack Register (England), 270, 275–77, 281, 282
Nurses, 50, 97, 98
Nursing homes, 116, 208

Odense University Hospital (Denmark), 263
Office of Health Economics (England), 283
Ontario, AMI care in, 12, 55–56, 58–70, 91, 389; financing of, 59–60; mortality and, 55, 59, 66, 68–69; queue management in, 109; technological change and, 59–66; trends in health outcomes, 66–70
Ontario Drug Benefit (ODB) plan, 58, 61
Ontario Health Insurance Plan (OHIP), 58, 59
Open-heart surgery, 217
Organisation for Economic Cooperation and Development (OECD), 124, 268–69, 345
Oxford Record Linkage Study, 270, 275, 278, 282, 284, 287

Payment systems, 10, 18, 307 (*see also* Fee-for-service system; Reimbursement); in Australia, 124; Belgium, 309; capitation payments, 254; in England, 274; in Italy,

326–28, 336, 338; in Japan, 159, 173; out-of-pocket, 11, 187, 193, 347, 354
Perth, Australia, 122, 125–32, 146
Pharmaceuticals, 116, 214, 243. *See also* Drugs; Thrombolytic drugs
Physicians (*see also* Cardiologists; Specialists; Surgeons): general practitioners, 253, 254, 268, 272, 292, 350; primary, 25, 212, 328; reimbursement of, 60, 75, 86, 90, 97 (*see also* Fee-for-service system); services of, 4
Physician supply regulation, 13; in Australia, 121; in Canada, 62; in European countries, 239–40, 258, 274, 294–95; in Israel, 361; in Taiwan, 197
Poor people, in Canada, 116
Prevention, 7, 233
Primary physicians, 25, 212, 328
Private hospitals, 122–23, 173, 191, 229n. 18, 256, 291, 359
Provider decisions, 294
PTCA (Percutaneous transluminal coronary angioplasty), 24, 298; in Australia, 127–31, 151; in Belgium, 310–14, 318, 319; in Canada, 55, 60–61, 63, 65–66, 67, 93, 95–97, 102, 109–11; in Denmark, 254, 255, 257–58, 259–60, 264, 265; in England, 271, 273, 277–79, 281; in Finland, 248; in France, 293, 295, 301; in Israel, 358–59, 366–67, 369, 377, 379; in Italy, 327, 331–32, 336; in Japan, 160, 164–66, 167–69, 171, 173–75, 176, 188–91; in Korea, 185, 186; in Sweden, 210, 214–16, 217–20, 227, 230nn. 28–29; in Switzerland, 349; in Taiwan, 196–97, 198, 199–200, 206; in the U.S., 29, 31
Public hospitals: in Australia, 121, 122; in Europe, 256, 291, 293, 296, 347

Quebec, AMI care in, 55–56, 72–86, 393–94; consequences of change in, 80–84; incentives for technological change in, 73–78; mortality and, 80, 83–84, 86
Queues, 109, 150, 210–11, 256, 257, 358. *See also* Waiting lists
Q-wave infarctions, 41, 102

Radiologists, 214, 392
Readmission, 124, 127, 150, 163, 313; in Australia, 132, 142, 145–46; in the U.S., 42–45, 49, 50
Recurrent AMI, 42–45, 127, 136, 139, 145–46, 151, 222
Régie de l'Assurance Maladie du Québec (RAMQ), 75, 79, 80, 83
Regional health authorities, 93
Regression models, 395–96
Regulation, 3, 10, 292–94, 357, 390; in Belgium, 308–9; in Canada, 60–62, 76, 92–93; of drugs and devices, 4, 293–94; in Israel, 360, 379; in Italy, 327–28; macro-, 12, 26, 384; micro-, 12–13, 348, 360, 384; in Taiwan, 197; in the U.S., 25–26
Regulatory Medical References, 294
Rehabilitation programs, 10, 371
Reimbursement, 10, 11, 174, 191 (*see also* Fee-for-service system; Financing of care; Insurance; Medical expenditures; Payment systems); to hospitals, 24, 359; in Israel, 376–77, 379; in Italy, 337, 338, 347; in Japan, 159–60, 176; of physicians, 60, 75, 86, 90, 97
ReoPro (inhibitor), 360
Resource use, 8, 380; in Australia, 142–46; in Manitoba, 113–15

Revascularization, 15, 237, 238, 259, 385, 394 (*see also* Angioplasty; Bypass surgery; CABG; PTCA); in Australia, 127, 131–32, 136, 149, 150, 152; in Canada, 55, 59, 60, 70, 76, 80, 109, 113; in Denmark, 257; in England, 271; in Israel, 360, 367; in Italy, 336; in Japan, 75, 171; in Korea, 188; in the U.S., 34, 41, 50

Service d'Aide Médicale d'Urgence (SAMU), 291, 293
Sex differences, 42, 95–97; in Australia, 142, 146; in Belgium, 321; in Finland, 247–48; in Israel, 369, 374, 375–76, 382; in Italy, 332, 343, 347; in Manitoba (Can.), 109, 113
Sickness funds (*see also* Insurance): in France, 290–91, 292; in Israel, 348, 359–60, 361, 372, 379
Singapore, 11
Smoking, 7, 136
Social Health Insurance system (Sweden), 212
Social Insurance Institution (Finland), 235
Social Medical Treatment Survey (Japan), 163
Socioeconomic status, 397
Specialists, 25, 27, 62, 253, 361–62, 392 (*see also* Cardiologists; Surgeons); in Australia, 122, 123, 150
Statins, 97, 263, 381
Stenting, 34, 128, 133, 220, 284, 360 (*see also* PTCA); in Denmark, 255; in France, 293; in Israel, 367, 369, 381; in Korea, 186; in Switzerland, 349
Strasbourg, France, 301
Streptokinase, 37, 60, 98, 263, 294, 309, 390; in Israel, 360, 370; in Switzerland, 352, 354
Stroke, 7, 139, 396
Surgeons: cardiac, 190, 197, 258; cardiothoracic, 286; cardiovascular, 171, 176, 392
Surgery, 4, 217. *See also* Cardiac surgery centers; Cardiothoracic surgery
Sweden, AMI care in, 11, 13, 208–27, 392; consequences of changes in, 220–22; global budget system of, 18; high-tech, 216–20; incentives for technological change in, 209–15; low-tech, 220; malpractice in, 214; medical expenditures and, 223–25; MONICA Project in, 216; mortality and, 209, 216, 220; regulation in, 12, 212–13; system of, 208–9; technological change in, 215–20
Swedish National AMI Register, 215–16
Swedish National Inpatient Register, 215
Swedish National Registry for Cardiac Intensive Care (RIKS-HIA), 216
Swedish Register for Coronary Angioplasty, 216
Swiss Federal Social Insurance Office, 345
Switzerland, AMI care in, 343–55; change in, 348–53; competition in, 348; financing of, 345–48; high-tech, 349; incentives for technological change in, 345–48; incentives for technology use in, 348; insurance competition in, 13; low-tech, 350–53; medical expenditures and, 343; MONICA Project in, 344–45, 349

Taiwan, AMI care in, 193–206; consequences of, 200–205; DRG system of, 11; financing of, 196–97;

high-tech, 199–200; incentives for technological change in, 196–98; low-tech, 200; mortality and, 198, 200; technology regulation in, 197
Taxation, 235, 236, 253, 307
Tax revenues, 22, 73
Teaching hospitals, 13, 106, 111
Technological Change in Health Care (TECH) Global Research Network, 9, 15, 18, 395
Thrombolysis, 285, 314, 373
Thrombolytic drugs, 16, 390 (*see also* Streptokinase; *and specific drugs*); in Australia, 136–39, 149; in Belgium, 309, 312–13, 318, 321; in Canada, 59, 70, 97–98, 113; in Denmark, 261, 263; in England, 279–81; in Finland, 245; in France, 291, 293–94, 302; in Israel, 370, 371, 381–82; in Italy, 334; in Japan, 164–65, 169; in Korea, 175; in Sweden, 216, 220, 227; in Switzerland, 350–53; in Taiwan, 200, 206; in the U.S., 36–37, 38, 48, 49, 50
Ticino canton, Switzerland, 352–53
Tissue plasminogen activator (tPA), 37, 60, 263, 294, 309, 318, 390
Tort Act (Sweden), 214

United Kingdom, 270, 271, 275, 284. *See also* England
United States, AMI care in, 4, 6, 21–50, 327, 332, 390; appropriateness of, 38–39; competition in, 13, 26–27, 49; consequences of changes in, 40–47; drug use in, 170; effects of incentives, 47–51; expertise in, 38–40; financing of, 22–25; high-tech, 29–36, 389; IHD in, 156; incentives for technological change, 22–27; life expectancy in, 115; low-tech, 36–38; malpractice and, 14, 329; medical expenditures in, 2, 22, 45–47, 124, 174; mortality and, 40, 41, 42, 109, 115; ownership of hospitals in, 13; payment system of, 18; physician supply in, 13; price levels of, 393; regulation and, 12, 25–26, 212; specialization in, 27; technological change and, 28–40; uninsured in, 24; utilization review in, 308
Urokinase, 390
Utilization review, 308, 348

Varsinais-Suomi, Finland, 241–43
Vaud, Switzerland, 344, 349, 352
Victoria, Australia, 125–26, 132–36, 150

Waiting lists, 268, 308, 336 (*see also* Queues); in Canada, 94, 97, 106, 111; in Denmark, 252, 256, 257, 259
Western Australia, 133, 136, 150
Western Australia Minimum Data Set, 132
Western Australian Centre of Health Services Research database, 126
Winnipeg, Manitoba, 107–8, 111
World Health Organization (WHO), 6, 264, 363. *See also* MONICA Project